Europ...y

Ian ...ken

EDINBURGH UNIVERSITY PRESS

© Ian Aitken, 2001
Edinburgh University Press
22 George Square, Edinburgh

Typeset in Monotype Apollo
by Koinonia, Bury, and
printed and bound in Great Britain by
Creative Print and Design, Ebbw Vale, Wales

A CIP record for this book is available
from the British Library

ISBN 0 7486 1167 3 (hardback)
ISBN 0 7486 1168 1 (paperback)

Contents

Introduction

This book examines the relationship between the two major traditions which dominate European film theory and cinema. The origins of the first of these, the intuitionist modernist and realist tradition, can be located in a philosophical lineage which encompasses German idealist philosophy, romanticism, phenomenology, and the Frankfurt School. The intuitionist tradition within European film theory and cinema emphasises aesthetic qualities such as irrationalism, intuitive insight, artistic autonomy, and indeterminate expression. Like the body of philosophical thought from which it stems, this intuitionist film culture is also concerned with both the role played by instrumental rationality within contemporary life, and the experience of alienation, or what Max Weber referred to as 'disenchantment', which afflicts the subject within modernity.

Early intuitionist, modernist film culture is often thought of as distinct from later European realist film theory and cinema, and distinctions between 'realism and anti-realism', or 'realism and modernism', are widely accepted within the field of media studies. However, these distinctions are misleading, and, in fact, early intuitionist film culture and later theories and practices of cinematic realism form part of one continuous tradition. There are, for example, clear intellectual and stylistic links between modernist movements such as Russian formalism, Weimar cinematic modernism, and French cinematic impressionism, the realist film theories of Grierson, Bazin and Kracauer, and the work of post-war film-makers such as Antonioni, Pialat, Fellini, Reitz and Erice. One of the central concerns of this study is to explore this intuitionist tradition, and to establish its relationship to the post-Saussurian paradigm of film theory and cinema. As a consequence, this book substitutes a conventionally upheld distinction between modernist and realist film theory and cinema for one between an intuitionist modernist/realist paradigm, and a post-Saussurian one.

The first three chapters of this book explore the interaction between intuitionist and rationalist tendencies within Russian formalism, Weimar cinematic modernism, and the work of Eisenstein, whilst Chapter 4 focuses on French impressionism: the European film movement most clearly identifiable with the intuitionist modernist tradition. Chapters 5 and 6 then provide an overview of the post-Saussurian tradition, and the structuralist, post-structuralist, political modernist and postmodern cinema which that tradition has fostered. Chapter 7 traces the continuities which exist between early intuitionist modernism and later intuitionist realism, and focuses on the theories of cinematic realism developed by Grierson, Kracauer and Bazin. Finally Chapters 8 and 9 explore post-war European realist cinema, and concentrate, in particular, on films which can be identified with the ideas of the above mentioned theorists.

This book does not attempt an exhaustive study of the post-Saussurian tradition. Such studies have been undertaken elsewhere, and there is no pressing need for this book to add to what is already a substantial literature on the subject. The principal focus of this book is on the intuitionist modernist and intuitionist realist traditions, and the post-Saussurian tradition is mainly considered in terms of the ways in which its underlying conceptions of representation, relativism, realism, structure, determinism and agency, relate to, and differ from, similar concepts deployed within the intuitionist modernist/realist paradigm.

This study also attempts to re-focus attention on a tradition within European film theory and cinema which has been neglected, and even dismissed as irrelevant to contemporary critical concerns. The critical opprobrium which has been directed at movements such as French impressionism, and at theories such as that advanced by Kracauer, is often remarkable in the extent to which it so confidently dismisses them as of little worth. However, such repudiations are largely the product of a failure to comprehend the complexity and sophistication of the intuitionist modernist/realist tradition, and this failure is, in turn, a consequence of the hegemonic hold which post-Saussurian thought has exercised over film studies. There is, however, growing evidence that this hold is beginning to weaken, as attempts are made to broaden and reconstruct the field. The emergence of 'post-theory', and of critical work on film studies drawn from disciplines as diverse as cognitive science, philosophical aesthetics, phenomenology, and philosophical realism, reflects this attempt at configuration. My hope is that this study will play a constructive role within this wider critical project, by re-focusing attention on the European intuitionist realist/modernist paradigm, and, in particular, on the intuitionist realist tradition.

This study has attempted to be as inclusive as possible within the constraints established by its central thematic concerns, and by available wordage. Nevertheless, although the period of time covered here extends from the 1900s to the early 1990s, it has not been possible to cover very recent films, or their makers. Similarly, the focus on the intuitionist and post-Saussurian traditions which this book adopts means that films and film-makers associated with the European art cinema have only been considered where they can be related to one or other of these two traditions. It has also been necessary to exclude, or cover only in outline, some areas which remain important to any study of cinematic realism. These include that of the nineteenth-century French realist and naturalist tradition, and its influence on both twentieth-century Marxist theories of aesthetic realism, and European film-making. However, although it proved possible to include an, albeit, schematic account of Lukácsian critical realism here, a detailed study of nineteenth-century realism and naturalism, Marxism, and Lukács, falls outside the parameters of this particular book. Similarly, the narrative set out here, which proceeds from an exploration of early intuitionist modernism, to an analysis of post-Second World War realism, means that it has not been possible to cover pre-Second World War cinematic realism, as in the films of Renoir and French poetic realism, in great depth.

Nevertheless, and despite these exclusions, a considerable amount of material is encompassed in this attempt to explore the intuitionist and post-Saussurian traditions within European film theory and cinema. In addition, this book is also intended to be the first in a two volume work. The second volume within this study will be dedicated to a study of realism, and will situate theories of cinematic realism within a wider critical perspective, which will encompass historical theories of realist representation, and contemporary approaches to realism emerging within the fields of phenomenology, perceptual psychology, the philosophies of science and mind, and artificial intelligence theory. This second volume will also include accounts of nineteenth-century realism and naturalism, Marxist aesthetic theory, Lukácsian critical realism, and the French poetic realist cinema of the 1930s. However, that is for the future, and this volume will commence with an analysis of the interaction between intuitionist and rationalist tendencies within Russian formalism and Weimar film theory.

I Didacticism and Intuition in Russian Formalism and Weimar Film Theory

Realist movements in Russian art and cultural theory began to emerge towards the middle of the nineteenth century, influenced by the French realist and naturalist traditions, and by a perceived need to create a new, national art form of popular appeal. In his *What is Art* (1897), for example, Leo Tolstoy asserted that 'Great works of art are only great because they are accessible to everyone'.[1] Similarly, in his *The Aesthetic Relations of Art and Reality* (1855) the writer Anatole Chernyshevsky claimed that 'Art does not limit itself only to the beautiful … it embraces the whole of reality … The content of art is life in its social aspect';[2] whilst the theatre director Konstantin Stanislavsky asserted that 'we are striving to brighten the dark existence of the poor classes … Our aim is to create the first intelligent, moral, popular theatre, and to this end we are dedicating our lives'.[3] This socially and politically oriented realist tradition was also reinforced by the emphasis on realism within the Marxist tradition. However, Russian realism in the arts pre-dated the emergence of Bolshevism, and was more closely related to movements such as populism, a political movement which lobbied for the liberation of the Russian peasant from serfdom, and with the various liberal, socialist or social-democratic movements which were active in Russia prior to the foundation of the Bolshevik Party.[4]

Although, as already mentioned, the development of a realist tradition in Russia towards the end of the nineteenth century was influenced by the aspiration to establish a more socially oriented art practice, it was also indirectly assisted by the systems of censorship and repression exercised by the Tzarist regime. One consequence of such totalitarian control of the public sphere was that open public debate on issues of major political importance was virtually non-existent.[5] However, yet another was that information about western modernist movements in the arts was kept from Russian artists and intellectuals, and, as a consequence, the realist tradition remained vital in Russia long after it had been superseded in the west by

4

various forms of modernism. It was only after the political hold of the ruling regime began to disintegrate following a wave of industrial strikes in 1903, military defeat in the war against Japan in 1904, and the formation of a constitutional government in 1905, that western modernism began to filter into Russia more forcefully.

Up to 1910, the most significant western modernist influence on Russian art had been that of symbolism. Russian symbolism, as in the work of individuals and groups such as Diagilev, Ryabushinsky, the Ballets Russe, Alexander Blok, and The Blue Rose Group, inherited the metaphysical millenarianism and anti-materialism of western symbolism, and the widespread concern for the mystical and the spiritual within this Russian symbolist tradition is summed up by Ryabushinsky's quixotic assertion that 'Art is eternal, for it is founded on the unchanging ... Art is whole for its single source is the soul ... Art is free for it is created by the free impulse of creation'.[6]

However, in addition to the aestheticism evident in the above remarks, Russian symbolism was also inspired by a desire to explore and represent aspects of Russian national identity. According to artists such as Natalja Goncharova, that identity was steeped in slavic, mystical, and folk traditions. Thus, a painting such as her *The Evangelists* (1910) refers back to earlier Russian traditions of ecclesiastical painting in its rendering of religious themes; whilst Mikhail Larionov's *Soldier in a Wood* (1908–9), combines representations of nature with an affirmation of Russian folk art traditions.[7] Although both these paintings display the influence of western modernism, they also exhibit a desire to re-experience the premodern in order to represent both authentic human experience, and an organic Russian national identity.

Between 1910 and 1921 Russian symbolism gradually evolved into a more characteristically modernist form of artistic practice, whilst preserving its initial interest in mysticism and the exploration of national identity. Artists such as Marc Chagall, Goncharova and Larionov also turned increasingly to eastern art in an attempt to both explore new formal languages of painting, and conceptions of national identity. This synthesis of modernism and mystical nationalist orientalism is well expressed in Goncharova's declaration that 'The East means the creation of new forms, and the extension and deepening of the problems of colour ... I aspire towards a sense of nationality and the East'.[8]

As their careers progressed, Larionov and Goncharova became increasingly concerned with questions of abstract formal composition, to the extent that they eventually abandoned figurative art altogether. In 1912 Larionov founded the rayonist movement, one which straddled the divide between figurative and abstract art. In 1914, Larionov asserted that 'Rayonism erases the barriers that exist between a picture's surface and nature ... that which is the essence of painting itself can be shown here best of all – the combination of colour, its saturation, the relationship of coloured masses, depth, texture'.[9] Although Larionov refers entirely to questions of pictorial form here, rayonism, like symbolism before it, remained concerned with the representation of spiritual realities, and such involvement with the abstract rendering of the metaphysical was also to emerge as a potent force later in Russian art, particularly in the suprematist movement, and in paintings such as Kazimir Malevitch's *White Square on a White Ground* (1918).[10]

In addition to rayonism, the increasingly modernist turn of Russian art from 1909 onwards was also influenced by the Italian futurist movement. The Italian poet Filippo Marinetti's *Manifesto del Futurismo* was first published in Russia in 1909, and, in 1916, the futurists' enthusiasm for the cinema led their *Manifesto del Cinema* to proclaim the supremacy of cinema over all other art forms.[11] The emphasis on speed, violence, power, lines of force, and modernity within futurist art influenced, amongst others, the Russian poet Vladimir Mayakovsky, whose work took on the jarring, disjunctive phonetic style which characterised futurist poetry. Mayakovsky joined the Russian futurist movement in 1911, and was later to influence the development of film culture within Russia through his association with the *avant-garde* journals *Lef* and *Novy Lef*.

In addition to the impact of symbolism and futurism, evolving Russian modernist movements in the arts were also influenced by Russian formalism. Following the formation of the Moscow Linguistic Circle in 1915, Opajaz (the Society for the Study of Poetical Language) was established in St Petersburg in 1916 to introduce formalist linguistic methods into literary theory. Here, linguists and literary theorists such as Roman Jakobson, Viktor Shklovsky, Osip Brik, Boris Eichenbaum, Vladimir Propp and the constructivist Boris Arvatov, attempted to identify the underlying laws and principles – or *literaturnost* – which made literature 'literary', and which distinguished the medium from other aesthetic practices.[12] At the same time, the Russian formalists also attempted this identification in combination with an exploration of the way that the art object was experienced by the observer.

The origins of the Russian formalist preoccupation with identifying *literaturnost*, and understanding the role of perceptual experience within the aesthetic encounter, are to be found in the work of Edmund Husserl, and, beyond Husserl, in the neo-Kantian idealist tradition. In his *Logical Investigations* (1900), Husserl sought to identify logical and mathematical principles which had an objective existence apart from their manifestation within empirical exposition. For Husserl, these underlying transcendental laws of logic constitute a model which all individual acts of reasoning stem from, and have, of necessity, to approximate to.[13] Husserl also argued that each separate theoretical practice contained its own autonomous set of objective underlying axioms, and that these both distinguished a particular practice from others, and determined the character and material manifestation of that practice. For example, Husserl sought to identify the general, fundamental concepts which made a science *scientific*, and it was a similar concern, inherited from Husserlian phenomenology, which motivated the Russian formalists attempt to define *literaturnost*.

The emphasis on objectivism within Husserl's phenomenology was also allied to a commitment to the analysis of immediate, conscious experience. Husserlian phenomenology 'brackets out' the question of the relationship between consciousness and reality in order to focus on the act of consciousness itself. Husserl did not claim that the question of the relationship between appearance and reality was a meaningless one, but that it must be 'put aside' for the purposes of phenomenological analysis. In his *Ideas for a Pure Phenomenology and Phenomenological Philosophy* (1913), for example, Husserl argued that, because the one thing which can truly be said to exist is that which is 'delivered' to us through an act of consciousness, it follows that such acts provide the only real foundation for knowledge.[14] Husserl's phenomenology is not, therefore, based in a solipsistic denial of reality, but on the provisional 'bracketing out' of the question of reality for the purposes of phenomenological analysis.

Although Husserlian phenomenology, as embodied in the *Logical Investigations*, is predominantly empirical, in both aspiration and practice, Husserl distanced himself from classical empiricist philosophy and methodology on the grounds that, whilst empiricism argued that 'laws' were generalisations from experience, he believed that underlying laws, or 'essences', existed, as in some Platonic or Kantian 'noumenal' realm, as universals which unite categories of phenomena. It is clear from this that, in addition to its empirical aspect, Husserlian phenomenology also has a pronounced idealist dimension. In addition to these empirical and idealist features, Husserlian phenomenology is also based in an intuitionist conception of knowledge. The noumenal 'essences' which Husserl refers to are beyond empirical description precisely because they are not material entities, and, consequently, can only be grasped through intuitive, rather than cognitive acts of understanding.[15] Husserlian phenomenological analysis proceeds from detailed empirical descriptions of appearances to the postulation of 'deep structures' which, at the level of the essence, are abstract and non-empirical.

One consequence of the emphasis on deep structures in Husserl's phenomenological method is that his writings occasionally betray a tendency towards reductiveness, as, for example, when analysing temporal experience, he arrives at very general formulations of underlying laws, and at phrases such as 'temporal relations are asymmetrical'.[16] In the *Logical Investigations*, Husserl prioritised the importance and value of the empirical, and this stress on the importance of the empirical, when carried into the Russian formalist tradition, was the source of some of that tradition's most important achievements. However, in the later sections of the *Ideas for a Pure Phenomenology and Phenomenological Philosophy*, Husserl developed the idealist tendency within his ideas further, and focused more on the essence, rather than the empirical. Husserl described this later stage of his thought as 'transcendental phenomenology', and distinguished it from the more empirical focus of the *Logical Investigations*. Such a shift from an empirical to a more reductivist, idealist approach, was also to occur within the later Russian formalist and structuralist traditions, and became a source of major problems in both.

Just as Husserl rejected what he considered to be the subjective psychologism of philosophers such as Brentano in his quest to uncover objective principles, Russian formalism also rejected the subjectivism of the symbolist tradition in its attempt to identify the objective underlying structures of literature. Russian formalism, which first emerged during the First World War, developed as a movement committed to an aesthetic of extended perceptual experience. Formalists such as Viktor Shklovsky argued that art should 'defamiliarise' reality, and, in doing so, stretch out the process of perception as an end in itself:

> The device which art uses is the device of 'making things strange' and of complicating the form, thereby increasing the difficulty and length of perception so that the perceiving process becomes an end-in-itself and has to be prolonged. (Mitchell 1974: 75)

When allied to his belief that perception of the art object should become an end in itself, Shklovsky's concept of *ostranenie* reveals the influence of both Kantian and Husserlian aesthetics. For Kant, as with Shklovsky, aesthetic judgement stands outside instrumental purpose, and constitutes an autonomous realm of freedom and self-realisation. According to Kant's theory of aesthetic experience, the mind freely seeks patterns of meaning in the object of aesthetic contemplation, thus bringing the 'understanding' and 'imagination' into a liberating unity within a 'harmony of the faculties'.[17] Kant also believed that the aesthetic judgement was impressionistic and non-conceptual in character. This, in turn, meant that, in order for the harmonisation of the faculties to take place, the object at which aesthetic contemplation was directed must possess the potential to stimulate a profusion of meaning in the mind of the perceiving spectator. The aesthetic experience is, therefore, based on the prolonged search for structures of meaning within the art object, and it is this which forms the basis of Kant's idea of 'natural beauty', or *Naturschöne*, in which the contemplation of nature is most likely to bring about the desired harmony of the faculties.[18]

The influence of *Naturschöne*, allied to Husserl's stress on detailed exploration of the concrete, eventually led to the emergence of Shklovsky's conception of *ostranenie*, and to the development of pre-revolutionary Russian formalism as a movement concerned primarily with the problematisation of subjectivity and experience through extending the process of perception. For the formalists, thus extended and problematised, perception provided the best means of engendering free creative activity within the spectator.[19] This conception of the aesthetic as a domain of freedom separated from an external instrumental reality, in which art existed only for the purpose of perception and contemplation, was, however, substantially mediated by a social and political context which eventually led the Russian formalists to adopt a more politically engaged, and less purely aesthetically aligned position. It is this latter phase which is referred to by Roman Jakobson, when he argued that Russian formalism should not be associated with either 'Kantian aesthetics' or 'l'art pour l'art', but with an exploration of the 'aesthetic function'.[20] For Jakobson, within the domain of poetry such an exploration takes the form of a study of 'poeticalness': the (in Husserlian terms) 'essence' of the poetic-aesthetic system.

However, Jakobson also links such a study to political ends when he argues that the exploration of poeticalness should also lead to analysis of how established sign systems represent reality in an ideologically compromised manner; and how new possibilities can be envisaged through the generation of alternative amalgamations of signifieds and signifiers. Nevertheless, and like earlier veins of Russian formalism, Jakobson insists on the importance of a formalist exploration of aesthetic systems and the aesthetic function, arguing that, without such an exploration, dominant ideological configurations would remain authoritative, so that 'the course of events ceases and consciousness of reality dies':

Why is all this necessary? Why need it be stressed that the sign is not confused with the object? Because alongside the immediate awareness of the identity of sign and object (A is A1), the immediate awareness of the absence of this identity (A is not A1) is necessary; this antinomy is inevitable, for without contradiction there is no play of concepts, there is no play of signs, the relation between the concept and the sign becomes automatic, the course of events ceases and consciousness of reality dies.[21]

Here, Jakobson distances Russian formalism from a Kantian, Husserlian preoccupation with problematising perception as an end in itself, and redefines the formalist project as one which attempts to defamiliarise experience, as a means of both exploring existing formations of social meaning, and of developing alternative configurations.

The *avant-garde* art movement most closely associated with Russian formalism was constructivism, which emerged out of the earlier suprematist movement just prior to 1917. The *Suprematist Manifesto* of 1913, which was drawn up by Kazimir Malevich and Mayakovsky, emphasised the necessity of exploring aesthetic form, as an end in itself, and as a means of expressing abstract, metaphysical intuitions, and rejected the idea that painting should 'represent' anything other than its own material reality. For Malevich, this meant that painting must achieve a 'degree zero' of pure art, in which the aesthetic surface of the painting was purged of all representational reference.[22] One consequence of such a radical rejection of representation was that the social and political was eliminated from artistic expression, as painters such as Malevich, Suetin, Chashnik and Leporskaja insisted on preserving the autonomy of the aesthetic. For example, Malevich's *White Square on a White Ground* (1918), an entirely abstract and formal composition, contains no reference whatsoever to the turbulent events which marked the year of its production.

Prior to 1917 the constructivist movement had also emphasised the exploration of aesthetic form as an end in itself, although, in distinction to suprematism's focus on expressive, abstract sensation, constructivism inherited the pre-revolutionary futurist enthusiasm for a machine aesthetic, and was premised on the idea of the artist as engineer, constructing art objects through a rational process of enquiry and experimentation.[23] However, after 1917, the constructivist movement divided along lines represented by artists such as Naum Gabo, who argued that the movement should focus primarily on formal, compositional concerns, and those such as Vladimir Tatlin, Aleksandr Rodchenko and El Lissitsky, who wanted art to develop in the image of industrial production, engineered like machinery, and able to play a worthwhile role within the Soviet Union's development as a modern, revolutionary state. Tatlin's *Monument to the Third International* (1919) is one of the most iconic examples of this 'productivist' tendency within constructivism, whilst El Lissitsky's poster *Beat the Whites with the Red Wedge* (1920) illustrates the movement's increasing political engagement.

This engaged, productivist tendency also led the constructivist movement to repudiate supposedly bourgeois aesthetic concepts such as 'vision' and 'genius', and to redefine the artist as a 'producer', or 'engineer', who made 'a useful and functional thing in a masterly way'.[24] Constructivist 'productivism' also foregrounded reflexivity in an attempt to retain Jakobson and Shklovsky's insistence on maintaining the 'contradiction between the concept and the sign'.[25] Thus, in Vsevolod Meyerhold's play *The Forest* (1922), the 'director-engineer' divides Ostrovsky's original five act play into thirty-three separate episodes, which are then 'assembled' to produce an array of dramatic effects.[26] Here, the initial formalist emphasis on revealing the devices of art in order to prolong and problematise the process of perception as an end in itself, an emphasis which pervades Shklovsky's pre-revolutionary essay *Art as a Device* (1916), is abandoned, and denounced as a remnant of decadent bourgeois ideology, as constructivism embraces the idea that art should serve a social and political, rather than solely psychological purpose.

In addition to the Russian formalist emphasis on the problematisation of subjectivity through the extension of perception, an emphasis which can be identified in both the suprematist and constructivist movements, reductivist tendencies within Russian formalism, as expressed in a Husserlian imperative to disclose deep structural axioms and 'essences', also continued to flourish during the 1920s. One of the most well-known examples of such reductivism, well known largely because of its later adoption by a number of western film theorists, was the structural analysis of Russian folk tales carried out by Vladimir Propp. In his *Morphology of the Folk Tale* (1928), Propp analysed 100 Russian folk tales and concluded that, underlying their apparent diversity, were thirty-one generative 'functions', which, when combined into differing arrangements, were chiefly responsible for the formation and narrative content of the tales. Propp also found that, underlying even these functions, a core meta-narrative could be discerned which was the ultimate source of both the thirty-one functions, and the entire corpus of folk tales.[27]

Propp's *Morphology of the Folk Tale* is an example of the way in which Russian formalist theorists attempted to explore the formal structural properties of an aesthetic object in order to both seek out an underlying generative grammar, and isolate the basic units of a particular aesthetic medium. It is also a good example of the way in which Russian formalism attempted to apply a rigorously 'scientific' methodology to cultural production in order to arrive at a more objective understanding of aesthetic laws.[28]

The formalist and constructivist legacy which was passed on to the Soviet cinema consisted of an incongruous fusion. On the one hand, an essentially mechanistic approach, in which basic representational units were combined in a deterministic way under the guidance of 'objective' underlying principles, was adopted; whilst, on the other hand, the role of defamiliarisation in creating more ambivalent pictures of reality was also emphasised. However, it was the latter, rather than the former tendency, which was to influence the work of one of the most important *avant-garde* Russian theorists and film-makers: Dziga Vertov.

In his most influential film, *Chelovek s kinoapparatom* (*The Man with the Movie Camera*, 1929), Vertov assembles what he refers to as 'cine-facts' (actuality shots) so as to build up an impressionistic, ambivalent, and non-directive portrayal of life within the Soviet Union. This degree of textual indeterminacy is also reinforced by the way that *Chelovek s kinoapparatom* explores the potential of film form and the new perceptual possibilities made available by the cinema. So, for example, *Chelovek s kinoapparatom* contains shots taken from the viewpoint of a speeding train and aircraft, as well as X-ray, micro and time-lapse photography.[29] *Chelovek s kinoapparatom* also exhibits a considerable degree of reflexivity, which finds expression in scenes in which the film-maker is seen setting up his equipment, and shooting the various sections of the film. Such reflexivity was important to Vertov, who regarded the average fiction film as a form of 'cine-nicotine', which pacified the spectator. *Chelovek s kinoapparatom*, on the other hand, was designed to be a proper 'cine-object', which gave the spectator the impression of 'a disagreeable-tasting antidote to the poison [of commercial cinema]'.[30]

In addition to the explorations in film form referred to above, Vertov was also committed to a documentary approach to film-making, and all the footage in *Chelovek s kinoapparatom* was shot on location. Vertov's emphasis on documentary arises from his theory of the 'cinema of fact'. Here, Vertov argued that literary and theatrical conventions which had their origins in bourgeois culture should be abandoned, and replaced by techniques drawn from the modern documentary film of everyday life. In attempting to realise this aspiration Vertov and his collaborators, the 'kinoks', made documentary newsreels which sought to capture *zhizn' v rasplokh*, or 'life caught unawares'.[31] This approach also provided the basis for Vertov's conception of *kinopravda*, or 'film truth', and for his newsreel series of the same name.

Vertov's desire to represent *zhizn' v rasplokh* can be related to the formalist and Husserlian stress on the exploration of everyday, perceptual experience. *Zhizn' v rasplokh* can also be associated, in particular, with Husserl's notion of the *Lebenswelt*, in that, as with the *Lebenswelt*, *zhizn' v rasplokh* contains features often missed by a human consciousness normally focused on more abstract, utilitarian concerns.[32] The idea of *zhizn' v rasplokh* is also the source of Vertov's concept of *kinoglaz*, or the 'film-eye', and it is the nebulous, semi-apparent aspects of everyday life which Vertov attempts to accentuate through the technique of montage, which transforms *zhizn' v rasplokh* into a work of *kino-fakty*, or 'film-facts'.[33] Vertov's insistence on the documentary method stemmed from his belief that both *zhizn' v rasplokh* and *Zhizn' kak ona est*, or 'life as it is', could only be discerned within a film founded on the orchestration of *kino-fakty*. However, Vertov believed that such orchestration should also employ all the formal and technical potential of montage editing in organising actuality material, and it is this documentary modernist model of film-making which finds expression in *Chelovek s kinoapparatom*.

Vertov's advocacy of the 'unstaged' documentary film, and rejection of the staged fiction film, also formed the basis of his well-known dispute with Eisenstein, during the course of which Vertov criticised films such as *Oktyabr* (*October*, Eisenstein, 1928) for their use of dramatised reconstruction. In criticising Eisenstein here, Vertov was following the policy on the 'cinema of fact' adopted by the journal *Novy Lef* in the late 1920s. For example, writing in *Novy Lef* in 1927, Sergei Tretyakov, a regular contributor to the journal, echoed Vertov in complaining that Eisenstein's films 'transformed reality' excessively, and, in so doing, 'deformed' it; whilst, in the same edition, Mayakovsky referred to the quasi-documentary representation of Lenin in *Oktyabr* as 'disgusting'.[34] Like others within *Novy Lef*, Vertov was uncompromising in adopting the formalist conviction on the need to create a new cinematic language of film, and to reject all 'bourgeois' conventions of cinematic representation, including the use of acting. This position led him to condemn Eisenstein's *Bronenosets Potemkin* (*Potemkin*, 1926) as an 'acted film in documentary trousers',[35] a criticism to which Eisenstein responded by condemning *Chelovek s kinoapparatom* as an example of 'cine-hooliganism'.[36]

In addition to their argument over the staged versus the unstaged film, the dispute which emerged between Vertov and Eisenstein during the 1920s was also founded on the fact that Vertov's approach to film-form was essentially impressionistic, and founded on the early formalist preoccupation with problematising experience; whilst Eisenstein's early aesthetic was founded both upon the far more deterministic axioms of Pavlovian behaviourist psychology, and on a perceived need to manipulate the spectator for specific ideological ends. It is this deterministic aspect of Eisenstein's thought which led him to criticise Vertov's films for their lack of 'purposeful intention', and to develop the more directive notion of the *kinokulaki*, or 'film-fist', in direct response to Vertov's more reflective concept of the 'film-eye'.[37]

Vertov's importance within film theory, and one of the reasons why, in the 1970s, anti-realist film theorists and film-makers turned to him as a source of inspiration, rests, to a significant extent, on the emphasis on self-reflexivity, formal experimentation and discursive indeterminacy which can be found in his work. Unlike more mechanistic, deterministic practitioners of Russian formalism, who sought to direct the spectator's understanding of social reality more substantively, Vertov's approach to montage and film form implied an active, self-directed spectator, able to scrutinise the impressionistic montage structures of *Chelovek s kinoapparatom* without being led to particular sets of conclusions. In this respect, Vertov's work avoids the reductivist tendencies implicit in the work of formalists such as Propp, and in the early Eisenstein.

* * *

If German philosophical idealism was a key influence on Russian formalism the same is true of Weimar film theory. Weimar film theory was founded upon a critical, and pessimistic conception of modernity which stemmed from classical German philosophy, and which viewed the contemporary world as one dominated by instrumental forces. The origins of this perspective lie in Kant's contentions that the modern world view inaugurated during the Enlightenment contained destructive elements which would inevitably come to disrupt the unity of society, and that the conception of reason which emerged from the Enlightenment embodied a rhetoric of control and exploitation. During the eighteenth and nineteenth centuries many German philosophers developed Kant's critique of capitalism and modernity further, and Hegelianism, neo-Hegelianism, German romanticism and Marxism can all be linked to this critical, pessimistic response to the emergence of modernity and capitalism.[38] Germany's distance from the centre of bourgeois power in Europe gave its intelligentsia insight into the way that the humanistic values of the Enlightenment had become transformed into an ideology which legitimated the interests of bourgeois capitalism.[39] For example, the philosopher and sociologist Max Weber argued that, under capitalism, the ordinary individual lived a 'disenchanted' existence, and was constantly manipulated by an 'instrumental rationality' which regarded him or her as little more than a 'function' within the system.[40]

Weber's convictions concerning the increasing rationalisation of modern life also influenced the Frankfurt School, which was established in 1923. The Frankfurt School, and its key members: Max Horkheimer, Friedrich Pollock, Theodor Adorno, Herbert Marcuse, Otto Kirchheimer and Leo Lowenthal, applied Weber's ideas on disenchantment and instrumental rationality to a contemporary context characterised by the rise of authoritarian ideologies (fascism and Stalinism), and the growth of systems of mass commercial manipulation within the field of popular culture. At the centre of the 'critical theory' which emerged from the writings of the Frankfurt School was a concern with the way in which dominant ideologies distorted reality in order to legitimate the interests of the ruling class, and this concern was most clearly expressed in Horkheimer and Adorno's Dialectic of Enlightenment (1944), which identified the emerging mass commercial 'culture industry' as the principal source of such legitimation. Alongside the members of the Frankfurt School, intellectuals and philosophers such as Siegfried Kracauer, Ernst Bloch and Walter Benjamin also argued that the human condition within modernity was characterised by alienation, and that questions of ethics and aesthetics had become subordinated to the imperatives of an instrumental rationality which pervaded the new mediums of mass culture.

Critical theory in Weimar was, therefore, marked by a very different intellectual atmosphere to that which inspired Russian formalism after 1917. In the Soviet Union, theorists such as Shklovsky, Vertov and Eisenstein felt confident about the prospects for the future, and developed aesthetic systems which reflected such assurance. However, critical theory in Weimar emerged against a context of the rise of fascism, and this darker context is reflected in the more pessimistic vision to be found within the critical and film theory produced in Germany between 1918 and 1930.

One characteristic feature of the theories of figures such as Kracauer and Adorno was a belief that the systemic structures which afflicted the individual within modernity were deeply inscribed within language, and that visual experience constituted a domain of potential freedom from linguistic determination.[41] The visual was also seen as embodying a primal and underlying mode of communication which pre-dated the rise of modernity, and which offered the possibility of a return to sensory contact, and, consequently, to a more valid form of human experience.

This overarching concern with the redemptive powers of the visual was also applied to the relatively new medium of the cinema, and the critical discourse on the cinema which emerged from this background included contributions by important figures such as Kracauer, Rudolph Arnheim and Béla Balázs, as well as lesser known critics such as Rudolf Kurtz, Rudolf Harms and Georg Otto Stindt, writing in journals such as the *Frankfurter Zeitung* and the *Deutsche Press*. This body of critical thought was characterised by an advocacy of non-cognitive and irrationalist forms of expression which, it was hoped, would be able to liberate the values and experiences repressed by instrumental rationality. Within these critical writings cinema was often regarded as a site of significant visual pleasure, and as a redemptive vehicle, through which the repressed 'real' could be made visible.[42]

In addition to a focus on the visual, this irrationalist critical discourse also emphasised the role of immediate experience and the concrete in disclosing reality through the veil of dominant ideology. As was the case with the Russian formalists, cinema's ability to represent the concrete in considerable detail was regarded as particularly important here. When applied to the film image, the formalist concept of *ostranenie* results in an extended problematisation of representation, which is further enhanced by cinema's ability to portray material density, and the focus on the concrete within Weimar film theory can also be related to a similar desire to problematise experience. Like *ostranenie*, Weimar film theory's preoccupation with the concrete also has its origins in Kant's conception of aesthetic contemplation through *Naturschöne*, and Husserl's idea of immersion within the *Lebenswelt*.

In addition to the concrete, Weimar film theory was also engaged with another important concern of the period: that of gesture. The concern with gesture had its origins outside the cinema, in a more general interest in an aesthetics of the body. A widespread fascination with the metaphysical and philosophical significance of the body characterised much of literature and the visual arts in Germany during the 1920s.[43] Within this context, gesture and facial expression were, like the visual more generally, regarded as a kind of primeval language, capable of transcending national, class, power and gender barriers, as well as the manipulative operations of language.[44]

The most well-known articulation of this emphasis on gesture and the body can be found in the writings of Béla Balázs, but it can also be found in the work of both Adorno and Kracauer, as well as in other writings of the period. In his *Der Sichtbare Mensch oder Der Kultur Des Films* (*The Visible Man and the Culture of Film*, 1924), Balázs argued that film possessed an ability to express a poetic reality which existed beyond the rational, and that the visual representation of physical gesture in film could express general truths which language could not. Balázs's belief that gestural expression could, ideally, amount to a 'spiritual experience' rendered visual, and that, on the contrary, words were 'mere reflections of concepts', amounted to a visual and non-cognitive aesthetic which also emphasised the ability of the documentary or actuality image to embody authentic gestural expression.[45]

Within Weimar film theory, the view of the modern condition as one characterised by fragmentation and ambiguity led directly to the emergence of the concept of 'distraction' as a major critical concern of the period. This amounted to the theorisation of a new form of visual and sensory experience of the modern environment, one in which an unfocused 'distracted' mode of understanding and consumption prevailed. This distracted form of experience inevitably led to an impoverished and 'abstract' encounter with the self and the world, and further reinforced instrumental rationality.[46]

Originally a negative term, defined in opposition to the contemplative forms of concentration and more unified modes of experience normally associated with the high arts, the notion of distraction eventually took on more positive and radical connotations during the 1920s, becoming identified with non-bourgeois, or proletarian modes of experience, and with alternatives to totalising systems of rationality.[47] The aesthetic theories of Kracauer, Benjamin and Adorno were all influenced by the concept of distraction. Adorno and Benjamin employed it to formulate modernist aesthetic systems based on the fragmentary and decentred nature of distraction, and on the need for art to reflect this in both form and content.

However, Siegfried Kracauer employed the idea of distraction, and the belief that the cinema could redeem the modern world for the individual through the cinematic representation of distraction, to develop a realist, rather than formalist aesthetic.

One of the most important German film theorists of the Weimar period, Rudolph Arnheim, was also a member of the *Gestalt* school of psychology, founded by Kurt Koffka, Wolfgang Köhler and Max Wertheimer around 1910. The basis of *Gestalt* psychology was the thesis that psychological experience should be treated as a whole, or *Gestalt*, rather than as a collection of disparate parts. This holistic approach to psychological experience, which reflects the concern for the idea of totality which characterises the German philosophical idealist tradition, led Arnheim to argue that the individual subject constructed psychological *Gestalts* by abstracting a coherent world of objects and events from the multiplicity of sense data. Arnheim described this process as a 'primary transformation': a distillation of what is general and typical from the mass of sense data confronting the subject. Although Arnheim regarded the process of primary transformation as a creative act in itself, in as much as it involved a degree of motivated selection on the part of the subject, he also argued that it served primarily functional purposes.

Arnheim's aesthetic theory was largely based on his conception of 'secondary', rather than 'primary' transformation. Here, the artist abstracted general or typical features from *Gestalt* fields and embodied them within works of art. As Arnheim put it, 'the artist uses his categories of shape and colour to capture something universally significant in the particular'.[48] Arnheim also argued that primary transformation was fundamentally different from secondary transformation, in which the artist used a variety of formal techniques to create or construct an aesthetic object.[49] This led him, like some of the Russian formalists, to reject naturalistic representation in the arts because it obscured the fundamental difference between ordinary perception and aesthetic construction. For example, in his *Film* (1933), Arnheim argued that the essence of film as an art form lay in the fact that it was 'fundamentally different' from reality, and not a mechanical recording of reality.[50] This advocacy of the specificity of the aesthetic, and the need to maintain the distinction between signifier and signified, medium and subject, can also be related to similar concerns emanating from Russian formalism.

In *Film*, Arnheim detailed the various ways in which the cinematic representation of reality differed from that of normal perception, and also set out a list of 'fundamental aesthetic concepts' which film must adopt in order to reinforce that distinction, and constitute itself as art. One of these concepts was that the 'special attributes of the medium should be clearly and cleanly laid bare' to the spectator, and Arnheim quotes Max Liebermann in asserting that 'True art is conscious deception'.[51] In addition, according to Arnheim, 'In order that the film artist may create a work of art it is most important that he should consciously stress the peculiarities of his medium'.[52] In other words, for film to be art, the formal devices of cinema must be foregrounded, and their impact maximised. Arnheim's advocacy of reflexivity here is largely motivated by his belief in the autonomy of the aesthetic, and in the role of the aesthetic in representing general truths, rather than by a more politically oriented desire to reveal the workings of dominant ideology. However, like the Russian formalists, Arnheim's theory of film is also motivated by a desire to constitute the spectator as an active agent within the film viewing process.

Arnheim's emphasis on film as art, on the need to make artistic technique explicit, and on the aesthetic as both an end in itself and a means of expressing general truths, could have led him to adopt as radical a formalist position as that espoused by the Russian suprem-atists. However, Arnheim's insistence that aesthetic 'secondary transformation' was a distillation of primary transformation led him away from a radical formalist stance. Arnheim argued that the 'interplay of object and depictive medium must be patent in the finished work',[53] and went on to assert that, although it was impor-tant that film should emphasise its formal devices, this should be done in such a way that 'the character of the object reproduced should not thereby be destroyed but rather be given force, defini-tion, emphasis'.[54]

Arnheim's insistence on the requirement to maintain a perceptible and evident relationship between primary and secondary representation within the film image is also apparent in his assertion – one which reveals the influence of the German philosophical tradi-tion – that 'film art was very near to nature itself'.[55] Despite the modernist and formative character of his film theory, therefore, the legacy of German romanticism and idealism, with its emphasis on both the sublime and Naturschöne, led Arnheim to argue that, whilst maximising its own aesthetic, formal potential, 'film art' must also remain circumscribed by, and committed to, the imperative of realistic representation. This position ruled out both the excessive formalism of aesthetic movements such as suprematism, and radical deconstructionist interpretations of concepts such as ostranenie.

Arnheim's attitude towards the relationship between represen-tation and reality also reflected a wider accommodation between modernism and realism which took place in both Germany and the Soviet Union during the 1930s, and which was influenced by philosophical debates, the failure of modernism to reach a mass audience, and the emergence of socialist realism within the Soviet Union. In the Soviet Union, for example, the concept of *ostranenie* elaborated by Shklovsky, Tomasevsky, Brik and others during the 1920s was increasingly opposed by theorists such as Jan Mukarovsky, who argued that *ostranenie* encouraged excessive formalism, which eliminated the art work's object of reference in the external world, and was, as a consequence, of little social or political value.[56]

Within the Soviet Union *avant-garde* formalism was also increasingly condemned as 'counter-revolutionary' by the Party hierarchy. RAPP (Russkaia assotsiatsiia proletarskikh pisatelei, Russian Association of Proletarian Artists), which was founded in 1928, adhered strictly to Party dogma on realism, and forced its members to do the same. In 1935, socialist realism also became established as the official policy within the cinema, and, in 1936, Zhdanov, in a report to the Party Congress of that year, insisted that socialist realism was now the only 'correct' method which could be adopted by the arts.[57] The period between 1936–8 also marked the peak of the Stalinist purges, in which artists and intellectuals such as Vsevelod Meyerhold, Sergei Tretyakov and Isaac Babel disappeared; and directors such as Eisenstein, Kuleshov and others, were forced to publicly renounce their formalist transgressions.

Just as the Soviet Union moved towards realism during the 1930s, in Germany, theorists such as Balázs, Kracauer and Arnheim also argued that film must remain committed to some form of realistic representation, and avoid the kind of radical application of *ostranenie* dismissed by Mukarovsky. The development of the *Neue Sachlichkeit*, or 'new objectivity' movement from the mid 1920s onwards also led to attempts to combine the foregrounding of aesthetic form with both realist representation and social and political purposiveness. In the cinema, *Neue Sachlichkeit* led to the emergence of such films as Fritz Lang's *M* (1931) and G. W. Pabst's *Westfront 1918* (1930), *Die Dreigroschenoper* (*The Threepenny Opera*, 1931) and *Kamaradschaft* (*Comradeship*, 1931).

In terms of film theory, the most important figure to emerge from the *Neue Sachlichkeit* period was Bertolt Brecht. Brecht, whose early plays, such as *Baal* (1918), can be associated with expressionism, moved towards a more realistic style during the mid 1920s. Brecht's involvement in the cinema was relatively limited, and he was only centrally involved in the production of one film, *Kuhle Wampe* (Slatan Dudow, 1932), during the 1930s. In addition, Brecht was unhappy with Pabst's adaption of his *Die Dreigroschenoper* and eventually arrived at the pessimistic conclusion that progressive art was impossible in such a capitalist dominated industry as the cinema.[58] However, it was Brecht's theory of epic theatre, rather than his involvement with film-making, which proved to be influential in respect to the later development of European film theory and cinema.

Just as the Russian formalist *avant-garde* rejected the canons of nineteenth century literary realism, and turned instead to an artistic practice which was strident and expressive, Brecht also distanced himself from the classical German poetry of Goethe and Schiller, and turned, instead, to popular traditions of plebian folk art and proletarian culture. Other influences on Brecht included the assertive rhetorical style of the *Old Testament*, Elizabethan drama, and an exotic, melodramatic view of the city (particularly London), which he derived from the novels of Rudyard Kipling, Charles Dickens and Jack London.[59]

In addition to these older influences, Brecht was also influenced by a range of more recent modernist artists and movements. These included the self-reflexive photo-montages of artists such as John Heartfield, and the productivist tendency within Russian formalism. Like post-revolutionary Russian formalism, Brecht also rejected the idea of the autonomy of the aesthetic, and committed himself to the development of a politically engaged theatrical practice. Like many others associated with *Neue Sachlichkeit*, Brecht also evolved his aesthetic ideas in deliberate opposition to earlier artistic movements such as dada and expressionism. Following his renunciation of the literary conventions and rhyming couplets of classical German poetry, Brecht adopted a style of blank verse in his plays and poetry which was jarring, harsh, and action-oriented. This provided the foundation for Brecht's concept of the *gestisch*, or *gest*, in which a form of language was used in which references to physical actions predominated over the representation of interior psychological states. This gestural, action-oriented form of language was also influenced by street chants, political marching songs, and the dissonant rhythms of jazz music.[60]

Like the Russian formalists, Brecht believed that the conventions of aesthetic realism which had developed within the nineteenth-century novel no longer corresponded to the needs of the twentieth century, and that a new type of art must be created in order to correspond to those needs. Like the Russian formalists, Brecht criticised the reliance upon empathetic identification, verisimilitude, diegetic coherence, narrative closure and characterisation within conventional realism, arguing that such techniques positioned the reader/spectator as a passive recipient of dominant ideology. In contrast, in Brecht's theory of epic theatre, narration takes place in a series of relatively autonomous tableaux, rather than, as in conventional theatre, within a series of smooth, unfolding scenes and scenarios. The object of such dislocation is both to foreground the fact that the play is a constructed artifice, and to disrupt processes of empathetic identification which might occur between spectator and characters and events within the play. In addition to this semi-dislocated tableaux structure, the various thematic strands of the play are also left partially unresolved, forcing the spectator to play a more active role in settling the dilemmas posed by the drama. In this respect, and as Brecht asserted, the epic theatre 'appeals less to the feelings than to the spectator's reason'.[61]

In addition to their disjointed, modernist profile, Brecht's plays are also expository and didactic. Characters speak out on different points of view, and make often conflicting statements, sometimes involving direct address to the audience, about how the contents of the play should be interpreted. This didactic aspect of Brecht's theory of epic theatre make his plays openly political, and can be associated with the various agitational propaganda movements which emerged in the Soviet Union following the October Revolution. However, Brecht's theory of epic theatre is by no means exclusively didactic and rationalist, but attempts to achieve a new balance between emotional identification and reason. Consequently, far from excluding emotion altogether, Brecht argued that 'it would be quite wrong to deny emotion to this kind of theatre'.[62]

One of the most influential concepts within Brecht's aesthetic theory, and the principal means through which his plays attempted to disrupt empathetic identification, is that of the *Verfremdungs-effekt*, or 'alienation effect'. Here, aspects of plot and *mise-en-scène* are organised so as to foreground the nature of the play as a constructed, signifying artifact. Writing about the use of alienation effects in Chinese acting, for example, Brecht argued that, in the Chinese theatre:

> the artist observes himself. Thus, if he is representing a cloud, perhaps, showing its unexpected appearance, its soft and strong growth, its rapid yet gradual transformation, he will occasionally look at the audience as if to say: isn't it just like this? ... The artist's object is to appear strange, and even surprising to the audience.[63]

Brecht's use of the term 'to appear strange' here indicates that the Brechtian *Verfremdungseffekt* can be associated with the concept of *ostranenie*, and both principles share the same modernist, deconstructionist character. In fact it is probable, although not entirely certain, that the idea of the *Verfremdungseffekt* was directly influenced by the earlier concept of *ostranenie*.[64] However, the *Verfremdungseffekt* also differs from *ostranenie* in that Shklovsky had initially intended that *ostranenie* should extend the process of perception as an end in itself, so that disinterested aesthetic contemplation could be distinguished from more instrumental forms of experience. However, Brecht always intended that the *Verfremdungseffekt* should be used to de-naturalise dominant ideology.

Brecht's writings did not become widely available in English translation until after his death, in 1956, and with the founding of the Bertold Brecht Archive in Berlin, in 1957. During the 1960s and 1970s European film theory adopted an increasingly anti-realist and modernist orientation, influenced by the appearance of translations of writings by Brecht, Shklovsky, Propp, Jakobson, Eisenstein, Vertov and others. One consequence of these developments was that the anti-realist film theory of the 1960s and 1970s focused on the more *avant-gardist* and deconstructionist aspects of Brecht's ideas, and Brecht soon became regarded as one of the most important sources for a new, *avant-garde* 'counter cinema'.

However, the characterisation of Brecht's theory of epic cinema as radically anti-realist and *avant-gardist* is problematic. Like Arnheim, Brecht wished to develop an appropriate balance between foregrounding and illusionism, and he did not reject the use of realism, or the 'classic realist text', to the extent that post-structuralist critics writing in the 1970s have suggested that he did.[65] Brecht also insisted on using popular, as well as modernist forms, in his plays, arguing that 'Popular means intelligible to the broad masses, taking over their own forms of expression and enriching them'.[66] Rather than adopt an entirely deconstructionist aesthetic, therefore, Brecht wished to base his theatrical practice on popular cultural forms, and to use devices such as the *Verfremdungseffekt* in order to make the spectator more politically and critically aware. As with most Weimar theory, therefore, realism still has an important role to play in Brecht's theory of epic cinema, a point which Brecht clearly signalled when he argued that 'The words Popularity and Realism are natural companions'.[67]

*   *   *

The philosophical origins of Russian formalism and much Weimar film theory are to be located within an intuitionist aesthetic tradition inherited from Kant and the German idealist tradition. However, in both Russian formalism and Weimar film theory, this intuitionist tendency entered into dialectical confrontation with others, premised on positivist, deterministic, didactic and rationalist principles. Almost from its beginning, therefore, European film theory and cinema was bifurcated by these two very different traditions. Both traditions can be found at work within the films and plays of Vertov and Brecht respectively. Despite his desire to be politically engaged in making films for a purpose, however, Vertov's *Chelovek s kinoapparatom* retains a degree of ambivalence which Brecht's plays do not, and it is this, combined with a pioneering, innovative exploration of film form, which makes *Chelovek s kinoapparatom* so important within the history of European cinema. Similarly, although Eisenstein accused Vertov of 'cine-hooliganism' in making *Chelovek s kinoapparatom*, there are grounds for arguing that it is from the more deterministic position adopted within Eisenstein's early film theory that most problems have emerged.

Notes

1. Elliot, David, *New Worlds: Russian Art and Society 1900–1937* (New York: Rizzoli, 1986), p. 8.
2. Ibid.
3. Ibid., p. 9.
4 Nettl, J. P., *The Soviet Achievement* (London: Thames and Hudson, 1967), p. 23.
5. Ibid., p. 20.
6. Elliot, op cit., p. 10.
7. Nettl, op cit., pp. 14–15.
8. Elliot, op cit., p. 13.
9. Ibid.
10. Parmesani, Loredana, *Art of the Twentieth Century: Movements, Theories, Schools and Tendencies 1900–2000* (Milan: Skira editore/Giò Marconi, 2000), p. 30.
11. Petrić, Vlada, *Constructivism In Film: The Man with the Movie Camera A Cinematic Analysis* (Cambridge and London: Cambridge University Press, 1987), p. 6.
12. Mitchell, Stanley, 'From Shklovsky to Brecht: Some preliminary remarks towards a history of the politicisation of Russian Formalism', *Screen* (Summer, 1974), vol. 15, no. 2, p. 75.
13. Passmore, John, *A Hundred Years of Philosophy* (London: Penguin, 1968), p. 187.

14. Ibid., p. 193.
15. Larrabee, Harold A. (ed.), *Selections From Bergson* (New York: Appleton-Century-Crofts, 1949), p. 111.
16. Passmore, op cit., p. 193.
17. Kant, Immanuel, *The Critique of Judgement*, trans. J. C. Meredith (Oxford: Oxford University Press, 1973), p. 176.
18. Kemp, John, *The Philosophy of Kant* (Oxford: Oxford University Press, 1968), p. 109.
19. Andrew, Dudley, *The Major Film Theories* (Oxford: Oxford University Press, 1976), p. 80.
20. Brewster, Ben, 'From Shklovsky to Brecht: A Reply', *Screen* (Summer, 1974), vol. 15, no. 2, p. 86.
21. Ibid., p. 87.
22. Parmesani, op cit., p. 31.
23. Petrić, op cit., p. 5.
24. Brewster, op cit., p. 91.
25. Ibid., p. 87.
26. Petrić, op cit., p. 7.
27. Propp, Vladimir, *Morphology of the Folk Tale* (Austin, TX and London: University of Texas Press, 1968). For analysis see Haney, Jack C., *An Introduction to the Russian Folk Tale* (New York and London: M. E. Sharpe, 1999), pp. 12–13.
28. Propp's *Morphology of the Folk Tale* will be considered in greater depth in Chapter 5.
29. Vertov, Dziga, 'Kino-Eye: The Embattled Documentarists', in Schnitzer, Luda, Schnitzer Jean and Martin, Marcel (eds), *Cinema In Revolution* (London: Secker and Warburg, 1973), p. 79.
30. Ibid., p. 81.
31. Petrić, op cit., p. 21.
32. Husserl's conception of the *Lebenswelt* will be considered in greater detail in Chapter 7.
33. Petrić, op cit., p. 4.
34. Ibid., p. 21.
35. Ibid., p. 10.
36. Ibid., p. 17.
37. Ibid., p. 55.
38. Hauser, Arnold, *The Social History of Art: Three: Rococo, Classicism and Romanticism* (London: Routledge and Kegan Paul, 1973), p. 94.
39. Hobsbawm, Eric, *The Age of Revolution* (London: Cardinal, 1962), p. 296.
40. Buck-Morss, Susan, *The Origin of Negative Dialectics* (London: The Harvester Press, 1977), p. 17.
41. Hake, Sabine, 'Towards a Philosophy of Film' in Hake (ed.), *The Cinema's Third Machine: Writing on Film in Germany 1907–1933* (London and Lincoln, NB: University of Nebraska Press, 1993), p. 131.
42. Kaes, Anton, 'Literary Intellectuals and the Cinema: Charting a

Controversy (1909–1929)', *New German Critique* (1987) no. 40, p. 24.

43. Hake, op cit., pp. 130–1.
44. Ibid., p. 132.
45. Balázs, Béla, *Der Sichtbare Mensche oder Der Kultur Des Films* (Wien and Leipzig: Deutsch-Osterreichischer Verlag, 1924), p. 40.
46. Rodowick, D. N., 'The Last Things Before the Last', *New German Critique* (1991) no. 54, p. 115.
47. Ibid., p. 117.
48. Arnheim, Rudolph, *Art and Visual Perception* (Berkeley and Los Angeles, CA: UCL Press, 1967), p. vi.
49. Ibid., p. 37.
50. Arnheim, Rudolph, *Film* (London: Faber and Faber, 1933), p. 18.
51. Ibid., pp. 44–5.
52. Ibid., p. 46.
53. Ibid.
54. Ibid.
55. Ibid., p. 47.
56. Mukarovsky, Jan, 'Standard Language and Poetic Language', in *Prague School Reader in Aesthetics: Literary Structure and Style*, trans. Garvin, Paul R. (Washington, DC: Georgetown University Press, 1964), p. 19.
57. Petrić, op cit., p. 69.
58. Walsh, Martin, *The Brechtian Aspect of Radical Cinema* (London: BFI, 1981), p. 11.
59. Esslin, Martin, *Brecht: A Choice of Evils* (London: Eyre Methuen, 1980), p. 103.
60. Ibid., pp. 105–6.
61. Willett, John (ed. and trans.), *Brecht On Theatre* (London: Eyre Methuen, 1979), p. 23.
62. Ibid.
63. Ibid., p. 92.
64. Mitchell, op cit., p. 80.
65. See Colin MacCabe's seminal 'Realism and the Cinema: Notes on some Brechtian Theses', *Screen* (Summer, 1974), vol. 15, no. 2.
66. Willett, op cit., p. 108.
67. Ibid., p. 107.

II

Determinism and Symbolism in the Film Theory of Eisenstein

Eisenstein's initial theory of montage was premised on the belief that a film's structure should be built up through the juxtaposition of contrasting elements. Eisenstein believed that this form of 'collision' montage would generate more powerful filmic effects, and, consequently, would also have a more forceful impact upon the audience. Eisenstein had studied mechanical engineering at the Petrograd Institute of Engineering before he became involved in first theatre and then the cinema, and he derived his initial conception of montage from this background, as well as from the constructivist emphasis on mechanistic assemblage. In *Film Form*, for example, he reveals the influence of both engineering and constructivism on him when he describes montage as a word 'borrowed from industry, a word denoting the assembly of machinery, pipes, machine tools. This striking word is "montage", which means assembling'.[1] Eisenstein's early training in engineering also led him to seek a unit of measurement for calibrating the influence of his films, and this became the 'attraction': the basic element of measure around which Eisenstein would assemble his montage chains.[2]

To this concern with mechanistic assemblage, Eisenstein also added an insistence that each attraction within the assemblage should retain a degree of autonomy, rather than be completely subsumed within the work as a whole. Thus, set design, costumery, lighting, plot, and other aspects of the film should retain a 'democratic harmony', rather than be ordered into a 'feudal hierarchy'.[3] This anti-realist aspect of Eisenstein's ideas was initially influenced by a context of *avant-gardist* criticism of the established Russian theatre. Newly formed *avant-garde* groups such as Vsevolod Meyerhold's R.S.F.S.R Theatre No. 1, Vladimir Mayakovsky's futurist theatre troupe, and the Proletkult theatre, all shared an antipathy towards the 'bourgeois' theatre practised by established institutions such as the Bolshoi, and argued instead for the establishment of a non-naturalistic, modernist form of theatre.

Within this general context of radical experimentation Eisenstein was particularly influenced by the ideas of Vsevolod Meyerhold. Meyerhold's method of theatrical performance combined experimental improvisation with a technique which he defined as 'biomechanics', where every aspect of stage presentation was determined by rigorous planning and measurement. Biomechanics also elevated physicality over the expression of psychological introspection, and one consequence of this was that Meyerhold's training courses for actors included sessions on acrobatics and other forms of physical activity.[4] Eisenstein joined Meyerhold's State School for Stage Direction in 1921, and the combination of functionalist biomechanics and experimental improvisation which he came into contact with there led him to develop a theory of the attraction which was characterised by a stylised, performative, positivist and reflexive approach.[5]

In addition to the influence of Meyerhold and theatrical anti-realism, Eisenstein's theory of film was also influenced by the behaviourist theories of the physiologist Ivan Pavlov. Pavlov's theory of the conditioned response was based on the prediction and control of observable behaviour. As with behaviourism in general, Pavlov's ideas were based on a deterministic conception of the human subject, which assumed that the individual could be conditioned to respond automatically to controlled stimulation. Eisenstein adopted Pavlov's notion of the conditioned reflex in the hope that it would provide an objective basis for a theatrical practice in which revolutionary ideals could be effectively communicated to the spectator.[6] However, the deterministic conception of human agency which underlies Pavlovian reflexology was to leave an indelible, and troublesome, imprint upon Eisenstein's later theory and practice of cinema.

The influence of Pavlovian psychology led Eisenstein to adopt an approach to artistic production, in which, as he himself made clear, the chief responsibility of the director was 'the moulding of the audience in a desired direction (or mood)'.[7] However, as a committed communist and 'disciplined Soviet citizen', Eisenstein wished to develop an artistic practice which could play an important role within the consolidation of the new Soviet regime. His advocacy of a normative artistic theory and practice was, therefore, the product of idealistic zeal, rather than of a less admissible attempt to manipulate the spectator *per se*.[8]

Eisenstein referred to his first theory of montage as the 'montage of attractions': a phrase which he first used in a theatre manifesto published in the radical *avant-garde* journal *Lef*, in 1923.[9] At this point in time, Eisenstein had yet to become familiar with Pavlovian reflexology, and the model of the attraction contained in the 1923 essay owes more to the influence of the combination of positivism and experimentalism which he had inherited from Meyerhold, than to reflexology. Nevertheless, the approach adopted within the 'Montage of Attractions' essay is fully compatible with, and looks ahead to, Eisenstein's later appropriation of Pavlov. Eisenstein's initial conception of the attraction was also influenced by the Russian formalist stress on identifying the basic underlying units and axioms of art, and the formalist preoccupation with 'scientific' method is similarly evident in Eisenstein's attempt to formulate aesthetic 'laws' similar in kind to those he had studied during his training as an engineer.[10]

These influences led Eisenstein to define the attraction as a particular type of 'aggressive quality' which would be embodied within all the individual events or gestures which made up a theatrical production, and Eisenstein hoped to be able to 'mathematically calculate'[11] the impact of these 'aggressive moments' upon the spectator:

> An attraction is in our understanding any demonstrable fact (an action, an object, a phenomenon, a conscious combination, and so on) that is known and proven to exercise a definite effect on the attention and emotions of the audience and that, combined with others, possesses the characteristic of concentrating the audience's emotions in any direction dictated by the production's purpose.[12]

Although not directly influenced by Pavlovian reflexology, the 'montage of attractions', with its rhetoric of mathematically calculated moments of aggression, conforms closely to Pavlov's positivist theoretical model. Elsewhere in the 'Montage of Attractions' essay Eisenstein also uses terms such as 'laws', 'verify', and these further attest to the character of his ideas at this stage.[13]

Eisenstein also derived his initial conception of the attraction from the circus act, where each stunt was both complete within itself, and delivered so as to achieve a maximum, stylised impact. Applying this approach to the theatre and cinema, Eisenstein argued that each stage event or film shot should function like a circus 'attraction', in that it should be dynamic in nature, and forceful in its attempt to attract the spectator's, attention. The play, or film's narrative structure would then be built up as a 'montage' of such attractions.[14] However, although Eisenstein derived the idea of the attraction from the circus he also made a crucial distinction between that idea and a typical circus stunt. According to Eisenstein, the latter was 'complete within itself [and therefore is] ... the direct opposite of the attraction, which is based on something relative, the reactions of the audience'.[15] In other words, the attraction does not exist in a finished form within the theatrical performance or film, and only achieves final resolution within the mind of the spectator. This does not, however, imply a significant degree of spectatorial autonomy, as, in line with Eisenstein's general orientation at this point in his career, the response of the spectator will remain conditioned by the force and character of the diegetic attraction.

Eisenstein used the models of collision montage and the attraction to develop an initial theatrical and film practice which was highly stylised and assertively didactic. He also designated this type of artistic *avant-garde* practice as an 'effective structure' because its principle objective was to impact upon the spectator. However, this directive tendency was undermined to some extent by Eisenstein's insistence that the various attractions within the film should not only possess a considerable degree of individual autonomy, but should also be 'arbitrarily chosen'.[16] This concern with the autonomy and arbitrary nature of the attraction was influenced by Eisenstein's belief that the attraction should have an unfinished character, in order to encourage the spectator to parti- cipate in the final production of meaning. Nevertheless, Eisenstein was equivocal about how such a randomly selected collection of incomplete attractions, which he designated with the appellation of 'free montage', would eventually coalesce into the 'specific final thematic effect' which he aimed to achieve.[17]

In his first attempt to resolve this problem, Eisenstein resorted to the idea of 'the dominant', a concept which was then widely discussed within formalist linguistic circles.[18] In his 1927 essay entitled 'The Dominant', Roman Jakobson argued that, although a literary text was comprised of a number of different codes, one of these always performed the role of organising the interactions of subservient codes across the body of the work.[19] In its identification of underlying generative structures, the idea of the dominant echoes the Russian formalist focus on deep textual structures, and can be associated with Vladimir Propp's concep- tions of the 'function' and 'meta-narrative', as set out in his *Morphology of the Folk Tale*, which was published less than a year after the appearance of Jakobson's essay. However, like Proppian morphological methodology, Jakobson's idea of the dominant also shares a potential for reductivism, and this was to have implications for Eisenstein's theory of the montage of attractions.

The montage of attractions was initially conceived of by Eisenstein as a method of film assembly which would link the dominant aspect of one shot, or attraction, to another, via the principle of collision. However, one consequence of this approach was that other aspects of the shot were largely ignored in the transition from shot to shot, as Eisenstein sought to develop a striking progression of evanescent 'dominant' stimuli across the body of the film. Later in his career Eisenstein qualified his use of the dominant, placing more emphasis on the ancillary aspects of the attraction, and this led him to regard the film shot as a locus for a range of interacting attractions, all of which could be developed in a number of ways, rather than merely as a vehicle for carrying a dominant theme. Eisenstein's mature conception of the attraction is based upon the premise that the attraction is a type of quality which exists both within and between shots, and, according to this formulation, any one shot can contain a number of visual, aural or intellectual attractions, all of which can evolve and enter into various relationships with each other.

Eisenstein initially applied the montage of attractions to the organisation of a film along five major axes, which he defined as 'metric', 'rhythmic', 'tonal', 'overtonal' and 'intellectual' systems of montage. Metric montage is generated through the juxtaposition of different lengths of shot, whilst rhythmic montage is developed through the juxtaposition of shots containing different types of movement, and direction of pace. However, although metric and rhythmic montage are relatively easily comprehensible and straightforward means of building up edited sequences, the categories of tonal and overtonal montage are more abstract, and, consequently, less easy to grasp. Tonal montage essentially refers to the overall atmosphere of a scene, or series of shots. It is the dominant 'tone' which colours the character of the individual shots within it. Overtonal montage extends the principle of tonal montage to larger sections of the film, and even to the film as a whole. All of these four categories of montage operate alongside that of intellectual montage (and in conjunction with musical compositional and dialectical structures which will be referred to later) to shape the development of the montage of attractions.

Although the four categories of montage referred to above make up the bulk of the edited narrative in Eisenstein's films, it is the fifth, that of intellectual montage, which has the most significant theoretical implications. Eisenstein's conception of intellectual montage is derived from a number of sources, including that of the Marxist philosophy of dialectical materialism, and is based on the premise that if two shots with radically different diegetic contents are placed in conjunction with each other the spectator can only explain their relationship by means of a concept which links the two at the level of symbolic meaning. A well-known example of intellectual montage can be found in the scene in Eisenstein's *Stachka* (*Strike*, 1924) where a sequence of shots of a cossack killing a child is cut against a sequence of a bull being killed in an abattoir. Because the two shots occupy two entirely different spatio-temporal and diegetic environments, the only means of linking them together meaningfully is through the abstract idea of 'slaughter', or 'butchery'. Eisenstein was particularly pleased with this sequence of intellectual montage, and discussed it in some depth in his *The Film Sense*.[20]

Despite the formalist nature of his theory of montage, and of the concept of intellectual montage in particular, Eisenstein's films themselves contain only isolated moments of modernist montage, and are, for the most part, largely made up of more conventional editing structures. In films such as *Stachka* (1924) and *Oktyabr* (*October*, 1928), for example, modernist montage sequences appear mainly at moments of dramatic or emotional climax, rather than throughout the body of the film, as Vertov was later to attempt in his *Chelovek s kinoapparatom* (*The Man with the Movie Camera*, 1929). It was partly his reaction to what he referred to as the 'cine-hooliganism' of *Chelovek s kinoapparatom*,[21] and the realisation that his initial conceptualisation of the montage of attractions could not provide a sufficient basis for the composition of an entire feature-length film, which eventually persuaded Eisenstein to adopt a less explicitly *avant-gardist* approach in his later work.

A number of important differences exist between Eisenstein's early theory of the montage of attractions and his later films and writings, and it has been argued that these differences are so great as to constitute an 'epistemological shift' from an earlier, cognitivist and 'materialist' aesthetic, to a later one based on notions of emotive indeterminacy and organic fusion. For example, David Bordwell has argued that a 'marked schism' exists between the 1923–30 and the 1930–48 phases of Eisenstein's career, and that 'two autonomous theories' can be discerned at work over this period.[22] The idea of the 'epistemological shift' was fashionable in the mid 1970s, and was largely derived from the French philosopher Louis Althusser's influential argument, set out in his *For Marx* (1965), that an epistemological shift could be discerned between the work of the early (humanist) and later (materialist) Marx. Following Althusser, and using Althusserian terminology, Bordwell applied the concept of the epistemological shift to Eisenstein, although he reversed Althusser's preference for the later Marx by arguing that the early, 'materialist' Eisenstein was preferable to the later Eisenstein, who had 'relapse[d] into Romanticism'.[23] However, the argument that a radical transformation had occurred within Eisenstein's thinking after 1930 has been challenged by many critics, both during the 1970s, when Bordwell was writing, and later, and the evidence suggests that, far from an epistemological shift, a consistent, although constantly evolving system of thought can be discerned within Eisenstein's films and written work.

One reason why Eisenstein's ideas evolved during the 1930s was that he became increasingly driven by a desire to ground his work in the theoretical principles of Marxist dialectical materialism.[24] In 1935 the influence of dialectical materialism on committed Russian intellectuals such as Eisenstein was reinforced by the appearance of two important and authoritative publications: the first translation into Russian of Engels's *Dialectics of Nature*, and Stalin's 'Dialectical and Historical Materialism'.[25] These works of Marxist philosophy attempted to systematise dialectics into a series of formal 'laws', which, it was argued, could be seen to determine all human and natural activity.

The appearance of such texts so soon after Soviet socialist realism had been confirmed, in 1934, as the official aesthetic doctrine of the new Soviet state, suggested to Eisenstein that a synthesis of dialectics and socialist realism might provide the basis for the development of a genuinely Marxist theory and practice of cinema. Eisenstein initially sought to establish a general film theory based on dialectics, and also planned the development of a film version of Marx's *Das Kapital*, which, he hoped, would be structured along dialectical principles, 'so that the humble worker or peasant can understand it in the dialectical manner'.[26] However, although neither of these challenging projects were ever realised, Eisenstein did draw extensively on the theory of dialectical materialism during the 1930s.

One aspect of dialectics which particularly influenced Eisenstein's later work was the idea that the dialectic was a natural force which pervaded all of life. This formulation caused him to modify his earlier conception of 'the dominant' as the organising principle in a film, and to develop a methodological model in which a single 'life force' or 'principle' permeated the entire film.[27] This emphasis on the synthetic unity of the art work was, in many respects, only an extension of Eisenstein's earlier conceptions of tonal and overtonal montage, whilst the idea of a single 'principle' shares a resemblance with the earlier model of the attraction as a 'quality' which determines the character of each and every shot. Nevertheless, the adoption of the idea of a 'single life-force' did lead to the emergence of very different films to the earlier *Stachka*, or *Bronenosets Potemkin* (*Potemkin*, 1925), and, in place of the fragmented, tableaux style of such films, Eisenstein's later films are more integrated and linear, and less overtly modernist.

Despite the emphasis which he had always placed on the relative autonomy of the 'attraction' or shot, throughout his career Eisenstein had always been primarily concerned with bringing his films into a final unified condition. As already argued, Eisenstein's preoccupation with the ideal of aesthetic unity stemmed from the influence of symbolism and romanticism, and that influence was such that Eisenstein has been described as the 'greatest exponent of symbolism within the cinema'.[28] However, Eisenstein's concern with concepts of aesthetic unity also stemmed from his conviction that, in order to play a positive role in promoting the cause of socialism, art must first attain the condition of coherent expression, and, in order to bring his interest in the unified work of art into conjunction with contemporary debates over dialectical materialism, Eisenstein turned to the conceptions of totality contained within Engels's *Dialectics of Nature*, and other key Marxist texts.

The model of organic totality put forward by Engels in the *Dialectics of Nature* was premised on the idea that, even though a complex organism may evolve as a consequence of a dynamic process of cellular differentiation, each cell within it will retain the character of its original, generative identity, or 'unifying principle'.[29] Eisenstein's adoption of the notion of a 'single expressive principle' was derived from this idea. Following Engels, he conceived the dialectic as an animating principle which pervaded all matter and thought, and argued that this animating force, 'movement', or 'principle', also 'lies at the basis of a work of art'.[30]

The dialectical model of an unfolding elemental process, characterised by both unity and contradiction, was an important influence on Eisenstein's later theory of film form. However, as his ideas developed, and under the influence of a symbolist aesthetic, Eisenstein began to place more emphasis on the importance of the first, or unifying principle, than on the category of differentiation, and this emphasis on an all-determining and pervasive 'unifying principle' increasingly distinguished his conception of the dialectic from that held within more orthodox, official circles. As we will see later, this, at first sight, apparently inconsequential philosophical divergence was later to have significant implications for Eisenstein's relationship with the Soviet establishment.

In addition to this philosophical digression, another issue which quickly led to the emergence of friction between Eisenstein and the Soviet authorities was that of Eisenstein's use of symbolist stylistic and thematic motifs. Eisenstein's late theory of film form combines the principle of organicism with the idea of the dialectic as an animating principle which suffuses all matter, and what emerges from this is a theory of film which draws on techniques and themes normally associated with romantic or symbolist art. However, the influence by what, in the official Soviet view, was a 'decadent', bourgeois movement, was to prove a source of continuous difficulty for Eisenstein. These difficulties emerged as early as 1928, when *Oktyabr* (1928) was strongly criticised for its excessive 'symbolist' content,[31] and continued throughout the 1930s and 1940s.

The symbolist orientation within Eisenstein's later films and writings also led him to utopian conclusions concerning the ability of film to represent, or come into proximity with, fundamental aspects of reality. For example, Eisenstein claimed that if a film was organised so as to accord with the structure of the dialectic – a structure which, following his reading of the *Dialectics of Nature*, Eisenstein believed to possess a fundamental ontological status – then that film would become one with the dialectic itself. This amounts to a utopian philosophy of metaphysical transcendent immersion, in which, as one critic has argued, 'the spectator, the film, and Eisenstein all participate, and in which ecstasy aims only at ensuring that one loses oneself, indefinitely'.[32] It is this metaphysical aspect of Eisenstein's film theory which marks that theory out as primarily symbolist, or idealist, rather than Marxist, and which reveals Eisenstein's abiding concern with the mystical, the religious and the irrational.[33]

Despite Eisenstein's increasing preoccupation with organicist conceptions of totality, his later aesthetic was also motivated by a desire to develop a theory of filmic composition which, whilst emphasising aesthetic unity, would also embody the dialectical principle of contradiction. Eisenstein's first attempt to develop a model of film form which would retain the oppositional autonomy of individual shots, yet contain that autonomy within the parameters of the film as a whole, was that of the 'complex ensemble':

I have deliberately used the term ensemble ... a skilful balance of individual expressions through proper orchestrations ... so that the entire complex of the expressive means of the film be used as to make each of them effective within the framework of the whole ... I repeat that mastery here means ability to develop each element of the expressive means to the utmost, at the same time orchestrating, balancing the whole so as to prevent any particular, individual element from undermining the unity of the ensemble, the unity of the compositional whole.[34]

Here, each 'individual expression' would be developed, as Eisenstein puts it, 'to the utmost', and each shot, theme and tone rendered individually expressive, vibrant and affective. However, these highly expressive units would also be 'neutralised' through the skilful balancing of elements within the whole, thus assuring that a unified aesthetic structure emerged.

Eisenstein also argued that the orchestration of these expressive units into a unified whole should be determined by a logic of dialectical development characterised by the antagonistic evolution of thesis and synthesis, and that such a logic should be embedded within the deep structural, narrative logic of the film. It is, therefore, the process of evolving counterpoint, in which 'themes interpenetrate each other ... and intertwine', which should determine the final aesthetic structure of the film.[35] This formulation led Eisenstein to criticise films in which the overall structure of the narrative did not flow from such an inner logic of thematic evolution as 'stylised' and 'formalist', and he differentiated his own theory of montage, based, as it was, on ensuring that every 'nuance of composition' in a film stemmed from such a logic, from what he considered to be a formalist approach to film form.[36]

Eisenstein based his denunciation of formalism here on a particular interpretation of the idea of 'theme'. By theme, Eisenstein means the ideational content of the film, and, according to Eisenstein, the 'primary' task of the film-maker was to establish of what such content should consist. For Eisenstein, this is not merely an aesthetic task, but a committed undertaking, driven by the Marxist film-maker's desire to ground his/her film in politically important, socially relevant issues. When the appropriate thematic matrix has been established, formal 'rhythmic proportions' of pictorial and narrative composition can then be applied. Where this is correctly accomplished, the rhythmic proportions of the film will express, and flow from, the 'inner content of the theme' and its dialectical evolution, and a satisfying, unified aesthetic form will emerge.[37] On the other hand, 'formalism' would inevitably emerge if the rhythmic proportions of the film did not embody the inner content of theme, but were laid across the film as a body of generic stereotypes, or ideological discourses. This 'dialectical' model of film form shares the same systematic nature which characterised Eisenstein's earlier model of the montage of attractions. However, the complex ensemble differs from the montage of attractions in that it is concerned with evoking an intuitive, rather than cognitive encounter with ideas, or 'themes'. In addition, the complex ensemble is a more unified aesthetic model than was the case with the montage of attractions, and deploys ideological discourse in a more obscure manner.

During the 1930s Eisenstein developed three separate approaches to film form, all of which were derived from the idea of the complex ensemble, and all of which were predominantly intuitionist and associative in character. The first of these aesthetic models was that of the 'interior monologue', which Eisenstein derived from James Joyce's *Ulysses* (1922). In *Ulysses*, Joyce structured dialogue in an impressionistic, associative manner in order to represent the way that the mind created interior monologues in a 'stream of consciousness'. Eisenstein believed that the sound film could take this approach further, and, when he visited Joyce in Paris in 1930, held discussions with the novelist on how processes of thought could be depicted in the medium of film.[38] Unfortunately, Eisenstein's Joycean model of associative representation soon came under attack from critics within the Soviet Union, who regarded *Ulysses* as an example of unacceptable modernist idealism. For example, in 1934, the Soviet Writers Congress denounced Joyce as a decadent intellectual, and, following this, Eisenstein was increasingly forced to abandon the Joycean inspired interior monologue.[39]

The second model of mental representation which Eisenstein explored during the 1930s was based on theories of proto-logical or 'savage' thought associated with figures such as the French anthropologist Lucien Lévy Brühl. One of the key ideas which Eisenstein derived from Lévy Brühl's *Primitive Mentality* (1930) was that of the underlying 'principle' which, Lévy Brühl argued, could be found within primitive systems of mimetic representation. Lévy Brühl claimed that, within primitive cultures, representational form was not merely used in order to depict the surface appearance of things, but was also deployed in order to distil a 'primeval generalisation' of the nature of that which was represented. Thus, when embodied within representational form, what Lévy Brühl referred to as 'sensuous thought', linked analysis and description with more intuitive representations of primeval generalisation, or 'principle', and Lévy Brühl argued that this amounted to a more holistic form of cognition than that which characterised contemporary modes of thought.[40]

'Principle', then, is that aspect of a particular representation which both gives it general significance, and sums up the essence, character or nature of the thing represented.[41] Following Lévy Brühl, Eisenstein argued that, in primitive mimetic representations, such as those found in the caves at Lescau and Cueva de los Caballos, generalising principle was realised, and made manifest, through the use of 'line'. According to Eisenstein, linearity is a fundamental aspect of perception, primarily because, in the act of visual perception, the eye 'runs over' a series of perceived objects in order to establish their relationship to each other. Again, after Lévy Brühl, Eisenstein went on to argue that it was this relationship between perception and linearity which determined the linear character of the primitive cave paintings found at Lescau and elsewhere.[42]

Eisenstein went on from this to argue that, whilst, in primitive art, the depiction of generalising principle was limited by the fact that artistic practice had yet to fully develop into a complex representational medium, and was, consequently, closely linked to the portrayal of an empirically perceived reality; the greater complexity and intricacy of contemporary art meant that principle could be expressed through *both* empirical, and far more abstract categories of linearity. Eisenstein's conception of the role of linearity within film art is, therefore, based on a conception of line as both a visually evident and an underlying, deep structural, organisational device. Line is that which both organises visual compositions into meaningful structures, and underlies the surface appearance of a film, linking all aspects of the film into an organic totality.

Eisenstein's conception of linearity as a kind of 'skeleton' located within the film allowed him to move on from the highly associative and paradigmatic model of interior monologue which he had derived from Joyce, and to develop a conception of film form which involved a greater degree of compositional and narrative organisation. A theory of film form based on Lévy Brühl's notions of sensuous thought and principle also enabled Eisenstein to synthesise this enhanced degree of compositional precision with his enduring consideration of organicism and totality more easily than would have been the case with a less structured, more impressionistic model derived from Joyce.

Although Eisenstein hoped that his adoption of an aesthetic model based on theories of primitive thought would prove more officially condonable than had been the case with his previous endorsement of Joycean *avant-gardism*, this proved not to be the case, and he soon came under aggressive criticism for what was perceived to be a politically regressive involvement with primitivism and quasi-religious iconography. Such criticism reached a peak in 1937, in a vitriolic campaign mounted against Eisenstein's *Bezhin Lug* (*Bezhin Meadow*) by, amongst others, the official critic Boris Shumyatsky, who declared Eisenstein's film to be 'anti-artistic and politically unsound'.[43] *Bezhin Lug* was eventually banned by the Chief Directorate of Soviet Cinema (GUKF), at the bequest of Shumyatsky.[44]

As the campaign against *Bezhin Lug* progressed, Eisenstein was forced to apologise for his 'mistakes', and admit that the use of Lévy Brühlian sensuous thought in the film had led to 'excessive symbolism' and 'formalism'. He also 'confessed' to the charge that *Bezhin Lug* had obscured the relationship of the characters and events within the film to their specific socio-historical context: that of Stalin's programme of the collectivisation of agriculture. It was this lack of socialist realist 'typicality', and apparent resort to idealist symbolism, which led to the banning of *Bezhin Lug*, and to Eisenstein's humiliating public apology for his film's 'elemental anarchy'.[45]

It was largely in response to the criticisms of 1937, and the furore over *Bezhin Lug*, that Eisenstein developed a third model of aesthetic representation: that of the associative image. Like the models of interior monologue and sensuous thought, Eisenstein's conception of an 'imagist' cinema rests on intuitionist, rather than cognitivist premises. Eisenstein defined the 'image' as an idea rich in associations. Thus, the representation of something in a film becomes a true 'image' of it when it is shown in conjunction with the various associations and connotations which might accrue to it as a consequence of its position and history within human experience.

Ironically, when combined with the conceptions of 'principle' and 'line', not only does Eisenstein's formulation of an 'imagist' cinema result in a highly associative, expressive and symbol-laden theory and practice of film-making, but, and despite Eisenstein's chastisement over *Bezhin Lug*, it also appears to mark a shift back towards the earlier *avant-garde* model inherited from Joyce. The key difference between the two models, however, is that, whereas the Joycean model was primarily concerned with the representation of subjective experience, the 'imagist' cinema focuses on the more objective associations and connotations which can be linked to particular representations of individuals, objects and events. Nevertheless, both models remain as intrinsically 'formalist' as the model of sensuous thought which was employed in *Bezhin Lug*.

The idea that a deep structural 'skeleton' of 'principle' could be discerned within a film also led Eisenstein to adopt a particular conception of authorship. For Eisenstein, the film-maker author was endowed with an ability to see through the 'flesh' of an evolving film, and to unearth its 'essential bone structure'. It is this ability to establish the 'generalised essence' of a phenomena, and then to construct a structure of generalising thematic lines and associative connotative images around that essence, which lies at the heart of the film director's activity.[46] As is the case with both dialectical materialist and romantic, expressive realist conceptions of authorship, therefore, Eisenstein's theory of film authorship is based on the notion that the director first seeks out processes which exist independently of him or her, and then goes on to create aesthetic structures which correspond to those processes. As with Eisenstein's account of the relationship between aesthetic composition and the dialectic, in which aesthetic form corresponds to the dialectic, rather than shapes something entirely new, Eisenstein's later conception of authorial agency leads him to reject the contention that the author should transform reality, and to endorse the view that the author is a perceptive observer and enabling vessel, through whose agency objective aesthetic form is brought into being.

The two final key components of Eisenstein's mature aesthetic are those of pathos and ecstasy, and it is these which finally bind Eisenstein's eclectic theory of film form into a coherent aesthetic position which is fundamentally symbolist in character. Eisenstein first employed the term pathos in 1926, as an alternative to the idea of the attraction. It will be recalled that the primary function of the attraction was to draw the spectator into an understanding of the ideological core of the film through effecting a series of shocks, or 'collisions', which were designed to disrupt both ideological preconceptions and passive spectatorship.

However, the emphasis on an *ostranenie* like process of cognitive distanciation within the model of the attraction increasingly came into conflict with Eisenstein's growing preoccupation with issues of aesthetic unity, and it was as a consequence of this that he turned to the idea of pathos as that quality within the film which would create a bond of emotional identification and empathy between film and spectator. The concept of ecstasy, which Eisenstein later derived from that of pathos, is based on the same principle of organic fusion which informs Eisenstein's understanding of pathos, and refers to that point within the viewing experience at which the spectator is 'lifted outside of himself' to achieve a particularly heightened and intense intellectual and emotional identity with the spirit of the film.[47]

It is important to understand that Eisenstein's formulation of the concepts of pathos and ecstasy did not imply that the viewing experience of the spectator should be in any sense a 'passive' one. On the contrary, Eisenstein argued that pathos and ecstasy should be used so as to achieve 'an awakening which puts the spectator's emotional and intellectual activity into operation to the maximum degree'.[48] For Eisenstein, therefore, pathos and ecstasy, like the earlier concept of the attraction, were means of both communicating knowledge to the spectator, and enabling the spectator to participate fully within the aesthetic experience. However, unlike the attraction, pathos and ecstasy were able to achieve such participation through an invocation of feeling, intuition and emotion, as well as conceptual judgement.

Eisenstein derived his understanding of the concept of pathos from contemporaneous debates then taking place over socialist realism, within which pathos was associated with both the theory of dialectical and historical materialism, and with the representation of socialist heroism. For advocates of socialist realism, pathos was objectively rendered when it emerged from the reality of the revolutionary subject-matter, rather than from the subjective imagination of the artist. In particular, the socialist realist expression of pathos would aim to epitomise and symbolise the drama of both the creation of a new revolutionary society, and the heroic, often tragic struggle which accompanied that creation.[49] It is clear from the above that the conception of pathos held within socialist realism was by no means a quietist one. Indeed, such quietism, based on the idea of pathos as an essentially reflective or immersive experience, was deliberately rejected as a residue of decadent bourgeois culture. Instead, pathos was conceived of as that which would enthuse and energise the spectator, and bring him or her into a dynamic connection with the work of socialist realist art. It is this more dynamic, catalytic conception of pathos which Eisenstein drew on when developing his ideas on film form.[50]

During the 1940s Eisenstein extended the concept of heroic, emotionally laden pathos into the notion of ecstasy, and it is with the idea of ecstasy that Eisenstein's aesthetic system begins to cohere into a unified whole. Eisenstein employs the idea of ecstasy in its medieval religious sense, to indicate a state of transcendent experience, or union with a transcendent object.[51] However, Eisenstein's use of such an emotionally charged, essentially non-cognitivist concept, led to the emergence of certain difficulties when he attempted to communicate ideological messages, or themes, through his films. Although Eisenstein still intended that ecstasy, like pathos and the attraction, should guide the spectator into a preordained identification with the ideological themes placed before him or her, the very excessive and charged nature of ecstasy also presupposed a degree of ideological disorientation, surrender of jurisdiction, and emotional saturation, which contradicted Eisenstein's more instrumentalist aspirations.

In the condition of exaltation which Eisenstein invokes through the idea of ecstasy, the spectator experiences a range of powerful and pleasurable emotions, whilst the film resonates with aesthetic substance. When this concept of ecstasy is employed in conjunction with Eisenstein's formulation of 'pathos', 'line', 'principle', and an 'imagist' theory of film, the result, as in *Ivan Grozny II* (*Ivan The Terrible Part Two*, 1946), is a work characterised by a considerable degree of expressive pictorial and symbolic signification. However, the problem for Eisenstein was that such highly charged aestheticism differed so greatly from the tenets of officially authorised socialist realism that *Ivan Grozny II* was bound to be criticised as unacceptably formalist, and Eisenstein's film became the object of such criticism from Stalin and others within the Soviet regime from almost as soon as it appeared.[52]

In *Alexander Nevsky* (1938) and *Ivan Grozny II*, Eisenstein employed the concepts of imagism, pathos and ecstasy in conjunction with the dialectical materialist notion of the 'leap' from quantitative accumulation to new qualitative states. As the various compositional 'lines' of these films build up ever more intense combinations of counterpoint, a climactic moment is reached when ecstasy emerges as a powerful emotion, and as a new category of quality. Eisenstein gives an example of this qualitative leap into the experience of pathos and ecstasy when referring to a novel by the Russian writer Victor Nekrasov, which had just been published when Eisenstein was writing in 1946. In the novel, *Stalingrad*, a German aircraft bombardment of Stalingrad has been taking place. All is a chaos of noise and fire. When the attack comes to an end there is a sudden cut to two men sitting quietly in the aftermath of the bombing. One turns to the other and asks 'Will you want to eat?'. Eisenstein regards this as a transcendant moment in the novel, as a heroic response to the violent chaos which had so recently taken place, and as 'the sound of something cosmic overcoming the enemy'.[53] For Eisenstein, this quiet utterance 'negates' the horror of the German bombardment, as antithesis negates thesis, and, therefore, achieves a qualitative transformation in the novel's generation of meaning.[54]

Perhaps the most complete realisation of pathos and ecstasy in Eisenstein's late aesthetic can be found in the 'Battle on the Ice' sequence in *Alexander Nevsky*. The entire sequence is orchestrated in considerable detail, so that every aspect of spatio-temporal arrangement, compositional design, chiaroscuro, gesture, movement and music is interwoven to produce one of the most highly composed sequences in the history of the cinema. Eisenstein points, in particular, to the sections in this sequence showing the attack of the German knights on the Russian soldiers.[55] In these scenes, the escalating, alternating montage sequences show the German attack building to a climax, and ending when the German knights smash into the ranks of the Russian soldiers. At this point the filming takes on a different quality, as the dynamic tension of the previous shots gives way to a scrambled mêlée, and the Russians fight back against their attackers. This transition from quantity to quality, through a dialectical leap which draws the spectator into an emotional and intellectual identification with the work, typifies the type of aesthetic approach which characterised Eisenstein's late aesthetic.

Despite the earlier focus on the orchestration of montage between shots in Eisenstein's writings, in films such as *Alexander Nevsky* and *Ivan Grozny* significant montage often takes place within the shot itself, and, in particular, at the juncture of sound and image. There is, in addition, little of the purely cognitively oriented 'intellectual montage' in these later films. Given all this, it could be argued that it was the arrival of both sound and colour which allowed Eisenstein to fully realise his abiding aesthetic concerns with organic totality within the artwork. If this is the case, then it is the films mentioned above, and particularly the 'Battle on the Ice sequence' in *Alexander Nevsky*, a sequence which Eisenstein devoted extensive sections of his book, *The Film Sense* (1942), to an analysis of, which should be regarded as examples of his real, and mature aesthetic, and not earlier films such as *Stachka*, or *Potemkin*. Nevertheless, there is no radical rupture between the early and late Eisenstein, as David Bordwell has argued, and the concern with the tableaux form, the aesthetic saturation of the image, and the orchestration of relationships within the frame, forms an evolving constant across both Eisenstein's films, and theoretical writings.

Eisenstein's conception of ecstasy, when combined with his organicist conception of the dialectic, leads to a theory of cinematic spectatorship, authorship and film form in which the state of ecstasy transports the spectator into the heart of reality itself, as film-maker, film and spectator become fused into an organic whole. In effect, Eisenstein's mature aesthetic theory is a theory of the cinematic sublime, yoked to the Marxist theory of dialectical materialism. However, it is the romantic concern with the sublime, rather than a concern with the dialectic, which dominates Eisenstein's later films.

Eisenstein's mature aesthetic was also more realist than his earlier, more deconstructionist one had been. During the 1930s and 1940s Eisenstein gradually abandoned the kind of cinematic *ostranenie* which, for Shklovsky, lay at the heart of aesthetic experience. However, Eisenstein's did not abandon such *avant-gardism* under the pressure of socialist realist orthodoxy, but because he became intellectually committed to finding his own symbolist approach to socialist realism. Thus, he developed a form of symbolist realism based on the dialectical leap, the ecstasy of imagism, and an almost Hegelian belief that, through film, a union with the absolute could be achieved. Ultimately, Eisenstein proved able to transcend both the reductivism implicit in much Russian formalist theory and practice, and the determinism evident in his own early film theory. In doing so, he carried on the more vital aspects of the formalist and Weimar film theory traditions.

Notes

1. Eisenstein, Sergei, quoted in Wollen, Peter, *Signs and Meaning in the Cinema* (London: Secker and Warburg/BFI, 1974), p. 32.
2. Aumont, Jacques, *Montage Eisenstein* (London: BFI and Indiana University Press, 1979), p. 41.
3. Andrew, Dudley, J., *The Major Film Theories* (Oxford: Oxford University Press, 1976), p. 46.
4. Barna, Yon, *Eisenstein* (London: Secker & Warburg, 1973), p. 55.
5. Aumont, op cit., pp. 42–3.
6. Leyda, Jay, *Kino: A History of the Russian and Soviet Film* (London: George Allen & Unwin, 1973), p. 194.
7. Eisenstein, Sergei, 'The Montage of Attractions', *Lef*, 1923, no. 3 (June/July), reprinted in Taylor, Richard and Christie, Ian (eds), *The Film Factory: Russian and Soviet Cinema In Documents 1896–1939* (London and New York: Routledge, 1988), p. 87.
8. Seton, Marie, *Sergei M. Eisenstein, a Biography* (London: Dennis Dobson, 1978), p. 154.
9. Aumont, op cit., p. 42.
10. Barna, op cit., p. 61.
11. Taylor and Christie (1988), op cit., p. 87.
12. Taylor, Richard (ed.), *The Eisenstein Reader* (London: BFI, 1998), pp. 35–6.
13. Taylor and Christie (1988), op cit., pp. 87–8.
14. Aumont, op cit., p. 44.

15. Taylor and Christie (1988), op cit., p. 88.
16. Ibid.
17. Ibid.
18. Andrew, op cit., p. 58.
19. Jakobson, Roman, 'The Dominant', in Matejka L. and Pomorska K. (eds), *Readings in Russian Poetics* (Cambridge, MA: MIT Press, 1971), p. 82.
20. Taylor (1998), op cit., pp. 38–9.
21. Petrić, Vlada, *Constructivism In Film: The Man with the movie Camera, A Cinematic Analysis* (Cambridge: Cambridge University Press, 1987), p. 17.
22. Bordwell, David, 'Eisenstein's Epistemological Shift', *Screen* (Winter, 1974/5), vol. 15, no. 4, pp. 32–3.
23. Ibid., p. 41.
24. Seton, op cit., p. 322.
25. Aumont, op cit., p. 66.
26. Seton, op cit., p. 153.
27. Andrew, op cit., p. 65.
28. Taylor, Richard and Christie, Ian (eds), *Eisenstein Rediscovered* (London and New York: Routledge, 1993), p. 103.
29. Engels, Frederick, 'Introduction to Dialectics of Nature', in *Marx Engels: Selected Works* (London: Lawrence and Wishart, 1968), p. 348.
30. Eisenstein, Sergei, *The Film Sense* (San Diego, CA, New York and London: Harcourt Brace & Company, 1975), p. 169.
31. Taylor (1998), op cit., p. 79.
32. Aumont, op cit., p. 65.
33. Seton, op cit., p. 150.
34. Eisenstein, Sergei, 'Colour Film', in his *Notes of a Film Director* (New York: Dover Publications, 1970), p. 120.
35. Eisenstein, Sergei, *film essays* (New York and Washington: Praeger Publishers, 1970), p. 158.
36. Ibid.
37. Ibid., p. 157.
38. Seton, op cit., p. 148.
39. Bordwell, David, *The Cinema of Eisenstein* (Cambridge, MA and London: Harvard University Press, 1993), p. 170.
40. Ibid., p. 172.
41. Taylor (1998), op cit., p. 188.
42. Ibid., p. 178.
43. Shumyatsky, Boris, 'The Film Bezhin Meadow', in Taylor and Christie (1988), op cit., p. 380.
44. Ibid., p. 378.
45. Taylor (1998), op cit., p. 139.
46. Ibid., p. 185.
47. Aumont, op cit., p. 58.

48. Ibid., p. 59.
49. Vaughn James, C., *Soviet Socialist Realism: Origins & Theories* (London: Macmillan, 1973), p. 91.
50. Bordwell (1993), op cit., p. 192.
51. Aumont, op cit., p. 59.
52. Barna, op cit., p. 265.
53. Eisenstein (1970), op cit., p. 172.
54. Ibid.
55. Eisenstein (1975), op cit., p. 174.

III

Aestheticism and Engagement in Weimar Cinematic Modernism and Soviet Montage Cinema

Between 1918 and 1925 three major modernist film movements appeared within mainstream European film industries. The first of these, the French impressionist movement (1918–29), will be explored further in Chapter 4 of this book, whilst this chapter will examine the origins, stylistic characteristics and thematic motifs of Weimar cinematic modernism (1920–33) and Soviet montage cinema (1925–33). A particular focus of attention here, as in previous chapters, will be on the dialectic between intuitionist and rationalist tendencies within these movements. However, this chapter will also explore the causal network which led to the appearance of the two movements, and, in particular, of Weimar cinematic modernism.

The modernist cinema which emerged in Germany during the 1920s was the product of a range of determining factors. These included philosophical traditions, such as romanticism and idealism; volatile economic and political conditions; and commercial strategies developed within the German film industry. The existence of such a range of factors makes Weimar cinematic modernism an ideal subject for investigations which seek to draw relationships between cinema and society. Given this, it is hardly surprising that Weimar modernism has been the focus of a number of such investigations, the most notable of which is Siegfried Kracauer's *From Caligari to Hitler* (1947).[1]

In *From Caligari to Hitler*, Kracauer employs a theoretical model drawn from the psychoanalytic theories of Freud, Fromm and others to interpret the German modernist cinema of the 1920s. However, whilst adopting Kracauer's premise that Weimar modernism should be related to the cultural, economic and political context from which it emerged, this chapter will circumvent Kracauer's predominant focus on 'psychological history' and national 'psychological dispositions',[2] and will attempt, instead, to apply a realist model of historical analysis to Weimar modernist cinema: one which seeks to establish the full range of determinations which led to the emergence of that

47

cinema.[3] What will be attempted here will not be an exhaustive study of the German modernist cinema of the 1920s (that would be the subject of an entire book), but an introductory outline of the industrial, political, social, cultural and philosophical influences which led to its emergence.

* * *

During the First World War Hollywood captured a substantial proportion of market share in European film industries, whose capacity to sustain pre-war levels of production had become seriously compromised by involvement in the war. The European film industry responded to this incursion by adopting a variety of counter-strategies, the most common of which, but also the most potentially financially hazardous, was that of funding big budget productions in an attempt to match American films in terms of budget, star quality and production values. However, in addition to this, producers in some countries also responded by developing alternative styles of film-making, and this commercial quest to develop alternative models to the Hollywood film influenced the emergence of both French cinematic impressionism and Weimar cinematic modernism.

As with other European countries which had participated in the war, film production within France declined steeply between 1914 and 1918, and, after the war, the French film industry failed to recover its pre-war levels of output. It was against this background that some French producers began to experiment with different styles of film-making, and it was partly as a consequence of this that the French impressionist movement came into existence in 1918. Just as French impressionism developed within a film industry which was willing to experiment with style and technique in the face of the challenge of Hollywood, so too did Weimar cinematic modernism. However, the conditions of the French and German film industries were very different at the close of the First World War. Unlike France, the German film industry emerged from the war in a position of strength, mainly as a consequence of the ban on most foreign films which the German government had introduced in 1916, and which remained in force until 1920. This allowed the German industry to escape the Hollywood invasion which afflicted the French film industry, and provided a foundation for a degree of expansion during the immediate post-war period.[4]

The German industry also went through a process of monopoly concentration during the war, and the formation in 1917 of the vertically integrated, government supported, Universum Film Aktiengesellschaft film company (UFA), initiated a chain of events which eventually resulted in a situation where German film production was second only to that of Hollywood in terms of output.[5] It was from this position of strength that UFA, 'the only film company ever to think that it could compete with hollywood ...', attempted to differentiate its films from those of its American rivals through the development of new styles, techniques and genres.[6]

In 1920 the first German expressionist film, *Das Cabinet des Dr Caligari* (*The Cabinet of Dr Caligari*, Wiene, 1920), was produced by the Decla film company. After the war, and against a context of foreign films once more entering the German home market, Decla, and its chief executive, Erich Pommer, decided on a strategy of producing a film which could be deliberately marketed as 'artistic'. Pommer believed that such a film would find a niche market in the international, and, particularly, American market, and drew on the pre-existing tradition of expressionism in order to develop *Das Cabinet des Dr Caligari*.[7] This suggests that *Das Cabinet des Dr Caligari*, and later 'expressionist' films, were mainly produced as part of a commercial strategy, which consisted of finding a niche market within the international middle-class audience. This interpretation has, in turn, led to the allegation that films such as *Das Cabinet des Dr Caligari* were not so much authentic works of art which carried on the aesthetic and oppositional mission of expressionism, but more an outcome of product differentiation within the more general commodification of the commercial cinema: 'Thus, a social economy of cultural prestige was articulated with a political economy of commodity production in establishing a distinctive class of film for a distinctive class of people: an "art cinema".'[8]

Das Cabinet des Dr Caligari was produced within a commercial studio system, and combines expressionist visual motifs with more conventional narrative devices. This fusion of modernist experiment and commercial convention led to criticism, by intellectuals such as Ezra Pound and Gertrude Stein, that *Das Cabinet des Dr Caligari* had degraded the high ideals of expressionist modernism.[9] The case that *Das Cabinet des Dr Caligari* was largely the product of a commercial strategy is also reinforced by the fact that Decla, which merged with the Deutsches Bioscope company in 1920 to become Decla Bioscope, was taken over by UFA in 1921. Between 1921 and 1927 Decla Bioscope, which remained a separate production unit within UFA under Pommer's directorship, then produced a substantial number of what became known as the German 'expressionist' films.[10]

However, the fact that Pommer and UFA recognised the economic potential of the German expressionist cinema does not mean that that cinema was entirely the product of a commercial, industrial strategy. As Kracauer has pointed out, Pommer may have grasped the 'timely atmosphere and interesting scenic potentialities' of *Das Cabinet des Dr Caligari* when the script was presented to him, but it is unlikely that he fully grasped the 'significance of the strange story'.[11] Like much Weimar cinematic modernism, *Das Cabinet des Dr Caligari* expresses various anxieties about the modern condition, and the nature of contemporary life, and a dialectic can be perceived within the film between a modernist resistance to commodification, and an appropriation of that resistance by the commercial industry as a means of product differentiation. Certainly, Kracauer is in no doubt that *Das Cabinet des Dr Caligari* is far more than merely an ingeniously crafted economic artefact:

> Whether intentionally or not, CALIGARI exposes the soul wavering between tyranny and chaos, facing a desperate situation ... Like the Nazi world, that of CALIGARI overflows with sinister portents, acts of terror and outbursts of panic ... The reappearance of these traits on the screen once more testifies to their prominence in the German collective soul.[12]

In addition to this context of industrial development and commercial strategy, the emergence of Weimar cinematic modernism was also influenced by a context of social, economic and political turmoil. On 28 June 1919, the defeated German leadership was forced to accept the punitive terms of the Treaty of Versailles, which, in addition to other demands, forced Germany to admit 'war guilt', and instructed the new German government to make substantial reparation payments to the allied powers. From 1918 onwards, German inflation also began to rise steeply, until, in 1923, the value of the German mark plummeted. A further economic collapse followed in 1929, in the wake of the Wall Street Crash.[13] This economic instability was also mirrored in the social unrest and political divisions which afflicted Germany over the lifetime of the Weimar Republic, and which eventually resulted in the abrogation of the Weimar constitution, and the ascendancy to power of Hitler and the National Socialist German Workers Party. These are the 'trauma' and 'dissolution of political systems' which Kracauer points to, and which, he argues, become indirectly reflected in the modernist films of the Weimar period.[14]

In addition to these influences, Weimar modernism also reflected, and responded to, the antagonistic cultural forces at work in Germany over the lifetime of the Republic. Weimar was established as a liberal, democratic, constitutional state. However, such demo-cratic constitutionalism was relatively foreign to a country which, during the period of the Austro-German alliance of 1879–1918, had become dominated by military, aristocratic and bureaucratic elites. It was this conservative establishment which was forced, through military defeat, to gave way to the Weimar Republic on 9 November 1918. However, this conservative culture could not be reconciled with Weimar, and, during the 1920s, found expression in a spirit of resurgent nationalism, reinforced by the sense of betrayal and humiliation felt over Versailles.[15]

In seeking an alternative model of national identity to that offered by Weimar, post-war right-wing German nationalists looked to the so-called 'Aryan nation' of Germanic tribes which had inhabited northern Germany and the Scandinavian countries during the middle ages. The conception of German national identity which emerged from this was also founded on the belief that 'traditional' German culture was superior to other forms of western culture, and one of the most influential proponents of this doctrine was Friedrich Naumann, who argued that German *Kultur* transcended the limita-tions of both 'decadent' western, and 'barbarian' communist society.[16] Like the conservative nationalism from which it arose, the doctrine of *Kultur* was also grounded in the values, myths and legends of the medieval Germanic empire, as well as the hierarchical culture which had developed during the years of the Austro-German alliance. Although this nationalist culture lost its hold on power after the military defeat of 1918, it remained an influential force during the Weimar period, and left its mark, on expressionism in particular, and Weimar cinematic modernism in general.

Another significant influence on the development of Weimar cinematic modernism was that of pre-existing artistic movements within German painting and literature. Prior to 1905 the term expressionism had been mainly used to refer to disparate artistic movements in Germany and the Scandinavian countries which had emerged from the 1870s onwards. However, after 1905, groups of painters began to emerge in Germany who explicitly defined them-selves as expressionist. These included Die Brücke (1905), Aktion (1910), Der Blaue Reiter (1911) and Sturm (1913), and, within them, artists such as Ludwig Kirchner, Erich Heller, Franz Marc, Wassily Kandinsky, Oskar Kokoschka and Max Beckmann.

German expressionist painting inherited the legacy of French symbolist art, and shared symbolism's preoccupation with the metaphysical and mystical. Both movements can also be associated with the emergence of various forms of millenarianism around the turn of the century. As was the case with many of these millenarian movements, the philosophical outlook of German expressionism consisted of a paradoxical combination of hope in the progress which might come with the dawn of a new era, and anxiety about the dangers that the new age might bring.[17] The expressionist world view was, therefore, made up of both nihilistic and utopian tendencies, and this dialectic between optimism and fatalism characterises much expressionist work, from the paintings of the Sturm group, to films such as Friedrich Murnau's *Nosferatu* (1924), with its invocation of both remorseless evil, and the transcendent power of love.

Expressionist theory and practice focused on the subjective nature of aesthetic experience, and, like symbolism before it, privileged intuition, emotional response and subjective expression over reason and rationality.[18] However, this subjectivist orientation was also mediated by German intellectual traditions premised on the idea that individual subjectivity could achieve an intuitive understanding of universal truths.[19] In addition, expressionism also shared a modernist concern for exploring the formal language of art, and this led expressionist artists to emphasise visual distortion as part of an attempt to move 'away from nature, back to the picture'.[20] At the same time, this emphasis on reflexive formal distortion reinforced the expressionist desire to represent subjectivity through the use of distorted imagery. This synthesis of formalism, anti-realism, and an intuitionist, subjectivist/objectivist aesthetic, led to the emergence of an artistic practice characterised by the foregrounding of formal devices, and by the use of distorted, anti-realist, violent, and forceful imagery.

One final influence on the development of Weimar cinematic modernism was that of the *Autorenfilm*, or 'authors film'. The *Autorenfilm* emerged out of a wider development taking place within European cinema around 1910, in which the cinema began to be increasingly regarded as a major new art form. However, like its counterparts in France and Italy, as exemplified in such films as *L'Assassinat du Duc de Guise* (*The Assassination of the Duke de Guise*, Charles Le Bargy and Albert Lambert, 1908), and *Quo Vadis?* (Enrico Guazzoni, 1913), the German *Autorenfilm* was not so much based on an exploration of the intrinsic aesthetic properties of film, as in the use of film as a vehicle for the recording of classic or prestigious plays. German *Autorenfilm* also represented the first attempt by the German cinema to reach a middle-class public, and countered the growing hegemony of Hollywood by adapting specifically German works of literature and theatre for the cinema.[21]

Most *Autorenfilm* were concerned with the more straightforward reproduction of theatrical performance, and did little to advance the further development of the cinema as an aesthetic medium. However, one film which did was *Der Student von Prag* (*The Student of Prague*, Stellan Rye, 1913). Thematically, *Der Student von Prag* builds on the German gothic and romantic heritage, but it also employs special effects techniques derived from the films of French directors such as Méliès.[22] The same thematic material and concern with formal experimentation in *Der Student von Prag* can also be found in *Das Cabinet des Dr Caligari*, with its references to Romanticism, and the tales of E. T. A. Hoffmann,[23] and, in this respect, as well as in others, there is a case for arguing that *Der Student von Prag*, rather than *Das Cabinet des Dr Caligari*, is the inaugurator of Weimar cinematic modernism.

It was the complex network of commercial, political, economic, aesthetic and cultural influences referred to above which led to the emergence of Weimar cinematic modernism, and, in 1920, to the appearance of *Das Cabinet des Dr Caligari*. The modernist cinema which emerged in Weimar between 1920 and 1933 can be divided into a number of different categories. Those films most clearly associated with expressionism include: *Das Cabinet des Dr Caligari* (Robert Wiene, 1920), *Der Golem* (*The Golem*, Paul Wegener and Carl Boese, 1920), *Von Morgens bis Mitternacht* (*From Morning to Midnight*, Karl Heinz Martin, 1920), *Destiny* (Fritz Lang, 1921), *Genuine* (Robert Wiene, 1921), *Das Haus zum Mond* (*The House on the Moon*, Karl Heinz Martin, 1921), *Nosferatu* (F. W. Murnau, 1922), *Dr Mabuse der Spieler* (*Dr Mabuse the Gambler*, Fritz Lang, 1922), *Schatten* (Artur Robison, 1923), *Der Schatz* (*The Treasure*, G. W. Pabst, 1923), *Raskolinikow* (Robert Wiene, 1923), *Erdgeist* (*Earth Spirit*, Leopold Jessner, 1923), *Der steinere Reiter* (*The Stone Rider*, Fritz Wendhausen, 1923), *Wachsfigurenkabinett* (*Waxworks*, Paul Leni, 1924), *Die Nibelungen* (Fritz Lang, 1924), *Orlacs Hände* (*The Hands of Orlac*, Robert Wiene, 1924), *Tartüff* (*Tartuffe*, F. W. Murnau, 1924), *Die Chronik von Grieshuus* (*The Chronicle of the Grey House*, Arthur von Gerlach, 1925), *Faust* (F. W. Murnau, 1926) and *Metropolis* (Fritz Lang, 1927).

In addition to these films, another group, known as the *Kammerspiel*, or 'intimate' films, can also be linked to the expressionist cinema within the larger parameters of Weimar modernism. These include *Scherben* (*Shattered*, Lupu Pick, 1921), *Hintertreppe* (*Backstairs*, Leopold Jessner, 1921), *Sylvester* (Lupu Pick, 1923), *Der Letzte Mann* (*The Last Laugh*, F. W. Murnua, 1924), and *Michael* (Carl Dreyer, 1924). After 1925 expressionist and *Kammerspiel* films increasingly adopted the social realist style of the *Neue Sachlichkeit*, or 'new objectivity' movement, and many of the characteristic themes of both groups of films were carried on into *Neue Sachlichkeit*, forming a continuous tradition of modernist film-making within Weimar from 1920 to the early 1930s. *Neue Sachlichkeit* films produced between 1925 and 1930 which can be associated with this tradition include *Die Strasse* (*The Street*, Karl Grune, 1923), *Variété* (*Variety*, E. A. Dupont, 1925), *Die freudlose Gasse* (*The Joyless Street*, G. W. Pabst, 1925), *Die Liebe der Jeanne Ney* (*The Loves of Jeanne Ney*, G. W. Pabst, 1928), *Die Büchse von Pandora* (*Pandora's Box*, G. W. Pabst, 1929), *Das Tagebuch einer Verlorenen* (*Diary of a Lost Girl*, G. W. Pabst, 1929) and *M* (Fritz Lang, 1931).

Many of the themes found in expressionist painting, literature and theatre can be found across the range of expressionist, *Kammerspiel* and *Neue Sachlichkeit* films. For example, the theme of alienation, and of the individual as subject to tyrannical or supernatural forces beyond his or her control, pervades films such as *M*, *Das Cabinet des Dr Caligari*, *Der Golem*, *Faust* and *Die Büchse von Pandora*; whilst that of insanity and nihilism appears in films such as *Das Cabinet des Dr Caligari*, *Nosferatu*, *Destiny* and *Die freudlose Gasse*. Another important theme which links expressionist films such as *Der Cabinet des Dr Caligari*, *Kammerspiel* films such as *Der Letzte Mann*, and *Neue Sachlichkeit* films such as *Das Tagebuch einer Verlorenen*, is that of loss of status and dignity. This is the central theme, for example, in one of the most influential Weimar films, Murnau's *Der Letzte Mann*, which depicts the psychological deterioration of a hotel doorman who becomes demoted to the post of lavatory attendant.[24]

Despite the thematic continuities evident within Weimar modernist cinema, a number of stylistic differences exist between expressionist, *Kammerspiel* and *Neue Sachlichkeit* films. Expressionist films such as *Das Cabinet des Dr Caligari* employ special effects photography to indicate the supernatural and transcendental; and distorted and aggressive imagery to indicate extreme feelings, and states of mind. *Kammerspiel* films, on the other hand, are more naturalistic, and use chiaroscuro lighting effects to create claustrophobic, intimate environments. The *Kammerspiel* films were also influenced by Max Reinhardt, who produced small-scale intimate plays, structured in such a way that the audience was able to attend to the smallest of gestures, and minutia of plot development. All the main German film actors of the period, including Conrad Veidt, Emil Jannings and Paul Wegener came from Reinhardt's troupe, and brought Reinhardt's slow-paced, metaphorical style of acting to films such as *Der Letzte Mann*.[25] Nevertheless, and despite these differences, a considerable number of stylistic continuities can also be established across the full range of modernist Weimar cinema. All these films emphasise pictorial composition within the frame, and employ long-take moving camerawork, and special effects techniques, in order to invoke subjective states of mind. Lighting effects are pronounced and highly composed, and, in comparison to Hollywood films, these films can also be identified by their slower pace, and gestural acting styles.[26]

In *From Caligari to Hitler*, Kracauer argued that Weimar modernist cinema revealed the influence of underlying mass psychological processes, a disturbed and pathological 'collective mentality' which eventually led to the emergence of fascism and Hitler.[27] Kracauer's thesis has been criticised on a number of counts. For example, it has been argued that, because they were only seen by a small section of the German public, this modernist cinema could not represent the underlying fears of the mass of the population.[28] However, such an argument fails to address the fact that, although a film such as *Nosferatu* was not made for a mass audience, it nevertheless appears to embody themes and anxieties which can be related to the general context of the period, rather than merely to the individual authorial concerns of its director.

Nor is there any logical reason why depictions of issues which affect the mass public should not appear in a minority, as opposed to mass cinema. If a broader analysis of the various influences on Weimar cinematic modernism is adopted, one which encompasses philosophical/ideological, cultural/aesthetic, commercial/industrial, and political/economic factors, then it becomes possible to argue that Weimar cinematic modernism is not merely the instrumental product of an industrial production strategy, nor just the work of a few atypical modernist German film-makers working within what was, otherwise, a commercial industry.

Weimar modernist cinema was influenced, in the first case, by a philosophical tradition stemming from idealism and romanticism, which privileged intuition over reason, and subscribed to a bleak view of the modern condition. Weimar cinematic modernism was also influenced by traditions of Weimar film theory which endorsed a primarily visual, non-cognitive, phenomenologically concrete, irrationalist and pre-modern form of aesthetic practice.[29] This aesthetic and critical tradition became reinforced during the 1920s by what Kracauer referred to as the 'collective paralysis of minds',[30] and the disruptive events and alienating conditions which threw 'inner life' into turmoil, and which found expression in films such as *Nosferatu* and *Der Letzte Mann*.[31] Both these films were directed by Murnau, and the role of individual authorship within Weimar cinematic modernism was clearly an important factor, as the emergence of important directors such as Lang, Murnau and Pabst attests. Set designers, actors, editors and cameramen also played an influential role in the creation of Weimar modernism, as did the influence of the *Autorenfilm* and other cultural tendencies. However, underlying these individual contributions is a philosophical/aesthetic tradition, reinforced by contemporary economic, social and political events.[32]

* * *

The context of the Soviet montage movement differed in many respects from that which influenced the development of Weimar cinematic modernism. Immediately after the First World War many Russian producers and film-makers fled to the west, taking much of their equipment and capital with them. This, a shortage of both capital and raw film stock, and hostility to the new regime expressed by many of those remaining within the film industry, ensured that film production in post-revolutionary Russia declined precipitously.[33] These circumstances led the Bolshevik regime to develop policies designed to both reconstruct the national film industry, and train a new generation of film-makers. The Peoples Commissariat of Education, or Narkompros, was the government agency given responsibility for supervising the development of the arts and education within the Soviet Union, and, in August 1919, Lenin issued a decree which nationalised the film industry, and charged Narkompros with the responsibility of regulating 'the entire photo and cinema trade and industry'. That same year Narkompros established the Moscow State Film School, from which many of the most important montage film-makers would later emerge.[34]

Following the Revolution of 1917, a politically engaged cinema soon emerged within the Soviet Union. On 27 June 1918 the Moscow Cinema Committee, which had been given responsibility by Narkompros for leading the development of Soviet film production, began work on the first real 'Soviet' film: *Signal* (Alexander Arkatov, 1918). This was quickly followed by *Underground* (Alexander Serafimovitch, 1918) and *Uprising* (Alexander Razumni, 1918): a semi-documentary account of the Russian Revolution which was premiered on the first anniversary of the Revolution, in October 1918.[35] Other politically engaged films to emerge during the period of the civil war included *For the Red Banner* (Vladimir Kasyanov, 1919), *Peace to the Cottage, War to the Palace* (Bonch-Tomashevsky, 1919), *Mother* (Alexander Razumni, 1920), *On the Red Front* (Lev Kuleshov, 1920), *In the Days of Struggle* (Ivan Perestiani, 1920) and *Sickle and Hammer* (Vladimir Gardin, 1921).

Many of the above films also fall into the category of a new genre of film-making which appeared during the civil war period: the *agitka*, or 'small agitational works'. Single-reel *agitka* such as *For the Red Banner* were mainly directed at raising the morale of the Red Army, and drew on formats already developed within the pre-revolutionary propaganda films which had appeared during the First World War. However, although the *agitka* were modest, straightforward propaganda pieces, they provided emerging film-makers with experience of a new, and different form of film-making. Films shot at the front had a documentary quality which distinguished them from more studio-bound, pre-revolutionary forms of film-making; whilst the imperative to complete films quickly led to the development of innovative editing, acting and other stylistic practices. The *agitka* film-makers also became actively involved in the fighting process, often filming in the midst of battle, and this degree of involvement was to breed a school of highly committed, politically engaged film-makers, which included Lev Kuleshov, Alexander Levitsky, Grigori Giber, Edward Tissé, Vladimir Kasyanov, Nikandr Turkin and Dziga Vertov.[36]

One of the most portentous developments to occur within committed Soviet film-making in 1918 was the departure of the first 'agit-train'. The mission of this particular train was to raise the morale of troops fighting to defeat the White Guard forces on the Eastern Front. To this end, the agit-train was equipped with a printing press, a troupe of actors, and a film crew headed by a cameraman later to become one of the most important within the Soviet cinema: Edward Tissé. Later agit-trains contained complete film-making systems, including laboratories and editing rooms, and this enabled films to be shot, processed, edited and projected at the front within a short space of time.[37]

In 1920, Vertov toured the south-western front on an agit-train which carried a print of his first, complete, edited film: *October Revolution*. Whilst on the move, Vertov also shot new footage of events at the front, and, when he returned to Moscow, he edited this footage into a series of films which formed the basis of his *Kinopravda* ('film truth') newsreel series. The *Kinopravda* both addressed contemporary political issues, and continued the exploration of film-form which had arisen from the work of those involved with the *agitka*. This provided Vertov with the theoretical and practical foundation for the development of his first film manifesto: 'Kinoki. Perevoret' ('Kinoks: A Revolution'), which was published by Mayakovsky, Nikolai Aseyev and Osip Brik in *Lef* in 1923.[38] However, Vertov's manifesto, in which he went so far as to declaim that 'what we have so far done in the cinema is 100 per cent mistaken', displayed a degree of *avant-gardism* which was soon to bring him into conflict with the Soviet authorities.[39]

That conflict first emerged in a series of disagreements which took place between Vertov and officials within Goskino, the successor body to the Moscow Cinema Council, which had been established in 1922. These problems eventually led Vertov to leave Moscow, and work with VUFKU, the pan-Ukrainian film production unit. Here, away from the constraints of the capital, he continued to experiment with his theory of the 'kino-eye', and eventually made *The Eleventh Year* (1928), *The Man with the Movie Camera* (1929) and *Enthusiasm, or Symphony of the Donbas* (1930). However, Vertov continued to experience difficulties with the Soviet authorities over the *avant-garde* nature of his films, and his career, from 1930, until his death in 1954, was beset by such problems.[40]

Vertov's problems with an increasingly dogmatic official Soviet film establishment mirrored those experienced by other montage film-makers. The establishment of Goskino in 1922 marked a period of increased official intervention in questions of film aesthetics, and Lenin's 'Directive on Cinema Affairs' of 1922 also made it clear that the regime expected the Soviet film industry to make commercially profitable, popular 'entertainment films', rather than *avant-garde* films such as the *Kinopravda*.[41] Tensions soon developed between such pressures and the interests of film-makers who, although committed to the regime, were also increasingly influenced by European modernism. For example, although 1922 marks the establishment of Goskino, and the publication of Lenin's Directive, it also marks the founding of the futurist influenced FEKS (Factory of the Eccentric Actor) group; the publication in *Lef* of the first kino-eye manifesto; the appearance of the first *Kinopravda*; and the publication of writings by Kuleshov, Alexei Gan and others. By 1925, when the first major montage film, Eisenstein's *Stachka* (*Strike*), was premiered, Soviet film-makers familiar with modernist movements such as formalism, cubism, constructivism and futurism were fully resolved on making films which drew upon these influences.

In 1920 Lev Kuleshov joined the State Film School, and established a workshop which aimed to explore editing techniques. In 1924 members of the Kuleshov workshop made their first feature film, *Neobychainye priklucheniya Mistera Vesta v stranye bolshevikov* (*The Extraordinary Adventures of Mr West in the Land of the Bolsheviks*), a comedy about western preconceptions of the Soviet Union, which also introduced the 'Kuleshov effect' into Soviet cinema. The 'Kuleshov effect' was the outcome of a whole series of experiments with montage combinations which Kuleshov had been working on from as early as 1917.[42] Here, editing is used in such a way that the meaning attributed to any particular shot is determined by its relationship to shots adjacent. Thus, an identical shot of a man's face placed next to a range of different images gives rise to different interpretations of the man's emotional condition, even though the same shot of the man is used in each case.

Kuleshov had initially embarked upon his experiments with montage in an attempt to develop editing techniques which would link shot to shot in such a way that coherent, large-scale narrative structures could be developed, which would have a predetermined effect upon the audience. For example, in his *Art of the Cinema* (1929), Kuleshov argued that, initially, he and his group were primarily concerned with discovering 'how this material was organised, what the fundamental impression-making means of cinematography is':[43]

> We went to various motion picture theatres and began to observe which films produced the optimum effect on the viewer and how these films were made – in other words, by means of which films and which techniques of film-making the film was able to take hold of a viewer and therefore to bring to his awareness what we had conceived, what we had intended to show, and, thus, what we intended to do.[44]

This aspect of Kuleshov's work also influenced the 'linkage' theory of montage developed by Vsevolod Pudovkin, who had been a pupil of Kuleshov's at the State Film School.[45] However, the real significance of the Kuleshov effect lay not in its ability to link shot to shot in order to create smooth narrative continuity, but in its power to generate ideas in the mind of the spectator through involving the spectator in a film's ultimate production and consumption of meaning. This aspect of the Kuleshov effect can be associated with concepts emerging out of Russian formalism, including Eichenbaum's conception of 'inner speech', and Shklovsky's concept of *ostranenie*, and went on to influence the development of the Soviet montage cinema.

Although not a true montage film, *Neobychainye priklucheniya Mistera Vesta v stranye bolshevikov* was a pioneering work, which showed the way forward for the evolving school of montage film-makers. The principal films produced within the Soviet montage film movement between 1925 and 1930 are: *Stachka; Bronenosets Potemkin* (*Potemkin*, Eisenstein, 1925); *Mat* (*Mother*, Vsevolod

Pudovkin, 1926); *Chyortovo koleso* (*The Devil's Wheel*, Grigori Kozintsev and Leonid Trauberg, 1926); *Shinel* (*The Cloak*, Grigori Kozintsev, 1926); *Zvenigora* (Alexander Dovzhenko, 1927); *Dom na Trubnoi* (*The House on Trubnoya*, Boris Barnet, 1927); *Konyets Sankt-Peterburga* (*The End of St Petersburg*, Vsevolod Pudovkin, 1927); *Moskva v Oktyabre* (*Moscow in October*, Boris Barnet, 1927); *SVD* (Grigori Kozintsev, 1927); *Oktyabr* (*October*, Sergei Eisenstein, 1928); *Potomok Chingis-khana* (*The Heir of Ghenghis Khan/Storm Over Asia*, Vsevolod Pudovkin, 1928); *Kruzheva* (*Lace*, Sergei Yutkevich, 1928); *Novyi Vavilon* (*The New Babylon*, Grigori Kozintsev and Leonid Trauberg, 1929); *Staoei novoe* (*Old and New*, Eisenstein, 1929); *Moja babuška* (*My Grandmother*, Kote Mikaberidze, 1929); *Goluboi ekspress* (*China Express*, Ilya Trauberg, 1929); *Chelovek s kinoapparatom* (*The Man with the Movie Camera*, Dziga Vertov, 1929); *Arsenal* (Alexander Dovzhenko, 1929); *Turksib* (Victor Turin, 1929); and *Zemlya* (*Earth*, Alexander Dovzhenko, 1930). After 1930 a few films continued to be made in the montage style, most notably Pudovkin's *Deserter* (1933); Eisenstein's *Alexander Nevsky* (1938); *Ivan Grozny* (*Ivan the Terrible Part One*, 1944, and *Ivan the Terrible Part Two*, 1946).

The first important montage film is generally recognised to be *Stachka*. *Stachka* was influenced by constructivism, and this influence can also be seen in the work of directors who emerged from the Leningrad theatre in the early 1920s. For example, Grigori Kozintsev, Leonid Trauberg and Sergei Yutkevitch, who formed the Factory of the Eccentric Actor, put on performances which, like Eisenstein's version of *Enough Simplicity in Every Wise Man*, employed acrobatics, forms of popular entertainment, and reflexive 'productivist' techniques. Kozintsev and Trauberg made their first major film, *Chyortovo koleso*, in 1926, whilst Yutkevitch made his, *Kruzheva*, in 1928.

In addition to Eisenstein and the FEKS group, the other major montage directors of the period were Lev Kuleshov, Vsevolod Pudovkin, Boris Barnet, Dziga Vertov and Alexander Dovzhenko. Pudovkin and Barnet had both been trained in Kuleshov's workshop at the State Film School, and their films display the influence of constructivism far less than was the case with the early films of Eisenstein and the FEKS group. On the other hand, Dziga Vertov, was strongly influenced by both constructivism and futurism, and his *Chelovek s kinoapparatom* displays those influences clearly. The final major film-maker, Alexander Dovzhenko, was Ukranian, and came to film-making relatively late, at the age of thirty-two. Whilst also influenced by the *avant-garde*, Dovzhenko's films drew on

Ukrainan folk traditions, and his best known film, *Zemlya*, displays a lyrical, regionalist, pantheistic quality which disintinguishes him from other montage film-makers, and looks forward to the work of later Russian film-makers such as Tarkovsky and Paradzhanov.

In terms of thematic content, the Soviet montage films of the 1925–33 period were quite different from those modernist films made in Germany between 1918 and 1933. The emphasis on the existential alienation of the individual found in many Weimar modernist films is largely absent from the Soviet films, unless that concern is deflected through the prism of the politics of class oppression, as in *Mat*; depictions of anti-social *lumpenproletarian* criminality, as in *Stachka*; or portrayals of upper-class decadence and corruption, as in *Ivan Grozny*. Another of the central themes of Weimar cinematic modernism, that of loss of bourgeois status, and decline into a proletarian underclass, is also largely absent from the Soviet films, which celebrate, rather than fear, the proletarianisation of society.

Although portrayals of strong leaders and leadership can be found in both Soviet montage and Weimar modernist films, such representations are rendered far less ambivalently within the former than the latter. Few critical reflections on the negative consequences of dictatorship are to be found within the Soviet montage cinema, unless directed at pre-revolutionary or counter-revolutionary subject matter, and even films like *Alexander Nevsky* and *Ivan Grozny*, both of which focus on pre-revolutionary figures, and indirectly refer to the authority of Stalin, do so in ways which ennoble the figure of the strong leader. Although these films emerged against a context of impending or actual war, a context which, it could be argued, necessitated an endorsement of potent leadership, both they, and Soviet montage cinema in general, failed to reflect the reality of the Stalinist dictatorship. This contrasts starkly with Weimar cinema's 'procession of tyrants',[46] in which it is the villains, rather than the heroes who 'have caught the imagination'.[47]

Whilst Weimar modernist cinema appeared against a background of continuous political instability, social unrest and economic fluctuation, the most serious political and economic difficulties within the Soviet Union had already been overcome by 1925, when the first montage film was made. By the time that Eisenstein had completed *Stachka*, for example, the revolution had been secured, the counter-revolution put down, famine more or less eradicated, and stable government installed.[48] These radically different contexts generated a sense of anxious cynicism and ironic 'neo-romantic decadence'[49] on the one hand, and confident, committed expectation on the other, and it was this which was responsible for both the prevalence of depictions of fatalism and nihilism in Weimar cinema, and the absence of such depictions in Soviet montage cinema.

As would probably be the case in any totalitarian State, Soviet film-makers were strongly encouraged not to depict contemporary Soviet social reality in a negative or equivocal manner, and such depictions which did emerge were often publically condemned as evidence of 'bourgeois idealism', 'formalism' or 'counter-revolutionary pessimism'. For example, in a Report to the Central Committee of the Communist Party, the architect of socialist realism, A. A. Zhdanov, charged the literary journal *Zvezda* with 'grave errors and failings' for publishing the work of the 'cheap and philistine' writer Zoshchenko:

> The point of this 'work' by Zoshchenko is that in it he portrays the Soviet people as lazy, unattractive, stupid and crude. He is in no way concerned with their labour, their heroism, their high social and moral qualities ... he chooses, like the cheap philistine he is to scratch about in life's baseness and pettinesses. This is no accident, it is intrinsic to all cheap, philistine writers, of whom Zoshchenko is one.[50]

The consequence of public tirades such as this, and their equivalent expression during the 1920s and 1930s, was that film-makers were forced to toe the party line on fear of public humiliation, or worse, and many of the Soviet montage films, despite their other qualities, and, in many cases, the intentions of their directors, came to embody the one-dimensional and instrumental view of social reality insisted upon by Zhdanov and other officials, as film-makers were forced to become 'engineers of the human soul'.[51] It was also almost certainly the German modernism of the 1920s that Zhdanov had in mind when he described contemporary 'bourgeois' art as 'absorbed in pessimism, doubt in the morrow, eulogy of darkness, extolment of pessimism as the theory and practice of art'.[52]

The stylistic characteristics of Soviet montage cinema also differed from those of Weimar cinematic modernism. In place of the long-take, moving camera of Weimar, montage films orchestrate elaborate structures of shots into overall montage patterns. Whilst the German films tended to exhibit a more coherent, heavily pictorialised diegetic space, Soviet films use principles of contrast and counterpoint to introduce a degree of temporo-spatial fragmentation less common in the German films. The acting styles which the modernist Weimar cinema had inherited from Max Reinhardt can also be distinguished from the acting found in many Soviet montage films. Reinhardt's theatre employed expressive gesture to represent psychological interiority, and had a direct influence on expressionist films such as *Nosferatu*, and *Kammerspiel* films such as *Scherben* and *Der Letzte Mann*.[53] The acting style found in a film such as *Stachka*, on the other hand, largely avoids depictions of psychological intro-spection, and emphasises physicality and social/political typicality.

The aesthetic style of Soviet montage cinema was also influenced by the rationalist, cognitivist tendency within Russian formalism, and by the instrumentalist aspirations of 'productivist' construc-tivism. The theory of montage itself emerged from objectivist preoccupations with discovering underlying aesthetic 'laws', preoccupations which are encapsulated in Eisenstein's positivist, early Pavlovian inspired theory of the stimulus-response 'attraction', with its objective of the 'moulding of the audience in a desired direction', and its endorsement of 'utilitarian theatre'.[54] Kuleshov's editing experiments, Pudovkin's theory of 'linkage' montage – with its intellectual basis in the 'laws of psychology',[55] Eisenstein's notion of intellectual montage and the more constructivist aspects of Vertov's film editing, are all primarily cognitivist models of artistic creation, which prioritise conceptual thought and reason, and deprioritise aesthetic categories such as interior vision, intuition and insight.

In contradistinction to Soviet montage cinema, Weimar cinematic modernist cinema can be defined as a non, or even deliberately anti-cognitivist cinema, which privileged the intuitive aspect of aesthetic expression. The visual style of Weimar also suggests an acknow-ledgement of existential uncertainty, an acknowledgement embodied in the flowing, indeterminate chiaroscuro which pervades so many Weimar films. In contrast, the term 'montage' implies order, and controlled orchestration. Weimar cinematic modernism also embodied the indeterminate character of an image-based aesthetic, whilst Soviet montage theory and cinema was based on an aesthetic of narrative structure, and reflected the rationalistic character of such an aesthetic.

The contrast between these two aesthetic positions is well illus-trated by Béla Balázs' essay 'The Future of Film', which originally appeared in the German periodical *Filmtechnic* in 1926, and by Eisenstein's response to that essay. In his essay, Balázs argues that the basis of film art lies in the quality of the photographed image, and that the film image is capable of embodying a 'powerful *figurative* and poetic force' which can express abstract, symbolic meaning.[56] Balázs is drawing upon his theory of the cinematic gesture here, as set out in his 1924 book *Der sichtbare Mensch oder Der Kultur Des Films*, in which he argued that film can express 'spiritual experience' which exists beyond the rational.[57] It is such experience which Balázs refers to in 'The Future of Film' when he argues that a scene from Eisenstein's *Bronenosets Potemkin* contains a 'hidden figurative quality' which has been brought to 'poetic expressiveness' by Eisenstein's cameraman, Edward Tissé.[58]

The scene in question is that in which a flotilla of small yaughts approach the Potemkin just prior to the massacre on the Odessa Steps. Balázs describes this shot as a 'sumptuous image' and a 'hymn of ecstasy' which evokes a general feeling of lyrical joy,[59] and argues that the poetic expressiveness of the scene is created, not by the motif, but by the photography, because 'cinema art of this kind emerges only through the lens; it can only be produced through photography'. Such an argument encapsulates the intuitionist, visual character of Balázs' film theory, and of Weimar film theory more generally.[60]

In contrast, Eisenstein's response to Balázs's essay, in his 'Béla Forgets the Scissors', which was published in the periodical *Kino* in 1926, encapsulates the underlying principles of much montage theory. In his essay, Eisenstein condemns Balázs' emphasis on the individual image, and criticises his approach as an example of bourgeois ideology rooted in individualism. In opposition, Eisenstein argues for greater emphasis on 'a "genetic" (constructive) amalgamation of the shots', and goes on to assert that such an emphasis on the relationships between shots, rather than on the 'individualised shot', is more politically progressive and correct.[61] In opposition to Balázs' focus on the image, Eisenstein compares filmic structure to language, and rejects Balázs' use of such aesthetic categories as insight 'creativity' and 'art' as 'unpleasant'.[62]

Although these altercations appear to indicate the existence of fundamental differences between Weimar cinematic modernism and Soviet montage, that which also links these two modernist cinemas together at the level of aesthetic style, and which, at the same time, reveals the underlying influence on both of the Kantian tradition, is pictorialism.[63] Just as Weimar cinema experimented with moving camerawork, special effects and evocative chiaroscuro lighting; so too, highly composed, vibrant and elaborate pictorial compositions are also common in Soviet montage cinema, and particularly in the later films of Eisenstein and Dovzhenko. This type of 'aesthetic saturation of the frame' also characterised French cinematic impressionism, and links these three modernist film movements together.[64]

As with the particular case of Eisenstein, a contradiction exists between the consciously theorised, cognitivist, often instrumental preoccupations of Soviet montage, and this underlying, more autonomous aesthetic tendency. Whereas, in principle, Soviet montage cinema was committed to playing a pedagogic role within the prescriptive formation and advancement of communist ideology, in reality, the sheer aesthetic beauty and power of the images in many montage films detracted from, and even undermined, that project. Underlying the Soviet montage film-makers concern for the transmission of political ideas, therefore, are a number of clearly discernable, and purely aesthetic preoccupations, and this reveals the intellectual origins of montage film theory and practice in a formalist, and, in Eisenstein and Dovzhenkos's case, symbolist concern for the aesthetic.

However, it was not possible for montage film-makers to directly confront this 'artistic' aspect of their work, as the conception of the aesthetic which it entailed was too closely associated with a romantic ideal that was politically unacceptable. Like the political censorship from which it habitually suffered, such denial and repression also impacted upon Soviet montage cinema, and led to a degree of containment of the sort of energies released to such effect within Weimar cinematic modernism. Where such energies did find expression within the Soviet cinema, in films such as *Alexander Nevsky*, *Ivan Grozny* and *Zemlya*, the central tradition of early European cinematic modernism becomes reinforced. That tradition, which has its origins in Kantian aesthetics, symbolism and phenomenology, also finds its most intense expression in the third major *avant-garde* film movement: French impressionism.

Notes

1. *From Caligari to Hitler* will be considered in greater depth in Chapter 7.
2. Kracauer, Siegfried, *From Caligari to Hitler: A Psychological History of the German Film* (Princeton, NJ: Princeton University Press, 1974), p. 8.
3. By realist, I refer to the methodology of historical analysis outlined by Allen, Robert and Gomery, Douglas in their *Film History: Theory and Practice* (New York: Alfred A. Knopf, 1985), pp. 1–24.
4. Bordwell, David, and Thompson, Kristin, *Film History: An Introduction* (New York: McGraw-Hill, 1994), p. 105.
5. Silberman, Marc, *German Cinema: Texts in Context* (Detroit, MI: Wayne State University Press, 1995), p. 2.
6. Elsaesser, Thomas, *Weimar Cinema and After: Germany's Historical Imaginary* (London and New York: Routledge, 2000), p. 3.
7. Ibid., p. 63.

8. Budd, M., 'The Moments of Caligari', in Budd, M. (ed.), *The Cabinet of Dr Caligari* (New Brunswick, NJ: Rutgers University Press, 1990), p. 24.
9. Ibid., p. 18.
10. Elsaesser, op cit., p. 18.
11. Kracauer, op cit., p. 65.
12. Ibid., p. 74.
13. Gay, Peter, *Weimar Culture: The Outsider as Insider* (London: Penguin, 1992), p. 162.
14. Kracauer, op cit., p. 9.
15. Gay, op cit., p. 90.
16. Ibid., p. 95.
17. Parmesani, Loredana, *Art of the Twentieth Century: Movements, Theories, Schools and Tendencies 1900–2000* (Milan: Skira editore, 2000), pp. 16–17.
18. Barlow, John, *German Expressionist Film* (Boston, MA: Twayne, 1982), p. 26.
19. See Solomon, Robert, C., 'Romancing the Self: Fichte, Schelling, Schiller, and Romanticism', in his *Continental Philosophy Since 1750: The Rise and Fall of the Self* (Oxford and New York: Oxford University Press, 1988), pp. 44–55. See also Eisner, Lotte, *The Haunted Screen* (London: Thames and Hudson, 1969), p. 12.
20. Barlow, op cit., p. 33.
21. Elsaesser, op cit., p. 65.
22. Ibid., p. 64.
23. Budd, op cit., p. 10.
24. Eisner, op cit., p. 218.
25. Ibid., p. 41.
26. Elsaesser, Thomas, 'Social Mobility and the Fantastic', in *Budd*, op cit., p. 178.
27. Kracauer, op cit., p. 6.
28. Salt, Barry, 'From Caligari to Who?', *Sight and Sound* (Spring, 1979), vol. 48, no. 2, pp. 119–23.
29. Hake, Sabina, 'Towards a Philosophy of Film', in her *The Cinema's Third Machine: Writing on Film in Germany 1907–1933* (Lincoln, NB and London: University of Nebrasca Press, 1993), p. 132.
30. Kracauer, op cit., p. 9.
31. Ibid., p. 7.
32. It has not been possible to explore the role of authorship in this brief outline of the system of determinations on Weimar cinematic modernism.
33. Leyda, Jay, *Kino: A History of the Russian and Soviet Film* (London: George Allen & Unwin, 1973), p. 123.
34. Ibid., p. 142.
35. Ibid., pp. 131–2.

36. Ibid., pp. 136–7.
37. Ibid., p. 132.
38. Michelson, Annette (ed.), *Kino-Eye: The Writings of Dziga Vertov* (London and Sydney: Pluto Press, 1984), p. xxiv.
39. Vertov, Dziga, 'The Cine-Eyes. A Revolution', *Lef* (June/July 1923), no. 3, pp. 135–43. Reprinted in Taylor, Richard and Christie, Ian (eds), *The Film Factory: Russian and Soviet Cinema in Documents 1896–1939* (London and New York: Routledge, 1988), p. 89.
40. Michelson, op cit., pp. xxiv–xxv.
41. Lenin, Vladimir, 'Directive on Cinema Affairs', 17 January 1922. Reprinted in Taylor and Christie (1988), op cit., p. 56.
42. Kuleshov, Lev, 'The Origins of Montage', in Schnitzer, Jean, Schnitzer, Ludu and Martin, Marcel (eds), *Cinema in Revolution: The Heroic Era of the Soviet Film* (London: Secker & Warburg, 1973), p. 70.
43. Kuleshov, Lev, *Art of the Cinema* (Moscow: Tea-Kino Pechat, 1929), selections reprinted in *Screen Reader 1* (London: SEFT, 1977), p. 338.
44. Ibid., p. 339.
45. Schnitzer et al., op cit., p. 70.
46. Kracauer, op cit., p. 77.
47. Elsaesser (2000), op cit., p. 19.
48. Nettl, J. P., *The Soviet Achievement* (London: Thames and Hudson, 1976), p. 99.
49. Elsaesser (2000), op cit., p. 20.
50. Craig, David (ed.), *Marxists On Literature: An Anthology* (London: Pelican, 1977), p. 514.
51. Zhdanov, A. A., 'Soviet Literature – The Richest in Ideas, The Most Advanced Literature', in *Maxim Gorky* et al., *Soviet Writers Congress 1934: The Debate on Socialist Realism and Modernism in the Soviet Union* (London: Lawrence & Wishart, 1977), p. 21.
52. Ibid., p. 19.
53. Eisner, op cit., p. 48.
54. Eisenstein, Sergei, 'The Montage of Attractions', *Lef* (June/July, 1923), no. 3, reprinted in Taylor and Christie (1988), op cit., p. 87.
55. Pudovkin, Vsevolod, 'On Film Technique', in his *Film Technique and Film Acting* (New York: Grove, 1960), p. 73.
56. Eisenstein, Sergei, 'Béla Forgets the Scissors', *Kino*, 20 July 1926 and 10 August 1926, reprinted in Taylor and Christie (1988), op cit., p. 147.
57. Balázs, Béla, *Der Sichtbare Mensche oder Der Kultur Des Films* (Vienna: Leipzig, Deutsch-Osterreichischer Verlag, 1924), p. 40.
58. Balázs, Béla, 'The Future of Film', *Kinogazeta*, 6 July 1926, reprinted in Taylor and Christie (1988), op cit., p. 144.
59. Ibid.
60. Ibid., p. 145.
61. Eisenstein (1926) in Taylor and Christie (1988), op cit., p. 147.

62. Ibid., p. 149.
63. See Chapter 1 on the influence of Kantian aesthetics on both Weimar film theory and Russian formalism.
64. O'Prey, Michael, 'The Frame and Montage in Eisenstein', in Taylor, Richard and Christie, Ian (eds), *Eisenstein Rediscovered* (London and New York: Routledge, 1993), p. 214.

IV

Into the Realm of the Wondrous

French Cinematic Impressionism

One of the first important schools of alternative film-making within French cinema was that of pictorialist naturalism.[1] Influenced by nineteenth-century traditions of realism, naturalism and impressionist painting, this school was characterised by a concern for landscape and the picturesque.[2] More specifically, films such as L'Herbier's *L'Homme du large* (*Man of the Ocean*, 1920), Louis Mercanton's *L'Appel du sang* (1920) and Jacques de Baroncelli's *Ramuntche* (1919) can be related to what has been referred to as the tradition of French, picturesque regional genre painting.[3] Many of these films, shot on location in regions such as Provence, Brittany and the Auvergne, attempt to invoke a landscape's atmosphere through a series of evocative impressions, and are centrally concerned with the relationship between regional communities and the surrounding natural environment.

A sense of lyricism, as well as veneration of the power and beauty of nature pervades these films as, for example, in Baroncelli's series of mountain films, or André Antoine's *La Terre* (*Earth*, 1921), which draws on the pictorial lyricism of the Barbizon school, and the paintings of Millet and Corot in particular. In addition to what might be referred to as an 'animated impressionism', clearly influenced by impressionist and post-impressionist painting, these films also draw on subject matter common to the naturalist tradition. So, for example, L'Herbier's *L'Homme du large* (1920), Antoine's *L'Hirondelle et la mésange* (*The Swallow and the Finch*, 1920) and *La Terre*, Mercanton's *Miarka* (1920) and Jacques Feyder's *Crainquebille* (*Old Bill of Paris*, 1923) all deal with issues of entrapment, obsession, alienation and mental illness.

The critical writings of Émile Zola were the single most important influence on this school of film-making, and, indeed, one critic has argued that it was Zola, rather than Louis Lumière and Georges Méliès, who was 'the father of the French cinema'.[4] In his *Le Naturalisme au théâtre* and *Le Roman expérimental*, Zola criticised the artificiality, lack of authenticity, and limited social perspective of nineteenth-century French popular drama, and, taking their cue from Zola's essays, French film-makers such as Ferdinand Zecca, René Hervil, Victorin Jasset, Henri Pouctal and Antoine took their cameras out of the studio and into the countryside, where they photographed local people within their domestic environments. As with nineteenth-century naturalism itself, this group of film-makers was also associated with the political left, and the representation of the poor within these films was frequently combined with demands for social reform, as, for example, in Zecca and Nonguet's *La Grève* (*The Strike*, 1903).

One of the most important figures within this genre of realist film-making was the theatre director André Antoine. In 1887 Antoine founded the Théâtre Libre group, an independent company which specialised in the presentation of plays derived from the novels of Zola, and from the writings of others within the naturalistic tradition.[5] Antoine dispensed with the traditional artifice of the French theatre in these plays, and encouraged his actors to speak and act as genuinely as possible. He also used real objects, as opposed to painted backdrops, in his sets, in order to achieve a greater sense of physical presence and authenticity.[6] In 1897 Antoine disbanded the Théâtre Libre and founded the Théâtre Antoine, which continued to perform plays in the naturalist manner until 1906, when it too was forced to close.

When Antoine eventually began to direct films he also drew on the naturalist tradition, using real people, as opposed to trained actors, and rejecting the artifice of the studio in favour of location shooting. In 1920 he directed *L'Hirondelle et la mésange*, a film set on the barges of the canals of Belgium and northern France. *L'Hirondelle et la mésange* displays typical naturalist thematic concerns with sexual jealousy, petty crime and poverty, and is largely shot on location using untrained actors. In 1921 Antoine also directed a film adaption of Zola's *La Terre*, in which he focused on the rural landscape and culture of the area around Beuce, where he had shot *La Terre* on location.[7] Both these films display concerns for the tribulations of the lower classes, and the lyrical representation of landscape, which were to influence cinematic impressionism.

In addition to his contribution as a film director, Antoine also contributed to the development of film theory in France during the period. Basing his approach on the established tradition of adapting prestigious works of literature for the cinema, Antoine argued that the cinema should seek its subject matter in already existing works of great art. However, he also added that such works should be recast using cinematic techniques.[8] Although, in recasting such works as Zola's *La Terre*, the techniques which Antoine drew on were largely derived from the naturalist canon, in addition to achieving a naturalist authenticity, Antoine's films also exhibit a use of complex pictorial compositions, and it is this combination of realism and pictorialism which characterises his films, and which gives them their particular quality.

Many of the film-makers who directed films within the pictorialist naturalist tradition during the period were associated with the Théâtre Libre and Théâtre Antoine, and Antoine himself was effectively the leader, around whom these film-makers gathered.[9] When he stopped making films after 1922, his protégées carried on the tradition. For example, Louis Mercanton directed *Aux jardins de Murcie* (*In The Gardens of Murcie*, 1923), a film about peasant disputes over water rights, whilst Léon Poirier directed *La Brière* (1924), a film set in a peasant community in Brittany. Mercanton also drew on pictorialist naturalism in his *Jocelyn* (1922), a film based on the novel by the nineteenth-century romantic writer and critic, Lamartine; and also combined pictorialist techniques with a documentary format in his *Verdun, visions d'histoire* (*Verdun, Visions of history*, 1928).[10]

A final major figure to emerge from the pictorialist naturalist school was Jean Grémillon, and it is also through Grémillon that a link can be established between pictorialist naturalism and the development of the poetic documentary tradition in France. In 1923 Grémillon directed a short documentary entitled *Chartres*, and, in 1926, *Un Tour au large* (*A Sea Journey*): a 'poetic' documentary about the voyage of a fishing boat. In 1928 he went on to direct his first feature film, *Maldone*, a big-budget film which, like the majority of films within the pictorialist naturalist tradition, focused on lower-class experience, whilst contrasting that experience with the 'sterile conventions of the *nouveau riche milieu*'.[11] Grémillon then went on to direct *Gardiens de phare* (*The Lighthouse Keepers*, 1929), a film about Breton lighthouse keepers. As with *Un Tour au large*, both *Maldone* and *Gardiens de phare* accentuate the lyrical representation of landscape, and the aesthetic saturation of the image. However, *Gardiens de phare* also contains elaborate cross-cutting in the impressionist style.[12]

After 1925 the pictorialist naturalism tradition gradually declined in importance, and was superseded by both the impressionist movement, and by other forms of cinematic modernism. Despite this, pictorialist naturalism continued to exert a significant influence on French film production during the remainder of the 1920s, and had a direct influence on a group of modernist, poetic documentaries which were produced between 1925 and 1930. These include *Rien que les heures* (*Nothing but the Hours*, Alberto Cavalcanti, 1926), *Voyage au Congo* (*Voyage to the Congo*, Marc Allégret, 1925), *Études sur Paris* (*Studies on Paris*, André Sauvage, 1928), *La Zone* (Georges Lacombe, 1928), *Nogent, Eldorado du Dimanche* (Marcel Carné, 1929), *Un Tour au large* and *À propos de Nice* (*On Nice*, Jean Vigo, 1930).

The documentary film flourished in France during the second half of the 1920s, as did debates over documentary theory and practice. For example, the film-maker and critic André Sauvage developed an approach to *avant-garde* documentary realism based upon a rejection of the conventional understanding of what documentary stood for, and on a categorical opposition to the use of the term *documentaire*.[13] Discussing Flaherty's *Nanook of the North* (1923), Sauvage argued that *documentaire* was a 'vulgar' expression, and that it would be more appropriate to use a term such as 'poetic realism' when addressing such a film.[14] *Nanook of the North* was one of the key influences on the development of this genre of French poetic documentary film-making. For example, the film-maker and essayist Hubert Revol argued that documentary film was the highest expression of 'pure cinema', and that *Nanook of the North* provided the model for the future development of the genre. For Revol and others, a revitalised form of documentary, inspired by the model offered by *Nanook of the North*, would consist of 'visual poems' which would 'touch the spectator through the beauty of their images':

> Documentary must be made by poets. Few of those within French cinema have understood that in our country, we possess innumerable elements and subjects to make, not just insignificant ribbons (of film), but splendid films lively and expressive ... The purest demonstration of pure cinema, that is to say of poetry which is truly cinematographic, has been provided for us by some remarkable films, vulgarly called documentaries, particularly *Nanook* and *Moana*.[15]

In addition to this conception of documentary as the highest form of pure cinema, Revol, Ricciotto Canudo and others also believed that documentary films such as *Nanook of the North* and *Moana* (Flaherty, 1926) were particularly suited to represent nature, and, consequently, the relationship between the documentary image and depictions of the natural environment was an important consideration for these film-makers.[16] Although critics and film-makers such as Sauvage, Canudo and Revol were influenced by cinematic impressionism, they were even more influenced by pictorialist naturalism, and this influence is revealed in Canudo's claim that the 'mission of documentary' was to 'fondre la vie de l'homme dans la vie des milieux' (to show man's relationship with the world around him).[17] Such a mission clearly draws on the French naturalist and realist tradition, and illustrates the extent to which these documentaries constituted a bridge between impressionist modernism and naturalist pictorialism.

As with cinematic impressionism, the documentaries referred to above were also centrally concerned with the representation of subjective experience. For example, in Cavalcanti's *Rien que les heures*, a number of special effects techniques are used to suggest the point of view of characters experiencing agitated emotional states. However, the concern with subjectivity in these films is also significantly mediated by their desire to evoke a poetic external reality, and one, moreover, which was often located within the urban milieu of Paris. For example, Jean Dréville argued that it was in the documentary, rather than the fiction film, that *photogénie* could best be realised, and he went on to argue that Walter Ruttmann's *Berlin: die Symphonie der Grossstadt* (*Berlin, Symphony of a Great City*, 1929), 'brought out the *photogénie* of urban life'.[18] *Photogénie* was the foundational concept of the cinematic impressionist movement, and will be discussed in depth later in this chapter. What is important to note here is that Dréville equates *photogénie*, and, therefore, what Revol called 'pure cinema', with the documentary, rather than feature film.

As the statements described above suggest, the documentary provided an ideal platform for the synthesis of the two traditions of pictorialist naturalism and impressionism, and the style of documentary which emerged from this was characterised by interlacing visual effects, impressionistic delineations of the urban or rural environment, indeterminate narrative structures, and fluid camerawork and montage, all of which were arrayed in order to create poetic, expressive effects. In these films, as in impressionist films, reality was transformed by the film-maker using film technique, but the use of documentary footage also ensured that it was a primarily external, rather than subjective world, which was evoked. So, for example, in addition to its use of subjective camerawork, *Rien que les heures* also contains a number of shots in which characters move against a complex background of streets, alleyways and apartment blocks within the environs of Paris.

In addition to these more *avant-garde* poetic documentaries, a number of other films made after 1925 also carried on the pictorialist naturalist tradition. One of the origins of both pictorialist naturalism and the poetic documentary style were two series of films directed by Louis Feuillade: *Fantômas* (1913–14) and *Les Vampires* (*The Vampires*, 1915–16). Although the films produced within these series contained many uncanny and bizarre motifs which would later be highly prized by the surrealists, they also included a considerable amount of footage which was shot within the streets of Paris, and which presented a poeticised urban landscape, suffused with mystery and uneasiness.[19] René Clair, who began his career as an actor in Feuillade's troupe, drew on these series when making both his *Paris qui dort* (*The Crazy Ray*, 1924) and *Sous les toits de Paris* (*Under the Roofs of Paris*, 1930). The Brazilian director Alberto Cavalcanti's *En Rade* (*Stranded*, 1927), Jean Renoir's *Nana* (1926), Henri Fescourt's *Les Misérables* (1926) and Jean Epstein's *Finis terrae* (*Land's End*, 1929) also carried on the tradition of pictorialist naturalism, to a greater or lesser extent, up till the end of the decade.

The stylistic developments which took place within the French cinema after 1920, and which included the emergence of pictorialist naturalism, were influenced by two major factors: the changing character of the French film industry, and the growth of an alternative film culture. After 1918 the French film industry found itself largely eclipsed by Hollywood, and, during the post-war period, companies such as Gaumont and Pathé continued to loose market share.[20] In response to this, and in the conviction that France would be unable to compete with Hollywood in the production of large budget films, many producers began to experiment with new and diverse approaches to film-making. This strategy eventually led to the appearance of a number of smaller production houses, which made more modest films for the home market, and this, in turn, acted as a catalyst for the stylistic development which occurred after 1920.

The other catalyst for that development was the growth of an alternative film culture, and one of the key figures in the emergence of such a culture was the critic and film-maker, Louis Delluc. In 1917 Delluc was appointed editor of *Le Film*, a weekly cinema magazine which was probably the first journal of its kind in the world.[21] Delluc also persuaded the newspaper *Paris-Midi* to begin publishing film criticism regularly from 1918, and, within three years of Delluc's first article appearing in *Paris-Midi*, all major Parisian newspapers carried regular film review columns. In 1918 Delluc left the editorship of *Le Film*, and went on to found the journal *Cinéa* in 1920, and to publish collections of his own film criticism in *Cinéma et Cie* (1919), and *Photogénie* (1920). Delluc also directed five films before his early death in 1924.

An intellectual film culture soon began to grow in France, building on Delluc's contribution. In 1919 the journal *Literature*, edited by André Breton, Louis Aragon and Philippe Soupault, began to publish film criticism. *Le Crapouilat*, edited by Jean Galtiére-Boisiere, followed suit in 1920, whilst, from 1920 onwards, the established journal *Mercure de France* also published film criticism by authors such as Jean Epstein and Léon Moussinac. In 1921 the impressionist film-maker Jean Epstein published his *Bonjour Cinéma*, and, in 1923, the journal *Cinéa-Ciné-pour-tous* was founded by Jean Tedesco. *Cinéa-Ciné-pour-tous* soon became the principal forum for debates on the cinema during the period, and exercised a major influence on the development of French film culture.[22]

In addition to Delluc, another influential critic, Ricciotto Canudo, also played an important role in the development of film theory over this period. In 1920 Canudo founded the journal *Le Gazette de sept arts*, in which he published essays by painters such as Fernand Leger, writers such as Jean Cocteau, and film-makers such as Jean Epstein.[23] Canudo also founded what may have been the worlds's first film club in 1920: the Club des amis du septieme art. The Club des amis du septieme art held informal gatherings attended by writers and film-makers such as Alberto Cavalcanti, Marcel L'Herbier, Epstein and Cocteau, and played an important role within the film culture of the period.[24]

In addition to film clubs such as the Club des amis du septieme art, an alternative cinema circuit also began to develop in the mid 1920s. In 1924 Jean Tedesco established the Vieux Colombier as a specialist art film theatre. This was soon followed by the Studio des Urselines, which was established by Armand Tallier in 1925. Finally, in 1929, the film producer Pierre Braunberger, whose production company Neo Film had made a number of *avant-garde* films during the mid 1920s, set up a distribution company called Studio Films, in order to distribute 'all the films of artistic quality (experimental films, documentary films, films called *Avant Garde*)'.[25]

It was the development of a critical discourse on the cinema, and the emergence of the new forms of film production, exhibition and distribution referred to above, which provided the basis for the expansion of *avant-garde* film-making which took place in France during the 1920s. The first major *avant-garde* film movement to emerge from this context was that of cinematic impressionism. Although differing in significant respects from the previous tradition of naturalist pictorialism, impressionism was also strongly influenced by that tradition, and the key development in the transition from the one movement to the other lay in the use of film to evoke extremes of subjective experience, in addition to the lyrical evocation of mood and landscape which had characterised pictorialist naturalism.[26]

This first period of impressionism can be described as impressionist pictorialism, in order to distinguish it from pictorialist naturalism,[27] and the first major film to emerge from the impressionist movement was Abel Gance's *La Dixième symphonie* (*The Tenth Symphony*, 1918). This was followed by *Rose-France* (Marcel L'Herbier, 1919), *J'Accuse* (*I Accuse*, Abel Gance, 1919), *Le Carnaval des vérités* (*The Carnival of Truths*, Marcel L'Herbier, 1920), *L'Homme du large* (*The Man of the Ocean*, Marcel L'Herbier, 1920), *Fièvre* (*Fever*, Louis Delluc, 1921), *El Dorado* (Marcel L'Herbier, 1921) and *La Femme de nulle part* (*The Woman From Nowhere*, Louis Delluc, 1922). Whilst these films retained the preoccupation with realist and pictorial qualities associated with the pictorialist naturalist style, they also deployed cinematic technique in order to indicate subjective psychological states. Thus, films such as *La Dixième symphonie* and *J'Accuse* employ superimpositions, slow motion photography, and distorted imagery, to represent psychological confusion, desire and anxiety.

The second phase of impressionism began in 1922, and lasted until 1925–26. This period was inaugurated by Abel Gance's *La Roue* (*The Wheel*, 1922), which was followed by *L'Auberge rouge* (*The Red Inn*, Jean Epstein, 1923), *Don Juan et Faust* (*Don Juan and Faust*, Marcel L'Herbier, 1923), *La Souriante Madame Beudet* (*The Smiling Madame Beudet*, Germaine Dullac, 1923), *Coeur fidèle* (*Faithful Heart*, Jean Epstein, 1923), *Crainquebille* (Jacques Feyder, 1923), *Le Marchand de plaisir* (*The Seller of Pleasure*, Jacque Catelain, 1923), *Gossette* (*The Little Kid*, Germaine Dulac, 1923), *Le Brasier ardent* (*The Burning Brazier*, Ivan Mosjoukine and Alexandre Volkoff, 1923), *Le Galérie des monstres* (*The Freak Show*, Jacque Catelain, 1924), *L'Inondation* (*The Flood*, Louis Delluc, 1924), *L'Inhumaine* (*The Inhuman One*, Marcel L'Herbier, 1924), *Kean* (Alexander Volkoff, 1924), *Catherine* (Albert Dieudonné, 1924), *La Belle Nivernaise* (*The Beautiful Nivernaise*, Jean Epstein, 1924), *L'Ironie du destin* (The Irony of Destiny, Dimitri Kirsanoff, 1924), *L'Affiche* (*The Poster*, Jean Epstein, 1925), *Visages d'enfants* (*Children's Faces*, Jacques Feyder, 1925), *Feu Mathias Pascal* (*The Late Mathias Pascal*, Marcel L'Herbier, 1925) and *La Fille de l'eau* (*The Daughter of the Water*, Jean Renoir, 1924).

The period between 1922 and 1925 was one in which cinematic impressionism developed a distinct identity, and in which many of the most characteristic films of the movement were produced. 1925 also marked the appearance of Léon Moussinac's *Naissance du cinéma*, a critical work which functioned as a manifesto for the impressionist movement, and which attempted to establish the key theoretical premises, convictions and stylistic repertoire of the new cinema.[28] Following the publication of Moussinac's book, Germaine Dulac then applied the term 'impressionist' to the group of film-makers around Abel Gance, when she argued that a new 'era' of cinema had arrived to replace the previous one, which had been dominated by realism:

> Another era arrived, that of the psychological and impressionist film. It seemed childish to place a character in a given situation without penetrating the secret domain of his inner life, and the actor's performance was annotated with the play of his thoughts and his visualised feelings. When one added to the unambiguous facts of the drama the description of multiple and contradictory impressions – actions being only the consequence of a mental condition, or vice versa – imperceptibly a dual development ensued which, to remain harmonious, had to follow a clearly established rhythm.[29]

Although the term impressionist had been applied to individual French films immediately following the First World War, it was not, therefore, until 1925–6 that the term began to be used to define a specific movement of film-making.

The conception of cinema which emerged from both Moussinac's and Dulac's assessment of the film-making of Gance, Epstein and others was one which emphasised interiority, and which employed special effects techniques, pictorial composition, rapid editing and musically derived narrative structures, in order to both express subjectivity, and explore the aesthetic potential of the medium of film. The narrative style of such a cinema would be impressionistic and indeterminate, as Dulac's comments make clear, and would also be based on musical compositional categories such as rhythm, counterpoint, lyrical interlude and crescendo. In such a cinema, the 'unambiguous facts of the drama' would be made enigmatic through the use of 'multiple and contradictory impressions', as the film-maker sought to both explore the formal potential of the medium, and penetrate the 'secret domain of … inner life'.[30]

However, the attempt to elevate the cinema of Gance and his associates into a movement with the canonic and culturally prestigious title of 'impressionism' did not remain unchallenged. Jean Epstein, who later went on to make one of the most modernist of films within the impressionist tradition, La Glace à trois faces (The Three Panelled Mirror, 1927), also retained links with the pictorialist naturalist tradition. Although Epstein's *Couer fidèle* had been strongly influenced by the rapid editing introduced into the French cinema by Gance's *La Roue* his next film, *La Belle Nivernaise* reverted to a lyrical naturalism which was closer to the style of André Antoine and his associates. After completing *La Belle Nivernaise* Epstein argued that the widespread rapid, rhythmic editing which had been introduced by *La Roue* had, by 1924, degenerated into a superficial and cliched cinematic device.[31] Voicing similar sentiments, René Clair also proclaimed that the whole cinematic model of impressionism, with its rapid editing, optical effects and cinematic trickery, added up to little more than 'false art'.[32]

By 1926 the aesthetic model of impressionism was also beginning to fragment under the impact of a variety of pressures and changing circumstances. One of these was the stylistic diffusion which followed from the emergence of a number of small independent production companies after 1924. Until then all the major impressionist film-makers had been employed in mainstream production companies. However, in 1924 L'Herbier established Cinégraphic, Gance established Films Abel Gance, and Epstein Les Films de Jean Epstein; whilst Renoir, Kirsanoff and Dulac also began to finance their own films.[33] This new context of relative freedom from commercial constraint influenced the stylistic diffusion which occurred after 1925, and, following this, many of the films produced, including those by Renoir, Kirsanoff, Epstein, Dulac and Cavalcanti, were shorter, more esoteric and elliptical, than earlier films had been.[34]

The final group of impressionist films to appear within the period of stylistic diffusion which lasted from 1925 to 1929 include *Ménilmontant* (Dimitri Kirsanoff, 1926), *Six et demi-onze* (Jean Epstein, 1927), *La Glace à trois faces*, *Napoléon vu par Abel Gance* (*Napoléon as Seen by Abel Gance*, Abel Gance, 1927), *En Rade* (*Stranded*, Alberto Cavalcanti, 1927), *Brumes d'automne* (*Autumn Mists*, Dimitri Kirsanoff, 1928), *La Chute de la maison Usher* (*The Fall of the House of Usher*, Jean Epstein, 1928), *La Petite marchande d'allumettes* (*The Little Match Girl*, Jean Renoir, 1928), *L'Argent* (*Money*, Marcel L'Herbier, 1929) and *Finis Terrae*. Although these films can still be classed as impressionist, as a group, they are far less stylistically consistent than the films made between 1923 and 1925.

This group of films also experimented with a number of new, innovative techniques. For example, *Ménilmontant* and *Six et demi-onze* discarded titles entirely, and relied only on the image track to advance the narrative; whilst *Napoléon vu par Abel Gance*, *La Glace à trois faces* and *L'Argent* deployed multiple subjective viewpoint scenarios, and lengthy tracking and crane shots. Although many of these films were relatively short, as a consequence of their dependence on uncertain and limited independent finance, the most well-known film from this group, *Napoléon vu par Abel Gance*, was conceived on an epic scale. *Napoléon vu par Abel Gance* is also a far more heterogeneous text than the earlier *La Roue* had been. Whilst *Napoléon* contains the same melodramatic tendencies and moments of impressionist 'pure cinema' as are found in *La Roue*, Gance's later film also employs chase and action sequences which are ultimately derived from the Hollywood western, and is a 'grand example of the French historical reconstruction film', the most popular film genre in France during the 1920s.[35]

In addition to the above context of stylistic differentiation within the movement itself, the congruity and pre-eminence of impressionism was also affected by the appearance of new modernist film movements after 1926. As already mentioned, the combined influence of impressionism and pictorialist naturalism led to the emergence of a group of modernist documentaries during the period. These documentaries, directed by Cavalcanti, Vigo, Sauvage, Allégret, Carné and Clair, can also be associated with the genre of the 'city symphony' film which appeared across Europe during the 1920s and early 1930s, and which included important films such as Walter Ruttmann's *Berlin: die Symphonie der Grossstadt* and Dziga Vertov's *Chelovek s kinoapparatom* (*The Man with the Movie Camera*, 1929).

In addition to these documentaries, another challenge to the ascendancy of impressionism stemmed from the entry into film-making of artists associated with French dada. Dada emerged as a movement in the arts immediately after the end of the First World War, although the first French dada film, Man Ray's *Retour à la raison* (*Return to Reason*), did not appear until 1923. This was followed in 1924 by René Clair's *Entr'acte* (*Intermission*), and Dudley Murphy and Fernand Léger's *Ballet méchanique*. The fourth major dada film of the period, Marcel Duchamp's *Anémic cinéma* (*Anemic Cinema*), appeared in 1926. These films appeared after dada had gone into decline as an influential force within the arts, were few in number, and had only a limited impact upon the development of French film culture during the 1920s. However, as dada film-making went into decline, emerging surrealist film-makers took over the dadaist mantle. The first French surrealist films, Man Ray's *Emak Bakia* and *L'Etoile de mer* (*The Starfish*), were both produced in 1927, and these were followed by Germaine Dulac's *La Coquille et le clergyman* (*The Seashell and the Clergyman*, 1928), and Salvador Dali and Louis Buñuel's *Un Chien andalou* (*An Andalusian Dog*, 1928) and *L'Âge d'or* (*The Age of Gold*, 1930).

In addition to dada and surrealist film-making, a third identifiable group of *avant-garde* films to emerge during the late 1920s can be grouped together under the heading of the *cinéma pur*. The *cinéma pur* attempted to isolate the fundamental formal properties of shape, form, rhythm and movement of the medium of film. Thus, Henri Chomette's *Jeux des reflets de la vitesse* (*The Play of Reflections and Speed*, 1925), as its name implies, studies the abstract patterns created by objects filmed at speed and from different angles, whilst his *Cinq minutes du cinéma pur* (*Five Minutes of Pure Cinema*, 1926) is even more minimalist and formalist in style. Germaine Dulac also made two films in the *cinéma pur* style: *Disque 927* (1928) and *Thème et varitions* (*Theme and Variations*, 1928), both of which explore the same sorts of formal relationships as do the films of Chomette.

In addition to those directly associated with impressionism, dada, surrealism and the *cinéma pur*, a number of other *avant-garde* film-makers active during the late 1920s were also influenced by these movements. These included Jean Renoir, Alberto Cavalcanti, René Clair, Jacques Feyder, Julien Duvivier and, towards the end of the period, Jean Cocteau. The eclectic style of many of these film-makers was also reinforced by the fact that they tended to work both within the mainstream film industry, and within the more experimentally inclined independent sector. This lack of any hard and fast demarcating line between art and mainstream cinema led film-makers such as Renoir, Cavalcanti and Clair to evolve varied film-making styles which combined both modernist and commercial techniques. However, this was also the case with impressionism, where, in addition to moments of 'pure' impressionist cinema, films such as *Napoléon vu par Abel Gance* also drew on melodramatic and other strategies derived from Hollywood and the popular French cinema.[36]

A number of distinctions can be drawn between impressionism and independent modernist groups such as dada, surrealism and the *cinéma pur*. Dada films such as *Entr'acte* display an anarchic and disorganised quality which can be distinguished from the more evocative, and highly composed aesthetic indeterminacy of impressionist film-making. In addition, the 'anti-art' posture of dada, as typified by Marcel Duchamp's 'found sculptures', and the deliberate crudeness, even vulgarity, of *Entr'acte*, was antithetical to an impressionist sensibility founded upon a romantic and visionary conception of art.[37]

Although the surrealist movement continued many of the thematic preoccupations of dada, including a pronounced hostility to the impressionist fixation with film as art, surrealism also differed from dada in its reliance upon psychoanalytic theory. In place of the anarchic *Entr'acte*, a film such as *Un Chien andalou* attempted to incorporate the logic of the dream into its narrative structure, and was preoccupied with darker, more sexually aligned subject matter than was the case with the more lighthearted work emerging from dada. However, the concern with the psychological unconscious in *Un Chien andalou* is quite different from the consideration of subjective, psychological and emotional experience in a film such as *Napoléon vu par Abel Gance*. In its attempt to depict what Dulac referred to as 'visualised feelings' and 'contradictory impressions', Gance's film focuses on a conscious and intentional, although emotionally saturated, form of psychological experience, as opposed to the subconscious psychological experience which is the primary concern of *Un Chien andalou*.

The crucial distinction to be made between impressionism, surrealism and dada is that, whilst the latter two groups were primarily influenced by twentieth-century modernist movements in the arts, impressionism was fundamentally influenced by the nineteenth-century traditions of naturalism and symbolism. More specifically, cinematic impressionism can be associated with the late symbolist aesthetic of Mallarmé, which emphasised the work of art's capacity for rendering the subjective vision of the artist through evocation, symbolic allusion and suggestion.[38] Jean Epstein, for example, defined cinematic impressionism as an 'aesthetic of approximation and the indefinite', in which pictorialist and modernist technique was used to suggest the presence of an underlying, and visionary authorial voice.[39]

The neo-symbolist conception of film art which characterised impressionism privileged the importance of the artist's vision and imagination, and the impressionists believed that, for film to evolve into a genuine art form, the film-maker must transform the material reality before him or her in some revelatory fashion.[40] In becoming transformed in this way, that material reality would also be rendered ambiguous, in order to reflect and express the subtlety of the artist's imagination. This degree of transformation necessitated a departure from the realistic style of the naturalist pictorialist tradition, where the filmic representation of the external world retained a considerable degree of verisimilitude, and the emphasis on the transformative power of imagination, and need to render ambivalent subjective experience and vision, led to the appearance of distorted, or non-naturalistic, images of external reality in impressionist films.

In addition to this preoccupation with the interpretation of subjective, revelatory vision, and in company with *avant-garde* movements such as the *cinéma pur*, cinematic impressionism also explored the specific properties of the medium of film for expressive ends. Although this was frequently pursued as a means of presenting subjective experience and vision, it was also pursued for its own sake, and as a means of distinguishing impressionist cinematic art from more literal commercial cinema. One critic has defined impressionism as 'an exploration of the processes of signification and representation in narrative film discourse', and, to this end, impressionist films explored the use of non-linear narrative structures, the fusion of objective and subjective imagery, graphic, rhythmic and associative forms of representation, connotative and symbolic forms of signification, and special effects techniques such as slow motion, rapid editing and superimposition.[41]

One of the most fundamental concepts within cinematic impressionism was that of *photogénie*. In his book *Photogénie* (1920), Louis Delluc argued that the source of *photogénie* was located in the ability of the moving image to render an object or character in an expressive way.[42] René Clair also argued that *photogénie* was based on the transformative power of the camera, claiming that, through this power, 'there is no detail of reality which cannot be extended here into the realm of the wondrous'.[43] *Photogénie* was, therefore, a latent power within the moving image, and was based on the camera's ability to poeticise the ordinary and prosaic through the use of framing, light and shade, and directional movement.

However, although this latent power to poeticise the prosaic differentiated the film image from other forms of representation, it was not, in itself, sufficient to amount to complete *photogénie*. Authentic, fully realised *photogénie* could only be manifested when this latent power was employed in order to express the vision of the film-maker, so that the inherent poetry of the cinema could be harnessed, and deployed in a revelatory manner by the *auteur*. *Photogénie* is that quality within the film image which aestheticises external reality, and which also engages in experimentation with the formal potential of the medium in order to achieve such a result. However that aestheticisation is primarily directed at displaying the essence of an object, or the spirit of an individual, as intuitively comprehended by the vision of the film-maker.[44]

The impressionist conceptions of authorship and *photogénie*, can also be situated within what Harold Abrams has called the dominant ideology of personal expression within western culture, and what Catherine Belsey has defined as the ideology of expressive realism.[45] Within this approach to authorship and aesthetic representation it is assumed that what is of primary importance within the work of art is the manner in which it exhibits the artist's personal intuition about some truth which exists within the world. This romantic ideology of expressive realism, in which the author expresses his or her imaginative sensibility about the essence of things, lies at the heart of the impressionist conceptions of authorship and cinematic representation.

In addition to its reliance on an ideology of expressive realism, and on a belief that film possessed aesthetic qualities which were intrinsic to the medium, the impressionist conception of *photogénie* was also based on the premise that the aesthetic experience of *photogénie* was, in some sense, beyond rational explication. For the impressionists, *photogénie* was an elusive and ineffable phenomenon, which could not be rationally conceptualised, as Louis Delluc made clear when he asserted that, in this case, 'Explanations here are out of place'.[46] Similar sentiments were expressed by Jean Epstein when he announced that 'The cinema is essentially supernatural. Everything is transformed ... The universe is on edge. The philosopher's light. The atmosphere is heavy with love. I am looking'.[47]

What lies behind Epstein's rhetoric is a belief that the film image is able to reveal aspects of reality normally unseen, and that the aesthetic experience which occurs when the spectator intuitively grasps that such a revelation is taking place is both intense and profoundly pleasurable. This belief on the part of the impressionists in the cinema's ability to bring hidden aspects of reality to the attention of the subject in a transcendent manner has been harshly criticised within much recent film theory, which has regarded such an approach as unnecessarily 'mystical', and as antithetical to the more rationalist paradigm of film theory which has dominated film studies since the 1960s. However, in many respects *photogénie* remains a concept which has often been poorly understood within this dominant paradigm. Furthermore, *photogénie* can also be related to both the intuitionist film aesthetic which emerged in Weimar during the 1920s, and with one of the most important and influential theories of film: the theory of cinematic realism developed in the 1940s by André Bazin.[48]

After 1930 the French cinematic *avant-garde* went into a decline precipitated by the arrival of the sound film, and by the rationalisation of the French film industry which quickly followed.[49] Between 1929 and 1930 film production in France almost doubled under the impact of the introduction of the sound film.[50] However, most of these were little more than filmed versions of successful boulevard stage plays. The first fully integrated French sound production was André Hugon's *Les Trois masques* (*The Three Masks*, 1929). Based on a stage play, *Les Trois masques* had to be shot at

Twickenham Studios in London because of the shortage of sound synchronisation resources then available in France.[51] The first talking picture filmed entirely in France was probably L'Herbier's *L'Enfant de l'amour* (*The Child of Love*, 1930), which was based on a play by Henry Bataille, and which L'Herbier had originally planned to make as a silent film. Both of these films suffered from the poor quality of sound synchronisation available at the time.[52]

The rapid expansion in sound film production soon led to the appearance of critical debates within the *avant-garde* over the implications which the sound film posed for an aesthetic of film which, up till then, had been founded on a belief that cinematic specificity was grounded in the visual. Critics and film-makers such as René Clair, Marcel L'Herbier, Jean Epstein, Benjamin Fondane and others initially reacted with suspicion and apprehension to the emergence of the sound film, whilst surrealists such as Artaud argued uncompromisingly that this unwelcome development constituted a threat to the survival of film as an art form.[53]

Despite this adverse critical reaction, however, others argued that the sound film provided the basis and potential for new and significant developments. For example, one critical response to the advent of sound in film was based on the notion that the silent film was an immature aesthetic form, which, it was argued, had achieved a level of maturity with the advent of sound. So, for example, in a 1929 paper entitled 'The Possibilities of a Broadened Art', Jacques Feyder argued that the lack of sound had arrested the development of film, making it an 'incomplete instrument'.[54] In a similar vein, Marcel Pagnol argued that sound would enable film to communicate a degree of psychological realism which the silent film had been unable to achieve.[55]

In addition to those who believed that the cinema had reached maturity with the emergence of the sound film, other French film-makers, theorists and critics acknowledged, with varying degrees of enthusiasm, that the sound film would soon be a permanent addition to the cultural landscape, and that a new aesthetic language and critical discourse would have to be created in order to accommodate it. Consequently, in the writings of Clair, Epstein, Feyder, Gance and others, increasing emphasis began to be placed on the need to experiment with new sound image relationships in an attempt to maximise the aesthetic potential of the sound film. René Clair argued that language should be considered as 'organised sound', and used as one formal element amongst others,[56] whilst Jean Epstein suggested that the sound-film should 'prospect' the natural sounds found in the contemporary environment in order to create a new tapestry of sound effects.[57] A similar approach to the experimental use of sound was adopted by Jean Renoir who used natural sounds in an attempt to capture the distinctive accents and timbres of urban life in his *La Chienne* (1931).[58]

One outcome of the advent of the sound film was a revival of earlier debates on the specific character of French national cinema. It was argued in some quarters that the French rationalist tradition, based as it was on dialogue and debate, provided an ideal basis for the growth of a successful French national sound cinema, and that the sound film was more suited to French cultural traditions than the silent film had been.[59] Another development closely related to this concern about the relationship between cinema and national culture was the way in which the sound film helped revive the practice of adapting great works of literature and theatre for the screen, a practice which had been a staple of the French film industry since its origins. Within this tradition adaption was not seen as a lesser category of film-making, as it had been by the impressionists, but as a valid way of augmenting and revitalising the historical legacy of French culture.

One important part of that legacy was the realist and naturalist heritage, and film-makers active within that tradition also believed that the sound film, with its capacity for verisimilitude, could reinvigorate some of the central concerns of realism. Jean Epstein argued that image, music and sound effects should be used to evoke atmosphere and environment, just as purely visual effects had in the earlier films of the pictorialist naturalist tradition.[60] Epstein later put his ideas into practice in his 'Breton trilogy': *Finis terrae, Mor Vran* (1931) and *L'Or des mers* (*Gold of the Seas*, 1932).[61] Closely related to this concern with realism and naturalism was the belief, held by Marcel Carné and others on the political left, that the sound film could make a new and more realistic portrayal of working-class experience possible.[62] These ideas became increasingly important during the 1930s, as internal political division grew in France, and as both left and right attempted to use the cinema to promote their respective agendas.[63]

* * *

Although French cinematic impressionism can claim to be the world's first modernist film movement it has been largely overlooked within Anglo-American film criticism, and has often been the object of pejorative dismissal.[64] In addition, few of the theoretical writings of the impressionists have been translated into English, whilst even fewer of the existing prints of impressionist films have been given English subtitles. Many important prints have also been irretrievably lost, and only a few are in current distribution. One important attempt to revive an appreciation of the movement occurred in 1979, when a reconstructed version of Gance's *Napoléon* received its premiere. However, although this event generated a considerable amount of publicity, it nevertheless remains the case that, compared to movements such as German cinematic expressionism and the Soviet montage cinema, French impressionism remains a largely overlooked area of film history.

In contrast to the relative disregard of cinematic impressionism, French modernist movements such as dada and surrealism have received considerable critical attention. This is despite the fact that only a few, and relatively short, dadaist and surrealist films were made during the late 1920s, whereas a considerable number of feature and epic length films were produced within the impressionist tradition. In addition, studies of dada and surrealist film-making are frequently carried out without reference to the overall context of French modernist film production during the 1920s, a context within which impressionism played a central role.

Despite this general critical orientation some attempts have been made to refocus attention on what was, in fact, the most substantial French *avant-garde* film movement of the silent period. For example, Richard Abel's *French Cinema: The First Wave 1915–1929* (1984) explores impressionism extensively, and provides detailed examinations of all the most important impressionist films, film-makers and theorists within the movement. Moreover, and in contrast to the prominence which he gives to impressionism, Abel regards dada and surrealism as having played only a minor role, both within the modernist film production of the period, and in the development of French film culture in general, and argues that the 'narrative avant-garde [impressionism], I contend, cries out for a critical re-evaluation'.[65]

The approach to impressionism, dada and surrealism advocated by Abel is, moreover, characteristic of the approach adopted by the majority of French film critical studies, in which impressionism has always been considered to have been the most important French film movement of the 1920s. This approach was influenced by the fact that impressionism could be so clearly linked to earlier French cultural traditions such as naturalism and symbolism. However, it should also be borne in mind that, in contrast to those within the impressionist movement, many modernist independent film-makers were not, in fact, French. For example, Cavalcanti was Brazilian, Dali and Buñuel Spanish, Man Ray and Dudley Murphy American, and Kirsanoff Russian. Within some French criticism, therefore, much modernist independent film-making was regarded as an emigre encroachment into French cinema, whilst impressionism was believed to be more firmly rooted within the national culture.[66]

There are a number of reasons for the lack of critical attention given to impressionism within relatively recent Anglo-American film criticism. During the 1960s and 1970s a theoretical approach developed within which those films and theories which explicitly challenged dominant bourgeois or capitalist ideology were regarded as the most progressive, and valuable. For example, in his 1975 essay, 'The Two Avant-Gardes', Peter Wollen distinguished between an aestheticised modernism, within which impressionism, the *cinéma pur* and various forms of structural and abstract cinema were located, and a, for him, more valuable *avant-garde* tradition, which included the work of Vertov, dada, surrealism, Brecht and Jean-Luc Godard.[67] Other writers followed Wollen, and, similarly, set an aestheticised, compromised modernism against a more vital tradition of the *avant-garde*. It is this which has largely been responsible for the fact that impressionism has been so neglected, and, as Nöel Burch has argued, 'misunderstood' and 'scorned'.[68]

However, the view that impressionism was a conservative force has also been reinforced by the political positions adopted by some of the impressionist film-makers themselves. Gance, for example, was wedded to a romantic view of genius which could, and has, been regarded as elitist; whilst his *Napoléon* has been strongly criticised for what was perceived to be an excessively enthusiastic valorisation of authoritarianism, as personified within the figure of Napoléon.[69] Other impressionist directors, including Marcel L'Herbier, were also of a conservative, or non-political disposition, and came from a distinctly haute-bourgeois background, whilst yet others displayed a tendency to shift their positions as self-interest dictated.

It was, however, primarily because impressionism was based on a romantic and symbolist tradition that the movement suffered so much critical opprobrium, both during the 1920s and afterwards. However, impressionism remains part of a significant French cultural tradition, which goes back to at least the early nineteenth-century, and includes both romanticism and symbolism. French nineteenth-century romanticism, in the literature of Sainte-Beuve, Dumas, Hugo, and the painting of Delacroix, Gautier and de Nerval, was characterised by an anti-bourgeois orientation which looked back to the feudal institutional structures and more settled traditions of the *ancien régime*, and to the spiritual preoccupations of medieval

Christendom.[70] This anti-bourgeois posture eventually evolved into the Jeune-France group, the *l'art pour l'art* movement, bohemianism and symbolism. Here, art was regarded as the principle means through which the perceived philistinism and barren materialism of capitalist culture could be transcended, and some kind of spiritual life maintained.[71]

That impressionism is the inheritor of this romantic tradition is clear, but what is less clear is the extent to which that tradition can be unequivocally defined as either reactionary or progressive. Although the origins of the French romantic tradition lie in the conservative, aristocratic world view of leading romantics such as Lamartine and Chateaubriand, during the period of the Restoration, when the achievements of the Revolution began to be challenged by an increasingly repressive ruling regime, the romantics allied themselves to the cause of social and democratic reform.[72] Impressionism was not as explicitly anti-bourgeois as the nineteenth-century romantics had been, and, in fact, the contempt for bourgeois materialism exhibited by the Jeune-France group of Gautier, de-Nerval and others in the nineteenth century can be more closely related to the anti-bourgeois posturing of twentieth-century groups such as dada and surrealism, rather than impressionism. Nevertheless, beliefs in the value of imagination, intuition, spirituality and the transcendent power of love were just as central to impressionism as they had been to the romantics, bohemians and symbolists.

Like Weimar cinema, French cinematic impressionism was less directly politically engaged than Soviet montage cinema, or the independent modernist cinemas of dada and surrealism. However, impressionism was neither detached, nor indifferent to the historical context from which it emerged. Like German expressionism, French impressionism was profoundly influenced by the impact of the First World War, and that influence was to lead both impressionist and expressionist theorists to develop an aesthetic theory grounded in the need for liberation from such future barbarism. In fact, the impact of the War may have been the principal source of impressionism, just as that same impact, alongside the emergence of fascism, may have been the principal source of German expressionism.

Notes

1. Williams, Alan, *Republic Of Images: A History of French Film-making* (Cambridge, MA and London: Harvard University Press, 1992), p. 113.
2. Abel, Richard, *French Cinema: The First Wave 1915–1929* (Princeton, NJ: Princeton University Press, 1984), p. 97.

3. Nochlin, Linda, *Realism: Style and Civilization* (Harmondsworth: Penguin, 1979), p. 88 and p. 112.

4. Andrew, Dudley, *Mists of Regret: Culture and Sensibility in Classic French Film* (Princeton, NJ: Princeton University Press, 1995), p. 26.

5. Braudy, Leo, *Jean Renoir: The World of His Films* (New York and Oxford: Columbia University Press, 1989), p. 26.

6. Williams, op cit., p. 115.

7. Andrew, op cit., p. 35.

8. Williams, op cit., pp. 116–17.

9. Braudy, op cit., p. 26.

10. Abel (1984), op cit., pp. 102–3.

11. Ibid., p. 214.

12. Ibid., pp. 512–13.

13. Ghali, Noureddine, *L'Avant-Garde Cinématographique en France Dans les Années Vingt* (Paris: Editions Paris Experimental, 1995), p. 287.

14. Ibid., p. 288.

15. Revol, Hubert, 'La Poésie du Cinéma', *Cinégraph*, vol. 111, no. 2 (February, 1930), p. 20.

16. Canudo, Ricciotto, 'Chronique du Septième Art: Films en culeurs', *Paris-Midi*, no. 4131 (31 August, 1923), p. 2.

17. Ibid.

18. Dréville, Jean, 'Le Documentaire, aimé du cinéma', *Cinémagazine*, no. 2 (February, 1930), p. 51.

19. Andrew, op cit., pp. 30–1.

20. Williams, op cit., pp. 82–3.

21. Abel (1984), op cit., p. 241.

22. Ibid., p. 250.

23. Ibid., p. 245.

24. Ibid., p. 249.

25. Ibid., p. 271.

26. Williams, op cit., pp. 101–2.

27. Bordwell, David, *French Impressionist Cinema: Film Culture, Film Theory and Film Style* (New York: Arno, 1980), p. 250.

28. Abel (1984), op cit., p. 260.

29. Williams, op cit., p. 101.

30. Ibid.

31. Bordwell, op cit., p. 236.

32. Ibid., p. 237.

33. Ibid., p. 240.

34. Ibid., p. 242.

35. Abel (1984), op cit., p. 431.

36. King, Norman, *Abel Gance* (London: BFI, 1984), p. 125.

37. Bordwell, op cit., p. 94.

38. Ibid., p. 96.

39. Ibid.

40. Ibid., p. 110.
41. Abel (1984), op cit., p. 290.
42. Bordwell, op cit., p. 106.
43. Ibid., pp. 107–8.
44. Ibid., pp. 121–2.
45. Abrams, A. H., 'Literature as a Revelation of Personality', in Caughie, John (ed.), *Theories of Authorship* (London: Routledge and Kegan Paul, 1981), pp. 18–21; and Belsey, Catherine, *Critical Practice* (London and New York: Routledge, 1980), pp. 7–14. See also Abrams, A. H. *The Mirror and the Lamp: Romantic Theory and the Critical Tradition* (Oxford: Oxford University Press, 1981), pp. 226–62.
46. Ray, Robert B., 'Impressionism, surrealism and film theory', in Hill, John and Church Gibson, Pamela (eds), *The Oxford Guide to Film Studies* (Oxford: Oxford University Press, 1998), p. 68.
47. Ibid., p. 74.
48. See Chapter 7 for a full analysis of Bazin's theory of cinematic realism.
49. Ghali, op cit., p. 48.
50. Armes, Roy, *French Cinema* (London: Secker & Warburg, 1985), p. 68.
51. Martin, John, W., *The Golden Age of French Cinema* (New York: Twayne, 1983), p. 26.
52. Ibid., p. 27.
53. Abel, Richard, *French Film Theory and Criticism: A History/Anthology 1907–1939* (vol. 2.) (Princeton, NJ: Princeton University Press, 1988), p. 47.
54. Ibid., p. 38.
55. Ibid., p. 57.
56. Ibid., p. 40.
57. Ibid., p. 66.
58. Andrew, op cit., p. 104.
59. Abel (1988), op cit., p. 9.
60. Ibid., p. 20.
61. Armes, op cit., p. 69.
62. Abel (1988), op cit., p. 21.
63. Ibid., p. 10.
64. Ray, in Hill and Church Gibson, op cit., p. 74.
65. Abel (1984), op cit., p. 281.
66. Ghali, op cit., p. 51.
67. Wollen, Peter, 'The Two Avant Gardes', reprinted in his *Readings and Writings: Semiotic Counter-Strategies* (London: Verso, 1982).
68. Burch, quoted in Abel (1984), op cit., p. 281.
69. Moussinac, Léon, 'A French Film: *Napoleon*', in King, op cit., pp. 34–41.
70. Hauser, Arnold, *The Social History of Art: Three: Rococo, Classicism and Romanticism* (London: Routledge and Kegan Paul, 1973), pp. 181–4.
71. Ibid., pp. 183–4.
72. Ibid., p. 182.

V

The World Well Lost[1]

From Structuralism to Relativism

At one level, the origins of structuralist methodology can be traced back to the 1880s, and to an emerging emphasis on the symbolic constitution of representational systems, within the disciplines of linguistics, philosophy and symbolic logic.[2] The work of the American philosopher C. S. Pierce, the German logician Gottlob Frege, and other theorists within these fields, was then taken up at the turn of the century by Polish, Czech, Swiss and Russian linguists such as Mathesius, Scerba, Baudouin, Jakobson, Saussure and Trubetskoy, as part of a general shift within linguistics from a historical, philological approach to the study of language, to one concerned with understanding the structural relations which existed within contemporary language systems. One of the most influential works within this emerging perspective on the study of language was the Swiss linguist Ferdinand de Saussure's *Cours de linguistique générale* (1916). However, the *Cours* was not, in fact, written by Saussure, but compiled three years after his death in 1913, from the lecture notes of students. Although the *Cours* is, as a consequence, an often uneven work, it did, nevertheless, prove an influential model for the development of structural linguistics within Europe from 1916 onwards.

After 1916 Saussurian structural linguistics also influenced the Russian formalist movement, and the work of formalist theorists such as Roman Jacobson, Viktor Shklovsky, Boris Eichenbaum and Vladimir Propp. However, debates on the symbolic and structural nature of linguistic and aesthetic representation had also taken place independently in Russia, with the establishment of the Moscow Linguistic Circle in 1915, and the St Petersburg-based Society for the Study of Poetic Language, in 1916. After 1916, this work was increasingly combined with Saussurian ideas, and with other studies emerging from centres of linguistic research in Geneva and Copenhagen, to form a European wide movement dedicated to research into the structural and symbolic components of language. This movement was further consolidated in 1926, when the Linguistic

Circle of Prague was formed by formalists and linguists such as Jakobson, Trubetskoy and Mukarovsky, and, in 1928, when members of the Prague and Geneva schools came together at the First International Congress of linguists.[3]

Although Saussure's influence began to spread rapidly after 1928, it must be borne in mind that he was not an isolated thinker, but part of a general shift then taking place within linguistics, symbolic logic and aesthetic theory, from a comparative, historical and philological approach, to one based on an investigation of the deep structures which determined linguistic, symbolic and representational systems. In addition, although Saussurian ideas remained influential during the 1930s, they were definitively challenged by Roman Jakobson in the 1940s, and eventually discarded in favour of the theories of generative grammar developed by Noam Chomsky and others in the 1950s and 1960s. Nevertheless, despite the fact that Saussurian ideas became increasingly less important within the field of linguistics over this period, during the 1940s they were enthusiastically adopted by the French anthropologist Claude Lévi-Strauss, and, thereafter, provided the theoretical basis for the French structuralist tradition.

It is important to appreciate that, besides the Saussurian tradition, a 'structural' approach to representational analysis also developed in other directions during the first half of the twentieth century. So, for example, within anthropology, British 'structural-functionalists' such as A. R. Radcliffe-Brown and Bronislaw Malinowski, and American anthropologists such as Franz Boas, Edward Sapir, Benjamin Lee Whorf and others, diverged significantly from Saussurian and Lévi-Straussian structuralism; whilst, in linguistics, the structural linguistics of Bloomfield and others within America also developed separately from the continental line.[4] Like continental structuralism, these developments were influenced by models of linguistic structure, and impelled by a need to introduce a greater degree of methodological rigour into their respective subject disciplines, but they differed from continental structuralism in respect of the core concepts and methods which they employed. Despite its importance, however, this Anglo-American legacy of structural analysis within the fields of linguistics and anthropology had little impact upon the development of structuralist and post-structuralist criticism within film studies, whereas the theories of Saussure had a profound impact.

Structuralist methodology was premised upon the conviction that, underlying the surface content of cultural artefacts, generative deep structures existed which ultimately determined that content. These underlying structures consisted of basic units and principles of combination for those units, and the chief objective of structuralist analysis was to reveal these units and principles. In line with this key distinction between deep and surface structures, Saussure made a fundamental distinction between *langue* and *parole*, where *langue* is the underlying system which makes possible the articulation of individual acts of speech, or *parole*. *Langue*, therefore, lies beyond, and influences, each manifestation of *parole*, and Saussure compared it to the system of rules and combinations of allowable moves which make up the game of chess.[5] However, both *langue* and *parole* also stem from a more fundamental category and human faculty which Saussure calls *langage*. Saussure defined *langage* as the entire field of linguistic activity, and argued that it should be conceived of as including both the totality of *parole* acts and the *langues* which underlie them, and what he called a 'linguistic faculty', 'which lies beyond the functioning of the various organs'.[6]

It is clear from the above that Saussure's conception of *langage* is far more than just a methodological definition which seeks to explain the conventional operation of speech acts, and their underlying organising principles. In fact, the idea of *langage* implies a particular approach to the theory of mind: one in which it is assumed that human communication is made possible through the existence of a mental, 'linguistic faculty'. Saussure conceives this faculty as a class of organisational codes within the brain, which function according to the principle of binary opposition, and it is this principle which is ultimately responsible for the production of 'signs': symbolic forms which possess both semantic and syntactic properties. It is because of the existence of this binary principle, one which causes human communication to take place through a process of placing one thing in opposition to another, that signs are generated in opposition to each other within an overall system of symbolic difference.

At the basis of the linguistic faculty, therefore, is a binary tendency, or principle, and this principle is also one of the deep structural organising principles of both *langue* and *parole*. However, the binary principle is not the only organisational axiom within *langue*. In addition to the binarism which emerges from the linguistic faculty, *langue* also consists of various ideomatic forms, such as conventionalised patterns of vocabulary and dialect, which generate regulatory structures that operate in conjunction with, and in addition to, binarism. According to Saussure, therefore, signs are generated according to both binary axioms, and other organisational principles of combination common to particular *langues*. These signs then combine into complex, linear semantic and syntactic structures at the level of *parole*.[7]

The theory of mind embodied within Saussure's notion of the linguistic faculty implies that the principle of binarism is innate, and coded into the genetic make-up of the human brain. However, Saussure's theory also implies that, although binarism may be innate, the other organisational principles or tendencies which exist within *langue* are not, but are, in contrast, the product of the language user's interaction with his or her environment. This means that, whilst binary coding may play an important role within the creation of concepts, the ways in which *langue* evolves, in terms of vocabulary, idiomatic form, and grammatical principles, can also be influenced by factors which are not dependent on innate structures within the brain.

The co-existence of a basic category forming mechanism in the brain, alongside other regulatory principles derived from experience, gives Saussure's conception of *langue* a realist and universalist dimension at one and the same time. *Langue* is realist in that language is determined by experience, and universalist in that innate, causal, trans-contextual structures are also postulated. Despite the fact that it is possible to read a realist trajectory into Saussure's theory of *langue*, however, it is clear that it is a universalist, rather than realist imperative which governs his approach. This is so partly because of Saussure's postulation of an internal linguistic faculty, and partly because of the emphasis which he places on the self-regulating nature of *langue*. This stress on self-regulation also implies that, in addition to a universalist and realist dimension, the Saussurian conception of *langue* also possesses a relativist aspect.

All three of the above readings of what remains a vague and loosely defined concept remain theoretically possible. However, the structuralist tradition which sprang from Saussure's work focused on the innate, self-regulatory and relativist aspects of his ideas, whilst the issue of reference was relegated to the margins of critical concern. Nevertheless, and despite such relegation, questions of reference continued to be a problem for those working within a structuralist tradition founded on Saussurian principles, as the following quotation makes clear:

Language is self-defining, and so whole and complete. It is capable of a process of transformation: that is of generating new aspects of itself ... in response to experience. It is self-regulating. It has these capacities precisely because it allows no single unitary appeal to a 'reality' beyond itself. In the end it constitutes its own reality.[8]

This appears to be fundamentally contradictory, for, if language is a 'self-regulating' entity which allows for no 'appeal to a "reality" beyond itself', how can it also be determined by experience? One of the problems with post-Saussurian structuralism is this failure to provide a clear account of the relationship between language as a fully self-contained system, and that which exists outside of language; and the failure to address this problem fully is the source of a fundamental philosophical and methodological flaw within structuralism.

Another issue which clearly arises from the above quotation is the extent to which language is depicted in almost metaphysical, or idealist terms, as a sentient entity, an 'it' which is 'self-defining, whole and complete', and which is engaged in a perpetual struggle against 'a reality beyond itself' in order to maintain its own hegemony over the trans-linguistic real, so that, 'in the end, it constitutes its own reality'. In addition to this idealist conception of language, the quotation also suggests an almost Darwinian or Nietzschean notion of struggle for dominance, where language seeks to extend and defend its own hegemony over 'reality'.

The extent to which structuralism highlights the notion of the self-regulating nature of linguistic systems is well illustrated by the way in which structuralists have focused on – but also misinterpreted – Saussure's use of the model of the chess game to explain how language functions. Such a focus appears to ignore the extent to which Saussure's overall theory also addressed issues of contextual determination. According to Saussure, *langue* evolves, at least in part, under the pressure of evolving contextual circumstances. New signs are produced as a consequence of these circumstances, according to principles of combination which are both established and in the process of evolutionary development.[9] According to this reading, *langue* does not consist exclusively of a *fixed* inventory of units and principles of combination, and this, therefore, distinguishes *langue* from the game of chess: a totally self-contained system, with an inventory which strictly determines the character of *parole* acts (individual moves). The crucial difference between linguistic *langue* and the chess game is, then, that the chess game is entirely coded from within, whilst language is not.

The continued reliance on such analogies as that of the chess game reveals the extent to which structuralism favours, and depends upon, conceptual models which view the world as consisting of closed and self-regulating systems of meaning. However, such an approach, with its implicit positioning of real significance at the level of the determining deep structures of the system, fails to take into account the fact that, in the world of human experience, closed and self-regulating systems are extremely unusual. It is because of this that contemporary linguistic theory views *langue* as a more open system of linguistic 'competence' which evolves in interaction with contextual referents, rather than an internally regulated autonomous system.[10]

The structuralist conception of *langue* is also a potentially reductive methodological concept, for, although the critic might begin by examining a variety of *parole* acts, his or her principal intention is to disclose the underlying deep structures of langue, and this can lead the diversity of *parole* acts to become subsumed within a limiting and prescriptive framework. This potential for reductive critical analysis is also reinforced by the structuralist conception of *langue* as a unified system. This stress on the overall unity of the system necessarily marginalises issues of diversity and difference within the system, and causes structuralist analysis to turn away from such issues, in order to search for unifying structures and principles. The structuralist elevation of *langue* over *parole* did have some beneficial consequences, and these will be explored later in this chapter. However, as the above makes clear, this elevation also resulted in the formulation of a critical methodology which was frequently deterministic and reductive.

Another problem with Saussurian structuralism lies within the conception of structure which it employs. It has been argued that Saussure's conception of *langue* is particularly significant because it constitutes a shift from an 'item centred' view of the world, and a 'word centred' account of language, to a more 'relational' or 'structural' understanding of both. According to Saussurian structuralism, individual items have no intrinsic significance in themselves, but derive that significance from their relationships to other items.[11] However, the problem with this type of 'relational' understanding is, precisely, its claim that significance resides in relations, rather than things. That this is an overstatement is made clear from the fact that, even in such a closed system as a chess game, individual pieces have 'fixed' as well as relational properties: a Bishop, for example, has the fixed property of diagonal movement, as well as relational properties based on its conjuncture with other pieces at a particular point in the chess game.

Saussure's argument on relationality was derived from the fact that the individual phoneme possesses no intrinsic meaning in itself, but only acquires meaning when combined into sequences in accordance with the underlying principles of langue. So, for example, in English the chain of phonemes 'dtocetr', makes no sense, but their recombination into the morpheme 'doctor', does. However, once phonemes form into morphemes, meanings begin to persist, and relationality becomes less fundamental. The structuralist conception of structure as an intangible system of differential relationships without 'positive' terms, appears, therefore, to be an oversimplified one.[12]

In fact, relationality only really holds sway within language at the microscopic level of the phoneme, and, beyond that level, meanings become increasingly fixed. *Langue* is, therefore, not simply a relational system, where signs, items or terms have no identity across the shifting network of relations. On the contrary, terms and relations cluster in order to represent the experiences of language groups, and identities also persist across relations. This idea of 'clustering', has certain similarities with Wittgenstein's model of meaning formation as a relational conceptual network containing grouped 'families' of similarity and difference, and involves a shift from the idea of structure as consisting of binary oppositional relationships, to one based on groupings of terms and relations between terms.[13] This model of structure is also closer to Chomsky's notion of linguistic competence.[14]

At the heart of the structuralist concern with deep structures lies a prioritisation of syntax over semantics. Within structuralist methodology it is frequently the formal relational differences between items which are deemed most significant, and meaning is seen to be located within that differential ordering of elements. However, such an approach subsumes semantics (meaning) under syntax (form), and, although the syntactical arrangements of elements within *langue* enable meaning to be articulated, they are not meaningful in themselves. In addition, delineating a formal organisation of elements is not the same as explaining the meaning which such a taxonomy might possess by virtue of its function as a semantic structure, with meaningful relevance to a community of users.[15] In order to fully appreciate, and, above all, explain, the significance of such a taxonomy, it is not, therefore, sufficient merely to locate such significance within a deep structure of formal relationships.

The emphasis on the determining power of deep syntactical structures within structuralism also leads to the assumption that such structures must exercise an absolute determining hegemony, so that, ultimately, the very concepts a language expresses were defined and determined by its structure.[16] However, although the concepts of a language may be influenced by the structure of that language, they are not necessarily completely determined by it. The concepts which a language expresses are also influenced by the experience of language users, and this means that symbols are influenced by external reality, as well by internal syntactic structures. This means that there is no need to presuppose a determining structure whose syntactic organisational principles completely determine our experience of reality, and, what is revealed within such a presupposition is a predisposition within structuralism to locate significant causality at the level of deep structure, and not at any other level. Such reductivism is inevitably problematic, given that most phenomena, including cultural artefacts, are the product of multiple, rather than singular causality.

It was the application of Saussurian ideas on linguistics to other fields within the arts and humanities, and Saussure's claim that linguistics was only part of a general science of sign systems yet to emerge, which gave rise to structuralism. One of the most influential early attempts to apply structural linguistic methodology to cultural ephemera, and one influenced by Saussurian ideas, was carried out by the Russian formalist linguist and anthropologist, Vladimir Propp. In 1928, Propp, who was a member of the Opayez Society, a grouping of formalist theorists which also included figures such as Viktor Shklovsky, Boris Eichenbaum and Roman Jakobson, published his *Morphology of the Folk Tale*, a structural study of 100 medieval Russian fairy tales. Propp concluded that the different plots, characterisation and setting in these tales were all variations on a deep structural grammar of thirty-one different 'functions', which included those of 'absentation', 'violation', 'trickery', 'departure', 'the provision or receipt of a magical agent', 'struggle' and 'wedding'. However, underlying even this deep structure, was a single underlying narrative, which can be described as follows:

> In a quest, a hero responds to villainy which has worked harm or loss on a family. Tested, often pursued, the hero, often aided by a helper, exposes and defeats the villain, and accomplishes his task. He often rescues or wins a princess, so that the family's initial lack becomes his reward.[17]

The methodological approach adopted in the *Morphology of the Folk Tale* was influenced by the Russian formalist principle of 'transformation'. Transformations are the rules within a particular representational system which allow certain types of combination and transmutation of basic units. Thus, in the *Morphology of the Folk Tale*, basic plot elements of the folk tales are altered through subjecting them to transformational principles such as reduction, intensification, inversion, multiplication, and either positive or negative signification.

The principal methodological instruments used by Propp in the *Morphology of the Folk Tale*, are, therefore, the function, and the principle of transformation. According to Propp, although individual tales might omit one or more functions, no tale contained additional functions to the thirty-one which he had located. For example, although the names of particular characters might change, their functions of 'helper', 'hero' or 'villain' remained constant. Propp also argued that these functions clustered along a linear axis to form 'spheres of action'. So, for example, the first group of functions, or 'sphere of action', consists of 'initial situation', 'absentation', 'interdiction', 'reconnaissance', 'delivery', 'trickery', 'villainy', 'lack' and 'mediation'. When this group concludes, another sequence of functions begins with 'departure', as the hero sets out on a mission to counteract the initial harm done by the villain.[18]

The methodological model developed by Propp in *Morphology of the Folk Tale* was derived from his analysis of medieval Russian fairy tales, and Propp argued that this model could not be applied to any other group of texts. Despite this, however, a number of attempts have been made to apply the Proppian model to film studies, and the most well known of these is probably Peter Wollen's 1976 analysis of Alfred Hitchcock's *North by North-West* (1956). In relating Propp's morphology to Hitchcock's film, Wollen concluded that a correspondence could be discerned between the two. For example, Propp's opening function of 'initial situation' is related to the first scene in *North by North-West*, in which 'the hero talks to secretary'. This is then followed by Propp's second function, 'absentation', which is related to the following scene in the film, in which 'Thornhill (the hero) leaves his office for the Plaza Hotel'.[19]

Although Wollen concluded that 'the basic structure described by Propp is present in *North by North-West*', he also pointed to a number of ways in which the film differed from Propp's morphology.[20] However, his qualifications in this respect are relatively minor compared to the detailed correlations which he makes between the film and Propp's morphological analysis. Such qualifications are taken substantially further, however, by John L. Fell. Writing in 1977, Fell concludes that the Proppian morphology is unable to account for the complex patterns of characterisation and motivation found in feature films, and that subjecting such films to 'one meterstick standard' is a reductive exercise.[21] Patricia Erens, also writing in 1977, concludes that it is because so many different structures of meaning can be read into a feature film that it is possible to apply Propp's morphology to film analysis, and that, 'to a degree, any tale can be made to fit the formula'.[22]

These attempts to apply Proppian methodology to film studies reveals the potential for essentialism and reductiveness which is inherent in the structuralist project. For example, in interpreting *North by North-West* in terms of Proppian functions, Wollen is obliged to overlook many of the typically Hitchcockian themes which pervade the film. There are also grounds for arguing that the application of Propp's morphology to film must inevitably lead to an impoverished level of analysis. Film is a primarily visual medium, yet Propp's morphology only accounts for the exigencies of plot, and this is a serious shortcoming in a methodology which seeks to analyse *North by North-West*: a film in which visual and aural style is crucially important.

Finally, both Wollen and Erens fail to observe Propp's counsel that his morphology should not be applied to any group of texts other than the medieval fairy tales from which it was originally derived. Rather than apply Propp's morphology to *North by North-West*, therefore, a more appropriate course of action would have been to first examine a group of films, and then derive an entirely different morphological breakdown from that analysis. It could be argued, in Wollen's defence, that he was not bound to adhere strictly to Propp's methodology, and that his prime objective was to explore the efficacy of that methodology, with a view to its eventual reformulation and modernisation.[23] Nevertheless, even if this was the case, Wollen's approach remains characterised by a degree of essentialism which was not present in Propp, and which requires justification. For, whilst Propp cautioned that his morphology applied only to a particular group of tales, Wollen went significantly beyond this to argue that it was 'indicative of a more universal concept of the tale ...'.[24]

During the late 1930s a number of European intellectuals fled the rise of Nazism in central Europe, and many emigrated to America. Amongst this latter group was Roman Jakobson, the Russian linguist and former member of the Prague School of structural linguistics. In America, Jacobson was offered a chair in general linguistics at the Free School of Advanced Studies in New York, a newly established institution staffed by other French and Belgian exiles.[25] Jakobson delivered lectures in French to this francophone group, and, in 1942, the French anthropologist Claude Lévi-Strauss, who had also fled to America, attended these lectures. When he returned to France after the war, Lévi-Strauss introduced Jakobsonian methods of structural linguistics into anthropology, first, in his *The Elementary Structures of Kinship* (1949), and then, in *Structural Anthropology* (1958), a book which consisted of papers written between 1944 and 1957.

As with structuralism in general, Lévi-Strauss' structural anthropology was based on the assumption that groups of texts were exemplifications of underlying deep structures, and he attempted to locate such structures in his published analyses of the myths produced by tribes within the central Brazilian rain forest. However, *Structural Anthropology* is more than merely a study of primitive myth, and is, in fact, a structuralist manifesto in a way in which the *Morphology of the Folk Tale* was not. Influenced by Saussure's call for the development of a new science of semiology able to encompass all sign systems, and by Jakobson's convictions concerning the huge potential of structural linguistics, Lévi-Strauss sought to use structural anthropology in order to reach an understanding of universal social and mental processes.[26]

In developing his own approach to structuralist anthropology, Lévi-Strauss was strongly influenced by the linguist Trubetzkoy's assertion that 'The evolution of a phonemic system at any given moment is towards a goal … This evolution thus has a direction, an internal logic, which historical phonemics is called on to elucidate'.[27] This belief in the existence of an internal, goal directed logic within signifying systems led Lévi-Strauss to conceive of the internal structural dynamic within primitive myth as evolving in order to fulfil three interconnected objectives. These were: (1) the attainment of structural unity and logical consistency; (2) the articulation, mediation and resolution of social contradictions; and (3), the symbolic depiction of the 'architecture of the spirit'.[28]

Guided by his conviction that one of the functions of myth was to articulate social meaning, Lévi-Strauss employed methods derived from structural linguistics in order to locate and codify the constituent features within groups of myths. These features were then organised into sets of binary oppositions, which symbolised underlying contradictions within the primitive society from which the myths had emerged. The deepest level of binary oppositions, the 'master antinomies', expressed fundamental social predicaments, and it was these which generated the series of secondary oppositions which emerged at the level of surface content. The myths studied within a particular myth cycle were also regarded as variations on one master myth, and one group of foundational binary oppositions, as Lévi-Strauss made clear when he asserted that 'in all these instances we are dealing with the same myth'.[29]

It is clear that, at one level, Lévi-Strauss accounts for the purpose and function of myth by reference to its role in articulating social meaning. However, Lévi-Strauss also went significantly beyond such an endorsement of social causality to claim that the true function of myth was to represent 'the architecture of the spirit'.[30] Here, Lévi-Strauss maintains that mythical thought is motivated by an imperative which is not, ultimately, social at all, but has its origins in the need to depict the fundamental operations of the human mind. For Lévi-Strauss, the structure and function of myth, like that of all cultural artefacts, is congruous with that of language, and the structure and function of language is, in turn, derived from the binary classificatory system of the mind. It is, therefore, this formal, mental classificatory system, rather than social content and context, which ultimately determines the form and content of myth.

In *Structural Anthropology* Lévi-Strauss often employs the radically dissimilar causal categories of social context and the 'architecture of the spirit' interchangeably, and this imprecision leads to difficulties in understanding exactly which of these categories he privileges at any one point. This difficulty is further compounded by the fact that the influence of the 'architecture of the spirit' in generating cultural artefacts can be understood as operating in one of two different ways, both of which are employed by Lévi-Strauss. In the first case, Lévi-Strauss appears to argue that the binary classificatory system of the mind is merely a facilitating framework which makes the articulation of social meaning possible. Here, cultural artefacts still largely express a social content, although the conceptual framework of binarism dictates how that content is organised and manifested. Within this interpretation, therefore, 'the architecture of the spirit' is little more than a formal system, which expedites, but does not determine, the production of meaning.

However, Lévi-Strauss' use of such a pregnant phrase as 'the architecture of the spirit' suggests that he does not merely refer to a formal, enabling system when he applies this concept to an understanding of structural causality, and, in fact, he appears to argue that the principal role of cultural artefacts such as myths is not to articulate social meaning, but to represent the elementary binary structure of the human mind. Far from being merely a facilitating structure then, 'the architecture of the spirit' is, itself, the ultimate object of all cultural reference. Although the individual may commonly believe that cultural artefacts express aspects of social reality, he or she is misguided in so believing, and the primary purpose of such artefacts is, in fact, to engender the play of binary differentials which enables the 'architecture of the spirit' to live and breathe. It is not binarism which acts as a facilitating structure for the generation of cultural artefacts and social meaning, but cultural artefacts and social representations which facilitate the interminable, everlasting manoeuvres of the spirit. The component features of a particular myth exist within an intertextual, discursive domain, and possess meaning by virtue of the fact that they are involved in relationships with other components within the system: relationships which are ultimately generated by the binary propensity of the mind.

Lévi-Strauss' assertion that cultural artefacts do not represent the world outside the text, but are discursive expressions of the architecture of the spirit, reveals the extent to which a reliance on Saussurian concepts of relational structure and arbitrary signification inevitably leads from structuralism to post-structuralism. That transition is evident in Lévi-Strauss' writings from as early as the second volume of *Mythologiques*, where it becomes clear that he has already shifted philosophically from a concern with deep, determining structures, to a consideration of the cultural artefact as an articulation of conventions which refer to other conventions and principles, rather than to social reality.[31]

If put into practice, and taken to its logical conclusion, Lévi-Strauss' idealist structuralist metaphysics would make any analysis of cultural artefacts such as myth impossible. This is because all that could be shown is how particular myths are composed of systems of binary categories which interact with each other, and refer back to the principle of binarism itself. Furthermore, this can only ever be a descriptive, rather than explanatory exercise, given that, if causality resides only in the a priori abstract category of binarism, the scope and range of speculation into causality becomes severely limited. It was because of this lack of explanatory capacity that, in practice, and despite his quasi-metaphysical inclinations, Lévi-Strauss was continually forced to re-engage with the idea that myth also mediated social contradiction.

Lévi-Strauss' prioritisation of theory ultimately stems from his conviction that universal structural codes underlie empirical phenomena, and it was this which led him to place greater emphasis on the elaboration of theoretical models than on empirical analysis. Although he accepted that the anthropologist must first carry out such analysis in order to build theoretical models of social structure, after a certain point these models took on an autonomy of their own within Lévi-Strauss' writings, and developed without much further recourse to empirical evidence gathering. Lévi-Strauss fully endorsed this approach, and characterised his practice as an anthropologist as that of 'experimenting with models', rather than 'observing facts'.[32]

Lévi-Strauss' work has come under criticism for the way in which it imposes theory over evidence, and for the extent to which it reduces the complexity of primitive myths to a level of deep structural antinomies, which, in themselves, signify little, and frequently end up as a display of formal relationships.[33] Associated with this objection is the equally important criticism that Lévi-Straussian analysis says little about how myths are understood by the communities who produced them. Such criticism is clearly valid. However, Lévi-Strauss does not bracket out issues of reception from his analyses because he is methodologically lazy, but because he believes that those who actually produced the myths are unaware of their real meaning.

Lévi-Strauss' most forthright defence of his methods were set out in the essay in *Structural Anthropology* entitled 'Social Structure'. However, the substantial criticism which arose from the initial publication of this essay in 1953 also prompted him to write a 'Postscript' to it, which appeared alongside the original essay in *Structural Anthropology*. In the 'Postscript', Lévi-Strauss rejected the accusation that he disregarded empirical research, and that he sought to reduce the complexity of social affairs to a sterile, unitary structure.[34] On the contrary, Lévi-Strauss argued that his methods paid 'intense, almost compulsive attention to detail', and accepted that 'a concrete society can never be reduced to its structure'.[35] However, what lies behind these claims is not an endorsement of empirical fieldwork, but the post-structuralist conception of structure which Lévi-Strauss had already begun to adopt by as early as 1958. This is made clear when, in seeking legitimation for his approach, he refers to Saussurian theories of relational signification, when claiming that he is concerned with difference and diversity, rather than 'a frozen abstract type of structure':

> our ultimate purpose is not so much to discover the unique characteristics of the societies that we study, as it is to discover in what way these societies differ from one another. As in linguistics, it is the discontinuities which constitute the true subject matter of anthropology.[36]

In *Structural Anthropology Volume Two* (1973), Lévi-Strauss reinforced his position on these questions when he made a number of forthright criticisms of Propp's *Morphology of the Folk Tale*. In a chapter entitled 'Structure and Form: Reflections on a Work by Vladimir Propp', Lévi-Strauss argued that Propp had reduced the fairy tales he had studied to the level of a 'sterile morphology'. For the Lévi-Strauss of 1973, therefore, it seems that structuralism must be concerned with both the deep structure and the concrete surface content of cultural artefacts:

Formalism destroys its object. With Propp it results in the discovery that there exists in reality but one tale. Henceforth, the problem of explanation is only displaced. We know what the tale is, but as experience puts before us not an archetypal tale but a great number of concrete tales, we do not know how to classify them any more. Before formalism we were certainly aware of what these tales had in common. Since formalism we have been deprived of any means of understanding how they differ. One has passed from concrete to abstract, but can no longer come down from the abstract to the concrete.[37]

Here, Lévi-Strauss effectively abandons a structuralist for a post-structuralist position in arguing that what is required is to understand how concrete tales articulate underlying master antinomies differently. By 1973 Lévi-Strauss had become increasingly influenced by the post-structuralist theory of Lacan, Derrida and Barthes, and his concern with pluralism must be related to the general turn from structuralism to post-structuralism which occurred in France during the late 1960s, rather than to any commitment to empirical analysis. Lévi-Strauss also eventually came to adopt the post-structuralist belief that theoretical positions were merely forms of discursive fiction, rather than models which could provide a true or objective account of reality. Such an approach, which fundamentally contradicted the scientistic and essentialist aspirations which Lévi-Strauss had originally entertained for structuralism, also makes empirical analysis irrelevant, as it, too, is merely another form of discursive practice.

The application of Lévi-Straussian theory to film studies often encapsulated both the structuralist and post-structuralist aspects of the anthropologist's thought. In his *Signs and Meanings in the Cinema*, Peter Wollen selected one of Lévi-Strauss' master antinomies, that of 'culture versus nature', redefined it in terms of 'garden versus wilderness', and applied it to an analysis of three films by John Ford: *My Darling Clementine* (1954), *The Searchers* (1955) and *The Man Who Shot Liberty Valance* (1960). Wollen argued that Ford's films contained complex systems of oppositions, which were generated by the master antinomy of garden versus wilderness. These oppositions included those of plough-share versus sabre, European versus Indian, married versus unmarried, settler versus nomad, and civilised versus savage. Wollen went on to argue that, whilst these oppositions were largely resolved in *My Darling Clementine* and *The Man Who Shot Liberty Valance*, they remained complex, shifting, and ambiguous in *The Searchers*, and he concluded that it was the 'richness of the shifting relations between antinomies' which marked out Ford's films, and *The Searchers* in particular.[38]

Although Wollen's use of Lévi-Strauss led to detailed and useful analyses of films such as *The Searchers*, it also exhibited a number of problems characteristic of structuralist methodology in general. The most significant of these is the difficulty which structuralism has in bridging the gap between describing textual terms and relationships, and providing an account of the causal factors which brought those terms and relationships into existence. For example, although Wollen argues that the master antinomy in *The Searchers* is that of 'garden versus wilderness', he does not discuss how social contradictions affecting American society during the mid 1950s generated this master antinomy.

Wollen's approach here is influenced by the structuralist, rather than post-structuralist aspect of Lévi-Strauss' thought, and, although he refers to Lévi-Strauss when arguing that it is important not to analyse a text so that it is reduced to an 'abstract and impoverished' structure, his analysis echoes the universalist tendencies within Lévi-Strauss' thought.[39] Rather than historicise *The Searchers*, Wollen argued instead that the opposition between garden and wilderness 'has dominated American thought and literature, recurring in countless novels, tracts, speeches and magazine stories', and that this is why it is also the master antinomy of *The Searchers*.[40] This allows Wollen to avoid any attempt to explain exactly how the opposition between garden and wilderness affected American society during the 1950s. His analysis is, therefore, limited ('abstract and impoverished') in its use of historiography, and is also based on a universalist conception of discursive causality.

Wollen's approach illustrates the difficulty which structuralist methodology has in linking description to effective explanation, and that difficulty is further illustrated when yet another attempt to apply Lévi-Straussian methodology to *The Searchers* is considered. Unlike Wollen, Brian Henderson attempts to historicise *The Searchers* by placing the film within the context of concerns over issues of racial integration, concerns which, Henderson argues, were widespread in America during the mid 1950s. Henderson argues that *The Searchers* is primarily concerned with questions of kinship, race, marriage and miscegenation, and he sees the master antinomy in the film, not as that of garden versus wilderness, but of 'kinship by blood' versus 'kinship by adoption'.[41]

Henderson goes on to argue that *The Searchers* explores the social dilemma of the need to preserve the purity of blood kinship against the pressures and consequences of racial integration, and that, in doing so, *The Searchers* also explores issues such as the incest taboo, the overrating/underrating of blood relations, and rules concerning the marital exchange of women.[42] According to Henderson, the social contradiction which *The Searchers* seeks to mediate is that of the acceptance or rejection of a multiracial society, and Henderson argues that the film resolves this contradiction through championing the cause of integration, whilst, at the same time, exploring the dangers and problems inherent in that cause.[43]

Although Henderson brings greater historical detail to bear on his analysis of *The Searchers* than was the case with Wollen, that detail still, nevertheless, remains tenuous and unconvincing. This is largely because Henderson provides no empirical evidence to support his argument that the oppositions within *The Searchers* were influenced by a context of social concerns over racial integration and segregation, but merely assumes this to be the case. *The Searchers* may, or may not, have been influenced by debates on racial integration taking place in America during the 1950s, but Henderson's structuralist approach has ensured that he is unable to prove the case one way or the other.

Furthermore, although Henderson does move on from the less historicised model adopted by Wollen, like Wollen, he also proposes an antinomic relationship which is largely derived from Lévi-Strauss' analysis of primitive myths. However, no explanation is given as to why the same antinomy should be found in such widely differing cultures as that of a primitive Amerindian tribe, and the America of the 1950s, and the only conclusion to be drawn is that both Wollen and Henderson rely on a covert, universalist conception of human nature. Although neither Wollen nor Henderson use the phrase, such a conception leads on naturally to an eventual acceptance of the Lévi-Straussian notion that the antinomies found in a film such as *The Searchers* actually represent 'the architecture of the spirit'.

Perhaps the most systematic attempt to apply structuralist and semiotic methodology to an analysis of the cinema was carried out by Christian Metz in his *Essais sur la signification au cinéma* (*Film Language*, 1968). Metz's concerns in the *Essais* link him to the earlier traditions of Russian formalism and Lévi-Straussian structuralism, in that he is primarily interested in establishing what is specifically 'cinematic' about the cinema, and in uncovering the deep structures of basic units, and their principles of combination, which enable all films to signify. Following Saussure's call for the development of a new science of semiology, Metz hoped that his work would lay the foundations for a rigorous and systematic classification of film language.

Metz's principal conclusion was that linguistic methodology could not be directly applied to the cinema because the cinema did not possess a distinct body of phonemic units in the way that language did. In language, a group of up to forty phonemes (letters of the alphabet), are recombined to make an almost infinite number of meaningful units, or morphemes. However, Metz argued that the film image could not be broken down in this way because, unlike language, the image was too closely related to the object which it represented. This meant that meaning was fixed, and not arbitrary, as was the case with the linguistic phoneme. This, in turn meant that, although the cinema did consist of a kind of language, one made up of conventions, basic units, and rules for the combination of those units, it did not possess a *langue* in the linguistic sense.[44]

Metz's approach to deep structure here was influenced by the post-structuralist turn already evident in the work of Roland Barthes and Lévi-Strauss, and by the general reaction against formalism, foundationalism and authoritarianism which emerged following the events of May 1968. However, Metz was also influenced by the theory of cinematic realism developed by André Bazin, and it was under Bazin's influence that Metz both rejected a Saussurian conception of structure as a system of relational differentials without positive terms, and went on to argue that the 'impression of reality' engendered by the cinema stemmed from the fact that cinematic representations corresponded to reality in ways other than the purely symbolic.[45] Metz grounds his approach to cinematic realism in psychology, rather than, as Bazin did, in a synthesis of phenomenology and Catholic existentialism. Nevertheless, he shares the Bazinian conviction that the 'impression of reality' is both central to the medium of film, and a positive, rather than negative aspect of the cinematic experience.

Metz argues that, in viewing film, the spectator accomplishes a 'transfer of reality, involving a whole affective, perceptual and intellective activity', and that this activity can only come into being if the spectacle of the film resembles the 'spectacle of reality'.[46] Metz goes on to argue that, where a film does not sufficiently resemble 'the spectacle of reality', the full panoply of spectatorship cannot take place. Unlike later post-structuralist theorists, Metz does not accept that the spectator is duped by the impression of reality in the cinema, and argues, instead, that it is, precisely, the film image's closeness to perceptual reality which enables the spectator to effect an active and willing 'transfer of reality':

> In short, the secret of film is that it is able to leave a high degree of reality in its images, which are, nevertheless, perceived as images.

Poor images do not sustain the world of imagination enough for it to assume reality.[47]

Metz's conviction that the spectator was not *necessarily* ideologically or psychologically misled, or positioned, by the cinema's impression of reality was based on his belief that the spectator was able to distinguish between film and reality through a recognition that film, as an aesthetic medium, possessed certain characteristics which differentiated it from reality. Chief amongst such characteristics was that of narrativity, and Metz claimed that it was in the process of confronting the problems of narration that the cinema also evolved a 'body of specific signifying procedures'.[48] For Metz, film is a language chiefly because it imposes a narrative logic on the events it portrays, and, in his *grande syntagmatique*, Metz set out to describe that logic. The *grande syntagmatique* established a basic unit, the 'autonomous shot', and seven different systems of combination of those shots, which Metz called 'syntagms', and it was these which 'told the story of the film'.[49]

Metz's attempt to categorise the narrative language of the cinema can be, and was, criticised for the fact that his narrative categories were often difficult to apply in practice. For example, one sequence of film might be associated with a number of the categories of the *grande syntagmatique*, or none at all. In practice, Metz's *grande syntagmatique* proved to be far less than the systematic analysis of the language of the cinema which he claimed it to be, and more a relatively random collection of taxonomical categories. Metz's system also suffered from the familiar structuralist problem of reductivism. In arguing that the application of a semiotic analysis to the cinema must begin at the level of denotation, rather than connotation, Metz hoped to build a solid theoretical foundation for later work. However, the end result is that his system, like those of Propp and Lévi-Strauss before him, ends up by reducing the complexity of film to a series of formal categories such as those of the 'bracketing syntagma', the 'achronological syntagma' and the 'ordinary sequence'.[50]

Although these problems led to the emergence of a number of criticisms of Metz's methodology during the 1970s, they were by no means the principal source of such criticism. In fact, that source was the Bazinian legacy which Metz had both inherited and sanctioned, and which he had built his structuralist theory of the cinema upon. Metz believed that the realist text promoted active spectatorship, and that the language of the cinema had reached a pinnacle of achievement with the realist narrative form. He was also forthrightly critical of anti-realist or 'experimental' forms of film-making, with their 'avalanche of gratuitous and anarchic images against a background of heterogeneous percussions, capped by some over-blown avant-gardist text'.[51] However, such pronouncements were radically at odds with a gathering post-structuralist consensus of opinion in which the spectator was seen as positioned by the narrative, and in which realism was regarded as the most reactionary form of cinema.

It was, therefore, Metz's championship of realist cinema, rather than the technical problems associated with the *grande syntagmatique*, which ensured his marginalisation within film theory during the late 1970s. His view that the 'modern cinema' should be 'highly understandable', and that, far from a 'breakdown of narrative', a new realist, narrative cinema, characterised by films such as Antonioni's *Il Grido* (*The Outcry*, 1959) and Fellini's *Otto e mezzo* (*Eight and a Half*, 1963), was emerging during the 1960s and 1970s, was unacceptable to the champions of an anti-realist, deconstructive, post-structuralist cinema.[52]

The work of Propp, Lévi-Strauss, Metz, Wollen and others illustrate a number of fundamental theoretical inadequacies which structuralism was prone to. First, the concept of structure often employed appears to imply that 'structure' has an autonomy and volition of its own, as though it were some sort of sentient entity. This notion of structure is difficult to defend philosophically, as it is based on an unprovable metaphysical conception of being. In addition, the concomitant idea that such structures are complete, unified systems rules out the possibility that they might, in fact, not be unified at all. The idea of deep structure as autonomous and unified also lends structuralism a deterministic dimension. Deep structures appear to dominate individuals who are not in control of the social processes within which they find themselves, and this means that there is, therefore, a 'hidden metaphysical commitment to determinism' within structuralism.[53]

Structuralist analysis also tends to result in the production of descriptive, as opposed to evaluative criticism, and to reduce complex aesthetic objects to a skeleton of formal categories. The final conclusions which are drawn from such analyses are often mundane and prosaic. For example, and as already mentioned, Wollen's principal conclusion concerning *The Searchers* was that 'it is the richness of the shifting relations between antinomies' in the film which makes it superior to either *My Darling Clementine* or *The Man Who Shot Liberty Valance*.[54] However, such conclusions say little about one of the most important films in the history of the cinema. Two final problems with structuralist methodology are a tendency to impose theoretical models upon empirical evidence, and an inability to account for audience reception. These final two difficulties have led to the charge that structuralism is an insular intellectual tradition, which ignores that which falls outside its own boundaries. This was a charge which a number of anthropologists aimed at the work of Lévi-Strauss, and which is further reinforced by the rather narrow intellectual focus adopted by Metz in his *Essais sur la signification au cinéma*.[55]

These various problems and difficulties eventually precipitated the appearance of post-structuralism. Post-structuralist theorists rejected what they regarded as the authoritarianism of structuralism, and attempted, instead, to formulate a more pluralist model, which would, nevertheless, remain theoretically rigorous, and indebted to the Saussurian tradition. For example, following Claude Lévi-Strauss' adoption of a post-structuralist position in 1973, Roland Barthes attempted a less essentialist project of structuralist analysis in his *S/Z* (1974). Here, in an analysis of Balzac's novel *Sarrasine* (1830), Barthes sought to illustrate how a supposedly unitary text could be deconstructed into a number of distinct underlying codes, as opposed to one single, defining, deep structure.

Barthes approach in *S/Z* was also founded on the conviction that, whilst all texts contain the potential to engender a multiplicity of possible readings, only certain types of text are capable of realising that potential. Barthes referred to such texts as *scriptible* (writerly), and argued that they were superior to *lisible* (readerly) texts, which encouraged the reader to consume meaning passively, rather than produce meaning creatively. In *S/Z*, Barthes deconstructed *Sarrasine* in order to show how the effect of completeness, and the illusion of realism which the novel engendered, was fabricated from the interplay of five major codes: the 'enigmatic', 'action', 'referential', 'semic' and 'symbolic' codes. He then went on to demonstrate how the operation of such codes could be altered, so as to turn *Sarrasine* into a more *scriptible*, and less unified text.[56]

However, although *S/Z* displays the influence of post-structuralist conceptions of signification, it also displays the continuing influence of the structuralist tradition. For example, Barthes' definition of the writerly text as that which evinces a 'greater complexity of coding' echoes the quantitative, technical language often used by structuralists. The idea that five major codes underpin all textual narratives is also little more than a variation on the structuralist belief in the existence of deep, determining structures. Although Barthes' codes are far more loosely defined than either Propp's functions, Metz's syntagms, or Lévi-Strauss' binary oppositions, they must, therefore, in the final analysis, be associated with a structuralist, as opposed to a post-structuralist venture.

Nevertheless, other facets of Barthes' thought can be more easily defined as post-structuralist, and one of these was his notion of the 'death of the author'.[57] However, even this notion emerges logically from structuralist preoccupations and premises. Lévi-Strauss had already postulated the idea that the true 'authors' of myth were unconscious mental and social discourses, and such autonomous discursive structures do not require much of a concept of individual agency. The idea of the death of the author also reinforces the lack of consideration for issues of historical causality and reference to be found within both the structuralist and post-structuralist traditions. This orientation has already been illustrated when discussing the difficulties which emerged during the various attempts to contextualise *The Searchers*. However, Barthes takes this approach to causality and reference a stage further when he describes the writerly text as a 'galaxy of signifiers, not a structure of signifieds'.[58] Barthes' position here is now definitively post-structuralist, and based on the conviction that the critic should not attempt to provide a 'discourse of knowledge' (including one based on the ascription of authorial determination) which imposes a final interpretation on the text.[59]

The Barthesian methodology found in *S/Z* has been used less within film studies than was the case with Lévi-Straussian and Proppian structuralism, possibly because the highly speculative and digressive approach which Barthes adopts in his book is not as conducive to accurate application as is the case with the work of Propp and Lévi-Strauss. One of the most substantial application of Barthes can be found in Julia Lesage's 1976 analysis of Jean Renoir's *La Règle du jeu* (*The Rules of the Game*, 1939). However, although Lesage produces a commendably detailed analysis of *La Règle du jeu*, many of her conclusions could be arrived at without recourse to Barthesian methodology at all. This is partly because Barthes five codes are, in themselves, so loosely formulated that, in the end, they can only be applied using a considerable degree of subjective critical judgement. Unfortunately, this amounts to precisely the sort of *explication de texte* which Barthes had initially formulated his more 'rigorous' structuralist approach in opposition to when he wrote his 'Introduction to the Structural Analysis of Narratives', in 1966.[60]

In addition, although Lesage's use of Barthesian referential and symbolic codes should, in theory, enable her to discuss the content of *La Règle du Jeu* in relation to its historical context, this does not really occur. The fact that *La Règle du jeu* was made in 1939, after the demise of the Popular Front, and in the face of emergent war, collaboration, and threat of fascism, and by a director closely involved in political activity, cannot, in the end, be accommodated within Lesage's Barthesian analysis. For example, although Lesage discusses how *La Règle du jeu* positions its characters across a spectrum of power and social class relations, the dictum that a text is a 'galaxy of signifiers, not a structure of signifieds', causes her to marginalise questions of reference and authorship which were, at least, attempted by Wollen and Fell.

Such avoidance is deliberate, of course, as Lesage follows Barthes advice that the critic should not 'structure the text excessively ... (and) ... close it' through the attribution of definite causality.[61] The Barthesian emphasis on discursive and intertextual causality also leaves the role of Renoir, and that of the other contributors to the film, unexplained within Lesage's essay. Although Barthes' notions of the 'death of the author' and 'birth of the reader' leads Lesage to concentrate on discursive patterns within *La Règle du jeu*, the fact that, during the entire course of the essay, Renoir's name is mentioned only once, appears critically untenable.

Barthes emphasis on what he called 'polysemy', or multiple meanings, was partly influenced by the concept of *différance*, which he derived from a reading of Jacques Derrida's *L'Ecriture et la différance* (1967), and it is with the work of Derrida that structuralism develops fully into radical post-structuralism. Although post-structuralism, as a movement, was far less coherent than structuralism, it can be argued that it emerged across a range of disciplines as part of a perceived need to oppose both 'dominant' institutional and ideological structures of power and authority; and foundationalist, realist or humanist conceptions of the self, reason, intentionality and knowledge. Although those involved in this struggle often adopted highly politicised approaches, others adopted a form of utopian libertarianism at odds with allegiance to already established political ideologies, or direct party political activity, and, as post-structuralism evolved, from 1968 onwards, it developed along both of these, sometimes incompatible, trajectories.

The post-structuralism of Jacques Derrida is derived from a combination of Saussurian linguistics, Kierkegaardian existentialism and Heideggerian phenomenology, and was particularly influenced by Saussure's conception of the linguistic sign as arbitrary, and as possessing meaning only by virtue of its relation to, and difference from, other signs. The idealist and relativist implications of this position, which implies that meaning resides only in the articulated conjunctions of signs, rather than in the relationship of those signs to an external world, are clearly evident. However, it is important to understand that, despite the latent linguistic solipsism inherent in his theory of the sign, Saussure attempted to distance himself from a radical relativist interpretation of his work, arguing that the fusion of signifier and signified within the linguistic sign fixed meaning into a 'positive' term, which then entered into a substantive relationship with external reality.[62]

Saussurian linguistics is founded on the arbitrary nature of the phonemic signifier, and its function as a 'negative' term within a system of differences. However, as argued above, Saussure did not argue that signs *themselves* were arbitrary. Nevertheless, the idea that, like the signifier, signs were also intrinsically differential, was enthusiastically adopted by Derrida, who argued that Saussure had failed to take his own theoretical insights to their logical conclusion, because he feared the consequence of appearing to support a position in which a clear distinction was drawn between language and the world. Derrida, on the other hand, did not fear such consequences, and was only too eager to draw such a distinction. Furthermore, he went on to argue that the idea that linguistic signification referred to something which existed outside it amounted to an untenable 'metaphysics of presence', and that signification did, in fact, take the differential form suggested by Saussure's model of the linguistic signifier: 'Every concept is necessarily and essentially inscribed in a chain or system, within which it refers to another and to other concepts, by the systematic play of differences'.[63]

In his *De la grammatologie* (1967), Derrida argued that the process of linguistic production is characterised by the fabrication of an endless chain of signifiers, within which signifiers and signs refer to each other.[64] In addition, although it may appear that this ongoing process of the generation of signifiers is driven by an impulse to achieve signification, in fact, each 'signified' is also, simultaneously, the signifier of other signifieds, and is, therefore, incapable of achieving absolute signification. This means that signification is always deferred, rather than attained, and it is this tendency towards deferral which maintains and perpetuates linguistic communication, and fuels the evolution of the endless chain of signifiers.

These ideas of difference and deferral find expression in Derrida's notion of *différance*. As a concept, *différance* bears some resemblance to the Hegelian and Marxist concept of negation as the motive force behind all development.[65] However, Derrida employs *différance* in conjunction with a structuralist conception of structure, within which the linguistic system is conceived of as a self-motivating and autonomous entity which reproduces itself through the constant deferral of meaning. Just as, in Hegel, and in dialectical materialism, the dialectic is the 'pulse of freedom', as Roy Bhaskar puts it, for Derrida, that 'pulse' is *différance*.[66] Derrida also employs the notion of the self-referentiality and lack of signification within the endless chain of signifiers to celebrate the 'absence of the transcendental signified', by which he means 'objective', or 'true' explanation, and to rule out attempts at full closure of meaning.[67] One can clearly see how this model of signification led on to the Barthesian argument that the text is a 'galaxy of signifiers, not a structure of signifieds', and to Barthes' insistence that the critic should not 'structure the text excessively ... (and) ... close it'.[68]

Derrida's conception of *différance* is derived from both a belief that meaning and language are, as a matter of fact, based on the processes of difference and deferral referred to above, and on the conviction that the act of writing should seek to embody such processes as a matter of principle. Derridean methodology, therefore, both in practice and intention, is deconstructive in character, and seeks to both undermine established systems of conceptual categorisation, and unmask their 'fallacious' attempts at closure. This is the basis of Derrida's 'diagnostic' method, where, instead of seeking analytic explication, with its concomitant closure of signification, Derrida seeks to defer and perpetuate the signifying process through the use of such devices as association, metaphor, the pun, alliteration etc. In his *Disseminations* (1972), Derrida developed this deconstructive model further, and employed the organic metaphor of the 'seed' to conceive of the linguistic sign as a generative entity (the seed), which disseminates meaning, possesses no fixed meaning itself, and, therefore, cannot be channelled into definition.[69]

At the basis of Derrida's philosophy, then, is a refusal to advance 'systems' of knowledge, or to accept any form of foundationalism which would halt the dissemination of signification. Derrida argues that the whole of 'western philosophy' is based on such systems, and that, behind this, is both a misunderstanding of the signifying process, and an institutionalised predisposition towards the exercise of authoritarian jurisdiction. Accordingly, Derrida refuses to advance any system or method of his own, and insists that his deconstructionist grammatology is not a method, but a technique for deconstructing existing methodological systems and categories.[70]

Derrida's attitude to questions of signification and representation are clearly influenced by the philosophical repudiation of realism central to a structuralist, linguistic idealist tradition, which begins, if not with Saussure, then certainly with Lévi-Strauss. This tradition is marked by a shift from engagement with the notion of representation, to a concern with the internal coherence and operation of systems; and by a concomitant shift from realism to the position that all our knowledge is mind-dependent. However, Derrida's concern with interiority — with the mind-dependence of our knowledge of reality — is also influenced by a Nietzschean critique of Enlightenment conceptions of objective reason. Just as Nietzsche argued that concepts of truth, knowledge and reason are related to existing sets of interests, Derridean deconstruction also seeks to reveal the culturally determined character of such concepts. What is crucially important here is that Derridean deconstructionism, does, in fact, prove to possess analytic intent, and that Derrida's diagnostic approach is, in the end, not directed at exploding or rejecting foundationalism *per se*, but at examining how particular foundationalist conceptions of truth, reality and being are culturally determined.

In addition, whilst using deconstruction to critique existing normative values — values which are affected by relations of social power and interest, and are, therefore, at least in part, 'provisional and finite' — Derrida also insists that such deconstruction should proceed by respecting certain rational procedures of enquiry. Derrida does, therefore, posit a certain kind of foundationalism: one based on the need for reliance on what he calls an 'indispensable guardrail' of rational procedures, such as careful observation, balanced argument, attention to detail, and so on. This means that interpretation cannot develop 'in any direction at all and authorise itself to say almost anything'.[71]

There are, therefore, two identifiable dimensions to Derrida's thought. On the one hand, there is a post-structuralist emphasis on revealing the social and cultural formation of established norms, and, in this respect, Derrida can be classed as a cultural relativist working within the general parameters of post-structuralism. On the other hand, Derrida declared that he did not 'put such concepts as truth, reference, and the stability of interpretive contexts into question'.[72] This means that his philosophy cannot be characterised as completely idealist, but as what I will later describe as an example of 'representational realism'. However, and despite Derrida's refusal to put foundational concepts themselves into question, the emphasis on the notion of the self-referentiality of the endless chain of signifiers, together with an emphasis on the relativity of meaning and rejection of a 'metaphysics of presence' within his work, was to give rise, in the theories of post-modernists such as Jean Baudrilliard, to a full-blown idealism which rejected foundationalism *per se*, in its endorsement of a critical practice based on the free play of sign and meaning, and 'the pleasure of infinite creation'.[73]

Derrida's emphasis on critical practice as a free play of signs and meaning was also adopted within the American deconstructionist movement by literary critics such as Geoffrey Hartman and J. Hillis-

Miller. These critics often took Derridean post-structuralism to the logical conclusions implied by its Saussurian imperative, and advocated a theory of writing which rejected foundationalism, adopted a deconstructionist model of literary 'diagnosis', rejected 'metacritical' explanation, and proposed that all discourses be regarded as equally valid rhetorical structures.[74] Nevertheless, even here, Derrida's insistence that writing and interpretation must be constrained by an 'indispensable guardrail', and should not be 'authorised to say almost anything', still held some leverage. A distinction can, therefore, be drawn between, on the one hand the 'wild deconstructionism' of Hartman and Hillis-Miller, with its emphasis on the open-ended, libertarian, free play of style and speculation, and the more rigorous conceptual rationalism of critics such as Paul de Man.[75]

The form of post-structuralism which stemmed from Derrida's conception of *différance* emphasised the subversion of authoritarian and normative values through ironic defamiliarisation, rather than through the overt advancement of oppositional models. However, and in contrast to a Derridean legacy which, in much of its American manifestation, became cut off from direct political engagement, other forms of European post-structuralism did attempt to combine a critique of established norms with the formulation of alternative systems, and with involvement in political and social engagement.

This tendency towards engagement within European post-structuralism had its philosophical origins in the conviction that authoritative social discourses, institutions, and forms of practice reflected the interests of dominant power groups, and that it was possible to develop others which did not. Nevertheless, despite this activist dimension, European post-structuralism remained dependent upon a deterministic conception of human agency which contradicted the idea that such activism could ever be effective. That conception of agency was derived from a structuralist model premised on the determination of the particular by the general, and, when applied to contemporary society, this model led to a view of the modern subject as almost entirely shaped by manipulative and instrumental forces. The various attempts made during the 1970s to establish an alternative, post-structuralist 'counter-culture', all drew on this bleak account of the possibilities for human freedom, and all struggled to construct theories of progressive action, which, after increasingly tortuous processes of theorisation, eventually foundered on the rock of predestination and pessimism.

Although this deterministic account of agency was derived from

the structuralist legacy, it also developed in France in direct opposition to the then dominant intellectual paradigm of Sartrean
existentialism. Unlike structuralism, existentialism prioritised questions of human agency and choice, and celebrated the possibility and
necessity of human freedom. Developed during the years of the
German occupation, existentialism was premised on the belief that
only such an endorsement of free individual choice offered a means
of effectively challenging a system which so evidently oppressed
individuality, and, in *Being and Nothingness* (1943), Sartre argued
that only the 'free action' had the power to 'modify the shape of the
world'.[76]

In the immediate post-war period, when hopes of a radical
renewal of society could still be entertained by intellectuals on the
left, the emphasis on purposive activism within existentialism seemed
to offer a viable way forward to the creation of a more liberated
society. Consequently, in the journal *Les Temps modernes*, which
Sartre founded with Simone de Beauvoir and Maurice Merleau-
Ponty, attempts were made to synthesise the Sartrean existentialist
concern with individual freedom with a Marxist theory of society.[77]
However, Sartre's relationship with the French Communist Party
was always a strained one, and, in his *Search for a Method* (1957) and
Critique of Dialectical Reason (1960) he moved away from the
Communist Party line to develop a theory of existentialist Marxism
which focused on the role of agency, and its relationship to collective
struggle and social context.

Sartre's theory of existentialist Marxism was only one of a number
of different versions of 'western Marxism' which appeared around
1960, and which included contributions by François Lefebvre, Lucien
Goldmann, Raymond Williams and members of the Frankfurt School.
Western Marxism arose in opposition to the dogmatic authoritarianism of Soviet Marxism, and adopted a wide range of approaches
in attempting to develop a more liberal, flexible, tolerant, or just more
intellectually acceptable account of Marxism. However, the form of
western Marxism which was to influence film theory most, and which
also emerged most strongly in direct reaction to Sartrean existentialist-
Marxism, was that developed by Louis Althusser.

For Althusser, whose ideas had been strongly influenced by
structuralist and post-structuralist conceptions of ideology, the
Sartrean focus on the power of intentionality and individual agency
could not provide an adequate explanation for the continued
existence of, and mass support for, capitalist society. Accordingly,
Althusser's work focused on how agency was shaped and determined by more abstract institutional forces, and on the means

through which ideology worked to manipulate the subject in the interests of the ruling elite. Drawing on the psychoanalytic theories of Jacques Lacan, Althusser argued that dominant ideology conferred an identity on the individual which the individual then accepted because it provided him or her with a stable sense of social position and personal orientation.[78]

However, although the subject was positioned, or 'interpellated' by ideology, the possibility remained that, through an engagement with forms of what Althusser called 'theoretical practice', the individual could become aware of his or her own manipulation, and attempt to transcend or oppose it. Accordingly, Althusser argued for a distinction to be made between 'ideological' and 'theoretical' practice, in which ideological practice was fundamentally instrumental, manipulative and illusory, whilst theoretical practice was concerned with deconstructing dominant ideological forms in order to reveal their class-based origins and function. For Althusser, the most advanced form of theoretical practice was the Marxist philosophy of historical materialism, and it was this which provided the 'problematic' (theoretical system) and model for his attempts to expose dominant relations of power.

Althusserian Marxism was influenced by a general structuralist predisposition to accept the dominance of the system over the individual, the whole over the part, and this led Althusser to reject both existentialist, and other 'humanist' forms of Marxism grounded in notions of human agency. This position also led Althusser to make a key distinction between the early 'humanist' and later 'materialist' Marx, in which he argued that the work of the 'later' Marx transcended humanist delusions, and focused on the systematic mechanisms through which capitalism reproduced itself. For Althusser, humanist Marxism was unacceptable, because it was not 'systematic' enough, and he insisted that such a 'philosophical myth of man' should be 'reduced to ashes'.[79]

Following his repudiation of humanist Marxism, Sartrean existentialism, and much of the work of Marx, Althusser attempted to describe the systemic mechanisms through which dominant ideology both reproduced itself, and determined individual subjectivity. This provided the basis for his theory of the 'ideological state apparatus': the social institutions whose function was to socialise the subject in the interests of the system. According to Althusser, in an ideological state apparatus such as education or the media, 'it is ultimately the ruling ideology which is realised'.[80] However, Althusser also argued that, because it was not as easily controllable by the ruling class as was the 'repressive state apparatus' (the army, police, etc.), the ideological state apparatus also offered a potential site for the emergence of struggle and revolt.

It is this conception of the ideological state apparatus which provides the basis for Althusser's notion of 'theoretical practice', within which individuals are able to disclose, and then struggle against, the ideological trappings and functions of the institutions within which they live and work.[81] Despite his reliance on a deterministic theory of the subject, Althusser did, therefore, propose a certain conception of agency. However, within this definition, the ability to exercise such agency was restricted to those who were suitably trained in the appropriate forms of theoretical practice, whilst those who were not remained deluded and duped.

Althusserian post-structuralist Marxism has been criticised as inherently elitist by, amongst others, the English Marxist historian E. P. Thompson, who, in his *The Poverty of Theory* (1978), describes it as 'bourgeois elitist' and 'idealist'.[82] Thompson's charge of elitism is a response to Althusser's insistence that only an elect of theoretical practitioners, trained in the precepts of Althusserian Marxism, had access to 'the truth'; whilst that of idealism stemmed from Althusser's focus on the ideological superstructure, rather than the economic and political base of society. The emphasis on ideology within Althusserian Marxism stemmed from the conviction that, within capitalist society, the ideological superstructure enjoyed a degree of 'relative autonomy', and was not completely determined by the economic base. This differentiated Althusserian Marxism from the official Soviet model, in which the distinction between a determining economic and political base, and a determined ideological superstructure, was maintained.

Thompson's critique of Althusserian Marxism was also targeted at Althusser's conception of popular culture. Thompson's Marxism was premised on the belief that popular culture was a potential, and actual, site and arena of resistance to dominant ideology, and that it was not 'overdetermined' (to use the phrase which Althusser derived from Freud and Lacan) by dominant ideology. This view of popular culture provided the basic premise for the whole tradition of cultural studies which developed in Britain during the late 1960s and 1970s, often in direct and open opposition to the Althusserian post-structuralist tradition. However, such a view of popular culture as a site of active agency and resistance was incompatible with Althusser's 'materialist' philosophy, within which any 'apparatus' works to 'constitute' 'concrete individuals as subjects'.[83] Popular culture is, therefore, inevitably reactionary, and remains so until it is taken over by the shock troops of theoretical practice.

A form of cinema based on the Althusserian model of theoretical practice would reflect on its own 'materialist' process of production, deconstruct dominant ideology, and replace that ideology with an account based on the precepts of Althusserian Marxism. During the 1970s Althusserian approaches to subjectivity, ideology and cultural practice were adopted by French film journals such as *Positif*, *Cinétique*, *Tel Quel* and *Cahiers du Cinéma*, and by English journals such as *Screen*. Taking its cue from Althusser, and inspired by the events of May 1968, *Cinétique* contributors argued that, like the church and education, the commercial cinema was an 'ideological state apparatus', and that, in order to challenge dominant institutions and ideologies, a new, progressive counter-cinema must be created. Basing their approach on Althusser's notion of 'interpellation', both *Cinétique* and *Tel Quel* argued that the impression of reality engendered by the cinema served to reproduce existing dominant ideologies, and that the basic form which ideology took within the cinema was that of realism. As a consequence, both journals proceeded to advocate the development of an anti-realist and self-reflexive form of cinema.[84]

In contrast to *Cinétique* and *Tel Quel*, *Cahiers du Cinéma* initially took a more 'culturalist' line on the progressive potential of mainstream cinema, arguing that many areas of popular cinema undercut or critiqued dominant ideology. This was argued, for example, in relation to the American films of Douglas Sirk and John Ford, and in relation to European directors such as Carl Dreyer and Roberto Rossellini. However, In 1969, against the context of the continued radicalisation of Parisian film culture, *Cahiers* shifted its position, and fell in line with *Cinétique* in advocating the development of a more modernist counter-cinema. A crucial influence on this change of policy was Jean-Louis Comolli and Paul Narboni's 1969 essay 'Cinema/Ideology/Criticism', which argued for a classification of film production into those films which 'allow the ideology a free, unhampered passage ... (and those) which attempt to make it turn back and reflect itself, intercept it and make it visible by revealing its mechanisms'.[85] Nevertheless, although Comolli and Narboni focused mainly on films which overtly challenged dominant ideology, they still adhered, to some extent, to the previous *Cahiers* insistence that some mainstream films, although part of the dominant system of commercial cinema, 'dismantled the system from within', and, as a consequence, could be considered progressive.[86]

It was, however, in the pages of the English journal *Screen* that the most systematic attempt to weld structuralism and post-structuralism into a general theory of film was made. Drawing on Althusser and Lacanian psychoanalysis, critics such as Laura Mulvey and Colin MacCabe argued that mainstream feature films positioned the spectator within dominant ideology. For critics like MacCabe, even a politically progressive film such as Ken Loach's *Days of Hope* (1975) collaborated in the manipulation of the subject, because it depended upon a realistic approach which was intrinsically authoritarian.[87] In contradistinction, and following the example set by *Cinétique*, MacCabe and others writing for *Screen* called for the formation of a reflexive and anti-realist theory and practice of cinema.

The attempt made by *Screen* to develop an overarching theory of cinematic representation, one which set out to theorise 'the encounter of Marxism and psychoanalysis on the terrain of semiotics',[88] was initially influenced by the unifying imperative, inherited from both the structuralist tradition and Althusser, of discovering objectively true theoretical axioms. However, by the late 1970s, Althusser's attempt to identify the 'scientific' basis of Marxist theory was largely held to have been a failure, whilst the increasing rejection of 'meta-narratives' and 'grand theory' within post-structuralism led to a gradual abandonment of the attempt to develop a general theory of film. The decline in the importance of Marxism within the west, and the parallel growth of the new politics of race, gender and ecology, also led to an increasing engagement with more targeted areas of political and ideological struggle, and these developments eventually led to the abandonment of the *Screen* attempt to develop a meta-theory of cinematic signification.

However, if post-Althusserian post-structuralism's rejection of grand theory differentiated it from structuralism, its dependence upon a Saussurian conception of *langue* also linked it firmly to the structuralist tradition, and ensured that the conceptions of agency and subjectivity common within later forms of post-structuralism remained essentially deterministic. This problem forced post-structuralist theorists to return to the question of agency, although in a rather half-hearted and ambivalent manner. For some, Lacanian theory seemed to offer the possibility of conceptualising a role for agency through the notion that, although constituted, the subject was always engaged in a process of becoming, and was, therefore, never a fixed entity. This meant that agency could exist within a 'dialectic of subjectivity', in which the subject was able to explore meaning within a framework which was, nevertheless, ultimately determined by existing discursive practice. This idea of the 'dialectic of the subject' was later taken up by Stephen Heath, who argued that a 'give and take' occurs within psychological experience, where the subject enjoys a degree of autonomous, undetermined agency.[89]

However, this is, in the end, an extremely limited conception of agency and intentionality, where the subject still remains an 'effect' of the discursive 'text'.

Given the extent to which Althusserian and Lacanian post-structuralism was based upon determinist principles, any attempt to develop a viable and substantive conception of agency from these sources was bound to encounter severe difficulties, and, ironically, in turning to Lacan, Heath arrived at an even more restricted model of agency than was allowed for in Althusser's notion of theoretical practice. The same is true of Coward and Ellis' *Language and Materialism* (1977), in which the Lacanian idea of the 'subject in process' is drawn on to argue that the subject is 'an effect constituted in the process of the unconscious, of discourse, and of the relatively autonomous practices of the social formation'. Coward and Ellis claim that Lacan had developed a 'materialist theory of the subject consonant with that of dialectical materialism', but it remains a theory in which the subject is a determined one.[90]

During the 1980s, the deconstructive 'archaeologies' of Michel Foucault emerged as the leading form of post-structuralist theory. However, Foucault's investigation of the social and cultural formation of discourse was no different in kind from the deconstructive exercises of Derrida. The origins of both their methodologies lay in Nietzsche's pessimistic conviction that theoretical systems did not, in fact, seek to establish objective truth, but were bound up with struggles between different groups in society, who used theory to advance their own interests. However, there is a crucial distinction between the theories of Derrida and Foucault which must be made here, and which was to have significant implications for the relativist turn which European film theory was to take in the late 1980s.

As already mentioned, Derrida's deconstruction of discourse was aimed at highlighting problems with the notions of truth, reference and objectivity which had been handed down from the Enlightenment, rather than at an outright rejection of those notions. As has already been argued, Derrida did not adopt a fully relativist position, and did not argue that any one discourse was as viable as any other. In addition, his foundationalist insistence on the use of an 'indispensable guardrail' of rational procedures to adjudicate between discourses looks forward to later developments within philosophical realism. Foucault, on the other hand, fully adopted the Nietzschean model of the relativity of discourse, abandoning Derrida's rationalist foundationalism, and his commitment to a renewal of the central insights of the Enlightenment, and it was Foucault, rather than Derrida, that European film theorists turned to during the 1980s.

Postmodernism is the direct inheritor of the post-structuralist tradition which emerges from Foucault and American 'wild' deconstructionism, and postmodernism can also be regarded as the most extreme formulation of the Saussurian conception of signification as a system of differences without positive terms. Postmodernism is characterised by a rejection of grand narratives, a concern for creative activity, an avoidance of comparative value judgements, and a belief that systems of signification relate primarily to each other, rather than to an extra-discursive 'real world'. An overriding concern with the centrality of discourse, and the production of 'mini', as opposed to 'grand' narrative is also common in such works as Jean François Lyotard's *The Postmodern Condition*. For Lyotard, the engagement with such mini-narratives is a liberating experience, and he treats all such narratives as possessing equivalent value, refusing to make 'authoritarian' value judgements which would elevate one over the other.[91] Such a rejection of 'meta-critique' is taken even further by Jean Baudrillard, who argues that, in the postmodern world, representations refer to each other, rather than to reality. Baudrillard's theory of the existence of self-referential simulations, like postmodernism in general, is, in many respects, the ultimate conceptualisation of the idealist post-Saussurian vision.

Lyotard and Baudrillard's rejection of the meta-critique, and endorsement of discursive pluralism, stems from their understanding of 'postmodernism' as constituting a rejection of the central values of the Enlightenment. Lyotard's theory of postmodernism also draws from the German idealist critique of modernity, within which modernity is regarded as ushering in a new era of exploitation and authoritarianism. However, Lyotard misunderstands the central imperative of that critique. Kant, Hegel, Weber, Marx and Habermas saw the Enlightenment as possessing an emancipatory potential which had become derailed by the emergence of capitalism, and all accepted the inherent value of the 'Enlightenment Project'. Habermas, for example, rejects the postmodernist repudiation of science and reason, and designates theorists such as Derrida, Foucault and Lyotard as 'young-conservatives'.[92]

Semiotics, structuralism, post-structuralism and postmodernism can be identified as a branch of relativist thought which has its origins in Saussure and post-Saussurian theory. However, despite its pre-eminence within film and literary studies, this post-Saussurian tradition is, in fact, only a minor component within a far more widespread tradition of contemporary philosophical relativism. Moreover, the Saussurian conception of meaning as a system of differences without positive terms has also been largely abandoned by contemporary theories which seek to understand the relationship between representation and reality. It is important, therefore, to put the post-Saussurian tradition in proper perspective, as a minor player within a far larger philosophical debate.

The origins of post-Saussurian linguistic idealism are to be found – at least in terms of modern philosophy – in Kant's assertion that, to a significant extent, the mind creates its own reality, and that reality as such is unknowable. However, it is important to point out that Kant remained a dualist, who argued that reality existed independently of mind, and was not completely mind dependent. Kant's emphasis on interiority was developed in reaction to what he regarded as an oversimplistic empiricist conception of mind as constituted by empirical experience, but Kant did not accept the polar opposite of empiricism: that the mind created the world.[93] However, in the nineteenth and twentieth centuries, the idealist implications of the Kantian theory of knowledge have been adopted by philosophers as diverse as Kierkegaard, Heidegger, Nietzsche, Kuhn, Lakatos, Feyerabend Rorty and others.

The approach adopted by the theorists mentioned above can be defined as 'representational realism'. Representational, or 'causal' realism, asserts that we do not have any direct knowledge of reality but only an indirect knowledge through representations. According to this conjecture, representations are largely our own constructions, based on sense impressions and internal mental constructs, but they also have a substantive and authentic relationship to reality.[94] Representational realism, in its many forms, constitutes the basis of most contemporary theories of realism. However, the doctrine itself also contains the potential for the development of an alternative, sceptical and solipsist doctrine, based on the conjecture that we might only have knowledge of our own representations, and no knowledge of external reality at all. This may lead to the proposition that, because we cannot stand outside our concepts, we cannot even prove the existence of a world outside consciousness. Such a position could be defined as subjective idealism, and is illustrated by Berkeley's postulate that knowledge of the world arises from mind, and, ultimately, from God:

[All the] furniture of the earth, ... all those bodies which compose the mighty frame of the world ... have not any substance without a mind [If they] do not exist in my mind or that of any other created spirit, they must either have no existence at all, or else subsist in the mind of some eternal spirit.[95]

Such extreme idealist and solipsist theories are, however, difficult to maintain, because they lead to the inevitable conclusion that reality is completely dependent upon mind. Few idealist philosophers have been prepared to adopt such a position.

A less radical form of idealism, but, nevertheless, a significant extension of representational realism further away from the representation of reality towards the autonomy of signification, can be defined as conceptual idealism. This position is founded on the premise that, whilst external reality may exist, we only have substantive knowledge of our representations of it, and little knowledge of reality-in-itself.[96] According to this view, our representations are predominantly produced by symbolic concepts and processes, rather than by external factors, and cannot, therefore, be said to represent external reality. Our representations of reality, and conceptual schemes, may, at a distant remove, be means of marking distinctions and differences in reality, but they are primarily, and essentially, symbolic systems, in which the meaning of a particular category is determined by its relation to other categories within the system, rather than by relation to a reality external to those categories. This, as has been argued, is also the fundamental premise of Saussurean linguistics and much post-structuralist and postmodernist theory.

Conceptual idealist theorists do accept that there may be some sort of link between reality and our conceptual schemes, but argue that the main task of analysis should be to understand how our conceptual schemes construct reality-for-us, and how that reality then becomes extended into inter-subjective understanding, cultural convention and ideology. One consequence of this approach is that concepts of realism, objectivity and truth come to be regarded as being merely mutually agreed upon conventions: something is 'true' if it conforms to that which has been conventionally and contingently agreed upon (as a result of either inter-subjective debate or hegemonic authority within a particular community) to constitute truth. Truth is, therefore, relative, and the concepts of truth generated by societies are essentially the product of processes of cultural agreement and dispute. Richard Rorty adopts this position, for example, when discussing the ideas of Thomas Kuhn and Paul Feyerabend:

> their views about the incommensurability of alternative theories suggested that the only notions of truth and reference one really understood were those which were relativised to a conceptual scheme ... It seemed possible to say that the question of what was real or true was not to be settled independently of a given

conceptual framework, and this in turn seemed to suggest that perhaps nothing really existed apart from such frameworks.[97]

Philosophical positions such as that expressed by Rorty (which, by the way, includes a serious misreading of Kuhn, who was definitely not a relativist) represents a significant shift from causal realism to conceptual idealism, and to the view that representational systems can only be compared usefully with each other on grounds such as internal coherence, rather than on the grounds of any correspondence to what Rorty calls 'something out there in the world'.[98] According to Rorty, representational systems and conceptual schemes are merely part of the ongoing 'conversation of man-kind', and do not address a reality which lies beyond them.

The view that, whatever reality itself is, it is crucially transformed within theoretical schemes, dominates many contemporary fields. In the discipline of psychology, for example, the dominant tradition of cognitivism contends that our understanding of reality is largely the product of innate mental structures and processes, rather than of external factors. Perceptual data is transformed into symbols which are informed by innate structuring principles, and access to any form of objective or 'real' knowledge in this process is massively overdetermined by the subjective processes involved.[99] Similar emphases on interiority and 'innateness' dominate many other contemporary disciplines, including linguistics, artificial intelligence theory and information science. In fact, according to one critic:

> It is difficult to think of an area of thought which has remained untouched by it [representationalism and relativism] in the last few years. In science, morality, politics, art, literature, history and philosophy the traditionally accepted methods and assumptions have been 'deconstructed' – undermined, revealed as baseless, as merely 'ideological' and relative.[100]

As a consequence of this, 'realism', or what Rorty calls 'universalism', is construed negatively, as a system of representational conventions which 'naturalises' established ideology, legitimates dominant values, and distorts the actual workings of representation. The true nature of representation, as value directed signification, rather than reflection, is obscured, and this also disguises the ways in which knowledge is conventionally coded and communicated within society in relation to dominant systems of power.

Structuralism, post-structuralism and postmodernism constitute one branch of the relativist position outlined by Rorty. Essentially, it is a position based on the primacy of interiority and relativity, and on a rejection of many of the foundationalist premises which stem from the Enlightenment. The value of this relativist tradition in the twentieth century lies in its critique of naive realism, just as the value of Kant's contribution lay in its critique of seventeenth century empiricism. However, as this chapter has outlined, there are major problems, both political and philosophical, associated with the post-Saussurian version of this sceptical, idealist tradition.

Notes

1. Rorty, Richard, 'The World Well Lost', *Journal of Philosophy*, no. 69 (1972).
2. Johnson-Laird, P. N., *The Computer and the Mind* (London: Fontana, 1989), p. 45.
3. Hawkes, Terrence, *Structuralism and Semiotics* (London: Routledge, 1988), pp. 59–60.
4. Ibid., p. 29.
5. Ibid., p. 20.
6. Quoted in Hawkes, op cit., p. 21.
7. Ferdinand de Saussure, *Course in General Linguistics* (New York and London: McGraw-Hill, 1966), p. 70.
8. Hawkes, op cit., p. 26.
9. Saussure, op cit., pp. 20–1.
10. Crystal, David, *Linguistics* (Harmondsworth: Penguin, 1985), pp. 119–22.
11. Hawkes, op cit., p. 22.
12. Tallis, Raymond, *Not Saussure: A Critique of Post-Saussurean Literary Theory* (London: Macmillan, 1995), pp. 88–9.
13. Wittgenstein, L., *Philosophical Investigations* (Oxford: Oxford University Press, 1953), pp. 30–1.
14. Crystal, op cit., pp. 103–4.
15. Searle, John, *Minds, Brains and Science* (London: Penguin, 1989), p. 31.
16. Kirk, G. S., *Myth: Its Meaning and Functions In Ancient And Other Cultures* (Cambridge: Cambridge University Press, 1978), pp. 42–3.
17. Paraphrased from Fell, John L., 'Vladimir Propp in Hollywood', *Film Quarterly*, vol. 30, no. 3 (1977), p. 20.
18. Ibid.
19. Wollen, Peter, '*North by North West*: a Morphological Analysis', *Film Form*, no. 1 (1976), pp. 20–1.
20. Ibid., p. 32.
21. Fell, op cit., p. 27.
22. Erens, Patricia, '*Sunset Boulevard*: a Morphological Analysis', *Film Reader*, no. 2 (1977), p. 30.
23. Wollen, op cit., p. 34.
24. Ibid.

25. Jackson, Leonard, *The Poverty of Structuralism: Literature and Structuralist Theory* (London and New York: Longman, 1991), p. 70.
26. Lévi-Strauss, Claude, *Structural Anthropology* (Harmondsworth: Penguin, 1963), p. ix.
27. Ibid., p. 35.
28. Kirk, op cit., p. 45.
29. Sim, Stuart, 'Structuralism and Post-structuralism', in Hanfling, Oswald (ed.), *Philosophical Aesthetics* (Oxford: Blackwell/Open University, 1992), p. 414.
30. Kirk, op cit., p. 45.
31. Ibid.
32. Lévi-Strauss, op cit., p. 280.
33. Kirk, op cit., p. 58.
34. Lévi-Strauss, op cit., p. 328.
35. Ibid., p. 327.
36. Ibid., p. 328.
37. Lévi-Strauss, Claude, *Structural Anthropology Volume Two* (Harmondsworth: Penguin, 1977 [1973]), p. 133.
38. Wollen, Peter, *Signs and Meaning in the Cinema* (London: BFI/Secker & Warburg, 1969), p. 102.
39. Ibid., p. 93.
40. Ibid., p. 96.
41. Henderson, Brian, 'The Searchers: An American Dilemma', *Film Quarterly*, vol. 34, no. 2 (Winter 1980/81), p. 19, reprinted in Nichols, Bill (ed.), *Movies and Methods Volume II* (Berkeley, CA, Los Angeles, CA and London: University of California Press, 1985), p. 444.
42. Ibid (Nichols), p. 434.
43. Ibid., p. 447.
44. Metz, Christian, *Essais sur la signification au cinéma* (Paris: Editions Klincksieck, 1974); *Film Language: A Semiotics of the Cinema* (New York: Oxford University Press, 1974), p. 93.
45. Ibid., p. 6.
46. Ibid., p. 12.
47. Ibid., p. 14.
48. Ibid., p. 95.
49. Cook, Pam (ed.), *The Cinema Book* (London: BFI, 1990), p. 229.
50. Metz (1974), op cit., p. 146.
51. Ibid., p. 225.
52. Ibid., p. 227.
53. Sim, in Hanfling, op cit., p. 416.
54. Wollen (1969), op cit., p. 102.
55. The published work which Metz draws on is taken almost entirely from French and central European authors, and makes few references to work published elsewhere.
56. Barthes, Roland, *S/Z* (New York: Hill and Wang, 1974), pp. 16–20.

57. Barthes, Roland, *Image-Music-Text* (London: Fontana, 1977), p. 148.
58. Barthes (1974), op cit., p. 5.
59. Ibid., p. 13.
60. Barthes, Roland, 'Introduction to the Structural Analysis of Narratives', *Communications*, 8 (1966).
61. Barthes (1974), op cit., p. 13.
62. Saussure, op cit., pp. 120–1.
63. Derrida, Jacques, *Speech and Phenomena* (Evanston, IL: Northwestern University Press, 1967), p. 140.
64. Derrida, Jacques, *Of Grammatology* (Baltimore, MD: Johns Hopkins University Press, 1974), p. 50.
65. See Chapters 2 and 7 for further analyses of dialectical materialism.
66. Bhaskar, Roy, *Dialectic: The Pulse of Freedom* (London: Verso, 1996).
67. Derrida (1974), op cit., p. 50.
68. Barthes (1974), op cit., p. 13.
69. Passmore, John, *Recent Philosophers* (London: Duckworth, 1985), p. 31.
70. Norris, Christopher, *Uncritical Theory: Postmodernism, Intellectuals and the Gulf War* (London: Lawrence & Wishart, 1992), p. 37.
71. Derrida (1974), op cit., p. 158.
72. Derrida, Jacques, 'Limited Inc abc', Supplement to *Glyph 2* (Baltimore, MD: Johns Hopkins University Press, 1977), p. 150; referenced in Jackson, op cit., p. 290.
73. Culler, Jonathan, *Structuralist Poetics: Structuralism Linguistics and the Study of Literature* (London: Routledge and Kegan Paul, 1975), p. 248.
74. Easthope, Anthony, *British Post-Structuralism Since 1968* (London: Routledge, 1991), p. 197.
75. Norris, Christopher, *Deconstruction: Theory and Practice* (London and New York: Routledge, 1988), p. 99.
76. Sartre, Jean-Paul, *Being and Nothingness* (London: Methuen and Co., 1969), p. 433.
77. Poster, Mark, *Sartre's Marxism* (London: Pluto, 1979), p. 11.
78. Althusser, Louis, *Lenin and Philosophy and Other Essays* (London: New Left Books, 1977a), p. 162.
79. Althusser, Louis, *For Marx* (London: New Left Books, 1977b), p. 229.
80. Althusser, Louis, *Essays on Ideology* (London and New York: Verso, 1984), p. 20.
81. Ibid., p. 21.
82. Thompson, E. P., *The Poverty of Theory and Other Essays* (London: Merlin Press, 1980), p. 204.
83. Althusser (1977a), op cit., p. 160.
84. Harvey, Sylvia, *May '68 and Film Culture* (London: BFI, 1980), p. 38.
85. Ibid., p. 35.
86. Ibid.
87. MacCabe, Colin, 'Realism and the Cinema: Notes on some Brechtian

theses', *Screen* (Summer, 1974), vol. 15, no. 2, p. 12. See also, MacCabe, Colin, 'Days of Hope: A Response to Colin McArthur', in Bennet, Tony, Boyd-Bowman, Susan, Mercer, Colin and Woollacott, Janet (eds), *Popular Television and Film* (London: BFI/Open University Press, 1985), pp. 310–13.

88. Easthope, op cit., p. 35.

89. Lapsley, Robert, and Westlake, Michael, *Film Theory: An Introduction* (Manchester: Manchester University Press, 1988), p. 53.

90. Coward, Rosalind and Ellis, John, *Language and Materialism: Developments in Semiology and the Theory of the Subject* (London: Routledge and Kegan Paul, 1977), p. vi and p. 92.

91. Norris (1992), op cit., p. 71.

92. Holub, Robert C., *Jürgen Habermas: Critic in the Public Sphere* (London and New York: Routledge, 1991), p. 138.

93. Seyers, Sean, *Reality and Reason: Dialectic and the Theory of Knowledge* (Oxford: Blackwell, 1985), p. 19.

94. Greere, R., in Bhaskar, Roy (ed.), *Harre and His Critics: Essays in Honour of Rom Harré With His Commentary on Them* (Blackwell, 1990), p. 17.

95. Woolhouse, R. S., *The Empiricists* (New York and Oxford: Oxford University Press, 1988), p. 109.

96. Trigg, Roger, *Reality at Risk: A Defence of Realism in Philosophy and the Sciences* (New York and London: Harvester Wheatsheaf, 1989), p. 7.

97. Rorty, Richard, *Philosophy and the Mirror of Nature* (Oxford: Oxford University Press, 1980), p. 275.

98. Rorty, Richard, 'Feminism and Pragmatism', *Radical Philosophy*, no. 59 (Autumn, 1991), p. 4.

99. Costall, Alan and Still, Arthur, *Cognitive Psychology Under Question* (London: Harvester, 1987), p. 9.

100. Seyers, op cit., p. 92.

From Political
Modernism to
Postmodernism

The emergence of a politicised, modernist, European art cinema and film culture during the 1960s and 1970s was directly influenced by the French structuralist and post-structuralist tradition. However, the anti-illusionist aesthetic which emerged from journals such as *Cinétique* was also influenced by Soviet montage cinema and film theory. As already mentioned, during the 1950s and 1960s, translations of essays published in *Lef* and *Novy-Lef* became more widely available in western Europe, and the demands for the creation of a revolutionary film language within these journals later went on to influence the growth of an anti-illusionist film aesthetic in France, Germany and other European countries. Many of the most important Russian formalist theoretical principles, including Shklovsky's conception of *ostranenie*, proved congruous with later Althusserian demands for the materialist demarcation and disclosure of dominant ideological forms, whilst the montage cinema of Eisenstein, Vertov and Medvedkin also furnished a historical canon upon which the anti-realist cinema of the 1960s and 1970s was able to build.

Formalist concepts such as *ostranenie*, and Eichenbaum's concept of 'inner speech', also had an impact on another important influence on the development of cinematic political modernism: that of Brecht. Brecht's theory of the *Verfremdungseffekt* was directly influenced by the concept of *ostranenie*, and by films such as *Stachka* (*Strike*, Eisenstein, 1925), *Potemkin* (Eisenstein, 1925) and *Oktyabr* (*October*, Eisenstein, 1928).[1] As with the Soviet writings of the 1920s, translations of Brecht first appeared in French and English during the late 1950s and early 1960s, and also went on to exercise a considerable influence over European film-makers and film theorists.

Although the combined influence of Russian formalism, Soviet montage, Brechtian aesthetics and French post-structuralism provided the foundation for the political modernist cinema which emerged in France during the 1960s, the basis of an anti-illusionist cinema had also been established some years earlier, with the emergence of the *nouvelle vague*. The *nouvelle vague* developed out of *Cahiers du Cinéma*, which had been founded in 1951. However, *Cahiers* did not develop as a journal committed to political modernism during the 1950s, but as one dedicated to exploring the question and role of authorship within the French, European and American cinema. This emphasis on authorship originally emerged as a response to what was perceived to be the shortcomings of existing French mainstream cinema, and was pre-figured in the writings of André Bazin and Roger Leenhardt, both of whom wrote on questions of film and authorship for the journal *La Revue du Cinéma* between 1946 and 1949.[2]

Another important contribution to the growing debate on film authorship was provided by Alexandre Astruc's essay 'Naissance d'une nouvelle avant-garde: la caméra-stylo', which was originally published in *L'Écran Français* in 1948. In his essay, Astruc argued that, just as the novelist used the pen, so the film-maker should employ the camera, as a vehicle through which to express his or her vision and sensibility.[3] After Bazin joined *Cahiers du Cinéma* in 1951 the issue of authorship quickly became the journal's dominant concern, and eventually evolved into *la politique des auteurs*: a concerted campaign of support for the work of those film-makers whom the *Cahiers* critics regarded as true *auteurs*.

In 1954 François Truffaut made what was to become a defining intervention within *la politique des auteurs* when he published his 'Une certaine tendance du cinéma français' in *Cahiers du Cinéma*.[4] In his essay, Truffaut criticised the French cinema of the *tradition de qualité* for its lack of individual creativity, reliance on pre-existing literary classics or scripts, and stylistic uniformity. In addition, Truffaut also advanced a distinction between the *auteur* and *metteur-en-scène* which was to shape the direction taken by *Cahiers du Cinéma* for some years to come. For Truffaut, the *metteur-en-scène* merely adapted existing works of literature, or worked within pre-given formula, whilst the true *auteur* used the cinema to express personal insight. Truffaut's polemical endorsement of *auteurism* set the tone for future *Cahiers* contributions to *la politique des auteurs*, and also provided a theoretical and stylistic underpinning for the emergent *nouvelle vague*.

Although the emphasis on *auteurism* within both *Cahiers* and the *politique des auteurs* was antithetical to the post-structuralist orientation of later cinematic political modernism, the films of the *nouvelle vague* themselves contained a number of stylistic characteristics which a more politicised cinema would later draw upon. So, for example, the films of François Truffaut, Jean-Luc Godard, Claude Chabrol, Jacques Rivette and Eric Rohmer combined an eclectic attitude to genre with an irreverent approach to the established conventions of French film-making. Such extemporisation, combined with a considerable degree of improvisation and experimentation with film style, led, in *nouvelle vague* films such as *Les Quatre cent coups* (*The Four Hundred Blows*, Truffaut, 1959), *Tirez sur le pianiste* (*Shoot the Piano Player*, Truffaut, 1960), *À bout de souffle* (*Breathless*, Godard, 1960) and *Les Cousins* (*The Cousins*, Chabrol, 1959) to stylistic innovations which provided a foundation for the later cinema of political modernism.

Although, the early films of the *nouvelle vague* display a spirit of rebellion against authority and convention, this was primarily directed against the institutions and practices of the *cinéma de papa*, and did not stem from any wider sense of political affiliation or commitment. It is not until the later films of Jean-Luc Godard that such commitment eventually appears, and, whilst Godard's first features, *À bout de souffle* (1960) and *Une Femme est une femme* (*A Woman is a Woman*, 1961), reveal little of the influence of post-structuralism, Brecht, Soviet montage or political engagement, films such as *Vivre sa vie* (*My Life to Live*, 1962), *Les Carabiniers* (*The Riflemen*, 1963), *Le Mépris* (1963) and, above all, *Deux ou trois choses que je sais d'elle* (*Two or Three Things I Know About Her*, 1966), reveal these influences more clearly.

The transition from the romantic anarchism of Godard's earlier films to the Brechtian political modernism of his work of the late 1960s and early 1970s was influenced by a number of different factors, but the most important of these was probably that of the general radicalisation of French intellectual life which emerged following the events of May 1968, when over 10 million workers went on strike in support of demonstrating students. This upsurge of political activity also reverberated within French film culture. For example, the Institut des Hautes Etudes Cinématographiques and the Ecole Nationale de Photographie et de Cinématographie were both closed by student direct action; whilst Godard and Truffaut succeeded in bringing the Cannes Film Festival to a premature end, arguing that the staging of such a festival was inappropriate, given the portentous nature of the events then unfolding on the streets of Paris. Godard was also involved in the formation and activities of the États Générales du Cinéma, an organisation formed by film-workers to establish an alternative system of film production, distribution and exhibition, and which aimed to 'denounce and destroy the reactionary structures of a cinema which has become a commodity'.[5]

Although little substantive reform of the film industry took place following May 1968, and mainstream French cinema continued on much as before, the events of May did precipitate an acceleration of what was already a quickly developing process of radicalisation within certain sectors of French film culture. For example, the Marxist inspired journal *Cinétique* published its first issue in 1969, whilst, in 1970, *Cahiers du Cinéma* sanctioned a new editorial policy which drew heavily upon Maoist precepts. These journals then provided a forum for the development of a post-1968 French film theory and culture which was strongly influenced by the post-structuralist Marxism of Louis Althusser.

In 1968 Godard and Jean-Pierre Gorin formed the Dziga Vertov Group, a grouping of politically committed film-makers inspired by Vertov, Althusserian Marxism and Brecht. Godard made eight films with the Dziga Vertov Group between 1969 and 1972: *British Sounds* (1969), *Pravda* (1969), *Vent d'est* (*Wind From the East*, 1969), *Luttes en Italie* (*Struggles in Italy*, 1969), *Jusqu'a la victoire* (*Till Victory*, 1970), *Vladimir et Rosa* (*Vladimir and Rosa*, 1971), *Tout va bien* (1972) and *Letter to Jane* (1972). Influenced by the context of post-1968 debates over the establishment of a Marxist-materialist, anti-realist film practice, this group of films combined non-linear narrative structures, documentary form, political slogans and non-synchronised sound effects in order to both deconstruct dominant forms of representation, and disrupt processes of spectatorial identification. However, although a film such as *Vent d'est* is far more radical in its rejection of realism and conventional cinematic pleasure than earlier films had been, the two final films which Godard made with the Dziga Vertov collective: *Tout va bien* and *Letter to Jane*, reintroduce a greater degree of both. *Tout va bien*, in particular, marks a move away from the 'rigorous' Althusserian influenced cinema of *Vent d'est*, to the more 'culinary' Brechtian approach adopted in the earlier *Deux ou trois choses que je sais d'elle*.[6]

In addition to Godard and the Dziga Vertov Group, another group of film-makers, often referred to as the 'Left Bank school', 'French new cinema' or *rive gauche*, also made films within a modernist tradition over this period. However, the *rive gauche*, which included film-makers such as Alain Resnais, Georges Franju, Jean Cayrol, Chris Marker, Alain Robbe-Grillet, Agnes Varda and Marguerite Duras, were even more diverse, and divergent in their film-making, than had been the case with the film-makers of the *nouvelle vague*. In addition, unlike the *nouvelle vague*, which was primarily influenced by Hollywood and a repudiation of the *cinéma de papa*, the *rive gauche* was influenced by a more explicitly modernist set of influences, which included the French poetic modernist documentaries of the 1920s, surrealism, and the *nouveau romain*. This combination of influences can be seen in films such as *Les Yeux sans visage* (*Eyes Without a Face*, Georges Franju, 1959), *Nuit et brouillard* (*Night and Fog*, Alain Resnais, 1955), *Hiroshima mon amour* (*Hiroshima My Love*, 1959), *L'Année dernière à Marienbad* (*Last Year At Marienbad*, Resnais, 1961) and *Trans-Europ Express* (*Trans-Europe Express*, Alain Robbe-Grillet, 1967).

Although the films of the *rive gauche* are often distinguished from the work of political modernist film-makers such as Godard, a number of correspondences can be drawn between the two. Like Godard, the *rive gauche* were influenced by a post-structuralist opposition to cinematic illusionism. Film-makers such as Resnais and Marker were also familiar with, and influenced by, both Soviet montage theory and Brechtian aesthetics, whilst Resnais, Varda and Duras used their films to comment directly on political issues. However, what differentiates a film such as Robbe-Grillet's *L'Homme qui ment* (*The Man Who Lies*, 1968) from Godard's *Weekend* (1967) is the extent to which the former is concerned with purely aesthetic issues. Although many of the *rive gauche* film-makers were influenced by the post-1968 concern to develop a politically progressive language of film, this degree of emphasis on the aesthetic places them outside the central trajectory of European political modernism: a trajectory which leads from Godard to the film-makers of the young and new German cinemas.

Just as the *nouvelle vague* emerged in response to the perceived complacencies of post-war commercial cinema, so also did the 'young' and 'new' cinemas in Germany. After the Second World War a Military Government was established in Germany, and the country was divided into four zones of occupation, controlled by British, French, American and Soviet forces respectively. The Military Government continued to exercise power up to 1949, when the Federal Republic of West Germany was formed from the British, French and American zones, and the German Democratic Republic (DDR) from the Soviet zone. However, whilst the DDR became a sovereign state in 1949, full sovereignty was only restored to the Federal Republic in 1955, when the military occupation came to an end, and the Republic joined NATO.

During the period of the Military Government, one of the central objectives of the occupying powers was to establish a post-war constitutional structure in Germany which would inhibit the re-emergence of right-wing nationalist tendencies. In order to meet this objective the constitution which was imposed upon the fledgling Federal Republic in 1949 distributed significant amounts of political power to the eleven regional governments, or *Länder*, rather than to central government. Similarly, in order to make it impossible for the degree of State control of public communication which had characterised the Nazi regime to re-occur, the Basic Law, the judicial charter upon which the constitution of the Federal Republic was founded, also inscribed the rights to freedom of expression and freedom from censorship into West German law.[7]

Nevertheless, the Basic Law did not frame such freedoms in absolute terms, but, rather, in terms which circumscribed and limited their autonomy of practice within a legal obligation of loyalty to the political institutions of the Federal Republic. Although this institutionally qualified expression of the libertarian ideal was initially formulated in order to shield the embryonic, and politically vulnerable Republic, against the various perceived threats to its sovereignty, it also placed judicial restrictions upon freedom of expression, and it was this, in conjunction with other factors, which eventually led to the growth of political protest during the 1960s and 1970s, and, in turn, to the emergence of the young and new German cinemas.

During the period of the Military Government, official campaigns of denazification, censorship and information management were applied to various sectors of civil society. Many film-workers who had collaborated with the Nazi regime were expelled from the film industry during this period, whilst German film production was closely regulated and censored. However, within the western sector the political imperative of managing the discursive content of film also went hand in hand with a covert economic pressure, exerted by American interests, to ensure that the new film market would be dominated by Hollywood.

The German cinema which eventually survived the encumbrances of denazification, censorship, and subjugation to Hollywood, was also forced to depict the current condition and recent history of Germany in ways which accommodated the ideological perspective of the occupying powers. Thus, a film such as *In jenen Tagen* (*In Those Days*, Helmut Käutner, 1947) represented the course of German history between 1933 and 1945 in terms of a struggle between decency and tyrany, just as the Military Government sought to draw distinctions between 'good' and 'bad' Germans as part of the process of institutional and intellectual reconstruction.[8]

However, during the 1950s, and after the advent of the Cold War, the dominant policy of anti-fascism, a policy formally inscribed within the Basic Law itself, gradually gave way to one of anti-communism. At the same time, during this period, West Germany also experienced an economic revival, which brought increased prosperity in its wake. The commercial film culture which emerged from this context was characterised by a tendency to avoid the appraisals of the recent Nazi past which had appeared in films such as *In jenen Tagen*. Instead, escapist genres such as the rural *Heimatfilme*, consoling 'nostalgic' war films, costume romances and comedies proliferated, as West Germany attempted to re-invent itself as a modern, liberal, consumer society.[9]

Many former film-workers purged in 1946 also re-entered the West German film industry during this period, and this led to the emergence of the *Heimatfilme*: the most popular genre of West German film-making during the 1950s. The post-war *Heimatfilme* had its origins in the 1930s mountain films of Arnold Franck, Luis Trenker and Leni Riefenstahl. Films such as Riefenstahl's *Das blaue Licht* (*The Blue Light*, 1932) set courageous German mountaineers against a landscape endowed with grandeur and nobility, and draw on the legacy of German romanticism in attempting to define national identity. However, it was the more prosaic observance of the relationship between individual and rural community in these films, rather than their representation of solitude and the romantic sublime, which was to influence the later *Heimatfilme*.

In addition to the mountain films, the post-war *Heimatfilme* was also influenced by the genre of *Blut und Boden* (blood and soil) films which emerged during the Nazi period. In *Blut und Boden* films, the romantic pantheistic ruralism of the mountain films was converted into a vehicle for the expression of populist, Nazi ideology. A film such as *Ewiger Wald* (1936), which emphasises the inherent superiority of the German people and culture, was even advertised as produced by, and for, the 'National Socialist cultural community'.[10] Although films such as *Ewiger Wald* were saturated with both the ideology of national socialism, and themes and imagery drawn from romanticism, in a way that the later *Heimatfilme* were not, their deification of rural life was to provide a model for the less overtly political, and more domestic representation of German rural arcadia which were to appear in the later genre.[11] The argument that a continuity can be traced from the *Blut und Boden* films to the *Heimatfilme* is also corroborated by the fact that, of the 300 or so *Heimatfilme* produced during the 1950s, many were re-makes of films made during the Third Reich, and a considerable number were made by directors who had worked under the Nazis.[12]

Although *Heimatfilme* such as Hans Deppe's *Grün ist die Heide* (*Green is the Heather*, 1951), and equivocal war films such as Helmut Käutner's *Des Teufels General* (*The Devil's General*, 1954), were extremely popular during the 1950s, by the early 1960s they had begun to lose their appeal, as a younger generation of Germans, who had not experienced the war directly, created a demand for films which displayed a more critical appreciation of recent German history. This loss of support for established generic film-making practices was also accompanied by an increase in Hollywood's penetration of the German home market: a factor which led to yet a further decline in both the quality, and quantity, of German film production. This decline was then further exacerbated by the growth of television, and a concomitant fall in cinema attendance, and, finally, by continued under-investment in home film production.[13]

By the early 1960s the West German film industry was in a state of near collapse, and it was against this background that, at the Oberhausen Film Festival of 1962, Alexander Kluge and twenty-five other young film-makers presented a Manifesto calling for radical reform. The 'Oberhausen Manifesto' launched what soon came to be known as the 'young German cinema'. Like the French *nouvelle vague*, the young German cinema sought to supplant the 'old' cinema of the 1950s, and, in place of the escapist commercialism of the *Heimatfilme*, the Oberhausen film-makers demanded the establishment of a cinema which would be publicly funded, critical in aspiration, and 'free from the conventions of the commercial film industry'.[14]

The young German cinema was founded on a combination of auteurist, modernist and socially purposive axioms, and employed a deconstructive realist aesthetic, influenced by post *nouvelle vague* French post-structuralism, and political modernism.[15] Most of the film-makers within the Oberhausen group also emerged from a background of sponsored, documentary film-making, and this, together with their antipathy towards the gaudy affectations of the *Heimatfilme*, led them to endorse an austere, actuality-based style of modernist film-making. This combination of modernism and documentary realism is particularly evident in the films of the most important Oberhausen film-maker: Alexander Kluge, who drew on Derridean post-structuralism in deploying a form of 'antagonistic realism' in his films. Here, established power relations and conventions were cinematically deconstructed, through the use of techniques which combined fantasy and ironic realism. Kluge also drew on Derrida's concept of *différance* when arguing that his intention was to have his films represent 'difference', or 'differentiation', as a means of both enlarging the consciousness of the spectator, and enabling him or her to escape incorporation within dominant ideological discourses.[16]

However, Kluge repudiated the radical, anti-normative relativism embodied in the idea of *différance*, and drew on the German concept of *Erfahrung* (experience) instead, to argue that the inculcation of an

'ability to differentiate' must be combined with social contextual-
isation, in order that a critically animated spectator might attend to
'social interest', as opposed to mere difference.[17] For Kluge, therefore, the representation of *Erfahrungszusammenhang*, or 'context of
experience', was an essential correlative to the type of associative
film-making style best able to depict differentiation, and he intended
his films to raise the consciousness of the spectator, whilst, at the same
time, presenting a politically interpreted 'horizon of experience'.[18]

In addition to their film-making activities, the new German film-
makers also lobbied for increased state support and subsidy for
German film production. The government, wishing to raise the
cultural status of the German cinema as part of a larger exercise in
national promotion, responded positively to such lobbying, and,
two years after Oberhausen, the Kuratorium Junger Deutscher Film
(Kuratorium) was established by the Federal Minister of the Interior
to support the first and second works of new film-makers. Following
the formation of the Kuratorium, the Films Subsidies Board was also
established in 1968 to provide funds for films deemed to be
culturally 'valuable' and 'extremely valuable'.[19] In addition to these
measures, the Federal Ministry of the Interior also awarded annual
prizes for the best German films of the year, whilst, from the late
1960s onwards, German television began to invest substantially, if
patchily, in film production, until the Television Framework Agreement of 1974 provided a regular stream of funding for new film
production.[20]

One of the principal achievements of Oberhausen was to act as a
catalyst for the development of a film culture which, in addition to
the institutional framework referred to above, also generated a significant audience for a later, alternative art-house cinema. However,
no such ready-made audience existed for the Oberhausen film-makers
themselves, and this, combined with an uncertain sense of their own
aesthetic and political course, eventually led to the movement's
decline. Oberhausen films such as Jürgen Pohland's *Tobby* (1962)
and Peter Schamoni's *Schonzeit für Füchse* (*Closed Season for Foxes*,
1966) were also criticised for their disrespectful and superficial treatment of subject matter, whilst others were criticised for their modish
fixation on the travails of disenchanted German youth. This critical
reaction, combined with the commercial failure of many of the young
German films, eventually led to the break-up of the movement.[21]

By the late 1960s, the pioneering work of the young German
cinema, the introduction of new funding subsidies, and growth of an
art-house film culture, had established a foundation for the emergence of the new German cinema, and for the appearance of film-

makers such as Rainer-Werner Fassbinder, Volker Schlöndorff, Vernor Herzog, Wim Wenders and Hans-Jürgen Syberberg. The increased quantity of funding available to these film-makers also provided the new German films with a greater range of stylistic options than had been available to the Oberhausen group. However, and despite this, the increased resources which the new German cinema enjoyed still remained relatively limited. The funding received from bodies such as the Kuratorium was meant to act as starting capital for production ventures which were then expected to find additional sources of revenue. However, in practice, many new German films were unable to find such revenues, and, as a consequence, the new German cinema remained relatively under-funded throughout the 1970s.[22] One consequence of this was that new German films were unable to emulate the seamless diegetic narratives and *mise-en-scène* of Hollywood films, and, as a result, the films of Syberberg, Fassbinder and others remained characterised by the 'unfinished' quality which had been a feature of the young German cinema.[23]

The young and new German cinemas also came into being committed to an active intervention in social and political debate. One of the factors which influenced this activist orientation was the West German government and establishment's desire to encourage artists, intellectuals and cultural institutions to engage critically with current and historical issues. In promoting such involvement, the establishment hoped to present the international community with an image of the Federal Republic as a model constitutional state, endowed with a culture characterised by freedom of expression and critical engagement.[24] Such projection was important to a country attempting to distance itself from its fascist past, and it was because of this that West German artists and intellectuals enjoyed such licence to criticise the *status quo*. However, the degree of autonomy which film-makers enjoyed as a consequence of this also meant that many films went far beyond the dominant liberal social-democratic consensus, and this eventually led to conflict between film-makers and the political establishment.[25]

In addition to this context of government and official encourage-ment for cinema to participate meaningfully within the public sphere of political debate, the social orientation of the new German cinema was also influenced by the role played by television in fund-ing film production. After 1949 West German television production was divided amongst nine regional broadcasting companies, each of which was required to broadcast a percentage of programming on issues of social and political concern as part of its public service responsibilities. The structure of West German television put in place after 1949 reflected the aspirations and federal character of the Republic and its constitution, and, just as the constitution was fashioned in order to limit the emergence of nationalist tendencies, so, the regional structure of television was also fashioned in order to circumscribe the state's ability to exercise influence over national communications media.

The degree of autonomy which West German television enjoyed was further reinforced by a legal obligation that each broadcasting company should transmit programming which expressed a wide diversity of opinions. However, just as the classical libertarianism of the constitution was limited by the legal requirement to remain loyal to the ideals and political institutions of the Federal Republic, so too was the libertarian pluralism of West German television. What this meant in practice was that, although programming critical of the establishment was encouraged, broadcasters also felt obliged to give priority to consensual opinion.[26] These limitations on pluralism of expression would later pose problems for new German film-makers such as Fassbinder and Syberberg.

During the late 1950s, when the German film industry was close to collapse, German television companies began to buy up film studios in order to invest in film production. However, in accordance with their pluralist aspirations, the companies commissioned independent projects, instead of making films themselves. The public service orientation of television also led to the appearance of many films with a pronounced social and political dimension.[27] For example, one of the television stations with the most developed public service profile, Westdeutscher Rundfunk – which serviced the largest and most important state of North Rhine-Westphalia – commissioned a genre of documentary-based feature films known as the *Arbeiterfilme* (workers films) between 1968 and 1972, as well as Edgar Reitz's *Heimat* (1984).

The new German cinema was, in some respects, unique, in the extent to which its critical, oppositional autonomy was condoned and encouraged by the political establishment. However, conservative forces within the country disapproved of the image of West Germany presented in many new German films, and, after 1977, following a shift to the political right and the political protests which arose around the actions of the terrorist Baader-Meinhof group, support for politically controversial projects began to decline. In 1982 the Christian Democratic Union came to power under the leadership of Helmut Kohl, and immediately established legislation aimed at the privatisation of German television. In conjunction with other factors, this introduction of commercial forces eventually led much of the new German cinema to evolve into a more generic, and politically 'acceptable' form of cinema during the 1980s.

If the period from 1962 to 1978 can be characterised as one in which the young and new German cinemas were able to critically represent social and political reality, the varying predispositions of the film-makers, and differing priorities of the funding bodies, nevertheless led to the emergence of a diversity of stylistic responses to what was a common historical and contemporary situation.[28] For example, in addition to the minimalist approach adopted by Straub, Fassbinder and Syberberg, other types of film-making to emerge over the period included the expressive literary adaptions of Wenders and Schlöndorf, the documentary realism of Erwin Keusch and Christian Ziewer, and the stylistic flamboyance of Rosa von Praunheim and the later Fassbinder. However, within this diverse group of film-makers, the legacy of political modernism is carried on most clearly in the work of Straub, Syberberg and Fassbinder.

The films of Jean-Marie Straub and Danièle Huillet (Straub-Huillet) draw on post-structuralist, political modernist and Brechtian repudiations of illusionism and emotional identification in order to depict an often alienated and corrupt political context. Films such as *Nicht versöhnt oder Es hilft nur Gewalt, wo Gewalt herrscht* (*Not Reconciled or Only Violence Helps Where Violence Reigns*, 1965) and *Chronik der Anna Magdalena Bach* also employ the Brechtian technique of affording the elements of sound, image, language and acting a degree of autonomy from each other. However, the films of Straub-Huillet differ from the plays of Brecht in the extent to which they eliminate unessential elements from the diegesis. The result is an austere and ascetic style of film-making, from which all expressive emotion is purged. This kind of 'materialist' cinema is indebted to Althusserian post-structuralism, and predates the Althusserian inspired cinema and film theory which developed in France after 1968.

Straub-Huillet adopted this minimalist style of film-making out of a determination to create a form of cinematic practice which would be radically different from both the emotion-saturated cinema of the national socialist period, and the normative manoeuvres of the classical Hollywood film. Consequently, and in accordance with the political modernist tenets that the language of dominant cinema reinforces bourgeois ideology, and that early film language proffered a more authentic articulation of popular and working-class experience, Straub-Huillet sought to echo the greater narrative and visual simplicity of early cinema. In addition to this quest for a more authentic simplicity of style, Straub-Huillet also attempted to emulate the ability of early cinema to express symbolic meaning. This concern for the poetic, symbolic power of the image tempers the austere minimalism in the films of Straub-Huillet, and gives them what could be described as an almost transcendent quality.

In addition to the influence of political modernism, early cinema and an intuitionist conception of visual signification, the films of Straub-Huillet were also influenced by the films of Carl Dreyer and Robert Bresson. Straub-Huillet were particularly influenced by Bresson's *Les Dames du Bois de Boulogne* (*The Women of the Bois de Boulogne*, 1945), a film in which sound, gesture and *mise-en-scène* are used in order to minimise psychological realism, and create evocative, formal compositions, which draw the spectator's attention to the materiality of gesture, movement and action in the film. Straub-Huillet were also impressed by Bresson's ability to suffuse the imposing *mise-en-scène* and characterisation within *Les Dames du Bois de Boulogne* with an austere nobility, and by his success in expressing a moral discourse on alienation, anxiety, betrayal and revenge, without recourse to either extensive psychological realism, or artifice of plot.[29]

In *Chronik der Anna Magdalena Bach* (1967), Straub-Huillet seek to convey a sense of Johan Sebastian and Anna Magdalena Bach's moral integrity, and stoic endurance in the face of hardship and exploitation, through an austere cinematic style which also seeks to deconstruct dominant cinematographic conventions. *Chronik der Anna Magdalena Bach* also seeks to achieve a degree of documentary authenticity by chronicling Bach's life and career through a use of original documents, and texts derived from those documents, rather than through the elaboration of a fabricated scenario. This concern with authenticity is also further enhanced by Straub-Huillet's decisions to shoot *Chronik der Anna Magdalena Bach* in the areas where Bach actually lived, and to include music taken from the various stages of his career.[30]

Whilst a variety of means are used to confer *Chronik der Anna Magdalena Bach* with the degree of documentary authenticity referred to above, the film also employs a rigorous, symmetrical compositional structure which lends nobility to the story that is told. *Chronik der Anna Magdalena Bach* is divided equally into ten parts, which are also grouped into four larger sections, each of which correspond to the main narrative divisions within the film. The ratio of duration of shot used in *Chronik der Anna Magdalena Bach* also echoes the formal structure of the film as a whole. Shots range from one second to seven and a half minutes in length, and the duration of each shot is motivated by the overall compositional organisation of the narrative, rather than by the exigencies of plot development or characterisation. Most of the cinematography in *Chronik der Anna Magdalena Bach* is static and fixed. However, when the camera does move, it does so in carefully orchestrated manoeuvres which foreground the artifice involved. In addition, as *Chronik der Anna Magdalena Bach* proceeds towards its conclusion, the duration of shots in the film also becomes progressively shorter, as Bach's own mortality gradually begins to ebb away.

Chronik der Anna Magdalena Bach is, at one and the same time, a love story, a documentary about Bach, an exposé of class exploitation and an attempt to reclaim important aspects of German cultural history. *Chronik der Anna Magdalena Bach* is also one of the greatest achievements of European cinematic political modernism. Not only does it successfully deploy Brechtian alienation and Althusserian 'materialist' devices in order to disrupt audience identification, but it also combines that central objective of political modernism with an imposing expressive quality. This combination of austerity and transcendent expression clearly owes a debt to Bresson, but *Chronik der Anna Magdalena Bach* displays a degree of uncompromising asceticism which goes beyond even Bresson, and which reflects Straub-Huillet's convictions concerning film language, and the cinematic representation of history.

Like Straub, Hans-Jürgen Syberberg was also influenced by both Brechtian aesthetics and a post-structuralist rejection of dominant cinematic form and language, to the extent that he described his *Ludwig: Requiem für einen jungfräulichen König* (*Ludwig: Requiem for a Virgin King*, 1972) as 'a declaration of war against the dominant forms of the cinema of dialogue and the entertainment film in the tradition of Hollywood and its colonies'.[31] However, unlike the austere asceticism of Straub, and the ironic deconstructionism of Godard, Syberberg's films display a preoccupation with spectacle and theatricality which sets them apart from other attempts to establish a 'materialist' counter-cinema.

Syberberg's concern with spectacle stems from his conviction that the early cinema of the silent period was grounded in a use of the spectacular which was ultimately derived from the theatre. Unlike many film-makers and theorists who have insisted on distinguishing the cinema from the theatre, and who have condemned as un-cinematic films which were perceived to be overdependent upon theatrical convention, Syberberg locates the aesthetic origins of the cinema in the theatre's ability to create a self-contained diegetic world. However, Syberberg also argues that the cinema transcends the theatre by virtue of its capacity to take the generation of compelling diegesis to the point where the constraining laws of logic and reason are no longer an inhibiting factor.[32]

Syberberg's films foreground the cinema's impression of reality in a reflexive way, both drawing attention to use of artifice, and maximising the cinema's ability to create affective spectacle. This emphasis on diegetic spectacle is influenced by the cinema of Méliès and the theatre of Brecht. However, it is also derived from Wagner's conception of the *Gesamtkunstwerk*, or 'total work of art', and, whereas it was the more austere music of Bach and Schönberg which influenced Straub, it is Wagner who provides the musical sources for Syberberg's films. It was the influence of Wagner, in particular, which led Syberberg to compose his films so as to achieve spectacular expressive effects, and, just as he believed that the cinema was able to transcend the spatio-temporal limitations of the theatre, he also claimed that film represented the ultimate realisation of the Wagnerian *Gesamtkunstwerk*: a belief which he eventually put to the test in his *Parsifal* (1982).[33]

In basing his approach to film-making on the combination of two such apparently contradictory models as Brechtian political modernism and Wagnerian romanticism, Syberberg developed an eclectic, paradoxical film-making style, which is, at divergent points, alternatively emotionally drenched, anti-illusionist and didactic. At times, Syberberg seeks to re-create the fluidity and inclusiveness of the *Gesamtkunstwerk*, whilst, at others, he adopts the more fragmented, reflexive and tableau style of the Brechtian theatre. One consequence of this is that his films are characterised by striking shifts of mood and perspective, which are often difficult to account for.[34]

In addition to his belief that an affective, performative cinema best realised the intrinsic aesthetic potential of film, Syberberg also argued that a performative orientation was characteristic of the German cinema in general. According to Syberberg, the stylistic influence of the silent film by the theatre was more pronounced in the German cinema of the 1920s than in that of any other country during that period.[35] Syberberg also argued that the performative quality of silent German cinema not only had its origins in expressionism, but also in a German cultural history which encompassed both expressionism and romanticism. Syberberg believes that his films both contribute to this cultural tradition, and draw on it to help shape contemporary conceptions of German national culture and identity.

Syberberg's belief in the importance of the romantic tradition for German cinema and culture made him a controversial and anachronistic figure during the 1970s, when the iconography of romanticism was still associated with the political right, and with the culture of national socialism. However, Syberberg argued that it was not sufficient to repudiate those aspects of the romantic tradition which had been appropriated by the Hitler regime, and it is because of this, that, in his films, he returns to Wagner, romanticism and medieval German mythology. However, this return to romanticism is not undertaken in a spirit of naive approbation, but with the deliberate intent of emancipating what Syberberg regards as authentic expressions of German national identity from their debasement by fascist ideology. Thus, for example, he described his *Ludwig: Requiem für einen jungfräulichen König* and *Karl May* (1974) as 'positive mythologisings of history ...'.[36]

Luwig: Requiem für einen jungfräulichen König and *Karl May*, together with *Hitler: Ein Film aus Deutschland (Hitler: A Film from Germany*, 1977), form a trilogy, within which Syberberg explores the way that fantasy and myth are able to transcend a reality marked by disillusionment and disenchantment. The principal characters in each of these films (Ludwig, Karl May and Adolf Hitler) are flawed individuals, who embrace archaic myths as compensation for the hostile world around them. In *Hitler: Ein Film aus Deutschland*, Syberberg also shows Hitler's appropriation of mythology as both transforming and debasing the utopian myths of the romantic period, and the strategy adopted in the film is to immerse the spectator in the 'destructive element' of Hitlerism, so that a better understanding of how this recasting of the cultural heritage was effected can be reached.[37]

Syberberg has been criticised for turning to such politically controversial subject matter, and has even been accused of harbouring Nazi sympathies.[38] However, Syberberg is not a proto-fascist, but a critic of the way that attempts to understand romanticism have been marginalised within West German establishment and intellectual culture. For Syberberg, the modern German disavowal of the utopian longings which lie at the heart of romanticism has resulted in the 'emotional deadness of Contemporary German society'.[39] Furthermore, he believes that failure to recover the tradition so corrupted by Nazism could lead to new outbreaks of violence, as the forces of the right seek to appropriate the romantic heritage for themselves. For Syberberg, therefore, it is crucial that the romantic legacy is addressed, and, in his films, he seeks to find a way back to the 'spiritual home of the Germans': one which has been lost to a combination of fascism, materialism and rationalism.[40] *Hitler: Ein Film aus Deutschland* is, therefore, directed at 'a psycho-analysis and exorcism of the German unconscious': an unconscious intimately involved with, and unable to escape from, the romantic legacy, its contagion by fascism and its repression by contemporary liberal rationalism.[41]

The work of exorcism performed in *Hitler: Ein Film aus Deutschland* must also be related to a contemporary intellectual concern with *Trauerarbeit*, or, 'process of mourning'. At the basis of this notion is the belief, derived from Freud, that the individual can only overcome the loss of a loved one by undergoing a repeated, painful process of remembering, or *Trauerarbeit*.[42] Syberberg believes that such a work of *Trauerarbeit* must also be carried out in relation to the Nazi period and its legacy, and this is why *Hitler: Ein Film aus Deutschland* seeks to immerse the spectator in the 'destructive element' of Hitlerism.[43] It has been argued that no contemporary German artist has been associated more consistently with the tasks of mourning than Syberberg.[44] However, that process of mourning is not directed entirely at the Hitler period, but at what Syberberg believes to be the commodification of value and loss of utopian vision which has become widespread within modernity. Syberberg's films, therefore, constitute nothing less than a 'program of cultural revolution', directed against this legacy of commodification, repression and loss.[45]

Syberberg identifies German identity with irrationalist tendencies, and his criticism of both Nazism and contemporary liberal rationalism is based on his belief that the irrationalist tradition was first corrupted by fascism, and then repressed within contemporary German society:

> Hence everything that is mysticism, *Sturm and Drang* ... the Romantic period, Nietzsche, Wagner and Expressionism ... were surrendered, relocated, repressed ... Germany was spiritually disinherited and dispossessed ... We live in a country without a homeland, without 'Heimat'.[46]

The neo-romantic aesthetic which characterises Syberberg's work can also be found in the films of other directors active within the new German cinema, and, although evident at its most pronounced in Syberberg's films, is also apparent in the films of Wernor Herzog, Wim Wenders, Werner Schroeter, Rainer-Werner Fassbinder and Herbert Achternbusch.[47] This strand within the new German cinema was referred to at the time as 'sensibilism', and was contrasted with a 'contentist' tradition, which employed more realistic, didactic forms of social critique. As already argued, this sensibilist tradition was influenced by the German romantic tradition, and classical

German philosophy. However, the sensiblist rejection of reason and rationality was also reinforced by the failure of the left to effect significant radical change in West Germany, following the radical upsurge of 1968. One consequence of this is that sensiblist films such as Syberberg's *Karl May*, Herzog's *Jeder für sich und Gott gegen alle* (*The Enigma of Kaspar Hauser/Every Man For Himself and God Against All*, 1974) and Wender's *Im Lauf der Zeit* (*Kings of the Road*, 1976) abandon a direct engagement with social and political issues, to focus on more abstract themes of alienation and isolation.

Like Syberberg, Rainer Werner Fassbinder was also influenced by the anti-illusionist post-structuralist aesthetic which developed in Europe following the events of May 1968. Like Syberberg, Fassbinder also wanted his films to play a role in provoking political and social change in West Germany, although Fassbinder's contribution was on a far less monumental scale than was the case with Syberberg's epic *Gesamtkunstwerks*. Like Syberberg, Fassbinder also directed his own 'trilogy' of films dealing with issues affecting German society, but Fassbinder's films avoid epic subject matter, and focus instead on the 'micropolitics of desire'.[48] Thus, his 'FRG Trilogy', which consists of *Die Ehe der Maria Braun* (*The Marriage of Maria Braun*, 1978), *Lola* (1981) and *Veronika Voss* (1982), is conceived of as an 'allegory of the Federal Republic during the Economic Miracle', which is told through charting the biographies of three individuals, rather than the movement of abstract political and social forces.[49]

Fassbinder's films link the representation of individual characters to social problematics, through depicting the hopes, aspirations and frustrations of people caught up in concrete historical circumstances. Thus, although his films are always concerned with the personal, individual experience is always given a social dimension. Although many of the themes which he is concerned with in his films also have a universal relevance, Fassbinder also believes that they are particularly characteristic of a post-war German society which, in suppressing the memory of its own history, has adopted a configuration of more innocuous values, which exclude all utopian and spiritual possibilities. Fassbinder was particularly influenced by the radical, utopian, anarchic ideals of 1968, and went so far as to describe himself as a 'romantic anarchist'.[50] Like others within the new German cinema, he regretted the fact that post-war German culture had turned away from such idealism, and his films depict the replacement of these ideals by more functional forces. Although Fassbinder's view of the contemporary human condition is a generally pessimistic one, his films also suggest that one means of transcending alienation and exploitation can be located within the power of love. This veneration of interpersonal love appears often in Fassbinder's films, and particularly in scenes in which the ability of love to overcome social, racial, sexual and other forms of prejudice is depicted.

Fassbinder's concern with the micro-politics of desire and the exigencies of everyday experience also influenced his approach to the use of film form. Initially influenced by the austere stylistics of Straub, Fassbinder later rejected Straub's films as too lacking in emotion, and, therefore, as inaccessible to a mass audience. Fassbinder then became increasingly influenced by the American films of the German *emigre* director Douglas Sirk, and particularly by the way in which Sirk's films deployed *mise-en-scène*, music, melodrama and costumery to covertly critique the values and life-style of American society. After 1971 Fassbinder's films increasingly adopted Sirkian melodramatic forms, and, as a consequence, became more available to larger audiences. This eventually led to the commercial and critical success of *Die Ehe der Maria Braun*, one of the most widely seen films of the new German cinema.

The influence of Brecht is also clearly discernable in many of Fassbinder's films. However, Fassbinder combined Brechtian aliena- tion devices with melodramatic techniques derived from Sirk to make films which are often, and sometimes contradictorily, both affective and distancing. Fassbinder adopted this approach because he wanted to make his audience feel, as well as think, and went so far as to argue that he had 'gone further' than Brecht in achieving such a synthesis.[51] This combination of Brechtian distanciation and Sirkian melodrama is clearly apparent in *Die Ehe der Maria Braun*, where Fassbinder uses off-screen sound and noise, unusual camera angles, and chaotic crowd scenes, in order to create a distance between film and viewer during scenes in which events and dialogue are rendered in melodramatic fashion. Despite its use of conventional film form, therefore, *Die Ehe der Maria Braun* uses Brechtian tech- niques throughout to create intellectual and social, as well as indivi- dual and emotional readings of characters and events.

Whilst German political modernism took on board the full theoreti- cal import of French post-structuralism, British political modernism was, at least initially, more influenced by a combination of the anarchic rebellious spirit and stylistic eclecticism of the *nouvelle vague*, and by the work of Brecht. One consequence of this was that the political modernist theory of Lacan, Althusser, Foucault and Derrida entered the British cinema later than was the case in France and Germany, and a clear distinction must be drawn between the theoretically informed mainstream art cinema which appeared in

those two countries during the late 1960s, and the far less theoretically grounded films which emerged in Britain.

One of the sources of a Brechtian, rather than post-structuralist or
political modernist British cinema, was the 'free cinema' school of
documentary film-making. Although influenced by the earlier
British documentary film movement, free cinema rejected the models
of journalistic documentary film-making advanced by John Grierson
and others within the documentary film movement. However, free
cinema did distinguish between Grierson and his associates on the
one hand, and Humphrey Jennings, on the other. Films such as *Spare
Time* (Jennings, 1939) and *Listen to Britain* (Jennings, 1942) were
regarded as models upon which a new documentary film practice
could be created, and Karel Reisz, one of the founder members of free
cinema, has described Jenning's *Fires Were Started* (1943) as the
'source film for Free Cinema'.[52] The first programme of 'free cinema'
screenings took place in August 1956 and consisted of *O Dreamland*
(Lindsay Anderson, 1953), *Momma Don't Allow* (Tony Richardson
and Karel Reisz, 1956), and *Together* (Lorenza Mazzati, 1953). This
was then followed by five other screenings, which took place
between 1956 and 1959, and which included films such as *Everyday
Except Christmas* (Anderson, 1957) and *We are the Lambeth Boys*
(Reisz, 1959).

Free cinema film-makers such as Lindsay Anderson saw themselves as working within a British tradition of humanist realist
representation within the arts which had little connection with
developments within European modernism.[53] Anderson also proclaimed that, although free cinema was widely considered to be a
'movement', it had little or no theoretical base, and he went on to
characterise the underlying ideology of the free cinema film-makers
as one of 'humanist individualism'.[54] Such a position was, of course,
antithetical to the post-structuralist, political modernist cinema
which was later to develop in France and Germany.

In 1956, Tony Richardson produced John Osborne's play *Look
Back in Anger* at the Royal Court Theatre in London. This initiated
the Brechtian inspired British 'new wave' in the theatre, and, in
1958, Osborne and Richardson established the Woodfall Films
production company in order to introduce the new wave to the
cinema. In 1959 Richardson made his feature film debut with *Look
Back in Anger* (1959), and followed this with *The Entertainer* (1960),
A Taste of Honey (1961), *The Loneliness of the Long-distance Runner*
(1962) and *Tom Jones* (1963). In films such as *The Loneliness of the
Long-distance Runner*, *Tom Jones*, *Saturday Night and Sunday Morning*
(Karel Reisz, 1960) and *If ...* (Lindsay Anderson, 1968), Brechtian

techniques are combined with stylistic traits borrowed from the *nouvelle vague*. This fusion of Brecht and the *nouvelle vague* can also be found in a more ironic and pastiche manner in the 'Swinging London' films: *Darling* (Schlesinger, 1965), *Alfie* (Lewis Gilbert, 1966), *The Knack* (Richard Lester, 1965), *Georgy Girl* (Silvio Narizzano, 1966), *Morgan: A Suitable Case For Treatment* (Reisz, 1966), *Billy Liar* (Schlesinger, 1963) and *Blow Up* (Michelangelo Antonioni, 1967).

The majority of these films are better associated with the *nouvelle vague* than with cinematic political modernism, and even a film such as *If* ..., with its eclectic mix of light-weight surrealism and Brechtian distanciation devices, must be sharply distinguished from works of political modernism such as Straub's *Chronik der Anna Magdalena Bach* and Godard's *La Chinoise*: both of which appeared around the same time as *If* .... One British film from this period which could be more justifiably associated with European political modernism is Michelangelo Antonioni's *Blow Up*. *Blow Up* uses distanciation devices to deconstruct the superficiality of 'swinging London', and to show the sense of alienation and lack of meaning which Antonioni believes underlies that society. However, and as will be argued in Chapter 9, *Blow Up* is better defined as a work of phenomenological realism, rather than political modernism. In addition, although made in Britain, *Blow Up* is quite different from *nouvelle vague* inspired films such as *If* ..., and should be placed alongside other Antonioni films of the period, such as *Deserto rosso* (*The Red Desert*, 1964) and *Zabriskie Point* (1969).

In 1966 the London Film-Makers Co-Op was founded in order to establish an alternative system of film production, distribution and exhibition which would challenge the dominance of the commercial cinema. The *avant-garde* film-making which emerged from this and similar organisations was primarily concerned with formal experimentation, rather than political engagement, and film-makers such as Stephen Dwoskin and Malcolm LeGrice experimented with the formal structure, characteristics and potential of the film medium in much the same way as the French *cinéma pur* movement of the 1920s had. This rejection of the institutions and practices of mainstream cinema was, therefore, undertaken largely for aesthetic purposes, and this differentiated the British *avant-garde* of 'structural' film-making from most French and German political modernism.

This tradition of predominantly aesthetic, as opposed to political modernism, eventually gave way to the emergence of more politicised theories and practices of film-making during the 1970s. In his 1975 essay 'The Two Avant-gardes', Peter Wollen argued that two distinct schools of *avant-garde* cinema could be identified: a British and North American tradition of 'structural' *avant-garde* film-making; and a European tradition of political modernism associated with the films of Godard, Straub/Huillet and others.[55] Wollen's distinction between Anglo-American formalism and European political modernism reflected a broader distinction between modernism and the *avant-garde* which became widely accepted during the 1970s, and in which aesthetic modernism was generally condemned as either politically irrelevant or reactionary, whilst politically engaged *avant-gardism* was strongly endorsed.

These distinctions between modernism and the *avant-garde* were adopted by *Screen* in Britain, and the theoretical questions raised by *Screen* also influenced British independent film-making during the late 1970s and 1980s. Wollen and Mulvey's *Riddles of the Sphinx* (1977) and *Amy!* (1980) drew on the post-structuralist psycho-analytic theory of Jacques Lacan, and on *Screen* theory in general; whilst Sue Clayton and Jonathan Curling's *The Song of the Shirt* (1979) drew on a reflexive, deconstructionist tradition influenced by Godard's films of the 1968–75 period. Other films which fall into this category include *Telling Tales* (Richard Woolley, 1978), *In the Forest* (Phil Mulloy, 1978), *News and Comment* (Frank Abbott, 1978), *Thriller* (Sally Potter, 1979), *Often During the Day* (Joanna Davis, 1979) and *Taking A Part* (Jan Worth, 1979).[56]

All of these films conform more or less to Peter Wollen's model of 'counter-cinema', one which he derived from his analysis of *Vent d'est*, and which he set out in his essay 'Godard and Counter-Cinema: Vent d'est', in 1972.[57] For Wollen, the films of a progressive counter-cinema are characterised by indeterminate and fractured narrative structures, incomplete characterisation, a lack of diegetic closure, reflexivity, and the disruption of spectatorial identification. However, because such films as *Riddles of the Sphinx* rejected classical narrative forms to the extent that they did, they remained the province only of committed minority audiences. In fact, there are grounds for arguing that such films should not be classed alongside the political modernist, commercial art cinema which appeared in France, Germany and elsewhere in Europe during the 1970s, and are more appropriately placed alongside other experimental film traditions which developed during the same period.

Outside of France, Germany and Britain, political modernist commercial art cinema also flourished elsewhere in Europe. In 1970 the Yugoslavian director Dušan Makavejev made *WR: Misteriji organizma* (*WR: Mysteries of the Organism*), a film which deconstructs conventional attitudes towards sexuality through its treatment of cinematic genres. The Hungarian film-maker Miklós Jancsó's

Fényes szelek (*The Confrontation*, 1969), *Agnus Dei* (1970), *La Tecniqa e il rito* (*Technique and Rite*, 1971), *Még kér a nép* (*Red Psalm*, 1971), *Roma rivuole Cesare* (*Rome Wants Another Ceasar*, 1973) and *Szerelmem Elektra* (*For Elektra*, 1974) are political allegories which fuse past, present and future into a continuum. They are also filmed using highly stylised *mise-en-scènes* and very long takes: *Szerelmem Electra* being composed of only ten shots. Jancsó's films also embody a typically post-structuralist preoccupation with struggles for power. For example, his best-known film, *Még kér a nép*, is concerned with the struggle between Hungarian peasants and landowners. Drawing on a variety of symbols associated with revolutionary activity, *Még kér a nép* uses moving camerawork, and a tableau format which reveals the influence of both Brecht and Godard.

Like Jancsó, and, indeed, many other political modernist film-makers, the films of the Greek director Theo Angelopoulos also focus on issues of national history and political struggle. So, for example, his *Mères tou 36* (*Days of '36*, 1972), which focuses on the murder of a militant union leader, becomes an allegory of political repression in Greece in general, whilst *O Thassios* (*The Travelling Players*, 1975) covers political struggles in Greece over the period between 1939 and 1952. *O Thassios* also employs performative and reflexive techniques which, in combination with its formal use of camera movement, and long-take photography, leads to a degree of anti-illusionism clearly inspired by Brecht, Straub and others.

Films such as *O Thassios* reflected the kind of ascetic, anti-illusionist interpretation of Brecht which was prevalent during the early to mid 1970s. This type of spare style was also adopted by the Belgian film-maker Chantal Akerman, who deployed it in an attempt to represent the subjugated condition of women within patriarchal capitalist society. Like the films of Jancsó and Angelopoulos, Akerman's *Jeanne Dielman, 23 Quai du commerce, 1080 Bruxelles* (1975), also employs static, long-take and moving camerawork, and deploys such techniques in conjunction with classically choreographed framing and camera movement to both represent exploitation, and render the central character with a degree of dignity. Although *Jeanne Dielman, 23 Quai du commerce, 1080 Bruxelles* is a highly modernist film in the extent to which it both undermines illusionism and disrupts processes of spectatorial empathy, like other political modernist films, its use of formal technique is directed at the representation of political repression, resistance and exploitation, rather than at the production of a purely aesthetic artefact.

By the mid 1980s political modernism within the commercial art cinema was in decline. The product of a politicised period, it began to wither away as the hopes for radical political change in Europe also receded. However, the turn away from political modernism was also influenced by the fact that, by virtue of its reliance upon an anti-realist aesthetic, political modernist cinema was unable to attract a mass audience: a fact which effectively undermined its aspiration to play a vanguardist role within a hoped for process of revolutionary change. One consequence of this was that, from the mid 1980s onwards, the boundaries between political modernism and a more general European art cinema became less clear. However, yet another was the emergence of a number of films which have since been labelled postmodern.

The links between the European 'postmodern' cinema of the 1980s and 1990s, and the post-structuralist and postmodernist theory of figures such as Derrida, Lyotard and Baudrillard, are far from transparent, and few, if any, of the European films commonly referred to as postmodern have been directly or substantively influenced by the ideas issuing from such theorists. On the contrary French film-makers, such as Luc Besson, Léos Carax and Jean-Jacques Beineix, were primarily influenced by stylistic develop-ments which occurred within the American cinema, and it was films such as *Chinatown* (Polanski, 1974), *American Graffiti* (Lucas, 1973) and *Star Wars* (Lucas, 1977), rather than post-Saussurian theory, which were the inspiration for European 'postmodern' films such as Beineix's *Diva* (1982).

Despite this, a number of clear conceptual correspondences can be traced between postmodern philosophy and postmodern cinema. Postmodern philosophy emphasises creativity, libertarianism, avoid-ance of value judgements, eschewal of analysis and a rejection of both authoritarianism and grand narratives. Similarly, postmodern cinema erases distinctions between high and low art, mixes styles and genres together in defiance of existing (authoritarian) rules of taste, and employs irony, pastiche and historical indeterminacy in place of directive conceptual analysis. It is the existence of such correspondences which has led some to link films such as *Diva* and Luc Besson's *Subway* (1985) to the tradition of Derridean, post-Saussurian philosophy, and to the deconstructionist values contained within that philosophy.

Claims for the radical and progressive potential of postmodern cinema are often based on the perceived presence of these values. So, for example, Kobena Mercer has argued that *Handsworth Songs* (John Akomfrah, 1987) deconstructs dominant representations of race and ethnicity by creating a collage of actuality footage, interviews and reconstructions, which does not propose any final interpretation of the events which it portrays.[58] Mercer and others also argue that films such as *Handsworth Songs* form part of a postmodern critical practice which avoids the essentialism inherent in the post-structuralist modernist tradition, and which, therefore, establishes a 'counter-practice' in place of the more ideologically prescriptive 'counter-cinema' of the 1970s. Similarly, Ella Shohat and Robert Stam argue that it is qualities such as pluralism, lack of closure and difference that are the chief virtues of a postmodern cinema.[59]

This model of a postmodern *avant-garde* cinematic aesthetic practice can be distinguished from the more analytic thrust of earlier, post-structuralist cinema, and it is the refusal to provide any sort of ordering vision which divides postmodern from post-structuralist cinema. The emphasis on indeterminacy of meaning within a postmodern *avant-garde* cinema must also be distinguished from both the advocacy of indeterminate signification in the theories of Bazin and Kracauer, and the approach adopted by the modernist cinemas of impressionism, expressionism and surrealism. The essential difference between cinematic postmodernism and these realist and modernist theories and cinemas lies in the fact that, whereas postmodernism employs indeterminacy in order to defer and place limits on the search for an 'essential' core of meaning, Kracauer's conception of 'distraction', and the impressionist conception of *photogénie*, employ indeterminacy as a means of understanding underlying realities. Whilst postmodernist indeterminacy is structured so as to lead the spectator across a range of ideas, realist and modernist indeterminacy is structured so as to lead the spectator into insight.

Advocates of postmodernism regard this emphasis on insight as problematic, and as the inevitable consequence of an intellectual tradition founded on the need to establish ideological 'meta-critiques'. However, concepts such as distraction, surrealist *dépaysement'* and *photogénie*, were originally developed in order to expand the possibilities of signification within a context of the growing commodification of culture. The problem with much postmodern cinema is that, in limiting its analytic thrust, and achieving what Fredric Jameson has called a 'depthlessness' of representation, it often mimics the form of the commodity, and, in so doing, reinforces the ongoing commodification of cultural value to which the intuitionist realist and modernist tradition was so opposed.[60]

Jameson argues that postmodern culture is the outcome of a continuing intrusion of the logic of capitalist exchange into the field of culture: an intrusion which has the effect of turning cultural artefacts into consumable goods, rather than vehicles for the expression of complex and difficult ideas. Consequently, Jameson argues, postmodern cinema should not be regarded as an intrinsically progressive development, but, on the contrary, as a manifestation of the 'cultural logic of late capitalism'.[61] However, Jameson does draw distinctions between a film such as Brian de Palma's *Blow Out* (1981), which he regards as 'depthless' in the above mentioned sense, and a film such as *Diva*, which, he argues, critiques aspects of the post-modern condition.[62]

This distinction leads Jameson to argue that postmodern cinema includes some films which embody the commodity form, and others which, whilst employing postmodern stylistic characteristics, use those characteristics to effect significant critique. For example, Jameson argues that *Diva* can be related to a specific historical conjuncture: that of the appearance of the 'first left government in France for thirty-five years', and that the film can be regarded as a political allegory which seeks to propose 'imaginary solutions of real contradictions' which exist within French political culture.[63] Jameson uses this idea of the role of art as proferring such imaginary resolutions and 'conflictual reconciliations' to draw distinctions between a commodified and a more valuably progressive postmodern cinema.

Two recent movements of film-making which have emerged in France and England, and which are frequently defined as postmodern, are the *cinéma du look* and the heritage film. The first film made within the *cinéma du look* was probably Beineix's *Diva* (1980), which Jameson has described as the 'first French postmodern film', and the three directors most clearly associated with the *cinéma du look* are Beineix, Luc Besson and Léos Carax. Films usually asociated with the *cinéma du look*, include *Subway* (Besson, 1985), *Le Grand bleu* (*The Big Blue*, Besson, 1987), *37.2 le Matin* (*Betty Blue*, Beineix, 1986), *Nikita* (Besson, 1990) and *Les Amants du Pont-Neuf* (*The Lovers of the Pont-Neuf*, Léos Carax, 1991). All are characterised by a tendency towards intertextual reference, and the use of reflexive, spectacular visual style. Although criticised for their apparent superficiality, and lack of concern for contemporary social and political issues,[64] it has also been argued that the 'punk hyperrealism' found in a film such as *Les Amants du Pont-Neuf* reflects a 'profound nihilism', which is based (ironically, given the extent of the film's reliance on media forms such as advertising), on a rejection of the values of consumer society.[65]

In addition to the films of the *cinéma du look*, another genre of films often defined as postmodern are the *retro* films of the 'heritage' and 'cultural tourism' cinemas. As we have seen, Jameson has argued that, in a postmodern cinema, in which films increasingly refer to an all pervasive media reality, rather than to a reality lying outside media representations, depictions of historical reality loose their specificity, and become 'depthless'. Consequently, in both the English heritage cinema and the French cultural tourism cinema, history becomes a site for the mobilisation of familiar stereotypes, and, frequently, stereotypes which are grounded in an identification with, and audience awareness of, other media representations.

In an English heritage film such as *A Room With a View* (Merchant-Ivory, 1986), history is used both as a source of consumable visual spectacle, and for the deployment and reinforcement of already widely understood conceptions of identity. Films such as *A Room With a View* and *Chariots of Fire* (Hugh Hudson, 1981) use pastiche, irony and self-conscious reflexivity in order to contain reflective analysis and historical specificity, and the same approach is adopted in French 'cultural tourism' films such as *Jean de Florette* (Claude Berri, 1986), *Manon des sources* (*Manon of the Source*, Berri, 1986), *La Gloire de mon père* (Yves Robert, 1990), *Le Château de ma mère* (Yves Robert, 1990), *Cyrano de Bergerac* (Jean-Paul Rappeneau, 1990), *Tous les matins du monde* (Alain Corneau, 1992) and others.

Nevertheless, and following Jameson, distinctions must be made between a progressive postmodern film such as *Jean de Florette*, with its abrasive depiction of rural French recidivism, and films such as *Le Château de ma mère*, which are far more clearly associated with the heritage 'cultural tourism' cinema of commodified postmodern cinema. Many of the French films often described as heritage can also be associated with the *tradition de qualité*, a realist tradition of film-making which will be described in greater depth in Chapter 8. What matters most, in the best of these films, is the balance achieved between genuine critique, and what Jameson has referred to as the less significant 'acting out of the reproductive process',[66] and it remains the case that some films made within the English and French heritage cinema appear deeply marked by the demands of commodification. For example, although it has been argued that a film such as *A Room With a View* contains critical material on sexual repression within English middle-class society,[67] the depictions of sexual repression which the film mobilises are delivered within the parameters of the well-established, and marketable, stereotype that the English are, indeed, sexually repressed. *A Room With a View* does not throw this stereotype into question, but, on the contrary, reinforces it in order to enhance the film's marketability.

Notes

1. Walsh, Martin, *The Brechtian Aspect of Radical Cinema* (London: BFI, 1981), p. 129.
2. Andrew, Dudley, *André Bazin* (New York: Columbia University Press, 1990), pp. 146–7.
3. Astruc, Alexandre, 'The Birth of a New Avant-Garde: la caméra stylo', *L'Ecran français* (1948), reprinted in Peter Graham (ed.), *The New Wave* (Garden City: Doubleday, 1967).
4. Truffaut, François, 'Une certaine tendance du cinéma français', in *Cahiers du cinéma* (1954), no. 31.
5. Williams, Alan, *Republic of Images* (Cambridge, MA and London: Harvard University Press, 1992), p. 389.
6. Willett, John, *Brecht On Theatre* (New York and London: Hill and Wang and Eyre Methuen, 1978), p. 389.
7. Porter, Vincent and Collins, Richard, *WDR and the Arbeiterfilm: Fassbinder, Ziewer and Others* (London: BFI, 1981), p. 7.
8. Kaes, Anton, *From Heimat to Hitler: The Return of History as Film* (Cambridge, MA and London: Harvard University Press, 1992), p. 12.
9. Ibid., p. 18.
10. Petley, Julian, *Capital and Culture: German Cinema 1933–45* (London: BFI, 1979), p. 132.
11. Kaes, op cit., p. 15.
12. Ibid.
13. Sieglohr, Ulrike, 'New German Cinema', in Hill, John and Church-Gibson, Pamela (eds), *The Oxford Guide to Film Studies* (Oxford: Oxford University Press, 1998), p. 467.
14. Franklin, James, *New German Cinema* (London: Columbus Press, 1986), p. 27.
15. Elsaesser, Thomas, *The New German Cinema: A History* (New Brunswick: Rutgers University Press, 1989), p. 163.
16. Ibid.
17. Ibid.
18. Ibid.
19. Franklin, op cit., p. 32.
20. Elsaesser, op cit., p. 33.
21. Ibid.
22. Ibid., p. 25.
23. Sieglohr, op cit., p. 469.
24. Ibid., p. 467.
25. Elsaesser, op cit., p. 318.
26. Porter and Collins, op cit., p. 8.
27. Elsaesser, op cit., p. 34.
28. Sieglohr, op cit., p. 468.

29. Roud, Richard, *Straub* (London: BFI and Secker & Warburg, 1971), pp. 19–23.
30. Ibid., p. 82.
31. Kaes, op cit., p. 42.
32. Ibid., pp. 42–3.
33. Jameson, Fredric, *Signatures of the Visible* (New York and London: Routledge, 1992), p. 64.
34. Kaes, op cit., p. 45.
35. Ibid., p. 44.
36. Ibid., p. 59.
37. Jameson, op cit., p. 63.
38. Kaes, op cit., p. 71.
39. Santner, Eric, L., *Stranded Objects: Mourning, Memory and Film in Postwar Germany* (Ithaca, NY and London: Cornell University Press, 1993), p. 130.
40. Kaes, op cit., p. 68.
41. Jameson, op cit., p. 73.
42. Kaes, op cit., p. 69.
43. Jameson, op cit., p. 63.
44. Santner, op cit., p. 103.
45. Jameson, op cit., p. 63.
46. Kaes, op cit., p. 68.
47. Elsaesser, op cit., p. 49.
48. Kaes, op cit., p. 82.
49. Ibid.
50. Ibid., p. 100.
51. Franklin, op cit., p. 143.
52. Aitken, Ian, *The Documentary Film Movement: An Anthology* (Edinburgh: Edinburgh University Press, 1998), p. 60.
53. Orbanz, Eva (ed.), *Journey to a Legend and Back: The British Realistic Film* (Berlin: Edition Volker Spiess, 1977), p. 42.
54. Ibid.
55. Westlake, Michael and Lapsley, Robert, *Film Theory: An Introduction* (Manchester: Manchester University Press, 1988), p. 190.
56. Harvey, Sylvia, 'The "Other Cinema" in Britain: Unfinished Business in oppositional and independent film, 1929–1984', in Barr, Charles (ed.), *All Our Yesterdays: 90 Years of British Cinema* (London: BFI, 1986), p. 241.
57. Wollen, Peter, 'Godard and Counter-Cinema: Vent d'Est', republished in Wollen, *Readings and Writings* (London: Verso, 1982).
58. Mercer, Kobena, 'Recording Narratives of Race and Nation', in Mercer (ed.), *Black Film British Cinema* (London: ICA, 1988),p. 11.
59. Shohat, Ella and Stam, Robert, *Unthinking Eurocentrism: Multiculturalism and the Media* (London: Routledge, 1994), p. 10.
60. Jameson, Fredric, 'Postmodernism, or the Cultural Logic of Late Capitalism', *New Left Review* (1984), no. 146, p. 58.

61. Ibid.
62. Jameson, op cit., (1992), p. 62.
63. Ibid., p. 59.
64. Austin, Guy, *Contemporary French Cinema: An Introduction* (Manchester and New York: Manchester University Press, 1996), p. 119.
65. Williams, op cit., p. 401.
66. Jameson, op cit. (1992), p. 62.
67. Street, Sarah, *British National Cinema* (London and New York: Routledge, 1997), p. 105.

The Redemption of Physical Reality

Theories of Realism in Grierson, Kracauer, Bazin and Lukács

During the 1970s the ascendency of post-structuralism and political modernism drove the realist and intuitionist paradigm, which had dominated European film theory from the 1920s to the late 1950s, to the margins of critical consideration. One consequence of this paradigm shift was that the tradition of realist film theory, in particular, became ignored, ostracised, and seriously misinterpreted. For post-structuralists, realism was an effect of dominant ideological socialisation, and any theory based on realist, as opposed to deconstructionist premises, was complicit in such socialisation. It is only since the late 1970s that substantial critical re-evaluations of the major proponents of cinematic realism have appeared, and this process continues up to the present day.

One of the reasons why the realist film theories of John Grierson, Siegfried Kracauer and André Bazin have been so misinterpreted in the recent past is that critics have failed to fully understand the extent to which they stem from complex philosophical positions. Yet, as this chapter will make clear, the work of all three theorists is derived from the same philosophical tradition, and one which links them to intuitionist movements in European cinema such as impressionism, Weimar modernism, surrealism, and early Russian formalism.

The first major realist film theorist, John Grierson, developed a theory of modernist documentary realism during the 1920s. Grierson believed that film, and documentary film in particular, could play a crucial role within society by providing an effective medium of communication between the state and the public. Grierson initially developed this position during a visit to America between 1924 and 1927, where he undertook a programme of research into the impact of immigration on American society. Whilst in America, Grierson encountered right-wing theorists who argued that traditional systems and conceptions of democratic participation were no longer tenable, and that society should be managed by professional elite groups, which would not be subject to electoral mandate. One of the most prominent of these theorists was Walter Lippmann, who, in his *Public Opinion* (1922), and *The Phantom Public* (1925), argued that democracy was intrinsically flawed, and should be abandoned.[1]

Lippmann was an influential spokesman for a cultural movement which was often elitist, authoritarian and racist. However, Grierson rejected Lippmann's ideas, which he characterised as 'the intellectual's case against the people', and argued, instead, that the arguments put by 'technocrats and managerialists' such as Lippman were similar to 'those of fascism'.[2] In opposition to the hierarchical, elite managerialism espoused by Lippmann, Grierson came to the conclusion that democracy could be made effective if the public was kept properly informed, and he believed that the documentary film could perform this crucial function.

Nevertheless, whilst rejecting Lippmann's general prognosis, Grierson accepted Lippmann's argument that modern mass society was now so complex that the libertarian ideal could no longer apply. Lippmann had argued that the form of cognition common to the mass public was based on generalised subjective judgement, and that it was, therefore, inferior to rational and scientific modes of cognition.[3] Although Grierson rejected the idea that public cognition was necessarily inferior in this way, he accepted Lippmann's contention that the public was often forced, through contingency, to construct generalised 'mental images' from information provided, rather than engage in a rational, cognitive analysis of that information. This led Grierson to argue that the documentary film should not try to teach the public 'to know everything about everything all the time', but, on the contrary, should seek to instil a general, and intuitive, understanding of the significant generative forces active within society.[4] Grierson's approach here is based on a belief that intuition, rather than cognitivist rationalism, offers the best means of understanding complex events, and this intuitionist, anti-rationalist perspective defines Grierson's early theory of cinematic realism.

In addition to the influence of American mass society theory, Grierson's intuitionist theory of cinematic realism was also influenced by German philosophical idealism. Philosophical idealism has a long historical lineage, but achieved its most systematic expression in Germany during the eighteenth and nineteenth centuries, where it made Germany a focal point for metaphysical and anti-materialist ideologies, and for philosophical critiques of the emergence of modernity and capitalism within western Europe. As neo-Hegelian idealism grew in importance in Britain after 1860, it developed into an ideology which emphasised themes of social duty and reform, rule by enlightened elites, and the need to return to the social relations and values of pre-industrial, capitalist England.[5] The idealist tradition in Britain reached the zenith of its influence between 1880 and 1914, after which it declined in importance, and became absorbed into theories which focused on the role of the mass media and popular education in fostering national unity. In particular, the idealist contention that a 'clericy' of intellectuals should co-operate with politicians in order to communicate national objectives to the people, became assimilated into theories on how new mass communications technologies could create channels of consensus between the State and the public.

A concern with social communication and civic education was, therefore, central to idealist thought, and, after 1918, many idealists, including John Grierson, became involved in the establishment of a public service role for the new social media of radio and film. Grierson first gained access to idealist thought through his father, who introduced him to the work of Carlyle, Byron and Ruskin.[6] After this he studied idealist philosophy at Glasgow University, where he read Plato, Kant and Hegel, and became influenced, in particular, by the works of the neo-Hegelian philosopher F. H. Bradley, and the idealist-socialist philosopher, A. D. Lindsay.[7] From these various influences, Grierson developed an intellectual position based on a belief in the importance of the State and corporate institutional structures, an opposition to both unregulated capitalism and populist democracy, and a conviction that non-cognitive intuitive experience could achieve greater insight than rational understanding.

One of the central concepts within philosophical idealism is that of totality. Grierson rejected the Marxist idea that fundamental divisions existed within society, and argued instead that social life was characterised by a 'matrix of inter-dependent relations', and that, consequently, societies and institutions which were highly integrated were superior to those which were less so.[8] These views led Grierson to place considerable stress on the role of the State in ensuring social unity, and, according to Grierson, when the State constrained individualism or sectarianism in the interests of social unity, it exercised 'good totalitarianism'.[9] Grierson's stance here appears somewhat authoritarian. However, that authoritarianism is attenuated by a distinction which he drew between the 'institutions' and 'agents' of State, in which he argued that the individual should be free to pursue an oppositional agenda under circumstances where the institutions of State had been subverted by its agents for sectarian purposes. However, although this distinction mediates what would otherwise amount to a classical authoritarian theory of the media, and also provides some basis for the emergence of a critical film-making practice, Grierson's insistence that intellectuals and film-makers must not step beyond what he called the 'degree of general sanction' effectively ruled out fundamental criticism of the basic institutional structure of society.[10]

In addition to his influence by idealist conceptions of the relations between State and civil society, Grierson was also influenced by a number of idealist aesthetic positions founded on intuitionist premises. He was particularly influenced by Kant's assertion that the basis of aesthetic experience lay in the perception of complex unities and harmonies, and argued that the role of art was to present such harmonies to the spectator, so that they would symbolise the 'harmonised relations of life' which the individual sought.[11] Another important influence on Grierson was Bradley's conviction that the existential complexity of underlying reality could only be experienced intuitively, and not through conceptual reason.[12] Grierson's reading of Bradley was later reinforced by his encounter with Lippmann's ideas on social communication within modern mass society, and these influences led him to the conviction that, in order to communicate effectively, art must employ generalised and symbolic, rather than didactic or pedagogic modes of expression.[13]

From these various influences Grierson arrived at a definition of the principal function of the documentary film as that of representing the interdependence and evolution of social relations in a dramatic, descriptive and symbolic way. This function was simultaneously sociological and aesthetic: sociological, in that it involved the representation of social relationships; and aesthetic, in that it involved the use of imaginative and symbolic means to that end.[14] Grierson also argued that the documentary film was ideally suited to represent the interconnected nature of social relationships because it was 'the medium of all media born to express the living nature of inter-dependency ... (it) ... outlined the patterns of inter-dependency more distinctly and more deliberately than any other medium whatsoever'.[15]

Examples of such images of interdependency can be found in most of the major early films made by the documentary movement. For example, in *Drifters* (Grierson, 1929), montage is used to illustrate the way that the practices, labour, culture and institutions of the deep sea fishing industry combine to form a holistic whole. Similarly, in *The Song of Ceylon* (Basil Wright, 1934), the links between the traditional and the modern, the religious and the secular are emphasised; whilst, in *Night Mail* (Harry Watt, Basil Wright and others, 1936), the nation is shown as bound together through its communication processes. In all these films, and despite their documentary status, descriptive information is combined with, and often dominated by, impressionistic techniques whose primary function is to express a poetic sense of unity and fusion.

Grierson first elaborated his theory of documentary film in 1927, in an unpublished paper entitled 'Notes for English Producers'. In the second part of this paper, entitled 'English Cinema Production and the Naturalistic Tradition', Grierson postulated two different categories of film: one consisting of films between seven and nine reels in length, and the other of films of around four reels. The first of these categories had its origins in the theory of 'epic cinema' which Grierson had elaborated in America in the mid 1920s, in which individual characterisation within the feature film was to be set alongside representations of social and national institutions,[16] in order that the spectator's understanding was directed into a recognition of the 'continuing reality' of the underlying unity of social and interpersonal relationships.[17]

However, Grierson's model of epic cinema bore little relation to the limited budget and resources available when he joined the Empire Marketing Board in 1927; and, in the second section of his 1927 paper, he defined a form of cinema more appropriate to those circumstances. This second category of film production would consist of shorter films whose objective would be to represent 'social interconnection in both primitive cultures and modern industrial society'. Grierson believed that these films would mark a 'new phase in cinema production', and that they would be superior to, and different from, existing actuality film genres[18] in that, within them, visual material 'could be orchestrated into cinematic sequences of enormous vitality' through a sophisticated use of montage editing and visual composition.[19]

Although this initial formulation of the Griersonian documentary explicitly emphasised modernist, formative editing technique, the actuality content of the documentary image remained an important factor for Grierson, as is made clear by a distinction he drew between the 'real' and the 'actual'. Writing about *Drifters*, shortly after its premiere, Grierson argued that the empirical content (the actual) of its documentary images was organised so as to express general truths (the real), which existed at a level of abstraction beyond the empirical, and which could not be directly represented.[20] Grierson's conception of 'the real' was derived from the Hegelian notion of *Zeitgeist*, or 'spirit of the age', and covered the general determining factors and predispositions specific to a particular time and place. Grierson argued that documentary films should be organised so as to express the real, and his first definition of documentary was based on the revelation of the real through the use of documentary footage and formative editing technique. Grierson also believed that the documentary image was better able to signify the real than the image produced within the artificial environment of the film studio, because it registered and transcribed the 'phenomenological surface of reality'.[21]

One of the major influences on Grierson at the time was the Hungarian theorist Béla Balázs, who argued that film was able to express a poetic reality which existed beyond, but could only be comprehended through, the empirical. This emphasis on the importance of the empirical reinforced Grierson's conception of the relationship between the phenomenal and the real, and there is a considerable resemblance between Balázs's assertion that film 'could represent ... the soul's bodily incarnation in terms of gesture or feature', and Grierson's claim that the documentary film could represent 'the characteristic gestures and features which time has worn smooth'.[22] Both formulations are concerned with the way in which the naturalistic image is able to signify abstract realities, and it is this which links the ideas of these two theorists.

Grierson's early theory of documentary film consisted of three principal elements: (1) a concern with the content and expressive richness of the actuality image; (2) an emphasis on the interpretative potential of editing; and (3) the need to represent social inter-relationships. All these aspects can be found in his early film theory, and in some of the films produced by the documentary film movement between 1929 and 1935. After that, the poetic montage style of films such as *Drifters* and *Song of Ceylon* gave way to a more didactic, journalistic style, whilst the earlier concern with philosophical aesthetics was replaced by a more functionalist discourse based around issues of propaganda and instrumental 'civic education'. This radical change of style and emphasis in Grierson's ideas, from the pre-1936 to the post-1936 period, can be explained in terms of a shift from a concern with the phenomenological naturalism of the image, to a more directive style always implicit in Grierson's notion of the creative *interpretation* of reality.

Nevertheless, there is evidence to suggest that, towards the end of his life, Grierson returned to his earlier aesthetic position. In *I Remember, I Remember*, the film which he made for BBC TV in 1970, he described documentary almost entirely in terms of its artistic qualities, and this indicates that the dialectical tension between the aesthetic and the sociological, a tension always implicit within his theory, but one which had been skewed decisively in one direction during the 1937–67 period, had once again reverted to the kind of balance which had characterised his early theory of intuitionist, modernist documentary realism. Grierson's theory of cinematic realism is often criticised for its instrumental tendencies. However, what is often not taken into account in such criticism is that Grierson developed two different theories of documentary realism over the course of his career. Whilst the later model of documentary was philosophically limited, the earlier theory was influenced by a complex synthesis of philosophical idealism, mass society theory, Soviet montage and Weimar film theory, and bears the traces of this sophisticated intellectual heritage.

Like Grierson, Kracauer's theory of cinematic realism was either criticised, misunderstood or ignored during the period when structuralism and post-structuralism formed the dominant strand within international film theory. One of the consequences of this was that the intellectual roots and characteristic themes of Kracauer's ideas were often dismissed, particularly within Anglo-American film criticism, as amounting to a form of 'naive realism', normative system building, or 'conservative humanism'. For example, in The Major Film Theories, Dudley Andrew described Kracauer as a 'traditional democratic and liberal theorist ... solidly, unmistakenly, even fanatically on the realist side';[23] whilst Barry Salt has argued that Kracauer's From Caligari to Hitler imposed inappropriate interpretations upon films, and was a 'candidate for the worst work of film history ever written'.[24]

However, if Kracauer's work has often been criticised within Anglo-American and French critical literature (and the quotations given above are by no means untypical), this has not been the case in Germany, where it has been argued that From Caligari to Hitler and Theory of Film have 'shaped the face of cinema studies'.[25] Furthermore, the relatively recent translation into English of Kracauer's early writings of the 1920s, and of his final work: History, The Last Things Before the Last, makes it clear that his ideas cannot be characterised as either a form of naive realism, or of conservative liberal humanism. On the contrary, Kracauer's film theory is founded on the critique of modernity whose trajectory can be tracked within German philosophy from Kant, through Weber, to the Frankfurt School, and it is this which shapes his work, from his earliest writings of the 1920s to his posthumously published final work.

Kracauer argued that the human condition within modernity was characterised by alienation, and subject to manipulative ideologies. Individual consciousness was reified, and questions of ethics and aesthetics subordinated to the imperatives of a dominant instrumental rationality which pervaded the new mediums of mass culture. Kracauer also locates the origins of this contemporary malaise in the fundamental inadequacies of the concepts of reason generated by the Enlightenment, concepts which marginalise the moral, the aesthetic and the non-cognitive.[26] These positions on modernity and the nature of mass culture were broadly characteristic of the ideology of the Frankfurt School, and the collection of essays written between 1922 and 1933, and published under the title *Das Ornament der Masse* in 1963, advance arguments concerning the role of the mass media in contemporary society which are similar in many respects to those put forward by Horkheimer and Adorno in their *Dialectic of Enlightenment* (1947). Although there is some debate about the extent to which Kracauer's position shifted throughout his career, particularly after his enforced move to America during the Second World War, the evidence of a continued adherence to some of the central tenets of the Frankfurt School's positions on the nature and problems of modernity remains clear.[27]

Many of the Frankfurt School's positions on modernity were derived from Max Weber's analysis of contemporary society as controlled by bureaucratic systems of 'instrumental rationality' which dominated the modern subject. According to Weber, the individual experienced a 'disenchanted' sense of existence as a consequence of this, in which meaning, value and the sense of enchantment which accompanies religious, metaphysical or utopian convictions, had been replaced by a more materialist and functional set of values, which ultimately served the interests of the system. Weber's bleak view of the condition of subjectivity within modernity was to provide a foundation for the Frankfurt School's critique of the 'culture industry', and also for Kracauer's theory of cinematic realism.

Following Weber's contention that the individual was disenchanted, Kracauer argued that the modern subject's relationship to the world was a 'distracted' one.[28] As already mentioned in Chapter 3, the concept of distraction employed by Kracauer amounted to the theorisation of a form of visual and sensory experience of the modern environment, in which an unfocused 'distracted' mode of being prevailed, which led, in turn, to a sterile encounter between the self and the world.[29] Although originally a negative term, defined in opposition to the more contemplative and unified modes of experience associated with the high arts, the notion of distraction eventually took on more radical connotations during the 1920s, becoming identified with non-bourgeois, or proletarian modes of experience, and with alternatives to totalising systems of rationality.[30]

Similar, dialectically conceived conceptions of distraction can be found in Kracauer, where distraction is both the product of abstraction and the mode of cognition through which the mass public can understand and transform their own experiences.[31] This means that distraction, as experienced through the film, constitutes a legitimate mode of aesthetic experience which corresponds to the 'damaged condition of modernity' itself.[32] Kracauer, employed the concept of distraction to develop an aesthetic theory based on a supposed structural correspondence between the 'distracted' modern condition and the particular forms of indeterminate mimesis found in film and photography,[33] and one of the foundations of Kracauer's theory of realism is this contention that both film form, and the specific forms of spectatorship adopted within the film viewing experience, correspond to the condition of modernity.[34]

However, Kracauer not only argues that film is 'realist' in the above sense, but also that it is 'redemptive', in that, through its ability to disclose the sensuous and ephemeral surface of reality, it offers the possibility of transcending the abstraction inherent within modernity.[35] Kracauer argued that film came into being in order to fulfil two 'originating principles'. The first of these was that of representing the fragmentation and abstraction characteristic of the modern condition.[36] The second was that of transcending that abstraction, and redeeming reality, through the empirical attributes of the film image. The true value of film, therefore, lay in its potential to redirect the spectator's attention to the texture of life which had been lost beneath the abstract discourses which regulate experience.[37]

Kracauer argued that modern capitalist society had turned away from both concrete experience and enlightened, critical reason, to produce a form of culture which he referred to as the 'mass ornament', and which included new mediums such as the cinema, and events characterised by extensive ornamental configurations, such as military parades and sporting competitions. Here, according to Kracauer, the real world of the individual had become 'desubstantiated', and replaced by spectacle: the 'functional but empty form of ritual' and the 'aesthetic reflex' of the dominant social rationality;[38] whilst visual display had become presentational, iconic and emblematic, as opposed to representational.[39]

Kracauer also argued that the mass ornament marked a return of mythic thought into western culture because myth was yet another 'aesthetic reflex' of instrumental rationality. Far from representing a radical alternative to instrumental rationality, contemporary forms of mythic thought were often central to the legitimation of capitalism because, like instrumental rationality, they arrested the processes of liberating and enlightening reason. Nevertheless, and like the later 'sensibilist' cinema of a film-maker such as Hans-Jürgen Syberberg, in which mythic forms are employed to liberate areas of experience repressed by dominant ideology, Kracauer also believed that modern mythic consciousness could emerge as an oppositional force in relation to instrumental rationality. Here Kracauer made a distinction between the superficial mythic spectacles generated by the mass ornament, and the more profound mythological consciousness which he explored in *From Caligari to Hitler*.

Kracauer's use of notions such as distraction, abstraction and redemption was also influenced by his reading of Kant, and there is an inverted affinity between Kracauer's assertion that mythic thought and instrumental rationality distort the operations of reason and the imagination, and the Kantian model of the harmony of the faculties within aesthetic experience, in which the role of the understanding is to regulate the imagination, and to cause it to seek order within nature. Kant argued that the aesthetic judgement arose from an interaction between the faculties of understanding and imagination, which represent law and freedom respectively.[40] These two faculties come into a harmonious rapport during aesthetic contemplation and it is this which is the basis of aesthetic experience.[41]

Kracauer adopts this Kantian model of the relationship between reason and imagination, law and freedom, and uses it to argue that limits are set upon the exercise of critical reason within both dominant instrumental rationality and the mass ornament. One consequence of this is that, within the realm of aesthetic experience, a debasement of the imaginary occurs, and a form of 'lawless freedom' emerges. Far from seeking order, instrumental rationality and the mass ornament cause the imagination to seek more superficial, and ultimately less satisfying fulfilment, and, according to Kracauer, this eventually leads to both the reinforcement of instrumental rationality, and increased disenchantment.

In addition to providing a theoretical support for Kracauer's convictions concerning the regressive function of instrumental rationality and the mass ornament, Kant's model of the harmony of the faculties, and, in particular, the related conception of *Naturschöne*, also had a profound influence on his theory of cinematic realism, and particularly on his claim that redemption could be achieved through a re-engagement with physical reality. For Kant, unlike the judgement of reason, the aesthetic judgement is essentially impressionistic, non-conceptual and rich in connotations. It follows, therefore, that, in order to generate the experience of aesthetic judgement, the object at which aesthetic contemplation is directed must also possess the potential to stimulate a profusion of meanings in the mind of the perceiving subject. Kant argued that such potential was best found within nature, and this is the basis of the Kantian concept of 'natural beauty' or *Naturschöne*.[42]

The Kantian conception of *Naturschöne* had a considerable influence on Weimar film theory, and particularly on the work of Balázs, whose *Der sichtbare Mensch oder Der Kultur des Films* (1924) influenced many of Kracauer's ideas in *Theory of Film*. In his book, Balázs drew on *Naturschöne* and the romantic philosophy of *Lebensphilosophie* to argue that the aesthetic specificity of film was closely related to the ability of the film image to explore and unearth meanings within nature. The following quotation, which is also indebted to the art theory of Georg Simmel,[43] exemplifies the preoccupation with *Naturschöne* which Kracauer was also to draw on:

> A landscape is a physiognomy, a face which anywhere and unexpectedly may look at us like the tangled lines of a picture puzzle. A face of an area with a particular if undefinable emotional expression, with a precise meaning yet hard to describe ... To trace this physiognomy in nature's picture puzzle, to frame, to emphasise, that is the function of style in art ... by the soul of nature we always mean our own soul, which is reflected in the former.[44]

In addition to Balázs, Theodor Adorno also referred to the affinity between film and *Naturschöne* when he argued that film should base itself upon its own 'artistic character', one which, for Adorno, was 'intimately related to the beauty of nature'.[45]

It is this context of interest in *Lebensphilosophie* and *Naturschöne* which Kracauer drew on throughout his career, and particularly in *Theory of Film*. Influenced by the notion of *Naturschöne*, Kracauer argued that a form of autonomous aesthetic experience, and one based upon the active search for patterns of meaning which Balázs had called for, could be attained through direct engagement with physical reality. Through this return to the concrete, the regulative power of the understanding, which had been diminished and distorted within mass culture, would be restored, and the imagination and understanding brought into healthier rapport. It was this concept of free and autonomous aesthetic experience, brought about through contact with external reality, which provided Kracauer with his understanding of the redemptive and utopian potential of the cinema.

The concept of *Naturschöne* also led Kracauer to develop a theory of cinematic realism which emphasised the indeterminate nature of both reality and representation. For Kant, the contemplation of natural objects was the best source of aesthetic experience because such objects were devoid of human intentionality, and, as a consequence, were better able to provide a space within which the imagination and understanding could explore freely, emancipated from the determining constraints necessarily involved in the encounter with an object produced by human will. This formulation of *Naturschöne* as essentially indeterminate led Kracauer to argue that film had affinities with such aspects of the natural world as 'unstaged reality', 'chance', 'the fortuitous', 'the indeterminate', the 'flow of life' and 'endlessness'; and the endorsement of such qualities makes it clear that Kracauer's theory of realist cinematic representation is premised on the sort of indeterminate processes implied by *Naturschöne*, where it is the indefinite bountifulness of natural beauty which encourages the understanding to seek constructive order and meaning.[46]

In addition to the Kantian concept of *Naturschöne*, Kracauer also drew on Edmund Husserl's conception of the *Lebenswelt* in developing his theory of cinematic realism.[47] Husserl argued that the objectifying abstract discourses of science obscured the more transient and subjective meanings generated within experience. It is this phenomenological world, 'the world in which we live intuitively',[48] which constitutes the *Lebenswelt*, and Husserl argued that, in order to achieve true fulfilment, the modern subject must regain contact with this lost, and repressed, realm of existence.[49] The emphasis on the concrete and the transient within Husserl's phenomenology led Kracauer to develop a theory of film in which what he referred to as the 'anonymous state of reality' would be preserved.[50] Following Husserl, Kracauer defined human reality in two ways. On the one hand, there were the systems of abstract conceptual reason which had come to exercise too dominant a hold over modern life. However, and on the other hand, there was also the 'base' of life. This was an essentially experiential and psychological domain, made up of a 'multitude of interpenetrating and counterinfluencing objects and relationships', and a 'complexity of satisfactions, discords, wants and pursuits which often lie below the conceptual and the conscious'.[51]

Kracauer argued that film was a privileged medium, which had been generated by the condition of the *Lebenswelt* within modernity in order to 'redeem' the base of life for the modern subject. Such redemption was possible because of the existence of structural correspondences, or 'affinities', between the *Lebenswelt*, with its transient, indefinite structure, and the suggestive indeterminacy of the film image.[52] Underlying the empirical content of the film image are its 'basic principles and structures', just as axiomatic structures and principles exist beneath the phenomenological surface of the *Lebenswelt*, and, for Kracauer, the basic principles and affinities of film equated structurally with those underlying the *Lebenswelt*. This postulation of a structural homological relationship between film and the *Lebenswelt* provides one of the foundations of Kracauer's theory of cinematic realism, and also makes it clear that that theory was not based on naive realist premises.

The third major influence on Kracauer's conception of reality was the Freudian theory of the unconscious. Kracauer conceived of the *Lebenswelt* as a domain of experience in which repressed desire often emerged in the form of psychological symptoms, and *From Caligari to Hitler*, in particular, is an attempt to decipher such repressed desire. In his book, Kracauer argues that films embody psychological dispositions which 'extend below' the dimension of consciousness. However, because film cannot represent the unconscious as such, underlying psychological dispositions are made manifest as 'visible hieroglyphs' of the 'unseen dynamics of human relations'.[53]

The analysis of the cinema in *From Caligari to Hitler* is premised upon the assumption that the German expressionist cinema embodies the 'inner life of the nation' and the 'German soul'.[54] However, Kracauer's preoccupation with issues of national identity here is untypical of him, and more a reflection of the widespread interest in the question of German national identity which emerged following the end of the Second World War. In fact, although Kracauer refers frequently to issues of national identity in *From Caligari to Hitler* the 'inner psychological dispositions' which he focuses on have nothing specifically national about them, but are rooted in the human condition. Here, inner life is thrown into turmoil by disruptive events, and Kracauer argues that, in periods of radical disruption, 'core underlying motifs' rise to the surface and become embedded in cultural artefacts such as films.[55]

Far from being a consideration of national identity, *From Caligari to Hitler* is a study of the ways in which alienating conditions create trauma within 'the base'. These events of 'turmoil' disrupt the operations of the *Lebenswelt*, and reinforce both abstraction, and the systems of power which underlie abstraction.[56] The principal influences on

Kracauer's conceptualisation of the psychological content of the *lebenwselt* were Freud's *The Psychopathology of Everyday Life* and *The Interpretation of Dreams*, and Erich Fromm's *Escape From Freedom*.[57] However, the influence of both Freud and Fromm on Kracauer was not as great as that of Husserl, and Kracauer himself argued that Husserl's model of the *Lebenswelt* was superior to Freud's model of the unconscious, because it dealt with conscious, as well as subconscious realms of experience.

Kracauer believed that an aesthetic medium must build from its basic 'properties', 'affinities' and 'appeals'. The basic property of film is its capacity for 'recording' and 'revealing' physical reality. The basic affinity of film is for representing aspects of reality such as 'the unstaged', 'the fortuitous', 'endlessness', 'the indeterminate' and 'the flow of life'.[58] Finally, the basic appeals of film are to notions of truth and authenticity congruent with the transient effects of things, and to notions of aesthetic beauty compatible with the perception and generation of a multiplicity of meanings.[59] Because human experience is not 'synthesised', but fragmented, consisting of 'bits of chance events whose flow substitutes for meaningful continuity', Kracauer espouses a cinema characterised by 'vague indefinability of meaning' and 'uninterpretable symbolism'.[60] Natural objects and events represented in films should, therefore, have a theoretically unlimited number of 'psychological correspondences' and should be surrounded by a 'fringe of meaning'.[61] Images on the screen should also reflect the 'indeterminacy of natural objects', providing 'raw material' with multiple meanings. Similarly, the film shot should 'delimit without defining', thus preserving the 'essential neutrality' of reality.[62]

Kracauer argued that, whilst the film-maker must give each scene in a film a dominant meaning relevant to the plot, he or she must also strive to give signification a degree of ambiguity, so that 'a considerable degree of indeterminacy is retained', and the film is able to generate 'free hovering images of reality'.[63] Kracauer summed up his conception of an indeterminate cinema by recourse to the model of the 'flow of life', a term which he derived from the phenomenology of Bergson and Husserl. Experience was a continuum, exemplified by the 'image of the street and the experience of the modern city', and Kracauer believed that film should seek to depict such a continuum.[64]

It was this conception of experience as a continuum which, as mentioned above, led Kracauer to argue that the basic appeals of the cinema were to notions of truth and authenticity compatible with transience, and to notions of aesthetic quality based on polysemic signification. This, in turn, led him to favour forms of *avant-garde* film-making which deployed an impressionistic style, and to praise films such as Alberto Cavalcanti's *Rien que les heures* (*Nothing But the Hours*, 1926), joris Ivens' *Regen* (*Rain*, 1929), and Jean Vigo's *À propos de Nice* (*On the Subject of Nice*, 1930): films which form part of the 'city symphony' genre of the 1920s. These films conform closely to Kracauer's requirement to depict physical existence through types of representation which are 'cinematic'. For example, *Regen* depicts the 'aftermath of a rain storm', the 'movements of clouds in the city', 'smoke effects' and 'other transient things';[65] and Kracauer argues that these are subjects which the medium of film appears 'pre-destined (and eager) to exhibit'.[66]

Kracauer also claimed that *avant-garde* documentaries such as Cavalcanti's *En rade* (*Stranded*, 1926) and *À propos de Nice* revealed 'hidden aspects of reality', a claim which he clarified further by means of a quotation from Germaine Dulac, who had argued that the 'subjects of pure cinema could be found, for example, in the trajectory of a bullet, or the formation of crystals'.[67] Although such aspects of reality are hidden because they also exist beyond the boundaries of perceptual recognition, Kracauer includes them within the general category of objects which are 'hidden' because they are part of a world whose 'qualities and poignancies' are lost to the modern subject, as experience is increasingly organised within normative frameworks of functional rationality. In discussing the cinema's ability to reveal 'hidden aspects of reality', therefore, Kracauer is referring to the ability of film to turn our attention back to immediate experience and the everyday.

In one respect, Kracauer's use of a quotation from Dulac, one which was originally intended to endorse the *cinéma pur*, is anachronistic. Kracauer was opposed to the idea that film was an art form in the traditional sense, and criticised *avant-garde* films – including those associated with both the *cinéma pur* and cinematic impressionism – which 'used', rather than represented reality. Kracauer argued that films which functioned in this way functioned ideologically, and he went on to equate art with ideology when he argued that art which emphasised the transformation of the world through the use of aesthetic conventions 'covered reality', and, in doing so, 'sustained the prevailing abstractness'.[68] Kracauer argued that this emasculated the *avant-garde* because films then functioned as 'elements of composition' which 'shut out nature in the raw'.[69] This led him to praise a film like *Entr'acte*, which retained traces of a relatively unmediated external reality, and also possessed the added virtue of lacking any 'recognisable principle or message'.[70]

Kracauer's emphasis on the need for an impressionistic stance towards the communication of meaning also led him to argue that the 'episodic' film was of particular importance. In such films, the narrative emerges from and disappears back into the 'flow of life'. These films are also 'permeable', in the sense that the plot is constantly interrupted by images of physical reality. Kracauer includes Italian neorealist films such as *Paisà* (Roberto Rossellini, 1946), *La Strada* (*The Street*, Frederico Fellini, 1954) and *Ladri di biciclette* (*Bicycle Thieves*, Vittorio De Sica, 1948) within this category of 'permeable' episodic films, and describes *I Vitelloni* (*The Young Calves*, Fellini, 1953) as 'composed of instants whose only *raison-d'être* is their instantaneousness [and which] appear to be inter-linked at random, without any logic or necessity'.[71]

Kracauer also referred to French impressionist film-makers such as Abel Gance and Marcel L'Herbier as episodic film-makers, and quoted Germaine Dulac approvingly once more, when she advocated both the development of the episodic film, and an end to the hegemony of the unified story film. However, whilst praising the episodic qualities of impressionist films like Dulac's *La Souriante Madame Beudet* (*The Smiling Madame Beudet*, 1923), Kracauer also criticised the expressive aesthetic which underlay impressionism, and was particularly critical of one of impressionism's central principles: the concept of *photogénie*, because of the emphasis which it placed on the transformation of reality.

It was because Kracauer rejected the notion that film was 'an art medium in the accepted sense' that he was both critical of French impressionism and sympathetic towards surrealism. Kracauer approved of surrealism because, like him, the surrealists were also committed to the ideal of an indeterminate cinema which would be capable of engendering self-determined associative and revelatory activity in the mind of the spectator. It is partly because of this that Kracauer considered surrealist films such as *La Coquille et le clergyman* (*The Seashell and the Clergyman*, Germaine Dulac, 1928) and *L'Etoile de mer* (*The Starfish*, Man Ray, 1927), and the more Dadaist *Entr'acte*, to mark an important shift from the exploration of artistic form as an end in itself, to the investigation of subject matter associated with the *Lebenswelt*.

However, Kracauer's conception of the *lebenswelt* must be distinguished from the various conceptions of the unconscious held within surrealism. As already described, Kracauer believed that the Freudian notion of the unconscious was inferior to Husserl's idea of the *Lebenswelt*, and that, whilst films which represented the *Lebenswelt* were 'cinematic', those which represented the unconscious

were 'merely Surrealist'.[72] Because Kracauer argued that the film
image should be indeterminate he was also opposed to the anchoring
of cinematic signifiers to specific psychoanalytic concepts, arguing
that this was 'excessively prescriptive'.[73] In Kantian terms, such
symbolism also contradicted the proper relationship between the
understanding and imagination, because, in this case, the understanding dominated the imagination.

Kracauer's theory of cinematic realism is grounded in the conviction that the rich complexity of immediate experience has become
impoverished by the power of instrumental discourses, and that a
return to the 'concrete density of things' will provide the way
forward for the modern subject. Kracauer also believes that film is
uniquely equipped to redeem this base of life for the modern
subject, and that film is a privileged medium, which is generated by
the state of the Lebenswelt within modernity. It should be clear from
this, therefore, that Kracauer does not, as his critics have claimed,
advance a theory of naive realism. In fact, his theory of cinematic
realism is best described as a form of phenomenological realism
which, like the Kantian aesthetics and Husserlian phenomenology
from which it is derived, seeks a basis for knowledge and representation through close observation of the material world.

It has been argued that the dialectical position which Kracauer
adopted towards distraction and popular culture in the 1920s and
early 1930s changed after his emigration to America in the late
1930s.[74] Such an argument rests on the supposedly 'conservative'
nature of works such as From Caligari to Hitler (1947) and Theory of
Film (1960). The origins of this idea can be found in a 1965 essay by
Theodor Adorno, entitled 'The Curious Realist', in which Adorno
argues that Kracauer's American writings lacked the radical, critical
force of his early writings.[75] Recent commentators, such as Elsaesser
and Schlüpmann, have also adopted this position,[76] whilst writers
such as Andrew, who were generally unaware of Kracauer's early
writings, have characterised the two books mentioned above as
'conservative' and 'reactionary'.[77]

The idea of the 'two Kracauers' has, therefore, emerged, based on
the supposition of an 'epistemological shift' between the early and
later works. Within this argument, the early Kracauer of 'The Mass
Ornament' is characterised as the 'anti-capitalist practitioner of a
materialist dialectics' and the 'phenomenological observer of the
everyday and the ephemeral'. The Kracauer of From Caligari to Hitler
and Theory of Film, on the other hand, is characterised as a 'system
building', an 'anti-communist', a 'sociological reductionist' and an
'unredeemed humanist'.[78]

However, it is debatable as to whether this antinomic conception of an 'epistemological shift' in Kracauer's writings can be sustained. *From Caligari to Hitler* may have been influenced by the same reaction to the post-war context of American cultural imperialism and the decline of the left – a reaction also associated with a sceptical attitude towards popular culture – which influenced Horkheimer and Adorno's *Dialectic of Enlightenment*, but the same cannot be said to anything like the same extent of *Theory of Film*.[79] In fact, both this, and Kracauer's final book, *History: The Last Things Before the Last*, return to many of the same concerns found in the writings of the 1920s, indicating a continuity, rather than rupture, across Kracauer's writings.[80] That continuity consists, essentially, in the sustained adoption of a critique of mainstream cinema as a force for *both* the reinforcement of abstraction and dominant ideology, and the liberation of the subject.

* * *

There are considerable similarities between the film theories of Siegfried Kracauer and André Bazin. Both Kracauer and Bazin were influenced by the same critique of modernity which flows through continental philosophy from the late eighteenth century onwards. Both were opposed to what they saw as the systematisation of modern life, and the subordination of the individual to the demands of instrumental rationality. Both also believed that the cinema possessed the power to redeem the world for the individual. Nevertheless, Kracauer and Bazin came from two very different cultural contexts. Kracauer was influenced by German classical philosophy, Kant, Husserl and Freud, whilst Bazin was influenced by catholicism, the French rationalist tradition, Bergson and Sartre.

Of these four influences, it was probably phenomenology which provided the most important foundation for Bazin's theory of film, and Bergson, who dominated French philosophy during the 1930s, who provided Bazin with his model of cinematic realism.[81] Just as one of the central categories of Husserl's phenomenology was his concept of the *Lebenswelt*, so, in Bergson, it is the flux of existence, and the flow and duration of consciousness, which constitutes the primary object of phenomenological analysis. Just as Husserl argued for a need to return to the *Lebenswelt*, Bergson also argued that, in order to truly experience reality, we must 'dive back into the flux itself'.[82] Like Husserl, Bergson also argued that this experiential flux was concealed from the subject by abstract, functional ideologies, and both he and Husserl believed that the principal objective of phenomenological analysis was to expose the base of life through a process of description and scrutiny.

In addition to Bergson's emphasis on the flow of existence, Bazin was also influenced by Bergson's concept of creative evolution. Here, Bergson adapted Darwin's theory of natural selection to argue that species evolve by becoming progressively more complex, rather than solely as a product of adaption to a changing environment. Rather than a bestial, Darwinian struggle for survival, therefore, Bergson argued that an *élan vital*, or vital spirit, pervaded the evolutionary process. Furthermore, although *élan vital* caused organisms to branch out exploratively into evermore complex series of morphological transmutations, each individual organism nevertheless remained related to the whole, and to the environment which provided both the grounds and parameters for development.

As has already been argued, phenomenological analysis is based on a process of description, or reconstruction, which reveals the deep structures which would ordinarily escape notice, as human experience is driven on by more functional imperatives. In this process, and under the scrutiny of enquiry, phenomena 'appear', or 'show themselves in the light',[83] and this metaphorical model of deep structures of experience being 'brought into the light', has clear correspondences with the way in which mediums such as photography and cinema operate. This metaphor of a reality normally hidden, which is revealed to the spectator via the force of light, was also to influence the development of Bazin's ideas.

In addition to phenomenology, Bazin was also influenced by existentialism. For existentialists the subject is not only a thinking subject but an initiator of action, and source of intuitive understanding; and existentialists believe that these three aspects of the human condition combine together during moments of significant experience.[84] However, existentialists such as Jean-Paul Sartre also believed that the modern individual suffers from an absence of inner fulfilment, and that it is this, rather than the more affirmative Bergsonian *élan vital*, which drives and motivates human activity. Although Bazin rejected Sartre's view of external reality as necessarily oppressive, he was influenced by the existentialist insistence that the individual defined him or her self through action, free choice and a quest for meaning. This notion that consciousness is a creative domain, within which choice and exploration take place, lies at the centre of both Sartrean existentialism and Bergsonian phenomenology, and also influenced Bazin's later conceptualisation of the role which film could play in generating forms of self-motivated spectatorial activity.

Bazin was directly influenced by existentialism through his reading of works such as Sartre's *The Psychology of the Imagination* (1940). However, although strongly influenced by Bergsonian ideas, he had little direct acquaintance with Bergson's writings themselves, and came to Bergson through his contact with the work of Catholic intellectuals such as Charles DuBos, Albert Béguin and Marcel Legaut. In 1938, whilst studying to be a teacher at the Ecole Normale Supérieure at Fontenay St Cloud, Bazin joined a study group inspired by the ideas of Legaut. The Legaut group were Christian activists, committed to the reintroduction of religious values and debate into the French educational system, and Bazin was particularly influenced by the call for a revolution in consciousness, premised on the need to build a new spiritual community suffused by moral and social values, which he found in Legaut's *La Condition chrétienne* (1937).

During this period Bazin also became closely associated with the literary journal *Esprit*, which had been founded in 1932 by the French Jesuit Emmanuel Mounier. Mounier was associated with the personalist movement, a Christian existentialist movement opposed to what its members considered to be the widespread 'depersonalisation' of existence within contemporary society. Mounier propounded a personalist doctrine which attempted to bridge the gulf between the individualist existentialism of philosophers such as Kierkegaard, and the emphasis on social and political revolution within the Marxist tradition.[85] Although he described personalism as 'a branch of the existentialist tree',[86] Mounier nevertheless rejected the more nihilistic aspects of the existentialist philosophies of Kierkegaard, Nietzsche and Heidegger, and adopted a utopian position regarding the possibilities of human emancipation more attuned to Marxism, in arguing that personal and political regeneration remained a real possibility.[87]

Mounier, and, through him, Bazin, was also influenced by the ideas of the radical Christian theorist, Teilhard de Chardin. A geologist by profession, Teilhard aspired to establish a synthesis of scientific and religious values within his discipline, and this led him to develop a metaphysical theory of geological formation. One of Teilhard's key concepts in this respect was that of the *noosphere*, or 'earth spirit'. Here, the earth was conceived as possessing a consciousness, the *noosphere*, and Teilhard argued that the traces of this planetary consciousness could be discovered through the close observation of natural phenomena. Teilhard's mystical, empirical evolutionarism, when combined with the emphasis on social and spiritual renewal within personalism, was to provide Bazin with the utopian, metaphysical perspective which he would later use as the basis for his theory of cinematic realism.

In addition to the influence of Legaut, Mounier and Teilhard, Bazin's theory of cinematic realism was also influenced by the ideas of the protestant literary and film critic Roger Leenhardt, who began to write about film in *Esprit* from 1934 onwards. Leenhardt saw the development of the sound film as a major gain for the cinema, arguing that it augmented the existing naturalism of the medium. Leenhardt also argued that the purpose of film was not that of rhetorical manipulation, but of the 'transcription of reality'.[88] For Leenhardt, the film-maker was an observer, or explorer, whose primary task was to depict, and illuminate, the meanings and characteristics which already existed within nature. Adopting the Christian view of man as fallen, and as seeking redemption and atonement, Leenhardt argued that man sought truth and understanding from an ambiguous and uncertain world, and that the cinema had a crucial role to play within this endeavour.

The principal source of Bazin's inspiration as a theorist of the cinema can be located in his conviction that the modern world suffered from a loss of spirituality, and this led him to base his theory of cinematic realism on a particular conception of human nature. That conception can be divided into two, related aspects. First, Bazin drew on Leenhardt's characterisation of man as fallen from a state of grace to argue that the human condition was marked by mortality and temporality, and, therefore, by a transitory and ephemeral understanding of, and relation to, reality.[89] Second, Bazin, through Bergson, Sartre, Legaut, Mounier and others, drew on the notion that the modern individual was oppressed by dehumanising, instrumental systems and ideologies, and was, as a consequence, alienated from his or her true self.

The belief that humanity was profoundly marked by an existential condition of transient mortality, and was also oppressed within modernity, led Bazin to adopt what was, at one level, a bleak conception of the human condition. However, such pessimism was qualified by Bazin's conviction that the individual possessed the potential to transcend his or her own damaged condition. Throughout Bazin's writings on the cinema the term 'love' is employed to describe a particular type of revelatory experience generated by encounter with the cinema. What Bazin means by this term is not entirely clear, but he appears to employ it in its Christian derivation, as signalling a self-less form of religious experience, during which a state of grace is experienced. It is this state of grace, encountered through film, which, Bazin argues, allows the individual to transcend the existential and social fetters placed upon individual self-realisation.

Bazin argues that this euphoric state is experienced when the photographic or film image 'wrenches' phenomena from the flow of time, and he goes on to assert that the spectator's need to 'redeem' such phenomena from Bergsonian *durée* satisfies two fundamental human needs.[90] First, the corruption of time, which eventually leads to death, is arrested when the film image embalms and preserves the otherwise transient and temporal. Second, following the Christian idea of man as a fallen being seeking salvation, Bazin redefines man as a 'searching being', and goes on to argue that the film image offers man the opportunity to experience fulfilment by virtue of the fact that it enables autonomous, exploratory spectatorship to occur. Bazin's theory of spectatorship is, therefore, grounded in the idea that, when the spectator gazes upon the realistic film image, he or she seeks to both transcend the contingent forms of knowledge and experience imposed by mortality, and achieve a degree of self-realisation founded on free thought and action.

Bazin believed that cinematic realism was facilitated by a particular conjunction of representational conventions and psychological processes, and, although it was the psychological processes which were his principal concern, he also believed that their manifestation would be engendered by the use of representational conventions which corresponded to our experience of perceptual reality. This, in turn, led Bazin to argue that the development of 'plastic realism' in the arts, from the invention of perspective during the Renaissance, to the emergence of the cinema, was primarily motivated by a quest to discover, and disclose, the aesthetic forms which would bring the 'seeking being' into existence. Bazin did not, therefore, consider the attainment of complete plastic realism, or what he referred to as 'total cinema', as an end in itself, but as a means of generating the forms of spectatorship which he believed to be so crucial to the existential wellbeing of the individual.[91]

However, although Bazin argued that photographic realism was inherently valuable when used to bring about the above ends, he also claimed that its ability to both suppress the symbolic and manipulate the spectator gave it a potentially regressive dimension. For example, Bazin argued that the use of perspective within western painting had led to an increased emphasis on the reproduction of external reality, and to a concomitant decline in the representation of more symbolic, spiritual themes. Bazin was critical of this turn away from the symbolic, and argued that, in great art, realism and the symbolic existed in dialectical union.

Bazin believed that realist art was more effective in acting as a catalyst for human emancipation than modernist or formalist art because of the capacity of the realistic image to present the world to the spectator in considerable empirical detail, and it is, Bazin believes, the empirical density of cinematic realism which is largely responsible for enabling the type of spectatorship which he advocates to emerge. For Bazin, the experience of cinematic realism is based on an encounter between an active, inquisitive apprehension, and what one critic has referred to as the 'flood of correspondences' which are revealed 'under the pressure of the long hard gaze'.[92] It is the realistic film which enables the 'long hard gaze' to emerge, as the spectator sees, and makes correspondences between, the complex, structurally dense content of the film's images. It is also by virtue of this empirical and structural density that the spectator is able to overcome the manipulative aspirations of ideology, as the ideological discourses within the film lose their identity in the face of a plethora of empirical information.

The type of cinema which Bazin advocates contains substantial empirical information about the world, is discursively indeterminate, and encourages the spectator to gaze long and hard at the diegetic world before him or her. Bazinian cinema also discourages an over-expressive or over-ornamental style, as well as the overuse of formalist montage. The long hard gaze of Bazinian cinema would also dwell on those enduring aspects of the human condition which transcend the historically, socially and politically contingent. However, an important point to note here is that, although Bazin is primarily concerned with such contingency in so far as it illuminates trans-historical aspects of the human condition, he also values those films most which link individual and universal psychological experiences to historical circumstances.

Bazin's theory of cinematic realism led him to focus on a number of film-makers whom, he believed, had made films in accord with the model of film-making which he advocated. This canon, which spanned both the silent and sound eras, includes figures such as Robert Flaherty, Friedrich Murnau, Erich von Stroheim, Carl Theodor Dryer, Roberto Rossellini, Vittorio De Sica, Robert Bresson, Jean Renoir, Orson Welles and William Wyler. Bazin argued that these directors were important because they had 'put their faith in reality'.[93] However, whilst these directors made realist, or what Bazin sometimes referred to as 'non-expressionistic' films, Bazin also claimed that elements of a cinema which did not 'add to', but 'revealed' reality, could also be found in the films of directors whom he did not normally include within his primary cinematic pantheon. Thus, although made within what Bazin referred to as the 'classical', as opposed to the realist paradigm of film-making, films such as John Ford's *Stagecoach* (1939) and Marcel Carné's *Le Jour se lève* (1939) nevertheless contained episodes in which 'reality lays itself bare'.[94]

Bazin believed that the history of the cinema should be rewritten along what he calls a 'dividing line' between films which reveal reality and films which impose their interpretation on the spectator. This 'aesthetic crevasse' within the field of cinema can be discerned running across the films of both the silent and sound periods of film-making, and Bazin's central concern, in writing about films such as *Greed* (Erich von Stroheim, 1924), *Journal d'un curé de campagne* (*The Diary of a Country Priest*, Robert Bresson, 1951), *La Terra trema* (*The Earth Trembles*, Lucino Visconti, 1948), *Umberto D* (Vittorio De Sica, 1952), *Limelight* (Charlie Chaplin, 1952), *The Best Years of our Lives* (William Wyler, 1946) and *Ladri di biciclette*, is to describe how such films reveal reality, and, in doing so, establish the potential for active spectatorship to occur.

As he was shaping his theory of cinematic realism Bazin discovered that a type of cinema was emerging in Italy which appeared to correspond almost exactly to his developing ideas. For Bazin, films such as Roberto Rossellini's *Paisà* (1946) and *Germania anno zero* (*Germany Year Zero*, 1947), Visconti's *La Terra trema*, and De Sica's *Ladri di biciclette*, 'stripped away' expressionism, and abandoned montage in favour of a style which transferred 'the continuum of reality' to the screen.[95] Bazin also argued that Italian neorealism gave back to the cinema a sense of the ambiguity and mystery of reality, and, in so doing, embodied both the character of Bergsonian *durée*, and Mounier's catholic existentialist conception of the subject's relationship to reality.[96]

One of the neorealist films which Bazin felt most fully embodied the form of cinema which he advocated was *Ladri di biciclette*. Unlike most films made during the classical period, the plot of *Ladri di biciclette* is concerned with a relatively insignificant event: the theft of a bicycle. Bazin approved of this because it was associated with commonplace, rather than 'extraordinary events', and because this meant that the film was firmly focused on the base of life within which we experience everyday psychological existence.[97] What impressed Bazin most about *Ladri di biciclette*, however, was the way in which the film illuminated the social context of post-war Italy without imposing any particular 'thesis' about that context upon the spectator. Bazin fully accepted that *Ladri di biciclette* contained a core point of view, and defined it as follows: 'in the world where this workman lives the poor must steal from each other in order to survive'.[98] However, Bazin believed that the approach to cinematic realism adopted in *Ladri di biciclette* rendered this central thesis ambiguous,[99] and, like one of Bazin's other favoured neo-realist films, *Germania anno zero*, he argued that the ambiguous aesthetic style adopted in *Ladri di biciclette* also provided a framework within which the spectator could experience considerable autonomy.

That autonomy was made possible, in part, by the way that *Ladri di biciclette* shows character and event within a rich texture of contextual detail. For example, as the central characters walk through the streets of Rome, and the camera holds scenes in long-take, the spectator eventually turns his or her attention from the events taking place to gaze randomly at the visual *collage* of dress, gesture and architecture which permeate the various scenes of the film. It is this digressive, meandering style of narrative construction, and the underdetermined integration of central themes and con-textual frameworks which arises from it, which, in Bazin's view, limits the manipulative potential of the central thesis in *Ladri di biciclette*, and promotes more autonomous spectatorship.

For Bazin, it is also important that films such as *Ladri di biciclette* achieve a balance between the representation of psychological, social and historical contexts. The account of the individual tragedy of the bill-poster in *Ladri di biciclette* would not be sufficient in itself, for example, to make De Sica's film the great work of cinematic realism which Bazin believes it to be. According to Bazin, the individual experiences of the bill-poster in *Ladri di biciclette* illuminate more general contexts, and it is because *Ladri di biciclette* contains this combination of psychological and contextual repre-sentations that he claims it to be the 'only valid Communist film of the past decade'.[100]

Bazin's theory of cinematic realism is chiefly concerned with forms of film-making which correspond to our perception of perceptual reality, and which create a diegetic framework within which the spectator can explore freely. However, in addition to this emphasis on realism and spectatorship, Bazin's film theory also addresses the issue of authorship. At one level, Bazin's concern with authorship seems incompatible with his view that a film-maker should present a 'neutral' canvas to the spectator. However, as has already been argued, a concern with active agency is central to Bazin's theory of spectatorship, and it is this underlying concern with the question of agency which leads him to address the issue of authorship within his general theory of cinematic realism.

Bazin's theory of cinematic realism was developed at a point during the historical development of the cinema when the classical Hollywood style of the 1930s was breaking down, and important *auteurs* such as Renoir, Welles and Rossellini were emerging. In addition, Bazin had always associated the development of the realist paradigm within the cinema with the work of seminal directors such as Flaherty, Murnau, Von Stroheim and Dreyer; and with masterpieces such as *Nanook of the North* (Flaherty, 1921), *Greed* (von Stroheim, 1923), *La Règle du jeu* (*The Rules of the Game*, Renoir, 1939) and *Citizen Kane* (Welles, 1940). Despite its emphasis on reality and the spectator therefore, Bazin's theory of realism was also closely associated, both intellectually and circumstantially, with questions of authorship.

The most important theoretical influence which led Bazin to engage with the question of authorship was the stress on self-realisation which he encountered within the Christian existentialist tradition. From Sartre, but much more so from Legaut and Mounier, Bazin derived the belief that the individual must seek a personal understanding of his or her own existence, and, from this focus on the individual, Bazin went on to argue that a study of the cinema should also seek to establish how a personal vision of reality could be discerned within the films of particular directors. However, Bazin's theory of cinematic realism was by no means primarily concerned with questions of authorship, and must be clearly distinguished from the *politique des auteurs*: the doctrine of individualist, expressive realism which came to dominate *Cahiers du Cinéma* during the 1950s.

In contrast to the *politique*, Bazin's account of authorship was premised on the need to situate the role of the director within a framework of other determining forces. For Bazin, the evolution of the cinema was primarily driven by mans' need to re-inhabit the psychological domain of everyday experience, and to rediscover a sense of autonomous spiritual freedom. In this sense, the primary causal force influencing the evolution of the cinema was not that of individual authorship, but a fusion of Bergson's *évolution créative* and *élan vital*, and the sense of lack which Bazin, influenced by Christian existentialism, regarded as inherent within the human condition. In addition to these factors, Bazin was also influenced by French determinist traditions which emphasised the influence of environment upon individual, and it was this, in particular, which led him to ascribe a degree of social and historical causality to films. Underlying such causality, however, is the idea, drawn from Bergson and Teilhard, that the development of the cinema is something akin to the working out of an evolutionary process, and

Bazin often refers to the cinema as though it were a sentient entity, evolving according to its own needs and principles, rather than as a product of individual authorship.

One exposition of Bazin's conception of directorial agency can be found in his 'In Defence of Rossellini' essay, which appeared in the Italian journal *Cinema Nuovo* in August 1955. Here, Bazin accepts that a true neorealist film must, necessarily, embody the director's vision of the world. However, Bazin argued that neorealist authorial vision would, in addition, reveal 'reality as it is visible through an artist, as refracted by his consciousness'. Bazin also claimed that neorealist authorial vision must stem from the director's 'conscious-ness as a whole', that is, not simply from his or her reason, as would be the case with a *'film à thèse'*.[101] In insisting on this formulation of 'consciousness as a whole', Bazin advocated a model of auteurism which accommodated the director's conscious and subconscious, political, moral and emotional sensibility, and it is as a result of adopting such an inclusive approach that he came to reject *Cinema Nuovo*'s criticism that Rossellini's films contained insufficient, or inappropriate, political content.

This inclusive model of authorship also led Bazin to differentiate Rossellini's style of neorealism from the nineteenth century French naturalist tradition. For example, in comparing Rossellini's work to that of Émile Zola, Bazin argued that, in Zola's novels, reality was first 'analysed', and then reassembled in order to fit the writers pre-conceptions. However, in Rossellini's films, reality was not analysed, but 'filtered', and, consequently, represented more 'ontologically'.[102] According to Bazin, the 'filtered' material in Rossellini's films con-tained both depictions of perceptual reality, and more abstract qualities associated with *durée* and the flow of life: qualities such as the fortuitous, the unexplained and the ambivalent; and Bazin argued that it was the inclusion of such ontologically filtered material which distinguished the work of Rossellini, and that of other neo-realist directors, from forms of film-making which 'covered' reality.

Within this model of representation, the metaphor of 'filtration' employed by Bazin implies that the role of the director is to channel, shape and select the ontological material which appears in his or her film. This involves a degree of authorial 'analysis' and structura-tion, but one which is circumscribed by the imperative to allow sections of relatively 'unanalysed' material to appear in a film. For Bazin, neorealist authorial transformation of reality is directed at the selection and organisation of these 'blocks' of reality, and, although the neorealist director shapes these blocks into an overall narrative, he or she interferes less with what is contained within them than would be the case with a director working within the traditions of the classical Hollywood or expressive montage cinema. As a consequence of this, in the neorealist cinema of Rossellini, meaning is established more a posteriori, than a priori, and, therefore, for Bazin, less ideologically.

Although Bazin's theory of cinematic realism contains a model of directorial agency, it is chiefly concerned with more abstract conceptions of causality, and with questions pertaining to the evolving relationship between film and reality. In particular, Bazin was concerned to understand the reasons for the evolution in the language of the cinema which occurred towards the end of the 1930s, and, in order to explain that evoulution, he adopted terminology drawn from disciplines such as etymology, palaeontology and geology, which he then used in order to compare the development of the cinema with the evolution and maturation of natural phenomena.

One of Bazin's most frequently used metaphors in this respect is that of the maturation of a river. A river passes through various stages of development, from source to final destination. However, a river is also an integral part of the landscape through which it flows, and is closely associated with the contours and terrain surrounding it. In the same way, Bazin sees the evolution of the cinema as a passage from youth to maturity, and as a response to the evolving existential contours and terrain of the human condition. Thus, writing in the mid 1950s, Bazin compared the evolutionary stage which the cinema had reached by 1939 with the 'equilibrium profile' of a river:

> By 1939 the cinema had arrived at what geographers call the equilibrium profile of a river. By this is meant that ideal mathematical curve which results from the requisite amount of erosion. Having reached this equilibrium profile, the river flows effortlessly from its source to its mouth without further deepening of its bed.[103]

What Bazin refers to here is the classical, systematic state at which, he believes, not only Hollywood, but also most European cinemas, had reached by 1939. He characterises this classical, fully realised style as 'analytic and dramatic', and believes that, by 1939, it had also become formulaic:

> By 1938 there was an almost universal standard pattern of editing ... Thus around 1938 films were edited, almost without exception, according to the same principal. The story was unfolded in a

series of set-ups numbering as a rule about 600. The characteristic procedure was by shot-reverse-shot, that is to say, in a dialogue scene, the camera followed the order of the text, alternating
the character shown with each speech.[104]

Like a river which had reached its equilibrium profile, classical film-
making flowed effortlessly between production and consumption.
However, the equilibrium profile of a river can only be maintained
so long as the surrounding terrain remains suited to it. Once that
terrain changes, equilibrium begins to disintegrate:

> But if any geological movement occurs which raises the erosion
> level and modifies the height of the source, the water sets to work
> again, seeps into the surrounding land, goes deeper, burrowing
> and digging. Sometimes, when it is a chalk bed, a new pattern is
> dug across the plain, almost invisible but found to be complex
> and winding, if one follows the flow of the water.[105]

For Bazin, although the 'level of classical perfection' achieved by the
cinema between 1930 and 1938 amounted to a 'perfect balance ... a
complete harmony of image and sound', this equilibrium remained
compromised and fragile, and had never been fully congruous with
the surrounding terrain of evolving human consciousness. Bazin
believed that classical cinema was instrumental and normative, that
it analysed, rather than revealed reality, and that it failed to give
rise to emancipatory forms of spectatorship. Bazin argued that these
deficiencies were bound to cause classical cinema to evolve, just as a
river, artificially contained within a flood plane, will eventually
break out of the barriers which hem it in.

According to Bazin, this is what began to occur from 1938 onwards, with the development of long-take, deep-focus photography
in America, and neorealism in Italy. Resorting once again to the
geological terminology which he derived from Teilhard, Bazin argued
that these developments represented a 'stirring in the vast geological bed of the cinema',[106] and that the crucial cinematic break-
through, the point at which the equilibrium profile of classical
cinema began to erode, the point at which 'the water set to work
again', occurred within the films of Orson Welles and William Wyler.
In these films, classical cinematic language was succeeded by a style
of deep-focus photography which emphasised the spatio-temporal
continuity of perceptual experience, and which, for Bazin, was 'far
superior' to the classical cinema of the 1930s.[107] For Bazin, therefore,
depth of field cinematography was not merely a new technological

development, but a 'dialectical step forward in the history of film language'.[108] Like a river which has broken out of the constraints of its equilibrium profile, the films of Welles and Wyler constituted the cinema's renewed attempt to explore the potential which the medium possessed to adjust to the evolving contours of human consciousness, in the latter half of the twentieth century.

For Bazin, the 'geological movement' which occurred in the language of the cinema towards the end of the 1930s – a movement which included both the work of Welles and Wyler, and the 'vast stirring of the geological bed of the cinema' represented by the appearance of neorealism – was only indirectly caused by the inherent deficiencies of classical cinema, and Bazin argued that, underlying this, a more fundamental causal factor could be observed. According to Bazin, the emergence of both deep-focus cinematography and neorealism was caused by a change in human consciousness which occurred in response to a collective experience of war, totalitarianism, fascism and mass brutality from the mid 1930s onwards. Bazin argued that this traumatic experience resulted in a renewed demand for freedom, and that it was this, which, in turn, triggered the evolution in the language of the cinema which occurred between 1938 and 1950.

None of the three theories of cinematic realism examined so far in this chapter can be characterised as naive realist. The film theories of Bazin and Kracauer are realist in the sense that both contend that film corresponds to certain aspects of reality. But, and as is also the case with Grierson, this correspondence is a homological one, and not affected by naive realist assumptions about films relationship to perceptual reality. It was Grierson, for example, who rejected *ciné verité* on the grounds that the film-maker always 'interpreted' reality, whilst Bazin talked about the 'myth' of total cinema. Nevertheless, cinema's *relationship*, rather than correspondence, to perceptual, empirical reality was important to all three theorists, and all believed that it was this relationship which enabled the cinema to reveal important underlying realities.

Bazin and Kracauer also believed that the dense, empirical richness of the realistic image enabled film to transcend ideological indoctrination and this, in turn, makes it clear that their theories of cinematic realism emerged in response to what was perceived to be an overarching context of instrumental socialisation, and loss of individual freedom. Intuition is also preferred to reason, as the foremost means of effecting emancipation and insight, in all three of the theories of cinematic realism considered here, and this, in turn, reflects their origins in idealist philosophy and phenomenology.

These three theories of cinematic realism also have pronounced utopian dimensions. Grierson's theory of documentary film was developed in response to what he perceived to be the threat posed to social unity by capitalism and elitism. However, Grierson's concern with preserving social unity did not rest on liberal-consensualist premises, but on a more abstract conviction that, following Hegel, the world was an interconnected whole: a sort of material 'absolute'. Grierson's utopian aspirations for film stem from this conviction, and from a belief that it is the mission of the documentary film to portray this underlying reality of interconnection. Similarly, Kracauer's theory of realism was premised on the need to counter forces which, he believed, were transforming the modern subject into little more than a functional, and alienated cog; and Kracauer is centrally concerned with film's ability to 'redeem' the individual from this fate. Finally, Bazin believed that film could play a central role in the evolution of a more vital human consciousness, and in the reintroduction of a renewed spiritual dimension into social and public affairs. These three theories of cinematic realism can also be distinguished from the post-Saussurian tradition in terms of the conceptions of agency which they advance. All three theorists believe that the individual possesses the potential – a potential which film can realise – to effect change, and achieve self-realisation. This is quite different from the more limited, often pessimistic conceptions of agency adopted within post-Saussurian theory.

*   *   *

One final model of theoretical realism which must be briefly considered here is that developed by the Marxist philosopher and literary critic Georg Lukács. Although Lukács wrote very little on the cinema, his theory of critical realism has had a considerable impact upon film theory, and has also influenced some of the most important realist films to emerge within both eastern and western Europe since the 1930s. Like the realist film theories of Grierson, Kracauer and Bazin, Lukács' theory of critical realism was rejected and dismissed by many cultural theorists working within the parameters of the post-Saussurian tradition. However, and despite this, Lukács remains of considerable importance, and his is probably the most extensive, systematic and sophisticated aesthetic theory to have been developed within the Marxist tradition.

At the centre of Lukács' aesthetic is the concept of totality. Following Hegel, Lukács argued that the chief role of art was to represent the relationship of the part to the whole.[109] Lukács' critical realism involved the elaboration of a model, the 'intensive totality', which would advance an account of the interconnection of individual and social phenomena within a particular historical conjuncture.[110] However, Lukács did not suggest that the intensive totality should, or even could, create a simulacrum of external reality: the 'extensive totality'. On the contrary, Lukács argued that the verisimilitude of the account produced within the work of realist art would necessarily be limited by the perspective of the writer, and by what he referred to as the 'unevenness of artistic form', where the internal logic and conventions of a particular aesthetic practice mediate representations of reality, shaping their final state, and making them an 'imperfect' copy.[111] Like the film theories of Kracauer, Grierson and Bazin, therefore, Lukács' aesthetic theory cannot be characterised as naive realist.

One of the most important distinctions which Lukács drew on was that between realism, naturalism and symbolism. According to Lukács, in naturalism, only the surface appearance of reality is described, and not the underlying causal networks which bring phenomenal reality into being. This means that naturalism describes contemporary reality without adequately explaining it, and, for Lukács, as for the Marxist tradition in general, this is not sufficient.[112] Lukács also argued that the emergence of naturalism and symbolism was linked to the alienation experienced by artists and intellectuals within capitalist society. As a consequence of this experience, Lukács argued that intellectuals felt compelled to withdraw from the task of representing society as a whole, and, instead, felt the need to represent a fragmentary social experience which accorded more closely with their own predicament.[113] According to Lukács, this failure to represent social experience led naturalism to an unfocused immersion in the detailed observation of alienated, atomistic phenomena; and symbolism into the embrace of reactionary mystical irrationalism.

These criticisms of naturalism and symbolist modernism also formed the basis of Lukács' critique of the work of Franz Kafka, which, Lukács argued, was characterised by both a plethora of descriptive detail, and excessive symbolism.[114] Lukács took his cue here from Marx and Engels, who, in *The Holy Family* (1845), had criticised Eugene Sue's popular novel *Les Mystères de Paris* for turning concrete descriptions of the criminal environment in Paris into a metaphysical romance about 'the secret driving forces of evil'.[115] For Lukács, as for Marx and Engels, realism must dispense with such symbolist irrationalism in order to represent a historically specific, multi-layered and concrete social totality:

The problem of narrative detail, of naturalism, has thus to be seen in a wider context. Since human nature is not finally separable from social reality, each narrative detail will be significant to the extent that it expresses the dialectic between man-as-individual and man-as-social being. It is these tensions and contradictions both within the individual, and underlying the individuals relation with his fellow human beings – all of which tensions increase in intensity with the evolution of capitalism – that must form the subject matter of contemporary realism. The realistic writer must seek the nodal points of these conflicts, determine where they are at their most intense and most typical, and give suitable expression to them.[116]

Lukács' model of aesthetic realism, as set out above, appears to suggest that the central determining characteristic of realism is the imperative to express the dialectic between the individual and the social within a particular historical conjuncture. The emphasis which Lukács places on this imperative stems from the central place which the concept of totality occupies within his overall aesthetic theory, and it is this which shapes his understanding of aesthetic realism.

Lukács' aesthetic system was based on the Hegelian-Marxist dialectic. However, Lukács interpreted the dialectic in a way which owed considerably more to Hegel than Marx. According to Lukács, the 'central category' of aesthetics was *Besonderheit*, or 'speciality'. *Besonderheit* refers to the system of mediations and relations which connect particular instances or events to general contexts, and it is this system which, Lukács claims, is the 'true subject' of art.[117] Lukács argued that, whilst science seeks to moves from the particular, or *Einzelheit*, to the universal, or *Allgemeinheit*, art seeks to explore the intermediate, historically relative areas which lie between these two domains. This means that, for Lukács, artistic representations of reality must seek to depict what he refers to as the 'historical here and now' of a particular society at a particular historical conjuncture.[118] At one level, all art is, to some extent, an aesthetic reflection of the 'historical here and now'. However, superior realist art deliberately emphasises these socio-historically relative intermediate categories, and, in doing so, creates what Lukács called *der Mensch ganz*, or 'the many sided man'.[119] By this, Lukács means both the formation of a reader who will be aware of his or her own place within a complex, interactive web of social and political relationships; and the creation of literary, fictional characters which will be developed so as to depict such relationships.

Explicit references to the cinema are relatively scarce in Lukács' writings, a fact which appears surprising, given that the questions of narration, description, naturalism and realism which he devoted his career to exploring are so central to the film. Lukács's writings on film are limited to a 1913 essay entitled 'Thoughts on an Aesthetic for the Cinema'; a series of short articles which appeared in the Italian left-wing film journal *Cinema Nuovo* in the 1950s; a chapter in his *The Specificity of the Aesthetic* (1963); the 'Introduction' to the Marxist film critic Guido Aristarco's *Il dissolvimento della ragione* (1965); and, in the final few years of his life, a series of interviews which appeared in the Hungarian film journal *Filmkultura*.[120]

Given Lenin's dictum that cinema was the most important of all the arts, this is a remarkably slim collection of material from classical Marxism's most prominent twentieth-century aesthetician, and this dearth of critical concern for the cinema reinforces the view, widely held amongst Lukács' critics, that he was overly preoccupied with one aesthetic tradition: that of the nineteenth-century realist novel. However, at the very outset of his career, Lukács did engage to some extent with film theory, and displayed a willingness to accept the new cinematic forms and modes of representation made possible by the emergence of the medium. For example, in 'Thoughts on an Aesthetic of the Cinema' (1913), Lukács set out a schematic model of film theory, in which photographic reproduction and formal montage were given equal standing. So, for example, in discussing the American director Edwin Porter's *Dream of a Rarebit Fiend* (1906), Lukács emphasised the extent to which the cinema's ability to produce fantastic effects through the use of 'superimposition, trick shots and reverse motion', when combined with an ability to create highly realistic images, resulted in the emergence of a 'completely different metaphysics'.[121]

Lukács's early ideas on the cinema were influenced by a general context of interest in the aesthetic characteristics of the film which was widespread amongst European intellectuals during the 1920s, and this initially led him to accept the value of modernist film practices. However, by the 1930s, Lukács had adopted the orthodox Zhdanovist line over 'reactionary modernism', and was criticising modernist film movements such as German expressionism. During the mid 1950s, Lukács also participated in a debate over the future of neorealism, in which he censured the movement for its reliance on naturalist techniques. Similarly, when, in 1958, Lukács next came to write about film, he insisted on the overriding importance of the realist and mimetic aspects of the medium, and on the prominence of both his model of critical realism, and the Zhdanovist model of socialist realism.[122]

By 1958, Lukács had also adopted a largely negative position on the possibility that the cinema could ever produce great film art. Lukács believed that film, as a medium, was incapable of matching the intellectual levels which drama and literature were able to reach because it was a primarily visual medium, and because 'an intellectual problem cannot be expressed by a picture'.[123] Similarly, Lukács also argued that the cinema, as an institution, was unlikely to produce great realist masterpieces, because, more than any other aesthetic medium, it was firmly ensconced within the economic base of capitalism, and was, therefore, 'spiritually as well as technologically' a product of capital.[124]

Lukács' conclusion that a form of progressive realism could not emerge from the cinema explains why he devoted so little time to a study of film in his writings. Nevertheless, and as Chapters 8 and 9 of this book will make clear, the model of the Lukácsian intensive totality has had a considerable impact upon some influential European film-makers. Lukácsian ideas have also influenced the development of film theory within Europe, largely because they provide a model for a film theory and cinema which aspires to represent complex individual, social and political relationships. However, Lukács' rejection of the modernist and naturalist traditions, and dismissal of some of the most important artistic works of the nineteenth and twentieth centuries, creates considerable difficulty for any artist or intellectual who seeks to put Lukácsian ideas into practice, or use them as the basis of a coherent and feasible aesthetic theory.

It is the centrality of the concept of totality within Lukács' work which gives his aesthetic theory its prescriptive aspect, and which caused him to reject forms of artistic practice which departed too radically from the style adopted by nineteenth-century writers such as Balzac and Tolstoy, and twentieth-century writers such as Thomas Mann. However, if the concept of totality is given a less pivotal role within Lukácsian critical realism it is possible to imagine a different form of realist theory and practice. For example, a reconstructed Lukácsian realist practice might not necessarily have to be based on the detailed delineation of intra-social relationships and their place within an overall totality, but could, on the contrary, portray partial, fragmentary, and distorted pictures of reality.

It has been argued that the most important cultural debate over questions of aesthetic realism which has taken place this century was that which occurred between Lukács and Brecht during the 1930s.[125] This is an exaggeration, however, as the published discussion which took place between these two theorists was only part of a much more extensive controversy concerning the respective merits of realism and expressionism which took place during the period, and which included contributions from figures such as Hans Eisler, Max Horkheimer, Theodore Adorno, Walter Benjamin, Béla Balázs, Siegfried Kracauer and Ernst Bloch. Nevertheless, Brecht's argument with Lukács did take on a special importance for film theory during the 1960s, and it is the case that Brecht's critique of Lukácsian realism provided one of the foundations for the development of formalist, *avant-garde* film theory after 1968.

Brecht's chief criticism of Lukács was that the latter had developed what, to all extents and purposes, was a formalist aesthetic:

The formalistic nature of the theory of realism is demonstrated by the fact that not only is it exclusively based on the form of a few bourgeois novels of the previous century (more recent novels are merely cited in so far as they exemplify the same form), but also exclusively on the particular genre of the novel.[126]

In opposition to such a supposedly 'formalist', Lukácsian approach, Brecht proposed a definition of realism in which formal innovation was determined by the requirement to represent an ever-changing social reality:

Anyone who saw me at work would think I was only interested in questions of form. I make these models because I would like to represent reality. As far as [even] lyric poetry goes, there too, a realistic point of view exists.[127]

Brecht also argued that a continual process of experimentation was necessary in order to overcome 'naturalised', normative and ideologically compromised representations of the real. However, such an emphasis on formal experimentation was clearly at odds with Lukács' conception of best form as a compelling canon of conventions handed down from the past.

A similar position to that of Brecht has also been adopted by more recent Marxist theorists. For example, Roger Gaurady put forward a theory of what he called 'shoreless realism' in *D'un réalisme sans rivages* (1963), whilst Ernst Fischer developed a similar approach to realist representation in both *Von der Notwendigkeit der Kunst* (1959) and *Kunst und Koexistenz* (1966). Echoing both Brecht and Bloch, Fischer and Gaurady argued that the use of distorted stylisation in works of art did not indicate a disintegration, or corruption of realism, as Lukács had argued, but, instead, constituted a valid attempt to modify existing realist conventions in order to represent a changing reality more appropriately. Like Brecht, both Fischer and Gaurady also argued that realism should be understood as a method, rather than a particular set of conventions, and a method which consists in the construction of models able, analogically and symbolically, to represent social reality. For both Fischer and Gaurady, this means that the stylised, symbolic representation of an alienated atomistic world constitutes a valid form of aesthetic realism.[128] Fischer, in particular, regards many examples of contemporary art as modern embodiments of the realist method, and as models which are symbolically, if not photographically, realist.

The imperative to link the particular to the general in a detailed way is central to Lukács' system. However, the qualifications put forward by Fischer and Gaurady suggest that this imperative could be put into effect through the use of modernist modes of representation, as well as through techniques drawn from nineteenth-century literary realism. In addition, the imperative to link the particular to the general does not necessarily imply a totalising approach which effects complete diegetic closure. Bearing these qualifications in mind, it is, therefore, possible to envisage the development of a more indeterminate, modernist form of the Lukácian intensive totality, and this possibility will be explored further in the following chapter.

Notes

1. Aitken, Ian, 'John Grierson, Idealism and the Inter-war Period', *Historical Journal of Film, Radio and Television* (1989), vol. 9, no. 3, p. 251.
2. Ibid., p. 252.
3. Ibid., p. 251.
4. Ibid., p. 252.
5. Hobsbawm, Eric, *The Age of Revolution* (London: Cardinal, 1962), pp. 299–305.
6. Aitken, Ian, *Film and Reform: John Grierson and the Documentary Film Movement* (London: Routledge, 1990), pp. 24–6.
7. *Ibid.*, pp. 41–7.
8. Grierson, John, 'The Challenge to Peace', in Hardy, Forsyth (ed.) *Grierson On Documentary* (London and Boston, MA: Faber & Faber, 1979), p. 176.
9. Grierson, John, 'Education and the New Order', in Hardy, op cit., p. 130. Essay reprinted in Aitken, Ian, *The Documentary Film Movement: An Anthology* (Edinburgh: Edinburgh University Press, 1998), pp. 93–102.

10. Aitken (1998), op cit., p. 37.
11. Grierson, John, 'The Social Relationships of Cinema' (Grierson Archive, University of Stirling: G3. 9. 4, 1934), p. 1.
12. Bradley, F. H., *Essays on Truth and Reality* (London: Clarendon Press, 1914), p. 175.
13. Grierson, John, 'The Contribution of Poetry to Religion' (Grierson Archive: G1. 5. 2,1920), p. 2.
14. Grierson, John, 'Answers to a Cambridge Questionnaire', *Granta* (Cambridge: Cambridge University Press, 1967), p. 10.
15. Grierson, John, 'The Challenge to Peace', in Hardy op cit., p. 178.
16. Grierson, John, 'Better Popular Pictures', *Transactions of the Society of Motion Picture Engineers* (August, 1926), vol. IX, no. 29, p. 243.
17. Grierson, John, 'Preface', in Rotha, Paul, *Documentary Film* (London: Faber & Faber, 1952), p. 16.
18. Grierson, John, 'Notes for English Producers' (1927) (Public Records Office BT 64/86/5511/28), p. 21.
19. Ibid.
20. Grierson, John, undated untitled paper beginning 'Against this background some indication of the part of the cinema is possible' (Grierson Archive: G2. 8. 7, 1933), p. 1.
21. Ibid.
22. Grierson, John, 'Flaherty, Naturalism and the Problem of the English Cinema', *Artwork* (Autumn, 1931), p. 124.
23 Andrew, Dudley, *The Major Film Theories* (Oxford, London and New York: Oxford University Press, 1976), p. 129.
24. Salt, Barry, 'From Caligari to Who?', *Sight and Sound* (Spring, 1979), vol. 48, no. 2, pp. 119–23.
25. Schneider, Tassilo, 'Reading Against the Grain: German Cinema and Film Historiography', in Ginsberg, Terri and Thompson, Moana Kirsten (eds), *Perspectives on German Cinema* (New York: G. K. Hall and Co., 1996), p. 38.
26. Kracauer, Siegfried, *Theory of Film: The Redemption of Physical Reality* (London, New York and Oxford: Oxford University Press, 1978), pp. 289–90.
27. Petro, Patrice, 'Kracauer's Epistemological Shift', in Ginsberg and Thompson, op cit., p. 101.
28. Kracauer, op cit., pp. 292–3.
29. Rodowick, D. N., 'The Last Things Before the Last', *New German Critique* (1991), no. 54, p. 115.
30. Ibid., p. 117.
31. Kracauer, 'Cult of Distraction: On Berlin's Picture Palaces', *New German Critique* (1987), no. 40, pp. 94–6.
32. Ibid., p. 94.
33. Schlüpmann, Heide, 'Phenomenology of Film: On Siegfried Kracauer's Writings of the 1920s', *New German Critique* (1987), no. 40., p. 111.

34. Kracauer (1978), op cit., p. 299.
35. Ibid.
36. Ibid.
37. Ibid., p. 298.
38. Elsaesser, Thomas, 'Cinema: the Irresponsible Signifier. Or, the Gamble with History: Film Theory or Cinema Theory', *New German Critique* (1987), no. 40., p. 70.
39. Ibid., p. 79.
40. Kant, Immanuel, *The Critique of Judgement* (Oxford: Oxford University Press, 1973), p. 176.
41. Colinson, Diane, 'Aesthetic Experience', in Hanfling, Oswald (ed.), *Philosophical Aesthetics* (Oxford: Blackwell, 1992), p. 137.
42. Kemp, John, *The Philosophy of Kant* (Oxford: Oxford University Press, 1968), p. 109.
43. Koch, Gertrud, 'Béla Balázs: The Physiognomy of Things', *New German Critique* (1987), no. 40, p. 170.
44. Balázs, quoted in Koch (1987), op cit., pp. 169–70.
45. Adorno, Theodore, 'Transparencies On Film', *New German Critique* (Fall/Winter, 1981), p. 201. Translation by Thomas Levin.
46. Kracauer (1978), op cit., pp. 68–9.
47. Casebier, Allan, *Film and Phenomenology: Towards a Realist Theory of Cinematic Representation* (Cambridge: Cambridge University Press, 1970), p. 15.
48. Husserl, Edmund, *The Crisis of European Science and Transcendental Phenomenology* (Evanston, IL: Illinois University Press, 1970), p. 139.
49. Ibid., p. 139.
50. Kracauer (1978), p. 69.
51. Ibid., p. 299.
52. Ibid., p. 72.
53. Kracauer, Siegfried, *From Caligari to Hitler: A Psychological History of the German Film* (Princeton, NJ: Princeton University Press, 1974), p. 7.
54. Ibid., p. 3.
55. Ibid., p. 10.
56. Ibid., p. 9.
57. Freud, Sigmund, *The Psychopathology of Everyday Life* (Harmondsworth: Penguin, 1975) and *The Interpretation of Dreams* (Harmondsworth: Penguin, 1976); Fromm, Erich, *Escape From Freedom* (New York: Holt, Rinehart & Winston, 1941).
58. Kracauer (1978), op cit., p. 71.
59. Ibid., pp. 21–2.
60. Ibid., p. 298.
61. Ibid., p. 68–9.
62. Ibid., p. 69.
63. Ibid., p. 71.
64. Ibid., p. 72.

65. Ibid., p. 31.
66. Ibid., p. 41.
67. Ibid., p. 180. Quoting Dulac: 'le Cinéma d'avant garde' in L'Herbier, Marcel (ed.), *Intelligence du cinématographe*, pp. 346–7.
68. Ibid., p. 301.
69. Ibid., p. 185.
70. Ibid., pp. 182–3.
71. Ibid., p. 256.
72. Ibid., p. 191.
73. Ibid.
74. Elsaesser (1987) op cit., p. 85.
75. Quoted in Petro, in Ginsberg and Thompson, op cit., p. 98.
76. See their respective essays in *New German Critique* (1987), no. 40.
77. Andrew, op cit., p. 108.
78. Petro, in Ginsberg and Thompson, op cit., p. 97.
79. Ibid., p. 101.
80. For a full account of this, see Rodowick, D. N., 'The Last Things Before the Last', *New German Critique* (1991), no. 54, p. 109–39.
81. Macquarrie, John, *Existentialism* (Harmondsworth: Pelican, 1973), p. 8.
82. Passmore, John, *A Hundred Years of Philosophy* (Harmondsworth: Pelican, 1968), p. 106.
83. Macquarrie, op cit., p. 10.
84. Ibid., p. 3.
85. Gray, Hugh, 'Translator's Introduction', in Bazin, André, *What Is Cinema? Volume II* (Berkeley, CA and London: University of California Press, 1972), pp. 2–4.
86. Ibid., pp. 2–3.
87. Andrew, Dudley, *André Bazin* (New York: Columbia University Press, 1990), p. 34.
88. Ibid., p. 31.
89. Bazin, André, 'The Ontology of the Photographic Image', in *What Is Cinema?, Volume I* (Berkeley, CA and London: University of California Press, 1967), p. 14.
90. Ibid., p. 13.
91. Bazin, André, 'The Evolution of the Language of the Cinema', in Bazin (1967), op cit., p. 24.
92. Andrew, op cit., p. 122.
93. Bazin (1967) op cit., p. 24.
94. Ibid., p. 27.
95. Ibid., p. 37.
96. Ibid.
97. Bazin, André, 'Bicycle thief', in Bazin (1972), op cit., p. 49.
98. Bazin, André, 'In Defence of Rossellini', in Bazin (1972), op cit., p. 97.
99. Ibid.

100. Bazin, 'Bicycle Thief', in Bazin (1972), op cit., p. 51.
101. Bazin, 'In Defence of Rossellini', in Bazin (1972), op cit., pp. 97–8.
102. Ibid., p. 98.
103. Bazin, 'The Evolution of the Language of the Cinema', in Bazin (1967), op cit., p. 31.
104. Ibid., pp. 31–2.
105. Ibid., p. 31.
106. Ibid., p. 29.
107. Ibid., p. 34.
108. Ibid., p. 35.
109. Pinkus, Theodore, *Conversations With Lukács* (London: Merlin, 1974), pp. 17–18.
110. Lukács, Georg, 'Art and Objective Truth', in *Writer and Critic* (London: Merlin, 1978), p. 38.
111. Ibid.
112. Lukács, Georg, 'Tolstoy and the Development of Realism', from *Studies in European Realism* (1950), reprinted in Craig, David (ed.), *Marxists On Literature: An Anthology* (Harmondsworth: Pelican, 1977), pp. 283–4.
113. Ibid., p. 282.
114. Lukács, Georg, *The Meaning of Contemporary Realism* (London: Merlin, 1963), p. 69.
115. Bisztray, George, *Marxist Models of Literary Theory* (New York: Columbia University Press, 1978), p. 22.
116. Lukács (1963), op cit., p. 75.
117. Parkinson, 'Lukács and the Central Category of Aesthetics', in Parkinson, G. H. R. (ed.), *Georg Lukács* (London: Routledge, 1977), p. 118.
118. Ibid., p. 132.
119. Ibid., p. 136.
120. Levin, Tom, 'From Dialectical to Normative Specificity: Reading Lukács on Film', *New German Critique* (1987), no. 40, p. 36.
121. Lukács, Georg, 'Thoughts on an Aesthetic for the Cinema', first published in the *Frankfurter Zeitung* (1913), published in English in 1981, in *Framework*, no. 14, p. 3.
122. Levin, op cit., p. 36.
123. Ibid., p. 59.
124. Ibid., p. 48.
125. Heath, Stephen, 'Realism, Modernism and Language in Consciousness', in Boyle and Swales (eds), *Realism in European Literature* (Cambridge: Cambridge University Press, 1986), p. 103.
126. Brecht, Bertolt, 'Against Georg Lukács', *New Left Review* (1967), pp. 40–1.
127. Ibid., p. 41.
128. Bisztray, op cit., p. 168.

# VIII

Late European
Cinema and Realism

There are significant continuities between theories of cinematic realism and practices of post-war realist cinema. Of all the major theorists considered in the previous chapter, Grierson exercised the least influence during the post-war period. The more journalistic approach to the documentary film which he adopted in the late 1930s failed to provide an adequate model for documentary realist film-making after 1945. Similarly, the ideas of Siegfried Kracauer, particularly as expressed in *Theory of Film* (1960), emerged against the context of a poststructuralist tradition which consigned Kracauer's model of cinematic realism to the margins of critical concern, and it was not until at least the late 1970s that Kracauer's work began to influence western European film-making or film theory to any meaningful extent. In contrast to Grierson and Kracauer, Lukácsian and Bazinian theory exercised a greater impact on post-war cinematic realism. Lukács' theory of critical realism was influential amongst some left-wing and communist film-makers across Europe, and, although largely ignored by the majority of film theorists in western Europe during the 1960s and 1970s, became increasingly influential during the late 1970s and early 1980s. Bazin's ideas were also taken up by many French film-makers from 1945 onwards, although the extent to which they were properly understood remains open to debate.

In addition to the influence of theories of cinematic realism, post-war European realist cinema was also influenced by a range of other factors. Post-war French realistic cinema incorporated many of the stylistic traits and thematic motifs associated with both the poetic realist cinema of the 1930s, and the cinema of the occupation. One of the most important figures in this respect was Marcel Carné, whose *Les Enfants du paradis* (*The Children of Paradise*, 1945) and *Les Portes de la nuit* (*The Gates of the Night*, 1946) embraced many of the themes found in pre-war works of *réalisme poétique* such as *Quai des brumes* (*Port of Shadows*, Carné/Prévert, 1938), *Hôtel du Nord* (Carne,

1938) and *Le Jour se lève* (*Daybreak*, Carné/Prévert, 1939). These earlier films were centrally concerned with issues of alienation and powerlessness, and with the plight of marginal, damaged characters. The cinema of *réalisme poétique* also drew on the French realist and naturalist traditions, and films such as *La Bête humaine* (*The Human Beast*, Jean Renoir, 1938), adapted from Émile Zola's novel of the same name, expressed a fatalistic vision, filmed in noirish chiaroscuro, which stands comparison with the darkest of nineteenth-century naturalist writing.

Films such as *La Bête humaine* and *Quais des brumes* were admired by existentialists such as Jean-Paul Sartre and Simone de Beauvoir for their equivocal portrayal of the human condition, but criticised by many on the left for their inherent pessimism, and lack of concern with contemporary political issues.[1] However, the existential *angst* expressed in films such as *Quais des brumes* was not the only thematic trope to be found within *réalisme poétique*, and films such as Julien Duvivier's *Pépé le Moko* (1936) and *La Belle équipe* (*The Glorious Team*, 1936) also drew on the radical tendency within the naturalist heritage to explore issues of political, racial and class conflict.

During the war years films such as Grémillon and Prévert's *Lumière d'été* (*Summer Light*, 1942) attempted to revive the poetic naturalist, expressive realist style of late silent cinema. However, this did not prove to be the predominant course adopted by French cinema between 1940 and 1945, when *réalisme poétique* gradually evolved into a more polished, studio-based and literary form of cinema, exemplified by films such as Carne and Prévert's *Les Visiteurs du soir* (*The Visitors of the Evening*, 1943) and *Les Enfants du paradis*.[2] The austere symbolic *mise-en-scène*, focus on issues of suffering and spiritual isolation, and detached, often metaphysical *élan* of the occupation cinema, achieved its apotheosis in Robert Bresson's *Les Dames du Bois de Boulogne* (*The Women of the Bois de Boulogne*, 1944/5), a film which exhibits a concern for the symbolic materiality of objects and gestures that was later to influence German film-makers such as Straub and Syberberg.

After 1945 the cinema of the occupation gradually evolved into what, by 1953, was referred to as the 'tradition of quality'. The stylistic continuity found in many French films produced over this period was partly influenced by the fact that a number of the national cinema institutions established during the occupation were retained, largely unchanged, after the liberation. Thus, although the war-time Comité d'Organisation de l'Industrie Cinématographique was reorganised into the Centre National de la Cinématographie after 1945, it continued to play much the same role within the French cinema as it had during the war.³ Similarly, organisations such as the Institut des Hautes Etudes Cinématographiques and the Cinémathèque Française, both established during Vichy, continued relatively unchanged into the post-war era.

If the continuity between French war-time cinema and the tradition of quality was influenced by institutional congruity, it was also affected by a perceived need to compete with Hollywood. American films flooded into France during the immediate post-war period, leading many to the conclusion that, in order to compete effectively, the French cinema would have to raise its production values to the point where they would be comparable with those of Hollywood. This conviction resulted in a situation where the increased technical sophistication apparent in French war-time, and immediate post-war cinema, became progressively channelled into the production of higher budget films during the 1950s, and the result was the cinema of the *tradition de qualité*.

Although the critics of the *nouvelle vague* were later to attach the disparaging appellation of *le cinéma de papa* to some aspects of the *tradition de qualité*, a number of important films were made during this period. One film-maker who retained the *noirish* predisposition of 1930s poetic realism was Henri-Georges Clouzot, whose *Le Corbeau* (*The Raven*, 1943) so assailed conventional mores that it became one of the most criticised films of the period. With *Le Corbeau*, poetic realism shifts into the more generic, less ambivalently existential territory of the *film noir*, and Clouzot was to proceed further in this direction with *Quai des Orfèvres/Jenny L'Amour* (1947), *Le Salaire de la peur* (*The Wages of Fear*, 1953) and *Les Diaboliques* (1954). The nihilistic melancholia found in these, and other film noir, such as *Manèges* (*The Cheat*, Yves Allégret, 1950), marks a return to the more melodramatic naturalism of 1920s silent pictorialism, rather than to the more socially oriented existentialist pessimism of 1930s poetic realism, although it could be argued that *Le Corbeau* bridges the two schools.

Other important films made within the tradition of quality include Claude Autant-Lara's *Le Rouge et le noir* (*The Red and the Black*, 1954), *L'Auberge rouge* (*The Red Inn*, 1951) and *La Traversée de Paris* (*Four Bags Full*, 1956). These films are characterised by a sharply observed sense of social position, and ironic, distanced posture. *La Traversée de Paris*, in particular, is a darkly comic account of a German occupied Paris, which, in some respects, resembles the alienating cityscapes found in films from the poetic realist tradition. Max Ophuls's *La Ronde* (*Rondelay*, 1950), *Le Plaisir* (*House of Pleasure*,

1953), *Madame de ...* (1953) and *Lola Montès* (1955) also display a subversive irony which makes them much more than mere expressions of *le cinéma de papa*, whilst *La Ronde* exhibits a reflexive, stylistic self-consciousness which was later to influence the *nouvelle vague*.

Important new directors such as Jean-Pierre Melville, Alain Resnais, Georges Franju, Chris Marker, Agnes Varda and Robert Bresson also emerged from within the tradition of quality during the 1950s. Of these, by far the most important was Bresson, whose first two major films: *Anges du péché* (*Angels of Sin*, 1943) and *Les Dames du Bois de Boulogne*, were made within the stylised, cool expressive realist style which characterised the best of war-time cinema. Bresson's films are also firmly grounded in the subject matter of the French realist and naturalist traditions. Thus, *Anges du péché* and *Les Dames du Bois de Boulogne* are concerned with issues of revenge, suffering and the exploitation of innocence; whilst later films, such as *Le Journal d'un curé de campagne* (*Diary of a Country Priest*, 1951), *Un Condamné à mort s'est échappé* (*A Man Escaped*, 1956) and *Pickpocket* (1959), adopt an austere, minimalist approach in their portrayal of fragile individuals striving to cope with a threatening external environment.

However, Bresson's films are not exclusively despairing in their depiction of the human condition. His films of the 1950s were celebrated by the critics of *Cahiers du Cinéma*, partly because Bresson's persistence in making films as an auteur corresponded to the agenda of *la politique des auteurs*, and partly because the thematic concerns evident in those films conformed to the revelatory Christian existentialism which Bazin had endorsed within the pages of *Cahiers*. For example, in *Pickpocket*, despite the presence of an over-arching context of isolation and emotional introversion, redemption remains possible through the experience of love, and, in *Anges du péché*, through forms of religious revelation. Bazin praised this aspect of Bresson's work when he claimed that *Le journal d'un curé de campagne* was 'concerned with a single reality – that of human souls', and explored 'an uninterrupted condition of soul, the outward revelation of an interior destiny'.[4] However, in later films, such as *Au Hasard Balthasar* (*Balthasar, Here and There*, 1966), *Mouchette* (1967), *Une Femme douce* (*A Gentle Woman*, 1969), *Four Nights of a Dreamer* (*Quatre nuits d'un rêveur*, 1972), *Lancelot du Lac* (*Lancelot of the Lake*, 1974), *The Devil Probably* (*Le Diable probablement*, 1977) and *L'Argent* (*Money*, 1983), Bresson's vision became much darker, and the possibility that grace could be experienced, or release from suffering achieved, is no longer entertained.

After Bresson the next major exponent of the French realist and naturalist tradition is Louis Malle. Malle's first major film, *Les Amants* (*The Lovers*, 1958), can be associated with the anarchic experimentalism, and use of Hollywood iconography, which typified the early films of the *nouvelle vague*. After *Les Amants* Malle experimented with a variety of different generic and commercial formula, in films which included the Brigitte Bardot and Jeanne Moreau vehicle *Viva Maria* (1965), before adopting a more social realist approach in *Lacombe Lucien* (1974) and *Au revoir les enfants* (*Farewell, Children*, 1987).

Lacombe Lucien and *Au revoir les enfants* focus on the impact of the German occupation during the Second World War, and explore the social, cultural and psychological dispositions which made collaboration possible. In *Lacombe Lucien*, Malle suggests that the source of collusion is to be found in the existence of a culture of rural apathy and insularity, and he represents that context through a naturalist style, which avoids both Lukácsian forms of realist representation, and the experimentation of the *nouvelle vague*. The criticisms of national social and cultural predispositions in *Lacombe Lucien* also reflect a process of political change occurring in France at the time of the film's production, when, following the fall of Gaulism in 1974, a more critical exploration of the myths and realities of Vichy became possible. The nihilistic naturalism of *Lacombe Lucien* both reflects, and is the product of, this more general context of revisionist enquiry.[5]

After Malle, both the realist tradition and the tradition of quality are carried on in a group of historical dramas directed by Bertrand Tavernier during the 1970s and 1980s. Tavernier's rejection of the *nouvelle vague*, and deliberate return to the *tradition de qualité*, is underscored by his appointment of Jean Aurenche as scriptwriter for a number of his films. Aurenche was criticised by Truffaut in his seminal essay 'Une certaine tendance du cinéma français' as one of those most responsible for the inadequacies of *le cinéma de papa*. However, Malle employed Aurenche to work on four films between 1973 and 1981: *L'Horloger de Saint Paul* (*The Watchmaker of Saint Paul*, 1973), *Que la Fête commence* (*Let the Festival Begin*, 1975), *Le Juge et l'assassin* (*The Judge and the Assassin*, 1976) and *Coup de torchon* (*Clean Slate*, 1981).

This group of films are realistic in style, were produced on relatively large budgets, and are centrally concerned with the relationship between individuals and their historical and cultural contexts. However, they can be distinguished from the 1950s films made within the *tradition de qualité* by the extent to which they refer to contemporary political debates or events. For example,

L'Horloger de Saint Paul explores issues of individual conscience and public responsibility against a backdrop of the revolts of May 1968. In line with Tavernier's more conservative views concerning this period, and in accordance with the general perspective associated with the *tradition de qualité*, *L'Horloger de Saint Paul* depicts the events of May 68 as a temporary disruption of more traditional French cultural mores, rather than as a positive force for cultural renewal. Similarly, although *Que la Fête commence* is set during the Regency period of Philipe d'Orléons (1715–23), it also refers obliquely to the post-Gaulist period, and makes indirect associations between these two periods of change and transition within French history.

In both *Que la Fête commence* and *Le Juge et l'assassin*, Tavernier also adopts an approach to historical interpretation which is influenced by the 'new history' movement: a leftist strand within historiography which concentrated on oral history and the social history of the everyday. An identifiably naturalist conception of the human condition is also evident in these films. The naturalist trope of a bestial human nature, incompatible with the cultural qualifications of civilisation, is particularly evident in *Le Juge et l'assassin*, where it is also allied to a post-structuralist critique of authority as the self-interested and abusive exercise of power. However, the introduction of naturalist mores also generalises the subject matter of *Le Juge et l'assassin*, and one consequence of this is that the film's depiction of political and social context remains schematic.

It has been argued that the development of Tavernier's film-making between the early 1970s and the late 1980s exhibits a shift from a concern with the relationship between the personal and the public, as in *L'Horloger de Saint Paul*, to an increasing preoccupation with the relationship between individual and environment in films such as *Coup de torchon* (1981) and *La Passion Béatrice* (1988).[6] However, that shift, the consequence of Tavernier's deployment of a naturalist sensibility, couched within a humanist orientation always implicit within the *tradition de qualité*, is also accompanied by an increasing concern with the exploration of family, as opposed to class or social relationships, as, for example, in *Un Dimanche à la campagne* (*A Sunday in the Country*, 1985). This combination of naturalism, humanism and attention to the intimacies of close relationships, increasingly leads Tavernier's films away from analytical exploration of particular historical contexts, to focus on more universal features of the human condition, as, for example, in *La Vie et rien d'autre* (*Life, and Nothing But*, 1989).

Two other French film-makers who emerged in the 1970s, and who are associated with the birth of the 'new naturalism' in French cinema, are Jacques Doillon and Maurice Pialat. Doillon's *Les Doigts dans la tête* (*Head in Hands*, 1974) portrays a group of alienated and disenfranchised adolescents, and paints a claustrophobic picture of social inertia and exploitation. However, in later films, such as *La Drôlesse* (1979), *La Fille prodigue* (*The Prodigal Girl*, 1980), *La Pirate* (*The Pirate*, 1984) and *La Vie de famille* (*Family Life*, 1985), Doillon moves away from issues of social disadvantage in order to explore the emotional consequences of exploitation within the confines of family life. At the same time, Doillon also abandons the naturalist ethos of *Les Doigts dans la tête* to adopt a more self-consciously *auteurist* approach, influenced by the films of Bergman, and grounded in the depiction of intense, personal emotional experience.

Maurice Pialat also adopts a predominantly naturalist approach in films such as *L'Enfance nue* (*Naked Childhood*, 1969), *Passe ton bac d'abord* (1979), *Loulou* (1980) and *À nos amours* (*To Our Loves*, 1983), and, like Doillon, Pialat often focuses on the subject of youth as a manipulated, exploited or vulnerable sector of society. Like the early Doillon, Pialat's films employ documentary-based techniques and non-professional actors, and, like Tavernier, Pialat aims for a degree of literality which is formulated in response to *nouvelle vague* modernist experimentalism. The documentary qualities of Pialat's films were also influenced by the Left Bank School of poetic documentary of the 1950s, and, in particular, by the ethnographic approach practised by Jean Rouch in films such as *Chronique d'un été* (*Chronicle of a Summer*, 1961). These influences led Pialat to adopt a style of filmmaking in which everyday, interpersonal interactions are dwelt on, and in which the rituals of family life, and particularity of custom and gesture, are closely scrutinised.

Pialat's concern with the representation of the *quotidien* inherits both a Bazinian emphasis on the need to seek the significant within the mundane, and the concerns of the new history movement associated with the Annales school.[7] However, Pialat's cinema, with its rejection of aestheticism, focus on the minutiae and texture of everyday interaction and chance events, and use of non-professional actors, improvisation and indeterminate, loosely structured narrative compositions, can also be associated with Kracauerian conceptions of cinematic realism. The importance which Pialat's films place on the value of individual experience, however flawed that experience might be, can also be associated with the emphasis on the elevation of the particular over the general found in the work of Kracauer.

Pialat's realism also embraces a utopian dimension which can be related to the more transcendental aspects of both Bazin and Kracauer's thought:

The cinema creates a dream world ... it transforms what is sordid into something marvellous, it makes the ordinary exceptional, and turns what is filmed into a moment of death. That's what I understand by realism.

In addition to a reference to the revelatory aspect of film, an aspect discussed in depth by both Kracauer and Bazin, Pialat's allusion to the manner in which the cinema can transform the ordinary into a 'moment of death' is also reminiscent of Bazin's notion of the 'mummy complex', in which film and photography are able to redeem both psychological experience and physical reality from the deterioration implicit in temporality. Bazin's discussion of this aspect of the realistic image in relation to the family photograph album seems to embody much of what Pialat means when he talks about realism and the 'moment of death':

> Those grey or sepia shadows, phantomlike and almost undecipherable, are no longer traditional family portraits but rather the disturbing presence of lives halted at a set moment in their duration, freed from their destiny; not, however, by the prestige of art but by the power of an impassive mechanical process: for photography does not create eternity, as art does, it embalms time, rescuing it simply from its proper corruption.[9]

The episodic quality of Pialat's films can also be related to Kracauer's theory of cinematic realism. In a film such as *Police* (1985), for example, episodic scenes flow into each other, and only indirectly suggest a surrounding social context. The same approach is adopted in *Van Gogh* (1991), in which Pialat uses a fluid narrative structure in order to portray the depressive and suicidal Van Gogh's relationships with the local people and landscape of Auvers. As in other Pialat films, the focus here is on the ordinary and *quotidian*, rather than on Van Gogh's status as an iconic artist; and, like *Police*, there is an unfinished quality to *Van Gogh* which also links the film to Kracaurian notions of cinematic realism. Pialat's films also exhibit the sort of indeterminate style, in which the narrative emerges from, and disappears back into, the 'flow of life', and in which episodes appear to be 'linked at random', which Kracauer endorsed.[10]

Pialat's focus on the everyday interaction between individual and environment reflects the influence of the French nineteenth-century realist and naturalist traditions. However, his focus on small-scale social interaction also mirrors Benjamin's assertion that the past should 'become citable in all its moments',[11] and Kracauer's claim that film 'permits us, for the first time, to take away with us the objects and occurrences that comprise the flow of material life'.[12] Pialat often approaches such material through a focus on the close depiction of family relationships. Here, the family appears to represent a sanctuary from the alienating forces at large within society, and the focus on familial interactions in a film such as *À nos amours*, particularly during scenes set around dinner tables in which individual characters (in Kracauer's phrase), 'emerge from and disappear back into' the overall flow of the narrative, also reinforces the predominant, impressionistic, episodic character of Pialat's realism. Finally, like the Italian neorealist films which Kracauer admired, a film such as *Police* is also suffused by 'the image of the street and the experience of the modern city'.[13]

The influence of the new history movement led to the emergence of a genre of realistic history films in France during the 1970s and 1980s. These include *Que la Fête commence, Le Juge et l'assassin, Lacombe Lucien, Les Camisards* (René Allio, 1972), *Moi Pierre Rivière* (*I, Pierre Rivière*, Allio, 1976), *Souvenirs d'en France* (*Memories of France*, André Techiné, 1975) and *Le Retour de Martin Guerre* (*The Return of Martin Guerre*, Daniel Vigne, 1983). Tavernier's *Que la Fête commence* and *Le Juge et l'assassin* are made within the parameters of the *tradition de qualité*, whilst the films of Allio and Techiné reveal the influence of Brecht. *Le Retour de Martin Guerre*, on the other hand, is predominantly naturalistic in tone, and detailed in its evocation of peasant society. Despite their differences, these films share a common commitment to unearth disregarded working-class and peasant history, in the spirit of the new history movement and post-structuralist political modernism. This commitment is well illustrated by Allio's *Moi Pierre Rivière*, which was adapted from a text published by Michel Foucault, and was based on the prison diaries of a convicted murderer. Finally, a film such as *Souvenirs d'en France* also looks forward to Edgar Reitz's *Heimat*, in its synthesis of the 'family saga' genre with Brechtian technique.

Like French cinema from the 1900s onwards, the realistic cinema which developed in Scandinavia in the latter half of the twentieth century also drew heavily on the nineteenth century realist and naturalist traditions. Film-makers such as Carl Theodor Dreyer, Alf Sjöberg and Ingmar Bergman were influenced by the theatre of Henrik Ibsen and August Strindberg. Dreyer's *Vredens Dag* (*Day of Wrath*, 1943), *Ordet* (1954) and *Gertrud* (1964) employ static pictorial composition, long takes and rhythmic camera movement to express an atmosphere of ascetic spirituality. In these films realism has a strong theatrical presence, which is also combined with a degree of modernist reflexivity, whilst the themes of faith, redemption, love and sacrifice which recur in them are heightened by the use of expressive chiaroscuro lighting, classical compositional techniques and restrained acting performances. In contrast to the formal asceticism of Dreyer, Alf Sjöberg's films display a more highly charged blend of expressive cinematic style. For example, *Himlaspelet* (*The Heavenly Play*, 1942) combines pictorialist naturalism and symbolism, whilst *Hets* (*Torment*, 1943) deploys an expressive realism influenced by German expressionism. On the other hand, Sjöberg's *Fröken Julie* (*Miss Julie*, 1950) embraces the naturalist theatricality of Strindberg's 1888 play.

The most important Scandinavian director of the post-war period was Ingmar Bergman. Like Sjöberg, Bergman was influenced by a combination of the nineteenth-century Scandinavian naturalist theatrical tradition, and European modernism. Bergman's films combine modernist devices, such as extreme close up, superimposition and direct address, with a psychological realism suffused with mythical representations of good and evil, and an often fatalistic vision of the human condition. However, and like Bresson's films of the 1950s, Bergman's films of the same period depict an alienating world within which the individual can be redeemed through acts of love, faith and engagement with art. This is the case, for example, with films such as *Det sjunde inseglet* (*The Seventh Seal*, 1957) and *Jungfrukällen* (*The Virgin Spring*, 1960). However, like Bresson, Bergman's two trilogies of the 1960s: *Säsom i en spegel* (*Through a Glass Darkly*, 1961), *Nattvardsgästerna* (*Winter Light*, 1962) and *Tystnaden* (*The Silence*, 1963); and *Persona* (1966), *Vargtimmen* (*Hour of the Wolf*, 1968) and *Skammen* (*Shame*, 1968), express a more pessimistic vision of human possibility than do the earlier films. This view of the human condition is also applied to Bergman's depiction of a Swedish culture which is depicted as authoritarian, hierarchical and emotionally impotent.

In *Fanny och Alexander* (*Fanny and Alexander*, 1983), Bergman contrasts the innocence of children with an institutionalised authority embedded in the Protestant values of duty, service and obedience. *Fanny och Alexander* also departs significantly from the more modernist treatment used in films such as *Persona* and *Tystnaden*, to adopt a realistic approach which combines psychological and more 'magical' styles of realism in order to conjure up the experience of childhood. Bergman's films have a pronounced autobiographical element, and this means that they cannot be easily accommodated within a concept of realism derived from either nineteenth-century realism and naturalism, or Lukácsian, Bazinian or Kracauerian theories of cinematic realism. In a film such as *Fanny och Alexander*, however, Bergman goes beyond such autobiographism to produce a work of realism which also draws a picture of a surrounding culture. In this sense, *Fanny och Alexander* can be regarded as a type of 'intensive totality', whilst its meandering narrative, long-take photography and thematic content can be related to Bazinian models of cinematic realism.

Influenced by the British documentary film movement of the 1930s, a social realist cinema emerged in Britain during the Second World War. Films such as *In Which We Serve* (David Lean/Noël Coward, 1942) employ location shooting and other techniques derived from the documentary film, in conjunction with a narrative which portrays a united national community. British war-time cinematic realism differed from that of Hollywood in the extent to which it used documentary-based techniques. However, it also differed from mainland European cinematic realism in that it was hardly influenced at all by either European naturalism and realism, phenomenology, or Marxism. In addition, British war-time realism was, in the main, characterised by normative tendencies which differentiated it from the more critical realist cinema emerging elsewhere in Europe during the war years, and films such as *Nine Men* (Harry Watt, 1943), *The Way to the Stars* (Anthony Asquith, 1945) and *The Foreman Went to France* (Charles Frend, 1942) function mainly to reassert officially sanctioned, consensual, conceptions of national identity, rather than throw them into question.

The influence of European realism on the British cinema of the Second World War can be found in the work of film-makers who were familiar with traditions of mainland European film culture. Thus, Alberto Cavalcanti, who made films with the French *avant-garde* during the 1920s, and who had been influenced by French naturalism, cinematic impressionism and surrealism, deployed these influences in his *Went The Day Well?* (1943), and 'The Ventriloquist's Dummy' sequence of *Dead of Night* (Cavalcanti, Dearden, Chrichton, Hamer, 1945).[14] Similarly, Robert Hamer, who, like Cavalcanti, was familiar with French poetic realism and the films of Carné, revealed those influences in his *Pink String and Sealing Wax* (1945) and *It Only Rains on Sunday* (1947). These films undercut, and diverge from, the dominant, normative realist orthodoxies of British war-time realism.

European influences can also be seen at work in the films of Powell and Pressburger. Their *A Canterbury Tale* (1944) and *I Know Where I'm Going* (1945) combine an emphasis on realist observation with a mystical sense of place. The films of Carol Reed are also influenced by French poetic realism and German expressionism, as well as by native English traditions of literary and theatrical realism. For example, Reed's *Odd Man Out* (1947), *The Fallen Idol* (1948), *The Third Man* (1949), *An Outcast of the Islands* (1951) and *The Man Between* (1953) combine documentary naturalism with expressionist, noirish photography, and, at times, subjective camera-work. Many of these films were based on novels or screenplays by Graham Greene, and were also influenced by Greene's belief in the need to develop a British, social-realist cinema.[15]

Ken Loach was one of the most influential British directors to remain committed to a social realist approach during the 1960s, and beyond. Loach's *Kathy Come Home* (1966) used extensive location shooting and non-professional actors to criticise class inequality, and existing social policy over housing and child welfare. Loach's later *Days of Hope* (1976), addressed issues of class struggle in Britain over the period between the beginning of the First World War and the General Strike of 1926, and relied heavily on extensive and detailed historical reconstruction. A similar attention to the naturalism of place and environment can also be found in Loach's *Looks and Smiles* (1981), *Fatherland* (1986) and other films.

However, a film such as *Days of Hope* cannot countenance European naturalism's fatalistic vision of the human condition, because it is influenced by Loach's own, strongly held political convictions, which stress the need for active struggle and commitment to the cause. Loach's politics also leads him to insert a degree of didactic prescriptiveness, and ideological one dimensionality into films such as *Days of Hope*, and this means that *Days of Hope* lacks the ambivalent thematic complexity which Bazin and Kracauer called for, and which a contemporaneous French film such as *Lacombe Lucien* (1974) displays. However, a distinction can be made between *Days of Hope*, which deals directly with political issues, and films such as *Poor Cow* (1967) and *Kes* (1969), which address issues of social underprivilege and exploitation, and are, as a consequence, less overtly didactic. Despite its epic aspirations, and reliance on Marxist models, *Days of Hope*'s dependence on naturalism and political didacticism also means that it cannot be considered an exemplary model of Lukácsian critical realism.

In addition to Loach, Mike Leigh also worked within a realistic vein during the 1970s and 1980s. In films such as *Bleak Moments* (1971), *Abigail's Party* (1977) and *Grown-Ups* (1980), Leigh explored the anxieties and frustrations of urban, lower and lower middle-class life. Like Loach, Leigh's films are naturalistic, rather than realist in a Lukácsian sense. However, and unlike Loach, Leigh rarely addresses political questions directly. Like Pialat, Leigh is another film-maker who can be associated with Kracauerian conceptions of cinematic realism. Leigh's films retain their ironic ambiguity, and disparate, impressionistic naturalism, to the end, whilst their narrative structures are frequently non-linear or episodic, and often provide little more than a schematic account of social and political context. All these characteristics appear in a particularly pronounced form in *Naked* (1993), a film which, in its use of a fluidly structured, episodic and tableaux format, and in its illumination of social context through a focus on the interactions of particular individuals, can be compared to Pialat's *Police* and *Loulou*.

Like Loach, Bill Douglas was also committed to using realism within a social and political context. His early trilogy of documentary films: *My Childhood* (1972), *My Ain Folk* (1974) and *My Way Home* (1979), is as uncompromisingly dark, in its depiction of an oppressive environment which destroys the vulnerable, as the bleakest works of French or Scandinavian naturalism. The same is true of Douglas' *Comrades* (1986) a fictional epic which depicts the plight of the Tolpuddle Martyrs. Despite its increased scale, *Comrades* retains the naturalist concern for environmental background evident in the trilogy, and the same thematic concern for individuals who are exploited and brutalised. *Comrades* is one of the most important works of post-war British realism, a film which combines uncompromising naturalism with Brechtian distanciation devices and elements of 'magic realism'.

Although Douglas died in 1991 without making any further films, both Loach and Leigh continue to work within a realist vein up to the present, as does Terence Davies, whose *Distant Voices, Still Lives* (1988) combines art-house pictorialism with a naturalistic portrayal of working-class, Liverpudlian society. However, in many respects, these film-makers stand against the prevailing tendency which characterised British film-making during the 1980s and 1990s. If realism had been the dominant tradition within the British cinema up till the 1980s, it ceased to be so after that, as directors such as Peter Greenaway, Sally Potter and Derek Jarman emerged, who chose to work within the parameters of a cinema more disposed towards modernism and anti-realism, than realism.

Although realism was an important facet of both the young and new German cinemas it was habitually combined with political modernism in the films of Straub, Fassbinder, Kluge and others. However, one entirely realist genre of films which developed within the new German cinema was the *Arbeiterfilme*. As has already been mentioned, during the 1970s television played an important role in supporting and promoting the emergence of a critical and socially oriented national film culture in West Germany. The television broadcaster in which this public service ethos was most entrenched, and which was also responsible for the emergence of the *Arbeiterfilme*, was Westdeutscher Rundfunk Cologne (WDR). WDR had close links with the Berlin Film and Television Academy, and it was this, together with important changes of personnel within WDR, which provided the broadcaster with the intellectual and institutional means to produce the *Arbeiterfilme*.[16]

The first *Arbeiterfilme* were shown on WDR's Third Channel, a minority viewing channel whose remit was to produce mainly educational programming. One consequence of this was that early *Arbeiterfilme*, such as *Einsamkelt aus Metropolis* (Christian Ziewer, 1968), *Warum ist Frau B. glücklich?* (*Why is Mrs B. Happy?*, Erika Runge, 1968), *Ich heisse Erwin und bin 17 Jahre* (*My Name is Erwin and I'm 17*, Runge, 1970) and *Rote Fahnen sieht man besser* (*Red Flags Can Be Seen Better*, Theo Gallehr and Rolf Schüber, 1971) display a pronounced documentary, educational and didactic bias. For example, *Rote Fahnen sieht man besser* follows the course of an industrial dispute in a manufacturing plant, and provides detailed information on the various stages of the dispute. However, when the *Arbeiterfilme* were transferred from the Third to the more main-stream First Channel in 1971 the shift from documentary to fiction became more pronounced, in films such as *Liebe Mutter, mir geht es gut* (*Dear Mother, I'm OK*, Ziewer, 1971), *Der Angestellte* (*The White Collar Worker*, Helma Sanders, 1971), *Acht Stunden sind kein Tag* (*Eight Hours Are Not a Day*, Rainer Werner Fassbinder, 1972), *Schnee-glöckchen blühn im September* (*Snowdrops Bloom in September*, Ziewer, 1974), *Shirin's Hochzeit* (*Shirin's Wedding*, Helma Sanders, 1975) and the last *Arbeiterfilme*: *Der aufrechte Gang* (*Walking Tall*, Ziewer, 1976).

Although the *Arbeiterfilme* can be more easily associated with Lukácsian, rather than Bazinan or Kracaurian models of cinematic realism, the extent of naturalist description in the films of Ziewer, Runge and others also distinguishes them from the more tightly organised, plot-based model of the Lukácsian intensive totality. *Arbeiterfilme* such as *Rote Fahnen sieht man besser* and *Der aufrechte Gang* situate their narratives within working-class communities, and use non-professional actors and extensive location shooting. In these films, the principal objective is always to link the personal to the directly political, but the films also convey a considerable amount of information about the cultural trappings and life-style of its working-class subjects and participants. This naturalist orientation results in films which are relatively slow paced, contain little dramatic action and rely heavily, sometimes ponderously, on dialogue. Not all the *Arbeiterfilme* produced between 1971 and 1976 concentrated on the everyday travails of the blue-collar, white, and predominantly male West-German working class. For example, *Shirins Hochzeit* explored the impact of racial intolerance upon the minority Turkish community, and also contains a tragic dimension largely absent from most of the other *Arbeiterfilme*.

Fassbinder also made his contribution to the *Arbeiterfilm* with his epic, five part, 470-minute long, *Acht Stunden sind kein Tag* (1972). Here, Fassbinder attempted to introduce a radical dimension into an existing commercial television genre, that of the 'family series' film. Fassbinder's appropriation of the family series genre was influenced by his wish that *Acht Stunden sind kein Tag* should reach as large an audience as possible. However, the film's reliance on Brechtian alienation devices which 'create an unresolved uneasiness in the relation of the spectator to the characters and action of the spectacle' may have stood in the way of realising such an objective.[17]

Although *Arbeiterfilme* such as *Lohn und Liebe* (*Wages and Love*, Ingo Kratisch and Marianne Lüdcke, 1973) often achieved high viewing levels, and favourable critical response, the overtly leftist political position adopted by the film-makers was criticised by conservative opinion within West Germany. This criticism became more acute in the mid 1970s, when the political balance in North Rhine-Westphalia shifted towards the right. Following this, the *Arbeiterfilme* came under increasing attack, particularly for their use of a documentary-drama form which some in positions of power felt amounted to a 'political manipulation of the viewer'.[18] These pressures eventually took their toll, and the *Arbeiterfilme* came to an end in 1976, with Ziewer's *Der aufrechte Gang*.

As was the case with Fassbinder's appropriation of the family series genre within the *Arbeiterfilme*, the next major realist project within the West German cinema was also derived from a genre of popular film-making: that of the *Heimatfilme*. Edgar Reitz's *Heimat* (1984) is one of the most ambitious projects of European cinematic realism ever undertaken. With a duration of some sixteen hours, *Heimat* spans more than sixty years of German history, from 1919 to the early 1980s. However, despite this ambitious time-frame, *Heimat* employs a deliberately contained perspective, and focuses on the linked history of three families. The effect of employing such a circumscribed perspective is further enhanced by setting the film within the small (fictional) village of Schabbach, which Reitz situates in the provincial Hunsrüch region, a rural area within the southern Rhineland.[19]

The term *Heimat* does not translate easily into English. At one level, *Heimat* represents the myth of a lost utopian past, or an ideal homeland within which the individual hopes to experience a renewed sense of identity and belonging. This aspect of *Heimat* has its origins within German romanticism and the medieval myths of the Aryan nation, both of which stress the organic link between the individual and his or her place of origin. Ernst Bloch also defined *Heimat* in almost metaphysical terms when he claimed it to be the utopian antithesis of alienation: declaring that 'There arises in the world something which shines into the childhood of all and in which no one has yet been: homeland'.[20] *Heimat*, therefore, stands for the sense of affinity which occurs when the individual feels organically connected to his or her true origins and identity. However, as Bloch points out, such an affinity is impossible, because *Heimat* is a place 'where no one has yet been', or, for that matter, will ever go.

In addition to its origins within German romanticism, the idea of *Heimat* also has more recent historical derivations. The *Heimat* movement of the 1890s arose in opposition to the rapid expansion of urbanisation and capitalism in what remained a largely rural society, and was grounded in a conception of German national identity premised on rural, traditional and feudal values. During the 1930s and 1940s the values of the nineteenth-century *Heimat* movement were also assimilated into the xenophobic 'blood and soil' ideology of National Socialism, and, in the 1950s, the spirit of *Heimat* re-emerged yet again, within the genre of the commercial *Heimatfilme*.

These historical associations between the idea of *Heimat*, National Socialism and the ideologically suspect post-war *Heimatfilme*, led a majority of intellectuals active on the West German left between 1950 and 1970 to view *Heimat* as an intrinsically reactionary concept. However, during the 1970s, this situation began to change, as a renewed interest in the progressive potential of *Heimat* began to make itself felt. This renewed interest in *Heimat* was, in part, a reaction to the influence of the new history movement, with its emphasis on rural and folk tradition. However, it also emerged in response to the appearance of a new realignment of progressive political forces within West Germany during the 1970s and 1980s.

The radical political configuration which emerged in West Germany during the late 1970s and early 1980s was characterised by a degree of anti-Americanism, and by the rise of anti-nuclear, environmental and devolutionary regionalist movements. Within this latter grouping, the regional and local were elevated in value over a national culture which was perceived as increasingly dominated by the materialistic values of consumer capitalism. It was against this context of a renewed interest in regionalism, and reaction to what was perceived to be the increasingly materialistic culture of the Federal Republic, that intellectuals turned to the idea of *Heimat*. Edgar Reitz's *Heimat* must, therefore, be seen as part of this more widespread attempt to both locate authenticity within local and regional experience, and resist the threat posed to such experience by mass consumer culture.[21]

Heimat centres on close personal relationships, rather than larger-scale historical events, and, in this respect, can be related to the idea of *Alltageschichte*, or the 'historiography of the everyday'.[22] *Heimat* is also based on extensive research carried out in the Hunsrüch region by Reitz. During the course of this, Reitz, who was born and raised in the Hunsrüch, interviewed local villagers, and incorporated many of their stories into the final version of his film. This use of provincial minutia confers a convincing degree of authenticity upon the intertwined, and empirically dense plot of *Heimat*, and also enables the film to cover a broad canvas.

The narrative of *Heimat* is made up of a loosely co-ordinated network of mini-narratives, which focus on the experiences of three families over the course of four generations. One consequence of this collage-like approach is that *Heimat*'s account of the historical development of West German society between 1919 and 1980 is impressionistic and inconclusive, rather than grounded in explicit forms of analysis. Like film-makers such as Fassbinder, Syberberg and Helga Sanders-Brahms, Reitz makes no attempt to provide one overarching explanatory account of West German history in *Heimat*, but, instead, shows that history from a range of different perspectives, and, in particular, from the perspective of 'the small people who live their lives in dignity, albeit without greatness'.[23]

Nevertheless, and despite its undefined, polyphonic structure, *Heimat* does take a stance in relation to the events of recent and current German history. Like others within the young and new German cinemas, and in accordance with the political realignment of the 1970s and 1980s, in *Heimat*, Reitz criticises the extent to which contemporary West German culture has both embraced international capitalism and consumerism, and rejected more organic, regional values. Reitz also believes that the destruction of these values has reached such a stage that the very idea of *Heimat* itself has now become an unrealisable myth. Thus, at the end of his film, Reitz shows the old structures of village life gradually collapsing under the force of a cruder, more garish urban and international culture.

Heimat's detailed perusal of the gradual destruction of the traditional and everyday by a commercially driven modernity complements the microscopic perspective adopted within the film. The small-scale, gradual changes which Reitz documents have a direct impact on the culture of the village, and so can be easily depicted within *Heimat*'s mini-narratives of a commonplace world which is under constant threat. However, this focus upon the fine textures of familiar life also means that *Heimat* inevitably pays less attention to larger-scale historical events, and this aspect of the film has led to criticism that *Heimat* is a revisionary and reactionary text, which avoids the more problematic, darker aspects of recent German history.[24]

However, *Heimat* was not developed as an anti-Nazi project, as some American critics, in particular, wish it had been, but as a statement about the dangers posed by capitalist modernity. In addition, and like Syberberg's approach to the representation of Hitler in *Hitler: Ein Film aus Deutschland* (*Hitler: A Film from Germany*, 1977), Reitz does not believe that an event as horrific, as, for example, the Holocaust, can be represented in a film in any meaningful way. On the contrary, Reitz believes that the narrativisation of such subject matter both contains and neutralises it, removing the true horror from the event, and turning it into an object of spectatorial catharsis.[25] *Heimat* was also made in response to the impact produced by the screening of the American film *Holocaust* in West Germany, in 1979. Reitz believed that *Holocaust* used the horror of the extermination camps only as a background for a 'sentimental family story', and that the American film was a 'glaring example' of 'an international aesthetics of commercialism'.[26] It was partly because of this that *Heimat* avoided the representation of such epochal and emotion laden subject matter as the discovery of the concentration camps.

However, Reitz's objections to *Holocaust* were also based on his concern that it attempted to impose a foreign (i.e. American) interpretation on recent German history, and, in many respects, *Heimat* can be regarded as Reitz's attempt to recover Germany's 'stolen' history, and return it to the Germans.[27] *Heimat* was made during a period, when, following three decades during which West German society had attempted to disavow its own recent history, German artists and intellectuals attempted to re-take possession of that history. Thus, in an echo of the assertion of German intellectual agency implicit in the title of Syberberg's *Hitler: Ein Film aus Deutschland*, and in direct repost to *Holocaust*'s attempt at historical appropriation, *Heimat* is subtitled 'Made in Germany', as a repost to the forms of cultural imperialism and historical expropriation of which Reitz believes *Holocaust* to be only one example.

It has also been argued that, through its emphasis on *Alltageschichte*, *Heimat* can be directly related to Kracauer's theory of cinematic realism, and that Kracauer's conception of the 'base of life', with its 'sorrows and satisfactions, discords and feasts, wants and pursuits which mark the ordinary business of living', is analogous to the thematic preoccupations of Reitz's film.[28] *Heimat* does, as Kracauer advocates, represent the 'texture of everyday life' in the way that it tracks its characters as they grow older, marry, divorce, fight, suffer, rejoice and die. Reitz also believes that, through engaging with these innumerable stories of everyday life, a larger picture of German history will eventually emerge from the bottom up, and that this new image of German history will be less authoritarian than that produced within more officially sanctioned forms of historiography and cultural production.[29]

The style of editing and photography employed in *Heimat* also complements Reitz's account of the gradual decline of *heimat*. The greater part of *Heimat* is shot in a realistic style using a black and white photography which confers a degree of documentary authenticity on its subject matter. At the beginning of the film, the camerawork and editing is often slow and meditative, and long-take, moving camera shots are much in evidence. However, in addition to this lyrical documentary realism, Reitz also employs more formative techniques in *Heimat* in order to poeticise his images, and infuse them with a sense of larger symbolism. In such scenes, the camera often lingers over objects, which then take on added, though ultimately enigmatic, significance. This focus on the poeticised materiality of objects recalls Kracauer's demand for a cinema which can 'redeem' the physical world, and Reitz's claim that, in *Heimat*, he wishes to 'defend things in a society that consumes them and throws them away' warrants further comparison with Kracauer.[30]

Colour is also used in *Heimat* in a way which corresponds to Reitz's wish to poeticise the traditional life of the village. Colour is only used in brief sequences, in order to suffuse particular actions and objects with a more general significance. However, the use of colour, like the use of special lighting effects, complex multinarrative structures and extreme close-ups, also makes *Heimat* a reflexive film. In addition to its realism, therefore, *Heimat* employs a series of formative devices whose principal function is to reveal the film's artifice and formal construction. For example, as the film proceeds, and the traditional life of the village gradually gives way to the intrusion of a more modern, instrumental culture, the dominant realistic style of *Heimat* also breaks down. The meditative, poetic qualities which characterised the opening episodes of the film are gradually replaced by a more gaudy, abrasive and discordant style of film-making, which also signals the coming destruction of *Heimat*. These two contrasting styles of film-making not only symbolise the existence and loss of *Heimat*, but are also deployed in order to foreground the function and role of the film-making process.

During the immediate post-war period in the Soviet Union, the official policy of socialist realism was applied with renewed vigour, ensuring that western European movements such as Italian neo-realism had little influence. The films of this period were also highly regulated and censored in order to ensure that they remained within official guidelines. One of the most significant casualties of this period was Eisenstein's *Ivan Grozny* (*Ivan the Terrible: Part Two*, 1946) and 'Part Three'. *Part Two* was banned outright by the authorities, and not released again in the Soviet Union until 1958, whilst 'Part Three' was destroyed.[31] The death of Stalin in 1953, and subsequent rise to power of Nikita Khrushchev, led to the 'thaw period' of 1953–8, during which official censorship and regulation of the film industry was relaxed. As a consequence, although films such as Grigori Chukhrai's *Sorok prevyi* (*The Forty First*, 1956) and Mikhail Kalatozov's *Letyat zhuravli* (*The Cranes Are Flying*, 1957) were still produced within the normative framework of a socialist realist style, they were also able to be more critical and innovative than had been the case with films produced during the Stalin era, and it has been argued that Kalatozov's film, in particular, became the 'symbol and expression of the new epoch'.[32]

The period from 1953 to 1965–6 was one of relative liberalisation within both the Soviet Union, and within the Soviet film industry, and one of the most important directors to emerge during this period was Andrei Tarkovsky. Tarkovsky's *Ivanovo detstvo* (*Ivan's Childhood*, 1962) was influenced by the European cinema of Bergman and others, whilst his *Andrei Rublev* (1965) drew on both European art cinema and Russian regional folk traditions. Unfortunately for Tarkovsky, a new period of conservatism was ushered in when Khrushchev was replaced as Party leader by Leonid Brezhnev in 1964, and *Andrei Rublev* was banned immediately, along with Andrei Konchalovsky's *Asya's Happiness* (1966) and Alexander Askoldov's *Commissar* (1966), both of which were deemed to be too critical of official policies. *Andrei Rublev* did not manage to achieve a limited distribution within the Soviet Union until as late as 1972.[33] As the Brezhnev regime consolidated its power further, films such as these became increasingly scarce, and a more normative socialist realism re-established itself as the dominant orthodoxy, as in, for example, 'pedagogic realist' films such as *Babye tsartvo* (*Women's Rule*, Alexei Saltykov, 1967), and *Okroshcheniye ognia* (*The Taming of Fire*, Daniil Khrabrovitsky, 1971): a film about the development of Soviet rocket technology.[34]

Nevertheless, the period between 1964 and 1968 remained one of relative liberalisation within the Soviet film industry, as the fading influence of Khrushchev's thaw continued to make itself felt.[35] As a consequence, a number of films were produced within this period which departed from the officially sanctioned forms of socialist realism. One of the most important of these was Sergei Bondarchuk's *Voyna i mir* (*War and Peace*, 1967), an epic adaption of Tolstoy's novel. *Voyna i mir* conforms to the Lukácsian model of the intensive totality in a number of respects. It is based on one of the classic works of nineteenth-century realist literature which influenced Lukács' theory of aesthetic realism, and it also deploys the complex plot structure, and detailed relation of individual characters to social context, which Lukács endorsed.

However, *Voyna i mir* also uses some overtly modernist techniques, such as a symbolic, anti-realist use of colour, disembodied speech, rapid editing and reflexive, hand-held camera cinematography; and the film's chief importance lies in the extent to which it shows how the Lukácsian model of the intensive totality can be given a successful modernist inflection. Although an example of critical, as opposed to socialist realism, *Voyna i mir* was, nevertheless, politically innocuous enough to cause the ruling regime few problems, and, despite its modernist style, was promoted as a great achievement of Soviet cinema during the Brezhnev era. It was, however, followed by a number of similar, though far less innovative big-budget historical reconstruction films, including *Waterloo* (Bondarchuk, 1970) and the 'entirely sterile' *Osvobozhdenie* (*Liberation*, Yuri Ozerov, 1971).[36]

After 1968, and the Soviet invasion of Czechoslovakia, the Brezhnev regime clamped down severely on oppositional elements within intellectual and cultural life through a campaign of arrests, forced exile and public condemnation.[37] However, as the socialist realist style once again began to be imposed in the Soviet Union, filmmakers in the regional republics, often influenced by anti-Russian nationalist sentiment, developed a more poetic, symbolic style of film-making. The first of this group of films (labelled as 'difficult' by the authorities) was Sergei Paradzhanov's *Teni zabytykh Predkov* (*Shadows of Forgotten Ancestors*, 1965).[38] This was followed by *Sayat Nova* (*The Colour of Pomegranates*, Paradzhanov, 1969), Georgy Shengalaya's *Pirosmani* (1969) and Yuri Ilienko's *Belaya pititsa s chernoy otmetinoy* (*White Bird With a Black Spot*, 1971). Tarkovsky's *Andrei Rublev* and *Zerkalo* (*Mirror*, 1975) can also be related to this group of films, which explicitly reject socialist realism, and turn, instead, to a cinema of personal expression which emphasises the artist's poetic sensibility. After 1968, this school of film-making came under increasing political attack from the authorities, and this reached a peak with the release of *Sayat Nova*, a film about the medieval Armenian poet and minstrel, Sayat-Nova. *Sayat Nova* was criticised for its emphasis on religious values and allegorical mysticism, and was withdrawn from circulation shortly after its premiere.[39]

The best of the Russian cinema of the 1970s combined the influence of this critical, expressive-poetic tradition with that of European art cinema. Andrei Mikhalkov-Konchalovsky's *Siberiad* (1979), Nikita Mikhalkov's *Raba lyubvi* (*A Slave of Love*, 1976) and Andrei Tarkovsky's *Stalker* (1979) fall into this category. However, by the early 1980s, as the Brezhnev regime began to lose its grip, Soviet cinema once again began to return to critical realism. Elem Klimov's *Idi i smotri* (*Come and See*, 1985) was released the same year that Mikhail Gorbachev assumed the leadership of the Communist Party. Klimov's stark portrayal of the German occupation of Byelorussia during the Second World War heralded the arrival of a more critical cinema during the period of *glasnost* (openness) and *perestroika* (restructuring), which included such films as Vasily Puchul's *Malen'kaya Vera* (*Little Vera*, 1988), a film which undermined traditional communist stereotypes of the virtuous, socially responsible Russian woman.

Whilst socialist realism quickly became the dominant orthodoxy within the post-war Soviet Block of Eastern European countries, many of the film-makers within these countries nevertheless attempted to stretch the boundaries of official orthodoxy from the outset. This was particularly the case during the thaw period, when important work began to emerge in Czechoslovakia, Poland and Hungary. Of these three countries the most significant in terms of the development of a critical realist cinema was Poland, and the most important director to emerge from the 'Polish School' of the 1950s was Andrzej Wajda. Wajda's trilogy of films: *Pokolenie* (*A Generation*, 1954), *Kanal* (1957) and *Papiao diament* (*Ashes and Diamonds*, 1959) centres on the activities of the non-Communist Polish resistance during the Second World War, and celebrates the resistance in ways which contradicted the then official dogmas of the Polish Communist Party. *Kanal*, in particular, also draws on poetic realist stylistics in its claustrophobic evocation of subterranean guerrilla warfare.

In 1970 a succession of workers strikes led to an easing of

political regulation and censorship within Poland, and this, in turn, allowed a more critical, social realist cinema, which described itself as the 'cinema of moral conscience', to emerge. Following a period in which he worked in a range of film-making styles, Wajda returned to a social realist vein in the wake of the political ferment which erupted in Poland in 1976. Wajda's *Czlowiek z marmura* (*Man of Marble*, 1976) explores the role of propaganda, censorship and cultural socialisation in Stalinist Poland during the 1950s, whilst his *Czlowiek z zelaza* (*Man of Iron*, 1980) portrays the continued role of political manipulation, and development of political opposition forces, during the 1960s and 1970s.

Both of these films can be regarded as intensive totalities in the Lukácsian sense, in that they focus on the interrelationship between individual characters and an array of social, cultural, political and institutional forces. *Czlowiek z zelaza* also incorporates contemporaneous documentary footage of the Solidarity strikes at the Gdansk shipyard into its narrative about individual conscience, social action and the struggle between opposition forces and the state. *Czlowiek z marmura* and *Czlowiek z zelaza* are also reflexive films, which employ techniques such as the flashback, actuality footage, and various references to the film-making process, in combination with a Lukácsian realist model. As with Bondarchuk's *Voyna i mir*, this combination of Lukácsian critical realism and modernist reflexivity makes these two films particularly important.

Wajda later developed the Lukácsian documentary-drama approach of *Czlowiek z zelaza* further in his *Danton* (1982), a detailed reconstruction of the events leading up to the execution of one of the chief architects of the French Revolution. In *Danton*, Wajda explores the conflicts and tensions which emerged between Danton, Robespierre and the Jacobins, and describes the revolutionary events which took place between the rise to power of the Jacobins, and their eventual replacement by a bourgeois regime in 1794. Like *Czlowiek z zelaza* and *Voyna i mir*, *Danton* also suggests ways in which the Lukácsian intensive totality can be combined with a modernist approach. For example, whilst conforming to the overall model of the intensive totality, *Danton* uses a jarring, reflexive music and sound score, formative editing, complex narrative transitions and foregrounded camerawork.

In addition to Wajda, two other Polish film-makers who came to prominence during this period, and who were also associated with the 'cinema of moral conscience', were Krsysztof Zanussi and Krszyszlof Kieslowski. Like Wajda's *Czlowiek z zelaza*, films such as *Spirala* (*Spiral*, Zanussi, 1978) and *Przypadek* (*Chance*, Kieslowski,

1981), are concerned with issues of individual moral and political choice, set against a troubled social and political context. Like Wajda, both Kieslowski and Zanussi saw themselves as film-makers with a role to play in articulating themes which the ruling regime were attempting to suppress, or distort, and both made films which combined social realism with modernist and 'magic realist' techniques.

Kieslowski's most significant achievement was his series of ten television films *Dekolog* (*The Decalogue*, 1988), each of which was based on one of the Christian Ten Commandments. Two films emerged from this: *Krotki film o zabijaniu* (*A Short Film about Killing*, 1988) and *Krotki film o milosci* (*A Short Film about Love*, 1988). Like *Dekolog*, these two films combine a humanist moral discourse and art-cinema sensibility with the depiction of an alienating social and cultural environment. However, unlike Wajda's later films, Kieslowski's films are more concerned with individual psychological, rather than social and political reality, and this places him outside the main stream of European cinematic realism: a stream which runs from pictorialist naturalism, through poetic realism, the *tradition de qualité*, Renoir, Pialat, Leigh, Reitz and Wajda; and which also includes the Italian and Spanish directors to be covered in the next chapter.

Notes

1. Williams, Alan, *Republic of Images* (Cambridge, MA and London: Harvard University Press, 1992), p. 239.
2. Ibid., p. 264.
3. Ibid., p. 277.
4. Bazin, André, *What Is Cinema? Volume I* (Berkeley, CA and London: University of California Press, 1967), pp. 139 and 133.
5. Forbes, Jill, *The Cinema in France*, After the New Wave (London: BFI/ Macmillan, 1992), p. 244.
6. Ibid., p. 167.
7. Annales School: *Annales* was a journal founded by Marc Bloch and Lucien Febvre in 1929. The school's approach to history was based on a belief that long-term structural sociological trends should be studied, rather than a chronicle of major political events. The School's most prestigious member is probably Fernand Braudel, whose *The Mediterranean and the Mediterranean World in the Age of Philip II* is regarded as a classic of the *Annales* approach.
8. Forbes, op cit., p. 221.
9. Bazin, op cit., p. 14.
10. Kracauer, Siegfried, *Theory of Film* (Oxford: Oxford University Press, 1978), p. 256.

11. Benjamin, Walter, 'Theses on the Philosophy of History', *Illuminations* (London: Fontana Press, 1992), p. 246.

12. Kracauer, op cit., p. 300.

13. Ibid., p. 72.

14. Aitken, Ian, *Alberto Cavalcanti: Realism, Surrealism and National Cinemas* (London: Flicks Books, 2000).

15. Greene was closely associated with the documentary film movement during the 1930s, and took part in the public debate over the development of a national, realist cinema in Britain during the 1940s and 1950s.

16. Collins, Richard and Porter, Vincent, *WDR and the Arbeiterfilm: Fassbinder, Ziewer and Others* (London: BFI, 1981), p. 30.

17. Ibid., p. 53.

18. Ibid., p. 162.

19. Kaes, Anton, *From Hitler to Heimat: The Return of History as Film* (Cambridge, MA and London: Harvard University Press, 1992), p. 164.

20. Ibid., p. 165.

21. Hansen, Miriam, 'Dossier on *Heimat*', in Ginsberg, Terri and Thompson, Moana Kirsten (eds), *Perspectives on German Cinema* (New York: G. K. Hall & Co., 1996), p. 107.

22. Kaes, op cit., p. 172.

23. Karsten Witte, 'Dossier on *Heimat*', in Ginsberg and Thompson, op cit., p. 111.

24. Koch, Gertrud, 'Dossier on *Heimat*', in Ginsberg and Thompson, op cit., p. 116.

25. Kaes, op cit., p. 184.

26. Ibid.

27. Ibid.

28. Ibid., p. 171.

29. Ibid., p. 172.

30. Ibid.

31. Barna, Yon, *Eisenstein* (London: Secker & Warburg, 1973), p. 265.

32. Vronskaya, Jeanne, *Young Soviet Film-makers* (London: George Allen and Unwin, 1972), p. 18.

33. Liehm, Mira and Liehm Antonin, J., *The Most Important Art: East European Film After 1945* (Berkeley, CA and London: University of California Press, 1977), pp. 308–9.

34. Ibid., p. 318.

35. Shlapentokh, Dimitri and Shlapentokh, Vladimir, *Soviet Cinematography 1918–1991* (New York: Aldine de Gruyter, 1993), p. 147.

36. Liehm and Liehm, op cit., pp. 312–13.

37. Shlapentokh and Shlapentokh, op cit., pp. 147–8.

38. Marshall, Herbert, 'The New Wave in Soviet Cinema', in Lawton, Anna (ed.), *The Red Screen: Politics, Society, Art in Soviet Cinema* (London and New York: Routledge, 1992), p. 176.

39. Ibid., pp. 188–9.

Post-war Italian and Spanish Realist Cinema

Between 1922 and 1943 Italy was ruled by a fascist dictatorship which used mainstream cinema as a means of disseminating officially sanctioned conceptions of national identity. A national regulatory body, the Direzione Generale della Cinematografica, was established in 1934 in order to review and ammend film scripts, and to promote pro-fascist films such as *Vecchia Guardia* (*The Old Guard*, Alessandro Blasetti, 1933): a film which commemorated the tenth anniversary of Mussolini's ascendency to power. The Centro Cattolico Cinematografico was also established in 1934, with the task of policing the moral and religious content of Italian cinema, and, in 1935, the foundation of the Ente Nazionale Industrie Cinematografiche enabled the State to exercise more or less complete control of the film industry.[1]

Nevertheless, and despite this degree of state intervention, the majority of films produced within the Italian cinema of the fascist period were conventional, commercial vehicles, rather than platforms for explicitly pro-fascist propaganda. The films which emerged from this context of generic, commercial production included ornamental and overheated 'filmed operas', extravagant Roman epics such as Alessandro Blasetti's *La Corona di ferro* (*The Iron Crown*, 1940), and glossy 'white telephone' comedies of manners, such as Max Neufeld's *Mille lire al mese* (*A Thousand Lire a Month*, 1933). During the war years the Italian Government introduced protectionist legislation, and this led to an increase in the production of such films, until, by 1942, output had reached a peak of 119. However, the majority of these films were, according to one critic, characterised by 'artistic mediocrity and ... startling separation from reality'.[2]

It was in response to this that a group of Italian directors known as the 'calligraphers' appeared during the 1940s. The films of Renato Castellani, Mario Soldati and Alberto Lattuada were produced under the constraints imposed by a watchful regime, and were, as a consequence, restricted in their ability to express oppositional ideas. This led Soldati and others to withdraw from the representation of contemporary subject matter, and to direct films such as *Piccolo mondo antico* (*Little Old Fashioned World*, 1940), which were set in the past, and preoccupied with questions of style. Nevertheless, and despite this degree of withdrawal from an uncomfortable political context, the use of location shooting in films such as *Piccolo mondo antico* and *La Donna della montagna* (*Woman of the Mountains*, Carlo Lizzani, 1942) provided a foundation on which the cinema of neorealism would later build.

If one of the sources of Italian neorealism can be located in a desire to transcend the artificiality of the cinema of the fascist period, another can be found in the development of a critical film culture in Italy from the mid 1930s onwards. In 1935 the Italian central film school, the Centro Sperimentale della cinematografia, was founded under the direction of the anti-fascist Luigi Chiarini. In 1937 the Centro Sperimentale established its own journal, *Bianco e nero*, and this was quickly followed by the founding of the influential journal *Cinema*, in 1938. Between 1937 and 1943 these two journals published articles by film theorists such as Rudolph Arnheim and Béla Balázs, and, together with the Centro Sperimentale, laid the foundation for the development of a more critical and progressive Italian film culture. Future neorealist directors, such as Roberto Rossellini, Guiseppi De Santis, Pietro Germi and Michelangelo Antonioni, attended the Centro Sperimentale, and also contributed to *Bianco e nero*; whilst Luchino Visconti was closely associated with the *Cinema* group.[3]

The French poetic realist cinema of Carné and Renoir also played an important role in the development of neorealism. Luchino Visconti, whose *Ossessione* (*Obsession*, 1942) is considered to have inaugurated neorealism, worked with Renoir on *Une Partie de campagne* (*A Day in the Country*) in 1936, and the abandoned *La Tosca* in 1940; whilst Antonioni worked alongside Carné on *Les Visiteurs du soir* (*The Visitors of the Evening*, 1942). The influence of poetic realism on neorealism was also reinforced by the impact of American literary naturalism. During the 1930s, the novels of Hemmingway, Faulkner, Dos Passos, Steinbeck, James M. Cain and others were translated into Italian by novelists such as Cesare Pavese and Elio Vittorini, and this provided a model for Italian film-makers seeking an alternative to the standard commercial fare. Nevertheless, *Ossessione*, which was loosely based on Cain's novel *The Postman Always Rings Twice*, was the only neorealist film to be directly derived from an American novel of the 1930s.

In addition to poetic realism and American literary naturalism, neorealism was also shaped by a school of realist literature which emerged in Italy during the 1930s, which included prominent writers such as Alberto Moravia, Elio Vittorini, Cesare Pavese and Vasco Pratolini. These writers rejected the 'positive' portrayals of cultural life required by fascist ideology, and focused, instead, on the experiences of the poor and socially marginal. Realist novels such as Vittorini's *Conversazione in Sicilia* (1941) had a particularly strong influence on directors such as Visconti and De Santis, becoming a 'bible to the neorealists'.[4]

One final important influence on neo-realism was that of the nineteenth-century Sicilian *verist* novelist, Giovanni Verga. Verga's ideas shaped the approach to cinematic realism adopted by the journal *Cinema*, and Visconti's *La Terra trema* (*The Earth Trembles* 1947) was also based on Verga's best-known novel: *The House By the Medlar Tree*. Visconti, De Santis and others were particularly impressed by the way in which Verga combined a poetic, humanist sensibility with the detailed, concrete depiction of Sicilian landscape and society, and De Santis argued that, besides being a 'great poet', Verga had also created an *oeuvre* which:

> seems to offer the strongest and most human, the most marvellously virgin and authentic ambience that can inspire the imagination of a cinema seeking things and facts in a time and space dominated by reality so as to detach itself from facile suggestions and decadent bourgeois taste.[5]

The emphasis which De Santis places on 'things', 'facts' and 'reality' here also echoes one of the first formulations of the neorealist aesthetic, as elaborated by Arnaldo Bocelli in 1930, where Bocelli argues that neorealism was 'sunk as deeply as possible into things, adhering to the object'.[6] This emphasis on the concrete, when combined with opposition to both fascist ideology, and a literary culture grounded in 'autobiographical lyricism' and 'elegiac introversion', was to have a profound influence on later neorealist filmmaking.[7] However, Verga's affirmative humanism was also to prove as influential as his penchant for detailed observation. For example, Vittorio De Sica's claim that Verga's work amounted to 'a revolutionary art inspired by, and acting, in turn, as inspiration to a humanity which hopes and suffers', reflects the affirmative humanism found within many neorealist films.[8]

De Santis' designation of Verga's work as 'humanist' also indicates an important distinction which must be drawn between

French nineteenth-century naturalism and its Italian counterpart: *verismo*. During the nineteenth century, Italian critics such as Francesco De Sanctis, Luigi Capuana and Verga criticised French naturalism for its pessimism, scientism, and emphasis on the genetically flawed, Darwinian *bête humaine*. Whilst adopting the factual, observational style of French naturalism, these critics insisted on the infusion of a more hopeful dimension into the naturalist vision, and Verga's insistence that, in addition to showing things as they are, *verismo* should also indicate how they could, ideally, be, was later to influence the engaged, humanist orientation adopted by neorealism.[9]

These various influences led neorealist cinema to focus on the relationship between individual and environment, and on the suffering of 'the poor, the underprivileged, the ordinary'.[10] Consequently, films such as *La Terra trema* and *Ladri di biciclette* (*Bicycle Thieves*, De Sica, 1948) situate working-class characters within social and cultural environments marked by poverty, social hardship and injustice, and also depict the relationship between character and environment in considerable empirical detail, furnishing that 'concrete homage to other people, that is, to all who exist', which the critic and scenarist Cesare Zavattini called for in his influential 'A Thesis on Neo-Realism'.[11]

In addition to this concern with the concrete and the ordinary, neorealist films such as *Ladri di biciclette*, *Germania anno zero* (*Germany Year Zero*, Rossellini, 1947) and *Umberto D* (De Sica, 1951) also emphasise the ambivalent character of everyday experience. This concern to depict the ambiguous nature of existence was partly influenced by the unresolved *finales* of French films such as *La Bête humaine*, *Quai des brumes* and *Pépé le Moko*. However, it was also influenced by a rejection of the tendency towards superficial, and often highly normative, narrative resolution which typified the cinema of the fascist period. It was in reaction to what Luigi Chiarini called the 'web of censorship' which surrounded the fascist cinema that the neorealist films which appeared after the liberation deliberately attempted to depict post-war Italian society in all its unsettling complexities.[12] Consequently, even though neorealists such as Chiarini emerged from the liberation committed to a form of film-making which would make a positive contribution towards social reform, they also insisted on the right to depict the Italian social formation as, in Chiarini's words, ' a world in ruins'.[13]

Prior to the liberation, the most influential neorealist film to appear in Italy was Visconti's *Ossessione*, which was conceived as something of a manifesto for the *Cinema* group, and whose noirish, fatalistic tone was developed in deliberate repost to the obligatory optimism of the fascist cinema.[14] The neorealist films which were made directly after the liberation deal with the war and its immediate aftermath, and include *Roma città aperta* (*Rome Open City*, Rossellini, 1945), *Paisà* (Rossellini, 1946), *Sciuscià* (*Shoeshine*, De Sica, 1946), *Il Sole sorge ancora* (*The Sun Rises Again*, Aldo Vergano, 1946), *Vivere in pace* (*To Live in Peace*, Luigi Zampa, 1946) and *Germania anno zero*. In these films the humanist orientation of neorealism is reinforced by a context of the rise to power in Italy of a post-war popular front government uniting liberal, centrist and left-wing political parties, and films such as *Paisà* and *Roma città aperta* endorse the programme of the anti-fascist popular front, rather than any explicitly Marxist position.[15]

Neorealist film-makers regarded themselves as active participants in the process of post-war social reconstruction, and, consequently, after 1947, neorealism turned to the exploration of issues such as economic reconstruction and social reform. *Ladri di biciclette*, *La Terra trema*, *Il Mulino del Po* (*The Mill on the Po*, Alberto Lattuada, 1948) and *Riso amaro* (*Bitter Rice*, Giuseppe De Santis, 1948), all fall into this category of socially purposive film-making. This activist predisposition was partly influenced by the affirmative realist humanism of the nineteenth-century *verist* tradition, and partly by the extent to which the success of the resistance (many neorealists had been active members) led film-makers to believe they could continue to play an effective role in shaping the course of events.

Neorealism reflected a commitment to the broad-based, cross-party political consensus which typified post-war Italian political discourse, and which was embodied within the policies of the popular front. However, after 1948, neorealist film-makers came under criticism, as Italian politics moved further to both left and right. Following election victories by the conservative Christian Democratic party in 1948, neorealist films were increasingly criticised for their 'negative' depiction of Italian society, and neorealism also received a further blow in 1949, when the so-called 'Andreotti law' came into force. The Andreotti Law established a series of quotas and subsidies designed to raise the level of home film production. However, subsidies and export licenses could also be denied to films which, in the government's view, 'slandered Italy'.[16] As it transpired, many of the exclusion orders made under the Law tended to target neorealist films, and Andreotti even intervened directly to condemn De Sica's *Umberto D* as a 'wretched service to his fatherland, which is also the fatherland of … progressive social legislation'.[17] Such criticism mirrors the assault made on *Ossessione* by Vittorio Mussolini in 1942, when he asserted that 'this [*Ossessione*] is not Italy',[18] and also reflects the fact that, from 1942, until at least the early 1950s, neorealism retained its oppositional character in relation to the government of the day.

In addition to criticism from the centre-right, neorealism also came under censure from the communist left during the late 1940s. In 1948 the Soviet Union's attempt to incorporate the western sectors of Berlin into the Eastern Block led to a marked intensification of the Cold War. The official Soviet policy of the Popular Front had been abandoned in 1946–7 and replaced by one which revisited the 'class against class' politics of the early 1930s.[19] This also coincided with the reaffirmation of Zhadanovist Soviet socialist realism as the official aesthetic doctrine of the Communist Party. However, neorealism had evolved within the ideological configurations of popular frontism, and the humanist, social-democratic tendencies which characterised many neorealist films could not be squared with the new political context.

In 1948, De Santis's *Riso amaro* was castigated by the communist daily *L'Unita* for its lack of 'positive heroes' and 'decadent' displays of female flesh; whilst Visconti received the ultimate rebuke of having his films compared to what, in Stalinist eyes, represented one of the worst excesses of 'decadent', European bourgeois cinema: the *réalisme poétique* of Renoir, Carné and others. Just as Renoir's *La Bête humaine* had been condemned by the French Communist Party during the 1930s, *Ossessione* was also accused of taking up the 'worst and most condemnable aspects' of the pre-war French cinema, including 'the erotic ambience of Renoir's films'.[20] Over the period from 1948 to the mid 1950s virtually every neorealist film-maker came under critical assault from the communist left. This criticism reinforced that emerging from the Christian Democratic right, and, yet further censure arrived from the Catholic Church, which classified neorealism in general, and *Riso amaro* in particular, as 'forbidden for believers'.[21]

As neorealism declined as an identifiably coherent aesthetic position during the early 1950s, the films of the major neorealist directors also evolved stylistically. Lucino Visconti drew on Marxist theory in making films such as *Ossessione* and *La Terra trema*, both of which, and particularly *La Terra trema*, were made within the neorealist style. However, with *Senso* (1954), Visconti departed radically from the documentary style of *La Terra trema* (which he had made in close association with the Italian Communist Party). *Senso* adopts an 'operatic', melodramatic format in order to portray the final months of the 1883 Austrian occupation of the

Venetian provinces. *Senso* also marks Visconti's shift from a neo-realist practice grounded in naturalism, to a more Lukácsian form of cinematic realism, as Visconti himself made clear when he argued that his aim in making *Senso* was 'to use history as a backdrop for the personal story of Countess Serpieri, who was ultimately no more interesting than the representative of a certain social class'.[22]

Senso focuses on the love affair between the Venetian countess Livia Serpieri and Franz Mahler, an Austrian army officer. However, neither of these two characters are rendered as 'positive' in any sense. Serpieri is unable to contain her own emotional turmoil, whilst her relationship with a representative of the occupying forces constitutes a symbolic betrayal of the Venetian resistance. Similarly, Mahler is a corrupt coward, who is eventually executed for desertion. This negative characterisation is not, however, used as an end in itself, or, as in poetic realism, in order to foreground individual existentialist *angst*, but as a means of illuminating the larger context of *fin de siècle* decadence and instability which *Senso* identifies with the final stages of the defeated Austrian occupation.

However, although *Senso* can be described as an example of Lukácsian cinematic realism, Visconti's film also departs significantly from the type of plot-based critical realism which Lukács acclaims in a novel such as Thomas Mann's *Der Zauberberg*. In addition to using plot and dialogue in order to construct an 'intensive totality', Visconti also employs both melodramatic and operatic forms, and an expressive use of colour and music in *Senso*, in order to create what Visconti referred to as 'a romantic film, filled with the essence of Italian opera'.[23] The end result is a film with a complex, and often confusing plot structure, which focuses on the fatal emotional entanglement of two individuals, but which provides only schematic details of the surrounding social and political context, as it attempts to express the inner spirit of the period.

Senso was acclaimed by the communist left in Italy because of the extent to which it abandoned the 'negative naturalism' of neorealism, and because it appeared to adopt a model of realism more in accord with the dictates of Soviet socialist realism. For example, whilst criticising both Rossellini's *Viaggio in Italia* (*Voyage To Italy*, 1953) and Fellini's *La Strada* (*The Street*, 1954) as 'regressive', and as failing to advance a progressive political message, Guido Aristarco, the editor in chief of *Cinema Nuovo*, described *Senso* as 'a great historical film, a revolutionary film which brought our cinematic history to a new peak'.[24] Aristarco's admiration for *Senso* reflected his support for Visconti's attempt to transcend the kind of neorealist aesthetic which had been roundly condemned by the communist left from 1948 onwards, but may also have led him to ignore the extent to which *Senso* departed from the orthodox social realist model advocated elsewhere in the pages of *Cinema Nuovo*.

After *Senso*, Visconti switched between neorealism and more Lukácsian forms of realism. The metaphorical realism of *Senso* was continued in *Le Notti bianche* (*The White Nights*, 1957). However, this was then followed by the more neorealist *Rocco e i suoi fratelli* (*Rocco and his Brothers*, 1960). Visconti's most Lukácsian film is undoubtedly *Il Gattopardo* (*The Leopard*, 1963). Set during the period 1860–62, *Il Gattopardo* chronicles the unfolding tensions which develop between the revolutionary movement, led by Garibaldi, and the growing power of the Italian bourgeoisie. However, the critical realism of *Il Gattopardo* is undermined by its reliance on big-budget pretensions, an overcomplex and confusing narrative structure, and miscast international stars such as Burt Lancaster, Claudia Cardinale and Alain Delon. *Il Gattopardi* also fails because it departs from Visconti's characteristic approach to the linking of the personal and the political. In later films, such as *Vaghe stelle dell'Orsa* (*Sandra*, 1965) and *La Caduto degli dei* (*The Damned*, 1969), Visconti returned to the more intimate focus adopted in *Senso*, and made romantic and family relationships the basis for films which also explored alienating historical and political contexts. *La Caduto degli dei*, in particular, with its portrayal of power and corruption within an upper-class Nazi family, can, like *Senso*, be regarded as an example of Visconti's overwrought, melodramatic adaption of the Lukácsian intensive totality.

In contrast to Visconti, the films made by Fellini and Antonioni during the 1950s and 1960s display a concern for cinematic realism more readily associated with the theories of Bazin and Kracauer, than Lukács. Writing about *La Strada*, for example, Fellini referred to Bazin's mentor, Emmanuel Mounier, when arguing that *La Strada* did not depict 'socio-political life', but 'captured an experience [of] the communication between two human beings'.[25] Fellini's *La Strada*, *Il Bidone* (*The Swindler*, 1955) and *Le Notti di Cabiria* (*Nights of Cabiria*, 1956) distance themselves from Visconti's apocalyptic 'socio-political' considerations, and focus on the everyday world of human interaction. This leads Fellini to define 'realism', in a film such as *La Strada*, in terms of the portrayal of two people who 'reach out and find one another', and, thereby, rescue a relationship which, otherwise, would become 'indifferent, isolated and impenetrable':

If a film creates a microscopic image of this evolution of feelings (in art, historical dimensions do not count) and captures the

contrast between a monologue and a dialogue, then it fulfils a
contemporary need, clears up and penetrates some of its aspects:
this is what I call realism.[26]

As the quotation above suggests, the means of capturing such realism is not through the portrayal of Lukácsian/Viscontian 'historical
dimensions', but through the 'microscopic image' of the historical
which exists within the 'evolution of feelings'. Fellini reinforces
this point further when, again referring to La Strada, he argues that
'Sometimes a film that captures the contradictions of contemporary
feelings through an elementary dialectics is more realistic than a
film that depicts the evolution of a precise sociopolitical reality'.[27] It
is, therefore, the contradictions which are expressed within this
evolution of feeling, an evolution which occurs within a dialectic of
monologue (isolation) and dialogue (reaching out and finding),
which Fellini seeks to establish within La Strada, and which he
characterises as 'realism'.

Like Rossellini's Viaggio in Italia, La Strada was also criticised by
the communist left for its apparent lack of engagement with the
political. However, although not a film à thèse in Aristarco's sense
of the term, La Strada does take a stand on issues such as poverty
and exploitation, and also conforms to Bazin's dictum that
neorealism necessarily presupposes a particular 'attitude of mind'
on the part of the director: one which combines reason, intuition
and emotion. Neorealism is a synthetic, rather than analytic
aesthetic, and, in Bazin's terms, 'a description of reality conceived
as a whole by a consciousness disposed to see things as a whole ... a
presentation which is at once elliptic and synthetic'.[28]

Nevertheless, Fellini's films also invariably combine this holistic
and elliptical form of film-making with social critique. So, for
example, La Dolce vita (1960) debunks the cosmetic superficiality of
Italian high society, whilst Amarcord (1974) makes indirect reference
to the fascist regime of the 1930s. Later films, such as Ginger e Fred
(Ginger and Fred, 1986), also caricature the modern Italian media
industry. This ambivalent, metaphorical synthesis of the individual
and the social, the intuitive and the critical, places Fellini's work as
a whole, and a film like La Strada, in particular, squarely within the
framework of Bazinian, phenomenological cinematic realism.

Much the same is true of the films of Michelangelo Antonioni.
Antonioni's I Vinti (The Vanquished, 1952), Le Amiche (Girlfriends,
1955) and Il Grido (The Cry, 1959) are made within the neorealist
style, and explore the alienation of the individual within a shifting,
valueless milieu. At the centre of the most important of these three

films, *Il Grido*, there is, as in *La Strada*, a focus on the existential problem of experiencing meaningful contact with others. However, although Antonioni's thematic concerns in this respect appear close to those of Fellini there are no 'ways forward' suggested in Antonioni's films, as there are in Fellini's, and, in *Il Grido*, the itinerant hero, Aldo, moves restlessly from partner to partner, situation to situation, until, in despair, he throws himself to his death.

Although *Il Grido* portrays a culture and society marked by rootlessness, instability and transience, it is not entirely clear whether the existential isolation experienced by a character such as Aldo is caused by an external, determining social context, or by individual psychological make-up. This ambivalence between the psychological and the social also arises in Antonioni's *L'Avventura* (*The Adventure*, 1960), *La Notte* (*The Night*, 1961), *Eclisse* (*Eclipse*, 1962) and *Deserto rosso* (*The Red Desert*, 1964). Although these films move away from the neorealist emphasis on the socially marginal found in *Il Grido*, to focus on the Italian haute bourgeoisie, the same concern with lack of emotional connection pervades all of them. In *L'Avventura*, for example, a group of friends journey to an island, where one of them, Anna, disappears. Although her friends try to find her, two of them: Sandro, Anna's lover, and Claudia, her closest friend, form a brittle, compromised relationship of their own, and abandon the search for Anna.

It has been argued that Antonioni's principal concern in *L'Avventura* was to depict the vacuity and self-centredness of the Italian upper classes.[29] However, in many respects, *L'Avventura* appears more concerned with the reality of individual isolation, than with social class *per se*. In making *L'Avventura*, Antonioni was influenced by Husserlian phenomenology, the French *nouveau roman* and Sartrean existentialism, and these influences led him to adopt a neutral, observational style in *L'Avventura*. Thus, *L'Avventura* eschews dramatic development, overt symbolism, or emotive dialogue, and charts an unfolding story dispassionately. What emerges from this is the evocation of a human condition characterised by superficiality, alienation and 'erosion from within'.[30]

L'Avventura expresses this sense of alienation through its juxtaposition of characters against landscapes which dwarf and overwhelm them. At the same time, Antonioni's scrupulously composed camerawork also creates a degree of Brechtian distanciation, which further increases the sense of detached unease which the film exudes. All of this serves to make *L'Avventura*, like *Il Grido* (which portrays alienation amongst the working class, rather than, as in *L'Avventura*, the bourgeoisie), a film about individual, rather than class disaffection. However, the sense of estrangement which Antonioni's characters suffer is also portrayed as forming an integral part of the human condition within modern society, and, therefore, as also social in essence. It is this which makes *L'Avventura*, like *Il Grido*, a film about both individual nihilism, and an existentially oppressive external reality.

L'Avventura, *La notte*, *Eclisse* and *Deserto rosso* can all be related to Bazinian and Kracaurian conceptions of cinematic realism. Talking about the most important of these films, *L'Avventura*, Antonioni describes how he set about 'breaking up the action' by inserting into the film 'a good many sequences that could seem banal or of a documentary nature'.[31] This corresponds closely to Kracauer's belief that films should cut from character and event to show 'images of the environment'.[32] Similarly, the use of long-take deep-focus photography, elliptical narrative structure, real-time sequences and unresolved *finale* in *L'Avventura* accords closely with Bazinian models of cinematic realism.

Antonioni's use of film as a means of uncovering layers of meaning is also close to Bazin's theory of realist signification and spectatorship, where meaning is gradually revealed under the force of the 'long, hard gaze':

> We know that under the image revealed there is another which is truer to reality and under this image still another and yet again still another under this last one, right down to the true image of reality, absolute, mysterious, which no one will ever see.[33]

One of the clearest demonstrations of this process of peeling away the external layers of reality in order to find a submerged, though ultimately inaccessible inner truth, can be found in Antonioni's *Blow Up* (1966), in a sequence in which a photographer, through enlarging a series of photographs, discovers that one of them contains the hidden evidence that a murder has been committed. However, although this 'true image of reality' is finally revealed to the central character, it proves ultimately meaningless to both him, and the superficial, disaffected milieux which surrounds him. In this sense, and as in both *Il Grido* and *L'Avventura*, reality, or truth, remains existentially inacessible.

Pier Paolo Pasolini defined himself as a 'mythic realist' rather than a neorealist, and his films are centrally concerned with the opposition between archaic forms of consciousness and the destructive impact of modernity.[34] In films such as *Edipo Re* (*Oedipus Rex*, 1967) and *Medea* (1969), for example, Pasolini explores oppositions between a magical, mythical consciousness, and more instrumental, rationalist attitudes to reality. Pasolini's first feature film, *Accattone* (1961), retains a neorealist preoccupation with the imagery and thematic subject matter of naturalism, and can be compared to Antonioni's *Il Grido* in its uncompromising depiction of poverty and underdevelopment, and in its disavowal of the affirmative humanism common to earlier neorealist films. However, Pasolini's bleak depiction of the *borgate*, or shanty towns goes beyond the depiction of poverty attempted in *Il Grido*, and the central character of the film, the pimp Vittorio, possesses few, if any, of the redeeming features displayed by Aldo in *Il Grido*.[35]

The naturalism of *Accattone* is set within a narrative which has clear mythological dimensions, encompassing issues of transgression, exploitation and retribution, and Pasolini takes this form of mythological naturalism further in his *Il Vangelo secundo Matteo* (*The Gospel According to Saint Matthew*, 1964). Like *Accattone*, *Il Vangelo secundo Matteo* uses non-professional actors and long-take, deep-focus, moving-camera cinematography in the Bazinian style, and also embodies Pasolini's concept of 'technical sacracity', or the 'sacred shot', where the integrity of the slow, panoramic shot is foregrounded, and prioritised over montage editing. Pasolini's assertion that 'montage processes the film image in the way that death processes life' also appears to be derived from Bazin's views on montage and deep-focus cinematography.[36]

Il Vangelo secundo Matteo also illustrates how Pasolini's concept of 'technical sacracity' evolved into his later theory of 'semiotic realism'. Pasolini departed from both nineteenth-century realism, and Lukácsian critical realism, in developing a theory of 'semiotic realism' in which the film image was conceived of as a sign which combined both an image of the world, and 'the world of memory and dream'.[37] Pasolini's theory of semiotic realism combined realistic representation with subjective representation, and a post-structuralist and Brechtian insistence on fracturing diegetic continuity. This symbolic and reflexive conception of realism can be found in *Il Vangelo secundo Matteo*, in passages within which realistic images function to evoke mythological archetypes. In later films, such as *Uccellacci e uccellini* (*Crows and Sparrows*, 1966), *Edipo Re*, *Teorema* (*Theorem*, 1968), *Medea* and *Salò o le 120 giornate di Sodoma* (*Salò, or the One Hundred and Twenty Days of Sodom*, 1975) this reflexive, allegorical aproach is emphasised even more, and, despite his claims to have developed a form of 'mythic realism', Pasolini's films after *Accattone* and *Il Vangelo secundo Matteo* place him within the anti-realist, or political modernist, rather than realist, camp.

Bernardo Bertolucci was influenced by Pasolini, and worked with the latter on *Accattone*. However, Pasolini's influence is hardly evident in Bertolucci's first major feature, *Prima della rivoluzione* (*Before the Revolution*, 1964), which, in addition to revealing the influence of the *nouvelle vague*, also exhibits lyrical, elegiac qualities later to prove more typical of his later work. In *La Strategia del ragno* (*The Spider's Strategem*, 1970), *Il Conformista* (*The Conformist*, 1971) and *Ultimo tango a Parigi* (*Last Tango in Paris*, 1972) these qualities become more pronounced, as Bertolucci moves away from the Godardian inspired stylistics of *Prima della rivoluzione*, and towards a more realistic style, characterised by the use of melodramatic and 'operatic' overtones.[38] Both *La Strategia del ragno* and *Il Conformista* employ a realistic visual style, in conjunction with more flamboyant fantasy sequences, and multi-layered narratives based on the operation of dreams and the unconscious. *La Strategia del ragno* also marks the transition from Bertolucci's notion of 'cinema as poetry' to that of 'cinema as spectacle', in incorporating both subjective camera movement, and melodramatic, rhetorical forms.

La Strategia del ragno and *Il Conformista* apply Freudian psycho-analytic concepts to political analysis through linking the issue of political corruption within Italy to the psychological experience of power, manipulation and abuse. Bertolucci was influenced here by Wilhelm Reich's *The Mass Psychology of Fascism* (1933) and Erich Fromm's *Escape From Freedom* (1951), both of which explore the psychological roots of authoritarianism; and, in *La Strategia del ragno* and *Il Conformista*, Bertolucci accounts for the roots of Italian fascism in terms of displaced, psychological neuroses, which are then fostered by an oppressive and authoritarian regime. In *Il Conformista*, such displacement is expressed through the metaphor of homosexuality. It is anxiety over personal inadequacy, or deviation from the required standard, which leads the vulnerable individual to desire a compensatory, authoritarian State, and, in *Il Conformista*, Bertolucci uses the repressed, and self-denied homo-sexuality of his central character, Marcello, to suggest how fascism came to be ingrained within one particular sector of Italian society.[39] *Il Conformista* relies upon Freudian, rather than Marxist ideas, in delivering its account of the emergence of fascism within the Italian middle classes, but also attempts to draw the psychological and the political together, in order to create a form of Freudian, social realist cinema.

Although *Ultimo tango a Parigi* was a substantial commercial success, in a way that *La Strategia del ragno* and *Il Conformista* were not, the concern with themes of repressed sexuality and individual neurosis evident in *Ultimo tango a Parigi* place it firmly within the thematic parameters which configure the two earlier films. However, *Ultimo tango a Parigi* takes the themes of alienation and entrapment explored in *La Strategia del ragno* and *Il Conformista* much further, and the final result is a film characterised by an 'almost metaphysical despair' over the prospects for human freedom.[40] There are also echoes of Antonioni's *L'Avventura* in *Ultimo tango a Parigi*, most notably in scenes in which Bertolucci frames his characters against vast, impersonal backdrops. Pronounced use of subjective camerawork, repeated flashbacks, and indeterminate narrative structures also bear the stylistic cultivated in *Il Conformista* and *La Strategia delle ragno* to full fruition in *Ultimo tango a Parigi*. Again, as in the two earlier films, realism remains the dominant organising strategy, and there are grounds for relating both *Il Conformista* and *Ultimo tango a Parigi*, in particular, to Bazinian and Kracaurian conceptions of cinematic realism.

In *Novecento* (*1900*, 1976), Bertolucci moved away from both the intimate exploration of individual dysfunctionalism explored in *Ultimo tango a Parigi*, and the synthesis of individual and political neurosis investigated in *Il Conformista*, towards a more Lukácsian inspired style of film-making. Influenced by Visconti's *Il Gattopardo*, *Novecento* was the most expensive film ever produced in Italy, and has been described as a 'monumental melodramatic saga staged as a political epic'.[41] Like *Il Gattopardo*, *Novecento* juxtaposes national and family history, and does so through linking the key events of contemporary Italian history with the intertwined destinies of two families. The central characters are Alfredo, the grandson of a wealthy landowner, and Olmo, the grandson of a peasant. Both are born on the first day of the year 1900, and Bertolucci's film follows their evolving relationship against the backdrop of the rise and fall of Italian fascism.

However, although *Novecento* can be described as a Lukácsian intensive totality in terms of its scope and range, it is not a work of impartial critical realism in the Lukácsian sense. Part Two of *Novecento*, in particular, is given from an overtly Marxist perspective, and embodies Bertolucci's conviction that the Italian ruling class will eventually be forced to cede power to an alliance of peasantry and proletariat. *Novecento* offers an over-idealised vision of Italian history, seen from the perspective of inevitable proletarian triumph, and relies on a conspicuous deployment of parodic, stylised and melodramatic formats to validate its case. As in Bertolucci's earlier films, the influence of Freud is also present in *Novecento*, and appears in the conflicts which occur between fathers, sons and

grandsons, and in the association between fascism, repressed homo-
sexuality, and violent sexuality. However, the aspirations towards
social and historical critique in *Novecento* are, to some extent,
undermined by these Freudian concerns, which constantly refocus
the film's attention on depictions of individual abberation and
obssession.[42] Although such depictions are meant to act as metaphors for social and political dysfunctionality, the metaphorical
links between the personal and the political in *Novecento* remain
equivocal, and only vaguely drawn.

   Novecento also lacks the more intimate focus on entrapped,
vulnerable, and doomed subjectivity which characterises *Il Conformista* and *Ultimo tango a Parigi*. Beyond this, *Novecento* also points
to more general problems inherent in adapting Lukácsian realism
for the cinema. The Lukácsian model of the intensive totality entails
the use of narrative and plot structures which traverse extensive
historical, social and political configurations. The inevitable result
is a work such as *Novecento*, which, like *Il Gattopardo*, is designed
on a grand, and probably overambitious scale. However, although
Il Gattopardo suffers from an overly complex narrative, and poorly
drawn characterisation, it does, at least, achieve a level of critical
reflection on the Italian *Risorgimento* which *Novecento* fails to deliver
in relation to the decline and fall of Italian fascism.

   An engagement with political history and social realism can also
be found in the cinema of Francesco Rosi. Rosi's *Salvatore Giuliano*
(1962), uses factual, documentary evidence to reconstruct the
motives behind the killing of the Sicilian bandit Giuliano, in 1950,
and portrays Giuliano as a hapless pawn, used to further the
interests of Sicilian separatists, anti-communists, the mafia and the
State. *Salvatore Giuliano* begins with the death of its central pro-
tagonist, and the remainder of the film consists of a series of flashbacks which explore the circumstances which led up to the killing.
This form of investigative and 'documented' narrative structure
allows Rosi to use the figure of the bandit as a catalyst, through
which the political power configuration of the Italian south during
the 1940s and 1950s can be sketched out.

   Salvatore Giuliano is grounded in a naturalist approach which
uses non-professional actors, extensive location shooting, forms of
documentary evidence, and a loose, often confusing plot structure
which is made more perplexing through the repeated use of flashbacks and spatial/temporal discontinuities. The end result is a work
which, although difficult to engage with, also achieves moments of
emotional, poetic intensity, as Rosi situates his tale of rebellion and
betrayal within the harsh, unforgiving Sicilian landscape. Rosi

continued his 'documented drama' approach to film-making in *Il caso Mattei* (*The Mattei Affair*, 1972) and *Lucky Luciano* (1973). The model developed in *Salvatore Giuliano* also influenced Gillo Pontecorvo's well-known *La Battaglia di Algeri* (*The Battle of Algiers*, 1965). However, *La Battaglia di Algeri*, although widely acclaimed when it appeared, lacks the indeterminate ambiguity, and poetic, naturalist sense of environment and nature which characterises the superior *Salvatore Giuliano*.

Rosi's *Cristo si è fermato a Eboli* (*Christ Stopped at Eboli*, 1979) departs from the semi-Brechtian, documented drama approach of *Salvatore Giuliano*, and is characterised by a lyrical realist style influenced both by Carlo Levi's neorealist novel, from which the film is derived, and by Visconti's *La Terra trema*. Shot almost entirely in a remote, southern Italian village, *Cristo si è fermato a Eboli* charts the stay of exile of a dissident leftist intellectual (Levi), in the village of Gagliano, during the period of fascist rule. Like *La Terra trema*, *Cristo si è fermato a Eboli* has a large cast of non-professional actors, and contains a considerable number of scenes – many of which contain no dialogue – in which the texture, customs and habitat of peasant life is observed in plentiful detail. however, *Cristo si è fermato a Eboli*, is, in many respects, even more Bazinian than *La Terra trema* in the manner in which Rosi's film uses long-take, moving-camera cinematography, to linger reflectively over the people and environment of Cagliano.

Cristo si è fermato a Eboli is pervaded by the same anti-fascist humanist sentiment typical of many early neorealist films, and a central distinction between the peasantry, who are depicted as a source of authentic moral and cultural value, and the fascist representatives, who exploit and oppress them, is apparent. *Cristo si è fermato a Eboli* is at its best when delineating the austere texture of peasant life, much as De Sica's *Ladri di biciclette* had explored the trappings of a destitute urban, sub-proletarian existence in 1948. However, Rosi's film is weakened by its final framing scenes, which show Levi in his studio in Turin, first, discussing his stay in Cagliano with his sister and their friends, and then, as an elderly, possibly dying man, re-viewing the work which he painted in Gagliano. *Cristo si è fermato a Eboli* was commissioned for television, and this may have led Rosi to adopt what, in relation to the relatively unstructured narrative which makes up the bulk of the film, is a rather conventional, stock framing device. The framing story also effects a degree of closure on the film which the rest of *Cristo si è fermato a Eboli* studiously avoids.

Rosi's *Tre fratelli* (*Three Brothers*, 1989) is, arguably, more Lukácsian than *Cristo si è fermato a Eboli* in its attempt to relate the personal experience, motives and ambitions of three middle-class brothers to a backdrop of political tension and violence in contemporary Italy. *Tre fratelli* also provides more information about social and historical context than *Cristo si è fermato a Eboli* does, and, in doing so, represents a shift from the neorealist style which pervades the earlier film. However, the underlying ideological trope of *Tre fratelli* remains the same as that of *Cristo si è fermato a Eboli*: that political institutions, and bourgeois society in general, exploit the rural peasantry. As in *Cristo si è fermato a Eboli*, a nostalgia for the values of peasant life permeates *Tre fratelli*, and a return to the values of peasant society is put forward as a means of transcending the self-serving power play of politics, and the exploitative tendencies of the developed world.

A similar attitude to the oppressive nature of bureaucracy, and the intrinsic worth of peasant culture, can be found in the films of Ermanno Olmi. Olmi's *L'Albero dei zoccoli* (*The Tree of Wooden Clogs*, 1978) is a close, naturalistic study of life in a Lombard farmstead towards the end of the nineteenth century. Using location shooting, non-professional actors, a loosely composed narrative and improvised dialogue, *L'Albero dei zoccoli* comes close to Bazin's ideal conception of cinematic realism, and Olmi's application of a poeticised, often symbolic realism, also provides the poetic, revelatory moments which Bazin called for. Like *Cristo si è fermato a Eboli*, *L'Albero dei zoccoli* is a quiet, unpretentious homage to peasant culture, and, when it appeared, in 1978, was regarded as a riposte to the melodramatic excesses of Bertolucci's *Novecento*, which had been premiered two years earlier.

In contrast to the films of Rosi and Olmi, Paolo and Vittorio Tavianis' *Padre padrone* (*Father-Boss*, 1977), *Il Prato* (*The Meadow*, 1979) and *La Notte di San Lorenzo* (*The Night of San Lorenzo*, 1982) combine elements of the neorealist tradition with a more metaphoric, symbolic, sometimes Brechtian approach. *Padre Padrone* is uncompromisingly naturalist, in its portrayal of the relationship between an underdeveloped, abusive and impoverished rural culture, and a harsh hill landscape of rocks and moorland. However, *La Notte di San Lorenzo* is a far more reflexive film. Like *Cristo si è fermato a Eboli* and *L'Albero dei zoccoli* before it, *La Notte di San Lorenzo* portrays conflict between the peasantry and oppressive, this time alien military forces. Like these two earlier films *La Notte di San Lorenzo* is also firmly situated within a regional milieux, but differs from both, as well as from *Padre Padrone*, in the extent to which it both draws attention to its use of artifice to convey its account of Nazi atrocity and rural resistance, and in the manner in which it deliberately parodies the neorealist model.[43]

*   *   *

Whilst fascist dictatorship in Italy came to an abrupt end near the close of the Second World War, a fascist regime continued to rule in Spain up till the death of General Franco, in 1975. After that, a gradual process of democratisation began, which eventually led to the election of a socialist government in 1982. Between 1939, when Franco's alliance of the political right, military and Roman Catholic Church defeated the Popular Front Government of socialists, republicans and anti-clericalists, and the beginning of the post-Franco period in 1976, the Spanish cinema was closely regulated by the state, just as the Italian cinema had been under Mussolini. In Spain, the film industry was controlled by a government department, which censored film scripts prior to filming, and ensured that Spanish cinema reproduced and legitimated the ideologies, policies and image of the ruling regime. The result was a film output as divorced from critical interpretation of existing social realities as that of fascist Italy had been.

As with the fascist regime of Mussolini, Francoist fascism also looked to the heroic past as a source of ideological verification, although, whereas Mussolini's regime had appropriated the image of ancient Rome to this end, Spanish fascism turned instead to the 'golden age' of Spanish colonial expansion during the fifteenth and sixteenth centuries. Thus, *Alba de América* (*Dawn of America*, Juan de Orduña, 1951) presents Columbus' colonisation of America both as a religious mission, and as an attempt to disseminate civilised Spanish values amongst the pagan cultures of the new world.[44] However, in addition to such arrogation of the imperialist lineage, the ruling regime also drew on another prominent source of ideological authentication: that of the Spanish Civil War of 1936–39. The Civil War was an event of lasting importance for Spanish film-makers, an importance reaffirmed by Carlos Saura as late as 1976, when he claimed that 'the Spanish Civil War has been and is still weighing down on us'.[45] A number of *cine cruzada*, or films with Civil War themes, were produced during the Franco period, and most served to legitimate the ruling regime, and justify its historical genealogy. Thus, a film such as *Sin novedad en el alcázar* (*The Siege of Alcazar*, Augusto Genina, 1940) celebrates the 'bravery, honour and righteousness of the Nationalist cause'.[46]

In addition to films on the Civil War, the Spanish cinema of the Franco period also embraced other cinematic genres as part of a strategy to bolster the standing of the regime. These included the long-standing genre of classical literary adaption. So, for example, a 1947 film version of Cervantes' *Don Quixote de la Manche* compared an idealistic Don Quixote with Franco.[47] In addition to such overtly pro-Francoist films, the Spanish cinema of the period also included the *sacredotes* (religious films), as well as a series of folkloric musicals and 'bullfight' films. These, and other popular generic vehicles, served the function of suggesting that Spanish fascism enshrined the values of a traditional and conservative Spanish national identity.[48]

Films and genres such as those mentioned above largely avoided critical engagement with contemporary issues, and it was this degree of disengagement which eventually led to a reaction amongst more socially committed film-makers, who looked to Italian neorealism to provide the model for a reinvigorated Spanish film culture. In 1947 a national film school, the IIEC (Instituto de Investigaciones y Experiencias Cinematográficas), was established in Madrid. Here, student film-makers were able to view foreign films otherwise banned throughout the rest of Spain. In 1951 the ILEC held an Italian Film Week event, during which neorealist films such as *Ladri di biciclette*, *Paisà*, *Roma città aperta* and *Miracolo a Milano* (*Miracle in Milan*, De Sica, 1950) were screened. This eventually led to the founding of the left-wing journal *Objectivo*, in 1953. Between 1953, and its suppression in 1955, *Objectivo* adhered to the pro-Zhdanovist line adopted by Guido Aristarco and *Cinema Nuovo* in Italy, and endorsed the work of *Cinema Nuovo* 'approved' film-makers and theorists such as Visconti and Zavattini (the first edition of *Objectivo* contained eighteen pages on Zavattini alone), whilst criticising less overtly Marxist neorealist film-makers, such as Fellini and Rossellini.[49]

The formation of a Spanish neorealist cinema was further consolidated in 1955 when *Objectivo* published an edition in which some recent Italian films, including Fellini's *Il Bidone* and Antonioni's *Le Amiche* were discussed in depth. The journal also helped to organise a First National Film Congress, which was held in Salamanca, in May of the same year, and at which Italian neorealism was extensively debated. The Congress attracted a wide range of participants, ranging from members of the Communist Party, to members of the Fascist Party, all of whom were united in condemnation of the commercial Francoist cinema as 'politically ineffective, socially false, intellectually worthless, aesthetically nonexistent, and industrially crippled'.[50] However, the ruling regime quickly came to the realisation that these developments within Spanish film culture constituted a challenge to established orthodoxies, and, as a consequence, *Objectivo* was closed down.

During the 1950s Italian neorealism provided an aesthetic model for Spanish film-makers opposed to the normative superficiality and aesthetic redundancy of the Francoist cinema, and, in some, but by no means all cases, to the regime itself. What united these film-makers around neorealism was a desire that the Spanish cinema should cease to be a cinema of 'painted dolls', and that it should focus, instead, 'on the problems that arise from everyday life'.[51] It was, therefore, the social realist imperative within neorealism which was the prime motivating force behind the emergence of Spanish neorealism. However, the existence of political censorship meant that the more leftist neorealist inspired cinema which developed in Spain during the 1950s was forced to adopt a clandestine, often sardonic, posture, and to draw away from a more directly political agenda. For example, a film such as Luis Garcia Berlanga's *Calabuch* (1956) exhibits an ironic treatment of subjects otherwise considered beyond criticism by the authorities, whilst Berlanga and Juan Antonio Bardem's *Bienvenido Mr Marshall!* (1951), satirised stereotypical notions of Spanishness to an extent which would have been unacceptable in a more 'serious' film.[52]

Despite these constraints, the influence of Italian neorealism did, nevertheless, lead to the emergence of a number of more committed realist Spanish films during the 1950s. For example, José Antonio Nieves Conde's *Surcos* (*Furrows*, 1951) showed images of rural poverty and destitution which distinguished it sharply from other films of the period, and eventually led to its condemnation as 'seriously dangerous' by the National Board of Classification.[53] Although *Surcos* was a Falangist film, which drew on neorealism in order to establish a Spanish national cinema based around the ideals of the fascist Falange, its *exposé* of rural Spanish poverty nevertheless proved unacceptable to the ruling regime. In contrast to Nieves Conde, the left-wing Juan Antonio Bardem set out to undermine traditional provincial Spanish values in his *Calle mayor* (*Main Street*, 1956). Although heavily censored by the regime, *Calle mayor* retained sufficient critical and aesthetic impact to be awarded the International Critics Prize at the 1956 Vencice Mostra, whilst Bardem's earlier *Muerte de un ciclista* (*Death of a Cyclist*, 1955), which deployed neorealist techniques in order to undermine the conventions of the standard Hollywood and Francoist melodrama, was awarded the International Critics Prize at the 1955 Cannes Festival.[54]

As the examples given above suggest, during this period Italian neorealism was regarded, by both right and left, as a fitting model upon which a reinvigorated national cinema could be built. For example, a conservative such as García Escudero, who was the government's General Director of Cinema, before being sacked for describing *Surcos* as 'the first glance of reality in a cinema of *papier-mâché*', linked the affirmative, humanist orientation which Italian neorealism inherited from the *verist* tradition to his own brand of conservative, social catholicism. On the other hand, film-makers such as Bardem and Basilio Martín Patino believed that neorealism could also provide the basis for a Marxist, and anti-fascist cinema.[55]

In addition to its perceived value to Falangists such as Escuderos, Italian neorealism also furnished a model for a Francoist Government, which, during the 1950s, attempted to portray Spain as an enlightened, though traditionally conservative European nation, and Francoist officials hoped that support for a Spanish national cinema based on an internationally renowned and prestigious film movement, would advance such ambitions. The fact that neorealism had emerged from another latin country, and one with a fascist past, also led Government officials to believe that Spanish neorealism could be relied upon to play its part within a more general exercise of officially authorised national projection. It was the realisation that such an appropriation of the neorealist tradition was occurring in Spain which led the exiled Louis Buñuel to make *Los Olvidados* (*The Young and Lost*, 1950), a film which deliberately undermined the inherent affirmative humanism of neorealism. However, *Los Olvidados* was immediately banned, and remained largely unknown to Spanish film-makers during the early 1950s. In 1961 the film-maker Carlos Saura encouraged Buñuel to return to Spain in order to make *Viridiana* (1961). However, *Viridiana* was quickly condemned as blasphemous by the Catholic Church, and, like *Los Olvidados*, also banned. Nevertheless, and despite such bans, it is ironic that, at the same time that a democratic Italian State was actively attempting to suppress neorealism, the Spanish dictatorship was encouraging its growth and development.

The period between 1962 and 1969 was marked by a degree of liberalisation within Spanish society and film culture, and by the emergence of the 'new Spanish cinema'. As with the new German cinema of the 1970s, new Spanish cinema was promoted by the state as evidence that modern Spain was a European nation with a vibrant cultural life. However, such promotion required an easing of the regulatory constraints which had led to the banning of *Los Olvidados* and *Viridiana*, and this strategy was not risk free for the government. For example, García Berlanga's *El verdugo* (*The Executioner*, 1963) mounted an *exposé* of the misuse of capital punishment which led to complaints that Berlanga's film was 'one of the greatest libels ever perpetrated against Spain'.[56]

The period of liberalisation which accompanied the appearance of the new Spanish cinema came to an end in 1969, in the aftermath of a political scandal involving government ministers, and student revolts inspired by the events of May 1968. Between 1969 and 1973 rigorous censorship was again restored, and government aid to filmmakers severely cut.[57] The 'third phase' of the new Spanish cinema lasts from 1973 to 1982, and covers the period from the assassination of Franco's anointed successor, Carrero Blanco, to the election of a democratically elected socialist government in 1982. This period of 'soft dictatorship', or *dictablanda*, saw the appearance of such seminal films as *El espíritu de la colmena* (*The Spirit of the Beehive*, Victor Erice, 1972), *La Prima Angélica* (*Cousin Angélica*, Carlos Saura, 1973) and *Cría cuervos* (*Raise Ravens*, Saura, 1975). After Franco's death in 1975 more overtly oppositional films also began to appear, including Jaime Chávarri's *El Desencanto* (*Disenchantment*, 1976).

After the socialist election victory in 1982 censorship was further reduced, and more ground-breaking films emerged. Carlos Saura's 'flamenco trilogy' of the 1980s: *Bodas de sangre* (*Blood Wedding*, 1981), *Carmen* (1983) and *El amor brujo* (*Love, The Magician*, 1986) moved away from both his neorealist films of the 1960s, and his more expressive, social realist films of the 1970s, to adopt a performative mode of film-making based on musical and dance forms. In its use of performance to explore issues of social and cultural identity, Saura's dance trilogy can be related to the performative, political modernist cinema which emerged in Germany during the 1970s, in the films of Straub and Syberberg, as well as to a longer tradition within European cinema, dating from G. W. Pabst's *Dreigroschenoper* (*Threepenny Opera*, 1930) and Slatan Dudow's *Kuhle Wampe* (1931).

Feature films dealing more critically with contemporary Spanish history began to appear shortly after the death of Franco in 1975. Bardem's *Siete días de enero* (*Seven Days in January*, 1978) is an account of the political events leading up to the assassination of four labour leaders in 1977, and combines documentary reconstruction with a dramatic narrative structure derived from the genre of the political thriller. Bardem's influential *Lorca, muerte de un poeta* (*Lorca, Death of a Poet*, 1987) also draws on personal biography as a means of illuminating wider social, political and historical contexts. Films such as *Dragon Rapide* (Jaime Camino, 1986), *El lute I: camino o revienta* (*El lute I: Run or Die*, Vicente Aranda, 1987), *El lute II:*

Mañana seré libre (1988) and *Lorca, muerte de un poeta* combine period drama, the political thriller, personal biography and social realism to create a form of film-making which is frequently analytical and critical, but which also occasionally descends into hagiography. By as early as 1980, films such as Gillo Pontecorvo's *Operación Ogro* (*Operation Ogro*) also reveal the evolution of this genre of film-making into a more formulaic vehicle, based around the conspiracy/action film model.[58]

Just as the *Heimatfilme* of the 1950s located the source of authentic German national identity in the rural, so, in Francoist Spain, films which depicted rural life also established the Catholic, conservative countryside as the font of a national character which was also epitomised by the ruling regime.[59] During the 1970s, leftist film-makers in Germany, France and Italy began to reassess the rural, and to consider it as a valuable sphere of experience, and alternative to bourgeois society. This was the case, for example, in the films of Francesco Rosi, Ermanno Olmi, René Allio and Edgar Reitz. However, a leftist appropriation of the rural proved to be more problematic within a Spanish cinema which, until as recently as the mid 1970s, had commonly relied on representations of provincial, agrarian life in order to legitimate fascist ideology. Consequently, when the post-Franco oppositional cinema did turn to the depiction of ruralist subject matter it did so from a mainly negative perspective, emphasising the extent to which rural culture had influenced and nurtured fascism.

One of the most important works within this body of films which focused on the darker facets of rural experience was José Luis Borau's *Furtivos* (1975). *Furtivos* depicts a rural world in which acts of incest, murder and brutality occur, if not routinely, then with a degree of inevitability. The term *furtivos* means both 'poachers', and 'those who lead their lives in a secretive way', and, in his film, Borau wished to show that 'under Franco, Spain was living a secretive life'.[60] Realist in style, *Furtivos* is also a symbolic allegory of the way that officially sanctioned power was used as an instrument of oppression within fascist Spain, and uses cinematography which attempts to reproduce the chiaroscuro effects found in the paintings of El Greco and Ribera, in order to express an atmosphere and context of personal and public recidivism.[60] Through its portrayal of psychological obsession and betrayal, *Furtivos* is a work which seeks to counter Franco's view of Spain as '*un bosque en paz*' ('a peaceful wood'), with an image of the country as 'a secret hellish prison teeming with creatures bent on mutual destruction'.[62]

Like *Furtivos*, Ricardo Franco's *Pascual Duarte* (1975) paints a similarly pessimistic picture of a Francoist rural arcadia. Pascuel Durante is a peasant caught up in events during the Spanish Civil War. However, he has also been psychologically damaged by an overbearing family, an impoverished social environment and a class hierarchy in which he is positioned near the bottom. This leads him to lash out, kill, and, eventually, be killed himself. *Pascual Duarte* sets it depictions of violence, murder and matricide against images of a harsh, impoverished rural landscape, and is an allegorical account of an oppressive culture in which violence 'becomes the only viable language for a class that was stripped of any identity'.[63]

Both *Furtivos* and *Pascual Duarte* can be associated with the *tremendista* tradition of 'black' Spanish pictorial and literary realism, and *Furtivos* is directly influenced both by Goya's 'black' painting, *Saturn Devouring his Son*, and by Buñuel's *Tristana*.[64] The *tremendista* tradition of black realism can be traced back to the Spanish Inquisition, and to images of the atrocities committed against the ethnic populations of the new world during the Spanish Conquest. However, it has also been used in both literature and film to depict the fratricidal atrocities which occurred during the Spanish Civil War, and both *Furtivos* and *Pascual Duarte* draw on this tradition to depict a Francoist culture within which violence, oppression and cruelty are endemic.

Other films within the historical naturalist tradition of Spanish film-making which emerged during the 1970s include those which focused on the figure of the *maquis*: republican guerrilla fighters who remained active after the fall of the Republic. Films within this category include *Los días del pasado* (*Bygone Days*, Mario Camus, 1977), *El corazón del bosque* (*The Heart of the Forest*, Manuel Gutiérrez Aragón, 1978), *La luna de los lobos* (*The Moon of the Wolves*, Julio Sánches Valdéz, 1987), *La guerra de los locos* (*The War of the Mad*, Manolo Matji, 1987), *Pim, pam, pum fuego* (*Ready, Aim, Fire*, Pedro Olea, 1975), *Si te dicen que caí* (*If They Tell You I Fell*, Vicente Aranda, 1989) and *El espíritu de la colmena* (*Spirit of the Beehive*). The two most important of these are *Los días del pasado* and *El espíritu de la colmena*. *Los días del pasado* frames its narrative of the *maquis*, and their struggle against the Civil Guard, against a *mise-en-scène* which represents the surrounding culture and environment in evocative detail. This form of treatment, which aims to place individual characters within a specific, overarching cultural and natural environment, is reminiscent of the films of Olmi and Rosi. However, Camus's evocation of the people and landscape of Asturias embodies a darker vision than that found within *Cristo si è fermato a Eboli* or *L'Albero dei zoccoli*, and 'recreates the tragedy [of the Civil War] by means of symbols: the landscape, the house, the school, the children ... .the cold, the forest'.[65]

The most important *maquis* film, *El espíritu de la colmena*, is also one of the most critically successful Spanish films ever made, and has been described as marking the 'high point of Spanish cinema'.[66] Set in rural Castile, immediately after the end of the Spanish Civil War, Erice's film depicts the encounter between a young child and a wounded republican *maquis*. *El espíritu de la colmena* is presented from the perspective of the child (Ana), and one consequence of this is that it contains relatively little dialogue, and concentrates, instead, on evoking both the visual qualities of the rural Castilian landscape, and the subjective, aphoristic consciousness of childhood. Although *El espíritu de la colmena* employs some modernist devices, including subjective imagery and non-naturalistic jump-cuts, the overall approach adopted in the film is based on rendering objects, houses and vistas with a degree of resonance which extends beyond their narrative significance within the film. *El espíritu de la colmena* is also set within a specific historical context. However, rather than depict that context in a Lukácsian vein, the film suggests the moral climate of the period through the use of images of isolation and bleak landscapes, and, through these means, displays a 'powerful ability to describe the oppressive, sickly and perennially painful atmosphere of the post-war period'.[67]

Both *Los días del pasado* and *El espíritu de la colmena* can be associated with Kracauerian notions of cinematic realism, and Erice's later film, *El sol de membrillo* (*The Quince Tree Sun*, 1992) conforms even more closely to Kracauer's ideas on realist cinema. In its account of a painter's attempts to capture the ellusive qualities of a sunlit quince tree, *El sol de membrillo* can be related to the concept of *Naturschöne* which Kracauer draws on in *Theory of Film*. However, as with *Los días del pasado*, the 'blacker' realism of *El espíritu de la colmena* takes Erice's earlier film closer to Kracauer's conception of the cinematic sublime in *From Caligari to Hitler*, than to the theory of cinematic realism set out in *Theory of Film*.

The Spanish cinema's post-war involvement with realism can be traced back to the influence of neorealism in the 1950s. However, that influence was soon mediated by that of the French *nouvelle vague*. The consequence of this was that film-makers such as Carlos Saura began to distance themselves from neorealism, and to adopt the more modernist, reflexive techniques associated with the *nouvelle vague*. Saura and others also appropriated the emphasis on authorship within the *nouvelle vague*, although the prototype of the Spanish *auteurist* film-maker *par excellence* already existed, in the shape of Louis Buñuel. From 1960 onwards, Saura consciously modelled his own film-making style on Buñuel's surrealistic brand of realism, in an attempt to establish himself as the most important Spanish film-maker. The synthesis of ironic melodrama, realism and surreal fantasy in films such as *El ángel exterminador* (*The Exterminating Angel*, 1962), *Belle de jour* (1967) and *Cet obscur objet du désir* (*That Obscure Object of Desire*, 1977) also came to increasingly define the new Spanish cinema, and can be found in recent films such as Julio Medem's *Vacas* (*Cowherds*, 1992) and *La ardilla roja* (1993).

Vacas employs a degree of surrealistic reflexivity which distinguishes Medem's film from the more realistic *Furtivos*, *Los días del pasado*, *El espíritu de la colmena* and *El Sol de membrillo*. The synthesis of surreal, melodramatic excess and reflexive fantasy found in *Vacas* can also be seen in the films of the most important film-maker to emerge in the 1980s, and one who decisively inherited Buñuel's mantle of Spanish cinematic auteurism: Pedro Almodóvar. However, films such as the spectacularly successful *Mujeres al borde de un attaque de nervios* (*Women on the Verge of a Nervous Breakdown*, 1988), move substantially away from the central realist tradition, and the same is true of José Juan Bigas Luna's *Jamón jamón* (1992), *Huevos de oro* (1993) and *La teta y la luna* (1995), Alex de la Iglesia's *Acción mutante* (1992) and *El día de la bestia* (1995), and the films of Urbizu, Bajo, Ulloa and Calparsoro. These films fall outside the remit of this chapter, and must be related to the emergence of a European postmodern cinema during the 1980s and 1990s.

Notes

1. Liehm, Mira, *Passion and Defiance: Film In Italy From 1942 to the Present* (Berkeley, CA and London: University of California Press, 1984), pp. 7–8.
2. Armes, Roy, *Patterns of Realism* (London: Tantivy Press, 1971), p. 32.
3. Liehm, op cit., p. 6.
4. Ibid., p. 37.
5. Armes, op cit., p. 52.
6. Marcus, Millicent, *Italian Film in the Light of Neorealism* (Princeton, NJ: Princeton University Press, 1986), p. 18.
7. Ibid.
8. Deveny, Thomas, G., *Cain on Screen: Contemporary Spanish Cinema* (London: Scarecrow Press, 1993), p. 135.
9. Marcus, op cit., p. 14.
10. Armes, op cit., p. 185.

11. Deveney, op cit., p. 69.
12. Ibid., p. 149.
13. Ibid.
14. Liehm, op cit., p. 55.
15. Marcus, op cit., p. 26.
16. Bordwell, David, and Thompson, Kristin, *Film History: An Introduction* (New York: McGraw-Hill, 1994), p. 417.
17. Ibid., p. 418.
18. Liehm, op cit., p. 57.
19. Nettl, J. P., *The Soviet Achievement* (London: Thames & Hudson, 1976), p. 154.
20. Liehm, op cit., p. 93.
21. Ibid., p. 94.
22. Leprohon, Pierre, *The Italian Cinema* (New York: Praeger, 1972), p. 148.
23. Liehm, op cit., p. 150.
24. Ibid., p. 148.
25. Ibid., p. 159.
26. Ibid.
27. Ibid.
28. Bazin, André, 'In Defence of Rossellini', in Bazin, *What Is Cinema? Vol. II* (Berkeley, CA and London: University of California Press, 1972), p. 97.
29. Leprohon, op cit., p. 168.
30. Marcus, p. 190.
31. Liehm, op cit., p. 180.
32. Aitken, Ian, 'Distraction and Redemption: Kracauer, Surrealism and Phenomenology', *Screen*, vol. 39, no.2 (Summer, 1998), p. 135.
33. Marcus, op cit., p. 191.
34. Ibid., p. 245.
35. Liehm, op cit., p. 239.
36. Ibid., p. 243.
37. Marcus, op cit., p. 247.
38. Liehm, op cit., p. 275.
39. Marcus, op cit., p. 307.
40. Liehm, op cit., p. 277.
41. Ibid., p. 278.
42. Bondanella, Peter, *Italian Cinema From Neorealism to the Present* (New York: Ungar, 1983), p. 314.
43. Marcus, op cit., p. 390.
44. Jordan, Barry, and Morgan-Tamosunas, Rikki, *Contemporary Spanish Cinema* (Manchester and New York: Manchester University Press, 1998), p. 17.
45. Deveney, op cit., p. 3.
46. Jordan and Morgan-Tamosunas, op cit., p. 18.
47. Bordwell and Thompson, op cit., p. 430.

48. Borau, Luis José, 'Prologue: The Long March of the Spanish Cinema Towards Itself', in Evans, Peter William (ed.), *Spanish Cinema: The Auteurist Tradition* (Oxford: Oxford University Press, 1999), p. xix.

49. Kinder, Marsha, *Blood Cinema: The Reconstruction of National Identity in Spain* (Berkeley, CA and London: University of California Press, 1993), p. 26.

50. Ibid., p. 27.

51. Ibid., p. 28.

52. Rolph, Wendy, 'Bienvenido Mr Marshall! (Berlanga, 1952)', in Evans, op cit., p. 10.

53. Kinder, op cit., p. 29.

54. Roberts, Stephen, 'In Search of a New Spanish Realism: Bardem's *Calle Mayor* (1956)', in Evans, op cit., p. 19.

55. Kinder, op cit., p. 31.

56. Deveney, op cit., p. 8.

57. Kinder, op cit., p. 5.

58. Jordan and Morgan-Tamosunas, op cit., p. 23.

59. Ibid., p. 46.

60. Deveney, op cit., p. 211.

61. Evans, Peter William, '*Furtivos* (Borau, 1975): My Mother My Lover', in Evans, op cit., p. 116.

62. Ibid., p. 117.

63. Deveney, op cit., pp. 14–15.

64. Kinder, op cit., p. 234.

65. Deveney, op cit., p. 100.

66. Smith, Julian, Paul, 'Between Metaphysics and Scientism: Rehistoricizing Victor Erice's *El espíritu de la colmena* (1973), in Evans, op cit., p. 93.

67. Deveney, op cit., p. 124.

Conclusions

Rather than return to what has already been covered in this book, I want to take the opportunity afforded by what pages remain to look ahead, and suggest how ideas considered within this study can be pursued further. I have argued that the intuitionist realist tradition within European film theory and cinema is of considerable value. However, I also want to argue that the issue of realism itself is extremely important, and that it transcends the boundaries of film theory. That this is the case becomes clear, for example, from even the most cursory study of the theories of Kracauer and Bazin, both of which are concerned with far more than the technical elaboration of a theoretical system.

For both theorists, realist aesthetic experience is based on the flood of correspondences which are released, and revealed, under the pressure of the spectator's gaze. Following Bazin and Kracauer, one way of theorising the experience of aesthetic realism is to conceive of it as both consisting of a set of representational forms and techniques which correspond in a number of ways to our perception and memory, and the active contemplation, by spectators, of truth claims about the world, where those claims are assessed against the spectator's own experience. For, to judge that a film is true to life, or 'realistic', is to make a double judgement. First, it is to make a judgement about what it is that the film depicts. Second, it is to make a judgement about what life is like. Whilst the spectator is making this complex, double judgement, the film continues to tell its meandering, convoluted story, and the spectator is rarely in a position to fully assess the truth or falsity of particular truth claims. This implies that, as Bazin and Kracauer suggest, far from being inherently normative, cinematic realism is inherently indeterminate, and has an important role to play in creating what Bazin referred to as the 'seeking being'.

The above account of how the experience of aesthetic realism might be theorised is, inevitably, both brief and underdeveloped.

However, it is all that can be attempted here, and these issues clearly need to be explored further, in later work. Similarly, although critical work on cinematic realism involving studies of Kracauer and Bazin, and ideas drawn from subject areas such as phenomenology, cognitive science and philosophical realism, have borne fruit over the last few years, there remains scope for further development. Finally, considerable potential exists for the application of Bazinian, Kracaurian and other forms of realist theory to the interpretation of particular films and film-makers. This has been attempted here, to a limited extent, in relation to film-makers such as Antonioni, Fellini, Reitz, Pialat and Erice, but this is only a beginning, and the second volume of this study will seek to explore all of these areas further.

Select Bibliography

Abel, Richard, *French Cinema: The First Wave 1915–1929* (Princeton, NJ: Princeton University Press, 1984).

Abel, Richard, *French Film Theory and Criticism: A History/Anthology 1907-1939* (vol. 2.) (Princeton, NJ: Princeton University Press, 1988).

Abrams, A. H., *The Mirror and the Lamp: Romantic Theory and the Critical Tradition* (Oxford: Oxford University Press, 1981).

Adorno, Theodor, 'Transparencies On Film', *New German Critique* (Fall/Winter, 1981).

Aitken, Ian, 'John Grierson, Idealism and the Inter-war Period', *Historical Journal of Film, Radio and Television* (1989), vol. 9, no. 3.

Aitken, Ian, *Film and Reform: John Grierson and the British Documentary Film Movement* (London: Routledge, 1990).

Aitken, Ian, *The Documentary Film Movement: An Anthology* (Edinburgh: Edinburgh University Press, 1998).

Aitken, Ian, 'Distraction and Redemption: Kracauer, Surrealism and Phenomenology', *Screen*, vol. 39, no. 2 (Summer, 1998).

Aitken, Ian, *Alberto Cavalcanti: Realism, Surrealism and National Cinemas* (London: Flicks Books, 2000).

Allen, Robert and Gomery, Douglas, *Film History: Theory and Practice* (New York: Alfred A. Knopf, 1985).

Althusser, Louis, *Lenin and Philosophy and Other Essays* (London: New Left Books, 1977a).

Althusser, Louis, *For Marx* (London: New Left Books, 1977b).

Althusser, Louis, *Essays on Ideology* (London and New York: Verso, 1984).

Andrew, Dudley, *The Major Film Theories* (Oxford: Oxford University Press, 1976).

Andrew, Dudley, *André Bazin* (New York: Columbia University Press, 1990).

Andrew, Dudley, *Mists of Regret: Culture and Sensibility in Classic French Film* (Princeton, NJ: Princeton University Press, 1995).

Armes, Roy, *Patterns of Realism* (London: Tantivy Press, 1971).

Armes, Roy, *French Cinema* (London: Secker & Warburg, 1985).

Arnheim, Rudolph, *Film* (London: Faber and Faber, 1933).

Arnheim, Rudolph, *Art and Visual Perception* (Berkeley and Los Angeles, CA: UCL Press, 1967).

Aumont, Jacques, *Montage Eisenstein* (London: BFI and Indiana University Press, 1979).

Austin, Guy, *Contemporary French Cinema: An Introduction* (Manchester and New York: Manchester University Press, 1996).

Balázs, Béla, *Der sichtbare Mensche oder Der Kultur Des Films* (Vienna and Leipzig: Deutsch-Osterreichischer Verlag, 1924).

Barlow, John, *German Expressionist Film* (Boston, MA: Twayne, 1982).

Barna, Yon, *Eisenstein* (London: Secker & Warburg, 1973).

Barr, Charles (ed.) *All Our Yesterdays: 90 Years of British Cinema* (London: BFI, 1986).

Barthes, Roland, 'Introduction to the Structural Analysis of Narratives', *Communication*, 8 (1966).

Barthes, Roland, *S/Z* (New York: Hill and Wang, 1974).

Barthes, Roland, *Image-Music-Text* (London: Fontana, 1977).

Bazin, André, *What Is Cinema?, Volume I* (Berkeley, CA and London: University of California Press, 1967).

Bazin, André, *What Is Cinema? Volume II* (Berkeley, CA and London: University of California Press, 1972).

Belsey, Catherine, *Critical Practice* (London and New York: Routledge, 1980).

Benjamin, Walter, *Illuminations* (London: Fontana Press, 1992).

Bisztray, George, *Marxist Models of Literary Theory* (New York: Columbia University Press, 1978).

Bondanella, Peter, *Italian Cinema From Neorealism to the Present* (New York: Ungar, 1983).

Bordwell, David, 'Eisenstein's Epistemological Shift', *Screen* (Winter, 1974/5), vol. 15, no. 4.

Bordwell, David, *French Impressionist Cinema: Film Culture, Film Theory and Film Style* (New York: Arno, 1980).

Bordwell, David, *The Cinema of Eisenstein* (Cambridge, MA and London: Harvard University Press, 1993).

Bordwell, David and Thompson, Kristin, *Film History: An Introduction* (New York: McGraw-Hill, 1994).

Bradley, F. H., *Essays on Truth and Reality* (London: Clarendon Press, 1914)

Braudy, Leo, *Jean Renoir: The World of His Films* (New York and Oxford: Columbia University Press, 1989).

Brecht, Bertolt, 'Against Georg Lukács', *New Left Review* (1967).

Brewster, Ben, 'From Shklovsky to Brecht: A Reply', *Screen* (Summer, 1974), vol. 15, no. 2.

Buck-Morss, Susan, *The Origins of Negative Dialectics* (London and Lincoln, NB: University of Nebraska Press, 1993).

Budd, M., *The Cabinet of Dr Caligari* (New Brunswick, NJ: Rutgers University Press, 1990).

Canudo, Ricciotto, 'Chronique du Septième Art: Films en culeurs', *Paris-Midi*, no. 4131 (31 August, 1923).

Casebier, Allan, *Film and Phenomenology: Towards a Realist Theory of Cinematic Representation* (Cambridge: Cambridge University Press, 1970).

Caughie, John (ed.), *Theories of Authorship* (London: Routledge and Kegan Paul, 1981).

Collins, Richard and Porter, Vinvent, *WDR and the Arbeiterfilm: Fass-binder, Ziewer and Others* (London: BFI, 1981).

Cook, Pam (ed.), *The Cinema Book* (London: BFI, 1990).

Costall, Alan and Still, Arthur, *Cognitive Psychology Under Question* (London: Harvester, 1987).

Coward, Rosalind and Ellis, John, *Language and Materialism: Developments in Semiology and the Theory of the Subject* (London: Routledge and Kegan Paul, 1977).

Craig, David (ed.), *Marxists On Literature: An Anthology* (Harmondsworth: Pelican, 1977).

Crystal, David, *Linguistics* (Harmondsworth: Penguin, 1985).

Culler, Jonathan, *Structuralist Poetics: Structuralism Linguistics and the Study of Literature* (London: Routledge and Kegan Paul, 1975).

Derrida, Jacques, *Speech and Phenomena* (Evanston, IL: Northwestern University Press, 1967).

Derrida, Jacques, *Of Grammatology* (Baltimore, MD: Johns Hopkins University Press, 1974).

Deveny, Thomas, G., *Cain on Screen: Contemporary Spanish Cinema* (London: Scarecrow Press, 1993).

Dréville, Jean, 'Le Documentaire, aimé du cinéma', *Cinémagazine*, no. 2 (February, 1930).

Easthope, Anthony, *British Post-Structuralism Since 1968* (London: Routledge, 1991).

Eisenstein, Sergei, *The Film Sense* (San Diego, CA, New York and London: Harcourt Brace & Company, 1975).

Eisenstein, Sergei, *Notes of a Film Director* (New York: Dover Publications, 1970).

Eisenstein, Sergei, *film essays* (New York and Washington: Praeger Publishers, 1970).

Eisner, Lotte, *The Haunted Screen* (London: Thames and Hudson, 1969).

Elliot, David, *New Worlds: Russian Art and Society 1900–1937* (New York: Rizzoli, 1986).

Elsaesser, Thomas, 'Cinema: the Irresponsible Signifier. Or, the Gamble with History: Film Theory or Cinema Theory', *New German Critique* (1987), no. 40.

Elsaesser, Thomas, *The New German Cinema: A History* (New Brunswick: Rutgers University Press, 1989).

Elsaesser, Thomas, *Weimar Cinema and After: Germany's Historical Imaginary* (London and New York: Routledge, 2000).

Engels, Frederick, *Marx Engels: Selected Works* (London: Lawrence and Wishart, 1968).

Erens, Patricia, 'Sunset Boulevard: a Morphological Analysis', *Film Reader*, no. 2 (1977).

Esslin, Martin, *Brecht: A Choice of Evils* (London: Eyre Methuen, 1980).

Evans, Peter William (ed.), *Spanish Cinema: The Auteurist Tradition* (Oxford: Oxford University Press, 1999).

Fell, John L, 'Vladimir Propp in Hollywood', *Film Quarterly*, vol. 30, no. 3 (1977).

Forbes, Jill, *The Cinema in France, After the New Wave* (London: BFI/ Macmillan, 1992).

Franklin, James, *New German Cinema* (London: Columbus Press, 1986).

Gay, Peter, *Weimar Culture: The Outsider as Insider* (London: Penguin, 1992).

Ghali, Noureddine, *L'Avant-Garde Cinématographique en France Dans les Années Vingt* (Paris: Editions Paris Experimental, 1995).

Ginsberg, Terri and Thompson, Moana Kirsten (eds), *Perspectives on German Cinema* (New York: G. K. Hall and Co., 1996).

Grierson, John, 'Better Popular Pictures', *Transactions of the Society of Motion Picture Engineers* (August, 1926), vol. IX, no. 29.

Grierson, John, 'Flaherty, Naturalism and the Problem of the English Cinema', *Artwork* (Autumn, 1931).

Grierson, John, 'Answers to a Cambridge Questionnaire', *Granta* (Cambridge: Cambridge University Press, 1967).

Gorky, Maxim, et al., *Soviet Writers Congress 1934: The Debate on Socialist Realism and Modernism in the Soviet Union* (London: Lawrence & Wishart).

Hake, Sabine, (ed.), *The Cinema's Third Machine: Writing on Film in Germany 1907–1933* (London and Lincoln, NB: University of Nebraska Press, 1993).

Haney, Jack C., *An Introduction to the Russian Folk Tale* (New York and London: M. E. Sharpe, 1999).

Hanfling, Oswald (ed.), *Philosophical Aesthetics* (Oxford: Blackwell/Open University, 1992).

Hardy, Forsyth (ed.), *Grierson On Documentary* (London and Boston, MA: Faber and Faber, 1979).

Harvey, Sylvia, *May '68 and Film Culture* (London: BFI, 1980).

Hauser, Arnold, *The Social History of Art: Three: Rococo, Classicism and Romanticism* (London: Routledge and Kegan Paul, 1973).

Hawkes, Terrence, *Structuralism and Semiotics* (London: Routledge, 1988).

Hayward, Susan, *French National Cinema* (London and New York: Routledge, 1993).

Heath, Stephen, 'Realism, Modernism and Language in Consciousness', in Boyle and Swales (eds), *Realism in European Literature* (Cambridge: Cambridge University Press, 1986).

Hill, John and Church Gibson, Pamela (eds), *The Oxford Guide to Film Studies* (Oxford: Oxford University Press, 1998).

Hobsbawm, Eric, *The Age of Revolution* (London: Cardinal 1962).

Holub, Robert C., *Jürgen Habermas: Critic in the Public Sphere* (London and New York: Routledge, 1991).

Horkheimer, Max and Adorno, Theodor W., *Dialectic of Enlightenment* (New York: Herder and Herder, 1972).

Husserl, Edmund, *The Crisis of European Science and Transcendental Phenomenology* (Evanston, IL: Illinois University Press, 1970).

Jackson, Leonard, *The Poverty of Structuralism: Literature and Structuralist Theory* (London and New York: Longman, 1991).

Jameson, Fredric, 'Postmodernism, or the Cultural Logic of Late Capitalism', *New Left Review* (1984), no. 146.

Jameson, Fredric, *Signatures of the Visible* (New York and London: Routledge, 1992).

Johnson-Laird, P. N., *The Computer and the Mind* (London: Fontana, 1989).

Jordan, Barry and Morgan-Tamosunas, Rikki, *Contemporary Spanish Cinema* (Manchester and New York: Manchester University Press, 1998).

Kaes, Anton, 'Literary Intellectuals and the Cinema: Charting a Controversy (1909–1929)', *New German Critique* (1987), no. 40.

Kaes, Anton, *From Heimat to Hitler: The Return of History as Film* (Cambridge, MA and London: Harvard University Press, 1992).

Kant, Immanuel, *The Critique of Judgement*, trans. J. C. Meredith (Oxford: Oxford University Press, 1973).

Kemp, John, *The Philosophy of Kant* (Oxford: Oxford University Press, 1968).

Kinder, Marsha, *Blood Cinema: The Reconstruction of National Identity in Spain* (Berkeley, CA and London: University of California Press, 1993).

King, Norman, *Abel Gance* (London: BFI, 1984).

Kirk, G. S., *Myth: Its Meaning and Function In Ancient And Other Cultures* (Cambridge: Cambridge University Press, 1978).

Koch, Gertrud, 'Béla Balázs: The Physiognomy of Things', *New German Critique* (1987), no. 40.

Koch, Gertrud, *Siegfried Kracauer: An Introduction* (Princeton, NJ: Princeton University Press, 2000).

Kracauer, Siegfried, *From Caligari to Hitler: A Psychological History of the German Film* (Princeton, NJ: Princeton University Press, 1974).

Kracauer, Siegfried, *Theory of Film: The Redemption of Physical Reality* (London, Oxford and New York: Oxford University Press, 1978).

Kracauer, Siegfried, 'Cult of Distraction: On Berlin's Picture Palaces', *New German Critique* (1987), no. 40.

Kracauer, Siegfried, *The Mass Ornament: Weimar Essays* (Cambridge, MA and London: Harvard University Press, 1995).

Kuleshov, Lev, *Art of Cinema* (Moscow: Tea-Kino Pechat, 1929), selections reprinted in *Screen Reader* (London: SEFT, 1977).

Lapsley Robert and Westlake, Michael, *Film Theory: An Introduction* (Manchester: Manchester University Press, 1988).

Larrabee, Harold A. (ed.), *Selections From Bergson* (New York: Appleton-Century-Crofts, 1949).

Lawton, Anna (ed.), *The Red Screen: Politics, Society, Art in Soviet Cinema* (London and New York: Routledge, 1992).

Leprohon, Pierre, *The Italian Cinema* (New York: Praeger, 1972).

Levin, Tom, 'From Dialectical to Normative Specificity: Reading Lukács on Film', *New German Critique* (1987), no. 40.

Lévi-Strauss, Claude, *Structural Anthropology* (Harmondsworth: Penguin, 1963).

Lévi-Strauss, Claude, *Structural Anthropology Volume Two* (Harmondsworth: Penguin, 1977).

Leyda, Jay, *Kino: A History of the Russian and Soviet Film* (London: George Allen & Unwin, 1973).

Liehm, Mira and Liehm Antonin, J., *The Most Important Art: East European*

Film After 1945 (Berkeley, CA and London: University of California Press, 1977).

Liehm, Mira, *Passion and Defiance: Film In Italy From 1942 to the Present* (Berkeley, CA and London: University of California Press, 1984).

Lukács, Georg, *The Meaning of Contemporary Realism* (London: Merlin, 1963).

Lukács, Georg, *Writer and Critic* (London: Merlin, 1978).

MacCabe, Colin, 'Realism and the Cinema: Notes on some Brechtian Theses', *Screen* (Summer, 1974), vol. 15, no. 2.

MacCabe, Colin, 'Days of Hope: A Response to Colin McArthur', in Bennet, Tony, Boyd-Bowman, Susan, Mercer, Colin and Woollacott, Janet (eds), *Popular Television and Film* (London: BFI/Open University Press, 1985).

Macquarrie, John, *Existentialism* (Harmondsworth: Pelican, 1973).

Marcus, Millicent, *Italian Film in the Light of Neorealism* (Princeton, NJ: Princeton University Press, 1986).

Martin, John, W., *The Golden Age of French Cinema* (New York: Twayne, 1983).

Matejka L. and Pomorska K. (eds), *Readings in Russian Poetics* (Cambridge, MA: MIT Press, 1971).

Mercer, Kobena, *Black Film British Cinema* (London: ICA, 1988).

Metz, Christian, *Essais sur la signification au cinéma* (Paris: Editions Klincksieck, 1971); *Film Language: A Semiotics of the Cinema* (New York: Oxford University Press, 1974).

Michelson, Annette (ed.), *Kino-Eye: The Writings of Dziga Vertov* (London and Sydney: Pluto Press, 1984).

Mitchell, Stanley, 'From Shklovsky to Brecht: Some preliminary remarks towards a history of the politicisation of Russian Formalism', *Screen* (Summer, 1974), vol. 15, no. 2.

Mukarovsky, Jan, 'Standard Language and Poetic Language', in *Prague School Reader in Aesthetics: Literary Structure and Style*, trans. Garvin, Paul R. (Washington, DC: Georgetown University Press, 1964).

Nettl, J. P., *The Soviet Achievement* (London: Thames and Hudson, 1976).

Nichols, Bill (ed.), *Movies and Methods Volume II* (Berkeley, CA, Los Angeles, CA and London: University of California Press, 1985).

Nochlin, Linda, *Realism: Style and Civilization* (Harmondsworth: Penguin, 1979).

Norris, Christopher, *Deconstruction: Theory and Practice* (London and New York: Routledge, 1988).

Norris, Christopher, *Uncritical Theory: Postmodernism, Intellectuals and the Gulf War* (London: Lawrence & Wishart, 1992).

Orbanz, Eva (ed.), *Journey to a Legend and Back: The British Realistic Film* (Berlin: Edition Volker Spiess, 1977).

Parkinson, G. H. R. (ed.), *Georg Lukács* (London: Routledge, 1977).

Parmesani, Loredana, *Art of the Twentieth Century: Movements, Theories, Schools and Tendencies 1900–2000* (Milan: Skira editore/Giò Marconi, 2000).

Passmore, John, *A Hundred Years of Philosophy* (London: Pelican, 1968).

Passmore, John, *Recent Philosophers* (London: Duckworth, 1985).

Petley, Julian, *Capital and Culture: German Cinema 1933–45* (London: BFI, 1979).

Petrić, Vlada, *Constructivism In Film: The Man with the Movie Camera A Cinematic Analysis* (Cambridge and London: Cambridge University Press, 1987).

Pinkus, Theodore, *Conversations With Lukács* (London: Merlin, 1974).

Porter, Vincent and Collins, Richard, *WDR and the Arbeiterfilm: Fassbinder, Ziewer and Others* (London: BFI, 1981).

Poster, Mark, *Sartre's Marxism* (London: Pluto, 1979).

Powrie, Phil, *French Cinema in the 1980s: Nostalgia and the Crisis of Masculinity* (Oxford: Clarenden Press, 1977).

Powrie, Phil (ed.), *French Cinema in the 1990s* (Oxford: Oxford University Press, 1999).

Propp, Vladimir, *Morphology of the Folk Tale* (Austin, TX and London: University of Texas Press, 1968).

Pudovkin, Vsevolod, *Film Technique and Film Acting* (New York: Grove, 1960).

Revol, Hubert, 'La Poésie du Cinéma', *Cinégraph*, vol. 111, no. 2 (February, 1930).

Rodowick, D. N., 'The Last Things Before the Last', *The New German Critique* (1991), no. 54.

Rorty, Richard, ' The World Well Lost', *Journal of Philosophy*, no. 69 (1972).

Rorty, Richard, *Philosophy and the Mirror of Nature* (Oxford: Oxford University Press, 1980).

Rorty Richard, 'Feminism and Pragmatism', *Radical Philosophy*, no. 59 (Autumn, 1991).

Rotha, Paul, *Documentary Film* (London: Faber & Faber, 1952).

Roud, Richard, *Straub* (London: BFI and Secker & Warburg, 1971).

Salt, Barry, 'From Caligari to Who?', *Sight and Sound* (Spring, 1979), vol. 48, no. 2.

Sandford, John, *The New German Cinema* (London: Oswald Wolff, 1980).

Santner, Eric, L., *Stranded Objects: Mourning, Memory and Film in Postwar Germany* (Ithaca, NY and London: Cornell University Press, 1993).

Sartre, Jean-Paul, *Being and Nothingness* (London: Methuen and Co., 1969).

Saussure, Ferdinand de, *Course in General Linguistics* (New York and London: McGraw-Hill, 1966).

Schlüpmann, Heide, Phenomenology of Film: On Siegfried Kracauer's Writings of the 1920s', *New German Critique* (1987), no. 40.

Schnitzer, Luda, Schnitzer Jean and Martin, Marcel (eds.), *Cinema in Revolution: The Heroic Era of the Soviet Film* (London: Secker & Warburg, 1973).

Searle, John, *Minds, Brains and Science* (London: Penguin, 1989).

Seton, Marie, *Sergei M. Eisenstein, a Biography* (London: Dennis Dobson, 1978).

Seyers, Sean, *Reality and Reason: Dialectic and the Theory of Knowledge* (Oxford: Blackwell, 1985).

Shlapentokh, Dimitri and Shlapentokh, Vladimir, *Soviet Cinematography 1918–1991* (New York: Aldine de Gruyter, 1993).

Shohat, Ella and Stam, Robert, *Unthinking Eurocentrism: Multiculturalism and the Media* (London: Routledge, 1994).

Silberman, Marc, *German Cinema: Texts in Context* (Detroit, MI: Wayne State University Press, 1995).

Solomon, Robert C., 'Romancing the Self: Fichte, Schelling, Schiller, and Romanticism', in his *Continental Philosophy Since 1750: The Rise and Fall of the Self* (Oxford and New York: Oxford University Press, 1988).

Street, Sarah, *British National Cinema* (London and New York: Routledge, 1997).

Tallis, Raymond, *Not Saussure: A Critique of Post-Saussurean Literary Theory* (London: Macmillan, 1995).

Taylor, Richard and Christie, Ian (eds), *The Film Factory: Russian and Soviet Cinema In Documents 1896–1939* (London and New York: Routledge, 1988).

Taylor, Richard and Christie, Ian (eds), *Eisenstein Rediscovered* (London and New York: Routledge, 1993).

Taylor, Richard (ed.), *The Eisenstein Reader* (London: BFI, 1998).

Thompson, E. P., *The Poverty of Theory and Other Essays* (London: Merlin Press, 1980).

Trigg, Roger, *Reality at Risk: A Defence of Realism in Philosophy and the Sciences* (New York and London: Harvester Wheatsheaf, 1989).

Vaughn James, C., *Soviet Socialist Realism: Origins & Theories* (London: Macmillan, 1973).

Vronskaya, Jeanne, *Young Soviet Film-makers* (London: George Allen and Unwin, 1972).

Walsh, Martin, *The Brechtian Aspect of Radical Cinema* (London: BFI, 1981).

Westlake, Michael and Lapsley, Robert, *Film Theory: An Introduction* (Manchester: Manchester University Press, 1988).

Willett, John (ed. and trans.), *Brecht On Theatre* (London: Eyre Methuen, 1979).

Williams, Alan, *Republic Of Images: A History of French Film-making* (Cambridge, MA and London: Harvard University Press, 1992).

Wilson, Emma, *French Cinema Since 1950: Personal Histories* (London: Duckworth, 1999).

Wittgenstein, L., *Philosophical Investigations* (Oxford: Oxford University Press, 1953).

Wollen, Peter, *Signs and Meaning in the Cinema* (London: BFI/Secker & Warburg, 1974).

Wollen, Peter, 'North by North West: a Morphological Analysis', *Film Form*, no. I (1976).

Wollen, Peter, *Readings and Writings: Semiotic Counter-Strategies* (London: Verso, 1982).

Woolhouse, R. S., *The Empiricists* (New York and Oxford: Oxford University Press, 1988).

Index

266